Johnson's
Dictionary
and the
Language of
Learning

Johnson's *Dictionary* and the Language of Learning

Robert DeMaria, Jr.

The University of North Carolina Press

Chapel Hill and London

Library of Congress Cataloging-in-Publication Data
DeMaria, Robert.
   Johnson's Dictionary and the language of learning.
   Bibliography: p.
   Includes index.
   1. Johnson, Samuel, 1709–1784.   Dictionary of the
English language.   2. English language—Lexicography.
3. Johnson, Samuel, 1709–1784—Knowledge and learning.
4. Learning and scholarship—Terminology.   5. Learning
and scholarship—History—18th century.   I. Title.
PE1617.J7D44   1986   423   86-4285
ISBN 0-8078-1713-9

This publication was supported in part
by the Salmon Fund of Vassar College

To J. T.

Contents

Preface

In a critical description as dramatic as the fiery climax of his novel *The Name of the Rose* Umberto Eco concludes a recent statement on dictionaries. By assaulting the Porphyrian tree of distinctions that is so important to dictionary definition, Eco breaks dictionaries out of their usually authoritative and staid role: "The tree of genera and species, the tree of substances, blows up in a dust of differentiae, in a turmoil of infinite accidents, in a nonhierarchical network of *qualia*. The dictionary is dissolved into a potentially unordered and unrestricted galaxy of pieces of world knowledge. The dictionary thus becomes an encyclopedia, because it was in fact *a disguised encyclopedia*" (*Semiotics* 68). Eco dispenses with the fictions of definitions and leaves the dictionary in the condition of a passive tool that we are free to use when we need it (86). The subversiveness of Eco's operation is delightful, but there are other things one can do with dictionaries after one has realized that they are really encyclopedias in disguise. Malcolm X discovered this when he began reading his dictionary in prison, and he is only one of innumerable autodidacts who have sought by this means to liberate themselves.

After spending some time reading a dictionary as a disguised encyclopedia it is possible to describe its contents—to classify and name the "galaxy of pieces of world knowledge" that the book contains. This is an additional step that few readers have bothered to take, but it has seemed to me extremely worth while, at least in the case of the great dictionary I try to describe in this book. I began reading Johnson's *Dictionary* as part of a research project that I thought might turn out to be a history of reading. In order to understand something about Johnson's life of reading, I began looking for the passages cited by Johnson in the books he used to collect quotations for the *Dictionary*. My interest naturally spread to the sources themselves, and I tried to imitate Johnson's procedure of reading and selecting. When I had become fairly adept at guessing which quotations in a book Johnson would extract, I began to ask what the principle behind such selection might be. Although there are almost always philological reasons for his selections, there are usually other reasons as well, and these other reasons have most often to do with the contribution the quotation can make to useful knowledge. Johnson makes few attempts to disguise the encyclopedic qualities of his book, but any reader's overall vision of its contents is severely restricted by the alphabetical and philological restraints every lexicographer must labor under. To overcome the obscuring tendency of the alphabetical order, I began indexing the contents of Johnson's *Dictionary* and eventually came up with a computerized index of some 23,000 records, each of them representing an illustrative quotation or, much less often, an editorial remark that contributes to a topic of knowledge in the *Dictionary*. As I read I identified what seemed to me the most important topics. The list changed a good deal over my years of reading the *Dictionary*, but it maintained an identifiable central cluster of concerns: knowledge and ignorance, truth and probability, learning and education, language, religion and morality are all prominent topics in Johnson's galaxy of knowledge, and they are all heavily treated from the beginning to the end of his book.

My own book is largely a record, based on extensive indexing, of how these subjects are treated in the *Dictionary*. In one sense, the *Dictionary* is a chronicle of how these subjects have been treated by the authors Johnson cites and indeed by an important segment of English civilization; in this sense it is possible to see Johnson's configuration as a standard view of recorded knowledge on these subjects because, after all, he employs mostly "standard," well-accepted authors. In another sense, Johnson's book is itself an important event in the history of these central topics. He does not simply record everything available to him: he makes choices about which works to include and which to exclude. As I try to say in the introduction, these choices are not usually or mainly personal choices, but they are choices, and the vision of the intellectual world Johnson gives us is different from the vision in, say, Charles Richardson's *Dictionary* or *Webster's III*.

My method in forming my index and coming to conclusions has been a combination of deduction and induction, much like the method any close reader would employ on any text. Initially I found that Johnson's text has certain characteristics, especially thematic characteristics, and then in further reading I confirmed and often adjusted my findings. Inevitably I have left out a great deal, not only of what I originally recorded and wrote, but also of what I might have recorded. Some subjects, such as the politics of the *Dictionary*, seemed to me to require separate treatment so that adequate attention could be given to the contemporary background. Other subjects seemed slight enough that they could be handled in notes or should not be handled at all. I

saw no need for a description of the natural science and history in the
Dictionary because it already exists in *Philosophic Words*, William Wimsatt's fine, original study. I also neglected the very large area of
technical information in the *Dictionary*, partly because Wimsatt has
described some of it so well, and partly because it did not seem to bear
importantly on the main group of subjects I discuss.

What remains is what I believe to be the most central area of the
whole field of knowledge as Johnson chose to record it in the years
1746–55. The description of this large area is necessarily somewhat
uneven. The intellectual landscape itself is beset with unresolved
issues and unreconciled opinions. Johnson did not attempt to smooth
out his history of ideas, and I have felt caught between a wish to order
what I found and a wish to present it in all its variety and with all its
tangles. In practical terms this has meant a great many decisions about
how to divide the material. The smaller the units or topics I dealt with
at one time, the more consistent my report could be—but the less I
conveyed the overall shape of the field of knowledge I was finally trying
to describe. With a good deal of advice from readers and editors I have
attempted to synthesize my material into sections large enough to
provide a sense of Johnson's overall choices and predilections, but not
so large as to misrepresent the necessarily discontinuous nature of his
presentation. The chief reason for the discontinuity should not be
forgotten: whatever else he created in his *Dictionary*, Johnson also
produced an authoritative dictionary that served his nation and others
usefully for at least a hundred years and helped to form the basis of the
great dictionaries that finally superseded it in the late nineteenth
century.

Reminders of this important fact are only a small part of the debt I
owe to Gwin Kolb of the University of Chicago: he encouraged me
and saved me from many follies, and, along with David Fleeman of
Pembroke College, Oxford, he saved me literally years of work. I am
also very grateful to the late E. J. Thomas and his unrivaled knowledge
of how the huge body of quotations in the *Dictionary* made its way from
the books Johnson read to the book he published. The work of these
three scholars on the history of Johnson's *Dictionary* informs my work
throughout, even though I am primarily concerned to describe Johnson's book as a finished text and therefore omit a formal discussion of
its interesting and important evolution.

This project obviously could not have been done without the

facilities of several great libraries and help from patient librarians. It is my great pleasure to thank the staff members of the British Library, the Bodleian Library, the John Rylands Library, the Beinecke Rare Book and Manuscript Library, the Vassar College Library, the Aberystwyth University Library, and the Lichfield Cathedral Library. I also had support on this project in the form of grants from the National Endowment for the Humanities and the American Council of Learned Societies. In the final stages of preparing the manuscript I received invaluable assistance from James Day of Vassar College.

Unlike Johnson's *Dictionary* this book was written in the "shelter of academick bowers," and I must thank Vassar College for its continuous support of my work. Along with grants and encouragement, the college gave me numerous diligent assistants, among whom I ought to mention Megan Smith, Elizabeth Kaplan, and Colleen Hamilton. The college has also given me access to fine computing facilities and to tireless computer experts who have gone out of their way to help me scores of times.

A Note on the Form of Citation

Quotations of Johnson's *Dictionary* are from the first edition (1755). I have indicated their whereabouts by italicizing the word under which they appear, and, when Johnson records more than one sense, I have indicated the sense under which the quotation appears with a number enclosed in brackets. I have also made sure to cite the authors of the illustrative quotations I include. Johnson sometimes misquoted his sources, and I have noted some of the rare instances when his misquotations alter his author's sense (see below, pages 17, 62, 134, and 148–49). I have not, however, checked every quotation for accuracy of citation and attribution. My interest is primarily, though not exclusively, in Johnson's text rather than his authors'; Johnson's misattributions, misquotations, inconsistent spellings, and errors of accentuation are left, therefore, as I found them (although, unlike Johnson, I have thoroughly distinguished "i" from "j" and "u" from "v"). When the same quotation is used to illustrate more than one word, I have italicized all the words under which the quotation appears but have followed the text of the fullest version.

In citing all other works I have followed the recommendations of the Modern Language Association and given a short reference in the text supplemented by complete information in the bibliography at the end of the book.

Johnson's
Dictionary
and the
Language of
Learning

nefs, which our Fathers were utterly unacquainted with.

Another Thing that makes it neceffary for our Reafon to have fome Affiftance given it, is the *Difguife and falfe Colours in which many Things appear to us in this prefent imperfect State :* There are a Thoufand Things which are not in reality what they appear to be, and that both in the *natural* and the *moral* World : So the *Sun* appears to be flat as a Plate of Silver, and to be lefs than twelve Inches in Diameter : the *Moon* appears to be as big as the *Sun*, and the Rainbow appears to be a large fubftantial Arch in the Sky ; all which are in reality grofs Falfhoods. So *Knavery* puts on the Face of *Juftice*, *Hypocrify* and *Superftition* wear the Vizard of *Piety*, *Deceit* and *Evil* are often cloathed in the Shapes and Appearances of *Truth* and *Goodnefs*. Now Logick helps us to ftrip off the outward Difguife of Things, and to behold them and judge of them in their own Nature.

There is yet a farther Proof of our intellectual or rational *Powers* need fome Affiftance, and that is, becaufe they are fo frail and fallible in the prefent State ; we are impofed upon *at home* as well as *abroad* ; we are deceived by our *Senfes*, by our *Imaginations*, by our *Paffions* and *Appetites* ; by the *Authority* of Men, by *Education* and *Cuftom*, &c. and we are led into frequent Errors, by judging according to thefe falfe and flattering Principles, rather than according to the Nature of Things. Something of this Frailty is owing to our very *Conftitution*, Man being compounded of Flefh and Spirit : Something of it arifes from our *Infant State*, and our growing up by fmall Degrees to Manhood, fo that we form a thoufand Judgments before our *Reafon* is mature. But there is ftill more of it owing to our *original Defection* from God, and the

Logic by Isaac Watts; Johnson's copy with the marks he made when reading and selecting passages for inclusion in the *Dictionary*. Vertical lines indicate beginnings and ends of passages he wished his amanuenses to copy. Underlines indicate the word he was interested in illustrating. The letters in the margin are the first letters of the underlined words. The lines through the letters were drawn by an amanuensis when he had copied the quotation on a slip of paper to be alphabetized under the illustrated word and passed on to Johnson.

Introduction

The *Dictionary* as Literature

1. Johnson's Book

Few readers today ever think of reading a dictionary consecutively or even extensively, the way they read most other books. We think of the dictionary as a work of reference, a store of discrete pieces of information properly arranged for easy access. Instances of dictionary reading are heard of, but they are usually accounted the result of some personal or circumstantial peculiarity. Malcolm X, who not only read but copied out many pages of his dictionary, can be seen as the victim of his imprisonment and his total lack of education (172). Robert Burchfield had to read the *Oxford English Dictionary* in order to write the *Supplement*. Perhaps Hart Crane and Emily Dickinson read extensively in dictionaries because their peculiar, poetic natures required it, and the same sort of peculiarity may account for the fact that Browning read Johnson's *Dictionary* in order to qualify himself for literature and later started on the *OED*.[1] Yet, the further back in history we go, the less strange dictionary reading appears.

The dictionary's loss of literary stature was gradual, and its fate has always been involved with the history of literary relatives like the encyclopedia, but as late as the nineteenth century some readers still saw dictionaries as books. In his *Biographia Literaria*, for instance, Samuel Taylor Coleridge granted Johnson's *Dictionary* a double generic life, and he praised it on one hand while damning it on the other: "Of this celebrated dictionary I will venture to remark once for all, that I should suspect the man of a morose disposition who should speak of it without respect and gratitude as a most instructive and entertaining *book* . . . but I confess, that I should be surprized at hearing from a philosophic and thorough scholar any but very qualified praises of it, as a *dictionary*" (1: 237–38). Like so many of Coleridge's distinctions, the sharpness of this division between books and dictionaries is foreign to Johnson's literary understanding, but the expression of it throws light on the older system of generic relations with which Johnson lived. Johnson referred to his *Dictionary*, as he referred to none of his other works, as "my Book" (*Letters* 1: 71), and he worked in a tradition of lexicography that tended to see the dictionary as generically encyclopedic as well as in a class of its own. For him, as for many of his literary predecessors, the dictionary was both a word book and a combination of all other literary kinds, a quintessential book of books designed to perform all the tasks of entertainment and instruction germane to writing of any sort. Although Coleridge extends it in a patronizing fashion, Johnson would not have thought consideration of his *Dictionary* as a book demeaning in the least. Johnson certainly wished to make a lasting and scientific contribution to philology, but his highest hopes for his *Dictionary* were wrapped up in his conception of it as a book.

As a book, Johnson's *Dictionary* is generically related not only to dictionaries but also to a host of encyclopedic histories, poems, commentaries, educational works, commonplace books, and, of course, encyclopedias themselves. In this wider genealogy, the most important immediate ancestor of Johnson's *Dictionary* is Ephraim Chambers's *Cyclopædia or Universal Dictionary*, first published in 1728. Johnson knew Chambers's work well: he frequently quoted articles from it, and he once asserted that he formed his style on Chambers's preface.[2] Johnson's most active amanuensis, Alexander MacBean, learned his trade working for Chambers, and Johnson himself was deeply disappointed toward the end of his life when he failed to get the contract for a new edition of the *Cyclopædia* (Boswell 2: 203–4 n. 3). In one of the first notices of the *Dictionary* in the literary world, Thomas Birch compared it in size to Chambers's—but the likeness is not merely superficial (Clifford 126).

In his preface and in his *Considerations Preparatory to a Second Edition* Chambers makes several attempts to define the genre of the dictionary and to characterize the lexicographer in general. His deliberations reveal the same kind of ambivalence about the task and those who perform it that Johnson expresses in his preface. Chambers's uncertainty about the stature of lexicographers and their work is most clearly manifest in his speculations on their origins. Assuming an interesting correspondence between the character of the originator and the nature of the work, Chambers begins:

Were we to enquire who first led up the way of Dictionaries, of late so much frequented; some little grammarian would, probably, be found at the head thereof: and from his particular views, designs, etc. if known, one might probably deduce, not only the general form, but even the particular circumstances of the modern productions under that name. The relation, however, extends both ways; and if we cannot deduce the nature of a Dictionary from the condition of the author, we may the condition of the author from the nature of the Dictionary. Thus much, at least, we may say, that he was an *analyst*; that his view was not to improve or advance knowledge, but to teach or convey it; and that he was hence led to unty the complexions, or bundles of ideas his predecessors had made, and reduce them to their natural simplicity: which is all that is essential to a lexicographer. Probably this was in the early days of the Egyptian sages, when words were more complex and obscure than now; and mystic symbols and hieroglyphics obtained; so that an explication of their marks or words, might amount to a revelation of their whole inner philosophy: in which case, instead of a grammarian, we must put perhaps a priest or mystagogue at the head of Dictionaries. (*Cyclopædia* 1: xvi)

Chambers's uncertainty about whether lexicographers are essentially "little grammarians" or "mystagogues" appears in several other places. He knows "what Figure Lexicographers make in the Republick of Letters; with what Contempt they are treated by those who hold the first Rank therein . . ." (*Considerations* 4), yet he uses the grandest possible terms to outline the qualifications for their task: the lexicographer "must have a compass of learning more universal than was ever found in the most celebrated Polyhistors, an *Eratosthenes*, *Varro*, or *Bacon*; possess more languages than a *Postellus* or *Bibliander*, be . . . more skill'd in literary matters than a *Lamberius*, or *Fabricius*; have more Reading than a *Leibnitz* or *Le Clerc*; more Reflection than a *Hobbs*, *Malebranche*, or *Locke*; more Acquaintance with the Ancients than a *Gravius*; with the middle Age Writers than a *Du Cange*, with the Moderns than a *Boyle*" (3), and so on. Moreover, Chambers's second edition, never undertaken in its prospective form, was to be the key to all human knowledge, not only of all "Books, Libraries and Cabinets," but also of "Shops, Garrets, Cellars, Mines, and other obscure Places, where Men of Learning rarely penetrate" (4). In sum, it was to reveal "the whole vast Apparatus of unwritten Philosophy" (4) and become, like the Scriptures, an instrument of salvation, giving its readers greater "intimations of the Creator's will" (*Cyclopædia* 1: xxv).

Although he was fundamentally less optimistic than Chambers, Johnson inherited from him a similar ambivalence about the highest aims of lexicography and the stature of its practitioners. As everyone knows, Johnson defines "lexicographer" in the *Dictionary* as "a harmless drudge," and he makes several other derisive remarks about his task. But against these satirical remarks must be put Johnson's grand statement of lexicographical dreams in his preface:

> When first I engaged in this work, I resolved to leave neither words nor things unexamined, and pleased myself with a prospect of the hours which I should revel away in feasts of literature, the obscure recesses of northern learning, which I should enter and ransack, the treasures with which I expected every search into those neglected mines to reward my labour, and the triumph with which I should display my acquisitions to mankind. When I had thus enquired into the original of words, I resolved to show likewise my attention to things; to pierce deep into every science, to enquire the nature of every substance of which I inserted the name, to limit every idea by a definition strictly logical, and exhibit every production of art or nature in an accurate description, that my book might be in place of all other dictionaries whether appellative or technical. But these were the dreams of a poet doomed at last to wake a lexicographer. (par. 72)

Johnson's attribution of these dreams to poetry reveals his sense of that art as the crown of learning. The same sense appears in Imlac's impossible requirements for the poet in chapter 10 of *Rasselas* and in Johnson's description of epic poetry in his *Life* of Milton. But, like other inferior branches of learning, lexicography aspires to the dreams of poetry. Chambers certainly entertained what Johnson calls the "dreams of a poet" when he imagined that the second edition of his *Cyclopædia* would "furnish the best Book in the Universe; and abundantly indemnify us in the Want of what other Countries are so fond of—Royal, Imperial, Caesarian, and Ducal Academies, Palatine Societies, and the like" (*Considerations* 4). Like Chambers, Johnson both scorns the academies (preface, par. 90) and competes with them to realize a dream of comprehensive and universally available knowledge that flourished in the late Renaissance along with the rise of the printing industry.[3] The dictionary is historically and generically linked to this grand dream and the academies founded to promote it.[4]

The best and most copious evidence that Johnson wrote his *Dictionary* within an encyclopedic tradition of lexicography is the vast amount of illustrative quotation he included. In the preface he acknowledges that "authorities will sometimes seem to have been accumulated without necessity or use, and perhaps some will be found, which might, without loss, have been omitted" (par. 65). His early critics seized on just this point. Thomas Edwards, for example, wrote to the antiquarian Daniel Wray in 1755 and agreed with his correspondent that Johnson's "needless number of authorities is intolerable, were these properly reduced, and the long articles from Miller and Chambers together with the monsters from the Dictionaries left out, the work for ought I know might be brought into half the compass it now takes."[5] A letter to Johnson's printer, William Strahan, dated 20 November 1755 (not long after publication), also complained loudly about the excessive quotation: "What I would propose is that you should print an edition of Johnson in one volume Folio, & never give more than one quotation to prove any one sense of a word. This would shorten the present work by one half & yet not lessen its value; for, at present, one may find 3 or 4 citations out of the very same author to authorize one meaning of a word" (MS Lichfield 37 fol. 1).[6] To prove his point this correspondent might have adduced the fact that there are nine consecutive quotations from Addison under the twentieth sense of "to have" and fifty-six illustrations of "ill" used as an adverb. Johnson's linguistic rationale for such apparent superfluity should be taken seriously: he says in the preface, "those quotations which to careless or unskilful perusers appear only to repeat the same sense, will often exhibit, to a more accurate examiner, diversities of signification, or, at least, afford different shades of the same meaning" (par. 65). Like Chambers's imaginary first lexicographer, Johnson was "an *analyst*." I suppose few readers have ever been better at distinguishing the various senses in which a word is used, but Charles Richardson, whose *New Dictionary of the English Language* was endorsed by Coleridge, has a case when he says in his preface that Johnson's lexicographical method tends to "interpret the import of the context, and not to explain the individual meaning of the word" (1: 38).

Johnson's fundamentally empirical philosophy shows up in sharp relief against the linguistic idealism that Richardson imbibed from

Horne Tooke, and the multitude of quotations in the *Dictionary* is consistent with all of Johnson's Lockean thoughts on language. However, Johnson filled his *Dictionary* with quotations for encyclopedic as well as for linguistic purposes. He makes his encyclopedic intentions perfectly clear in the preface where he speaks in elegiac tones about his earliest dreams for the success of his book:

> When first I collected these authorities, I was desirous that every quotation should be useful to some other end than the illustration of a word; I therefore extracted from philosophers principles of science; from historians remarkable facts; from chymists complete processes; from divines striking exhortations; and from poets beautiful descriptions. Such is design, while it is yet at a distance from execution. When the time called upon me to range this accumulation of elegance and wisdom into an alphabetical series, I soon discovered that the bulk of my volumes would fright away the student, and was forced to depart from my scheme of including all that was pleasing or useful in *English* literature. . . . (par. 57)

Despite his complaints and those of his publisher,[7] Johnson was able to accomplish a remarkable portion of his scheme. Moreover, his accomplishment connects his book with a tradition of encyclopedic historical works that flourished in England in the seventy years after the Restoration. The general connection between dictionaries and historical works is, like so much that is generically relevant to the *Dictionary*, evident in Chambers's preface to his *Cyclopædia*. Chambers might have been laying the groundwork for the *OED* as well as for Johnson's *Dictionary* when he said flatly, "The Dictionary of an Art is the proper history of such art; the Dictionary of a language, the history of that language" (1: xvii). But language means learning to Johnson and the whole humanistic tradition, and thus a dictionary after Chambers's model is also a history of learning. Furthermore, Johnson equated literature and learning,[8] so his "scheme of including all that was pleasing or useful in *English* literature" is another indication of his intention to present a record of English learning in his book.

As a history of learning the *Dictionary* fits very neatly into the list of works that Johnson projected at about the same time that he was planning and composing the *Dictionary*. On the manuscript list that he gave to Bennet Langton, Johnson proposed to himself a "History of Criticism," an edition of Chaucer (with an etymological glossary), a

"History of the Heathen Mythology," a "History of the State of Venice," "A Dictionary to the Common Prayer, in imitation of Calmet's Dictionary of the Bible," a "Dictionary of Ancient History and Mythology," a "Treatise on the Study of Polite Literature, containing the history of learning," and, among a few others, a "History of the Revival of Learning in Europe, containing an account of whatever contributed to the restoration of literature; such as controversies, printing, the destruction of the Greek empire, the encouragement of great men, with the lives of the most eminent patrons and most eminent early professors of all kinds of learning in different countries" (Boswell 4: 381–82).

The combination of historical and philological work evident in these projects and in the *Dictionary* is just what characterizes the great historical works of the Restoration, and Johnson's book is importantly related to them. Johnson cites many of the historians in the *Dictionary*: Camden, for example, appears in Gibson's monumental edition; Hickes and Spelman are used in Latin for etymologies; an English work by William Wake supplies many quotations on the important subject of death; and Edward Stillingfleet contributes much from one of his long polemical tracts against Roman Catholic idolatry. In *Dr. Woodward's Shield*, a book that centers around a natural historian much quoted in the *Dictionary*, Joseph M. Levine accurately describes the scientific and historical methods of these scholar-clerics. These men were generally superb textual critics who looked upon the record of words, the accumulated testimony in literature, as the most significant material for research into any subject. The application of a philological approach to historical problems led to works in which the erudition is often amazing and the methodological ignorance appalling. Of the vast *Discourse of the True Antiquity of London*, for example, Levine says, "for Stillingfleet, the antiquarian evidence was a device to elucidate a text. On the whole the Bishop preferred the word to the thing. 'I have one great Argument,' he writes, 'to prove that Canterbury was built by the Romans, not from Roman coins found almost in all parts of the City, as Mr. Somner affirms; but from Caesar's Account of his 2nd Landing'" (*Dr. Woodward* 138). Because of their exegetical method, their frequent etymological speculations, and their margins crammed with cross-references, Stillingfleet's and his contemporaries' histories read like dictionaries of a specialized vocabulary. Conversely, Johnson's *Dictionary*, with its emphasis on historical content, as well as on definition and etymology, bears a relation to the solid, erudite folios that dominated the booksellers' shelves in the late seventeenth century and were replaced, not without lamentation, by the eighteenth century's more numerous little octavos and pamphlets.[9]

Not only Johnson's projected works but also a number of those he actually produced before writing the *Dictionary* focus on the history of learning. Early in his career Johnson earned half a year's salary working on a translation of Father Sarpi's *History of the Council of Trent*.[10] This is just the sort of philological antiquarian work that the scholar-clerics in England produced—in fact, William Wotton saw Sarpi's *History* as exemplary when he defended the modern historians against their more narrative and rhetorical ancestors (Levine, "Ancients, Moderns, and History" 48). Johnson continued his activity in the area of literary history by writing, between 1739 and 1749, the lives of the scholars Boerhaave, Morin, Burman, Barretier, and "the learned Sydenham." But Johnson's most important early scholarly experience was the enormous labor of cataloguing the Harleian Library. This was a task worthy of a legendary seventeenth-century scholar like Thomas Hearne or Humphrey Wanley, and no attempt to characterize the nature of Johnson's literary achievement should ever neglect it. In his "Account" of the library Johnson indicates the larger historical interest that informed the most ambitious work he did before undertaking the *Dictionary*. Clearly, Johnson is describing himself when he appeals to

> those whom Curiosity has engaged in the Study of Literary
> History, and who think the intellectual Revolutions of the World
> more worthy of their Attention, than the Ravages of Tyrants,
> the Desolation of Kingdoms, the Rout of Armies, and the Fall
> of Empires. . . . those that amuse themselves with remarking
> the different Periods of human Knowledge, and observe, how
> Darkness and Light succeed each other, by what Accident the
> most gloomy Nights of Ignorance have given Way to the Dawn
> of Science, and how Learning has languished and decayed, for
> Want of Patronage and Regard, or been overborne by the Prevalence of fashionable Ignorance, or lost amidst the Tumults of
> Invasion, and the Storms of Violence. (*Harleian Catalogue* 1:
> 3–4)

The interest in history evident in Johnson's early works and in his list of scholarly plans should explode the popular notion, encouraged by Boswell, that Johnson was not interested in history.[11] Among other

influential places, the myth appears in one of the few accounts of the
scholar-clerics of the Restoration, D. C. Douglas's inspirational *En-*
glish Scholars, 1660–1730. Douglas says, "Johnson adopted towards
historical scholarship in general, and towards medieval studies in
particular, an attitude so different from that of [his] erudite predecessors, that it is permissible to discern in the transition between them the
end of an age" (28). But, like his "erudite predecessors," Johnson is
mainly interested in language and learning, and his *Dictionary* is a
history book cast in the seventeenth-century mold. Toward the end of
the preface he is explicit about his sense of his book as literary history;
his expression is doubly significant, however, because he hopes in the
same breath to join the pantheon of seventeenth-century writers
whose works are the basis of his history: "The chief glory of every
people arises from its authours: whether I shall add any thing by my
own writings to the reputation of *English* literature, must be left to time
. . . but I shall not think my employment useless or ignoble, if by my
assistance foreign nations, and distant ages, gain access to the propa-
gators of knowledge, and understand the teachers of truth; if my
labours afford light to the repositories of science, and add celebrity to
Bacon, to *Hooker*, to *Milton*, and to *Boyle*" (par. 92). Both Johnson's wish
to have his name added to this particular list of authors and his
pleasure in recounting their learning attest to the truth of Alfred North
Whitehead's incisive remark that Johnson "is still of the essence of the
seventeenth century" (see Bate 295).[12]

2.   The Audience of the *Dictionary*

The history of dictionaries shows that their writers have educational aims and identify students as an important part of their audience. Starnes and Noyes demonstrate this clearly in their standard
work *The English Dictionary from Cawdrey to Johnson*. The point is
illustrated, among other ways, by their facsimile reproductions of the
title pages of early English dictionaries. Cawdrey's *Table Alphabeticall*,
for example, describes itself as not only "conteyning" but also "teaching the true writing, and understanding of hard usuall English words."
Later on, when the word "interpretation" generally replaces the word
"teaching," the title pages indicate the pedagogical nature of the books
they advertise by referring to their intended audience: the groups of
prospective readers usually include women, foreigners, and some

direct or euphemistic term for the unlearned. *The New World of English Words*, for example, describes itself as "*A Work very necessary for Strangers, as well as our own Countreymen, for all Persons that would rightly understand what they discourse, write, or read.*" Johnson's immediate predecessor and most important competitor for the market of dictionary buyers, Nathan Bailey, advertised on his title page, "The whole WORK compil'd and Methodically digested, as well for the Entertainment of the Curious, as the Information of the Ignorant, and for the Benefit of young Students, Artificers, Tradesmen and Foreigners. . . . "[13] The pedagogical intentions of dictionaries are even more obvious in the Latin-English dictionaries than in their monolingual relatives. Next to Bailey's, the dictionary Johnson cites most in his own book is Robert Ainsworth's *Thesaurus*. Ainsworth makes the direction of his book clear in his prefatory address "Eruditis et purae Latinitatis amatoribus"; roughly translated, he writes: "To the learned and the lovers of pure Latinity: This book was not prepared so much for you as for the education of children in the schools, but I should not be surprised if somehow or other it should come into your hands, for all fathers and tutors who care about their children and their pupils and who might not themselves be experienced in languages will, if they are wise, be sufficiently assisted in their designs by buying such a book as this one" (ix).

Johnson's and his publishers' sense of their audience is deeply influenced by the educational tradition of lexicography. This influence is more obvious in the earlier documents relating to the *Dictionary* than in the final product, but it is powerful throughout. In the preface of 1755 there are only two references to learners (pars. 21 and 55), and these are especially concerned with foreigners. However, in the "Plan" of 1747 Johnson clearly indicates his intention to write a dictionary that "instructs the learner," is of "advantage to the common workman," and is "designed not merely for criticks, but for popular use" (*Works* 5: 3, 5); and further back toward its inception there is even clearer evidence that the *Dictionary* was thought of as an educational work. The earliest really important document relating to the history of the *Dictionary* is "A Short Scheme for compiling a new Dictionary of the English Language." A couple of notes jotted on the back of this manuscript provide evidence that in making the *Dictionary*, as Scott Elledge has remarked, Johnson "thought of students, of men in the process of educating themselves" (271). The author of the jottings was a reader whom Johnson evidently trusted for a response, probably the

Reverend Taylor, to whom Johnson is known to have given the first draft of *Irene* for comment.[14] On the back of sheet 7, apparently reacting to what looked to him like a plan to arrange the vocabulary according to etymological roots, Johnson's reader queried, "Is not Fabers Method quite thro', the best? If the Words are not alphabetically placed, a Man must understand the Language only to find a Derivative, & then he has no Occasion for your Dictionary. This would spoil the Sale of it to Schools & Foreigners. . . ." The second significant note was written in response to Johnson's stated intention "to quote when it can be conveniently done such sentences as besides their immediate use may give pleasure or instruction by conveying some elegance of language or some precept of Prudence or of Piety" (fols. 17r and 18r): the commentator adds, "All Examples should be compleat Sense & Grammar, (not the Author's whole Sense) for without that a Learner can not judge how, why, in what Sense a word is employed . . ." (fol. 18v). When Johnson reiterated in 1755 his intention to print quotations that would give "pleasure or instruction," he subtly maintained the relation of his book to educational works. Paragraph 57 of the preface ends, "Some passages I have yet spared, which may relieve the labour of verbal searches, and intersperse with verdure and flowers the dusty desarts of barren philology." This is a silent reference to William Walker's *English Examples of the Latine Syntaxis*, one of many schoolbooks that Johnson used as a source of quotations in the *Dictionary*. The passage in question comes from Walker's instructions to teachers (A8r), and Johnson prints the injunction more correctly inside the *Dictionary* in illustration of "philology": "Temper all discourses of *philology* with interspersions of morality."

Like Walker, Johnson uses philology for educational and therefore, of course, for moral purposes, but this particular way of combining linguistics and more fundamental educational goals was not at all new to lexicography. Johnson's extensive use of illustrative quotations distinguishes his book from its English forerunners, but in this and in the pedagogical use of these quotations it is closely related to a number of continental dictionaries.[15] The relation is perhaps closest in the case of Basilius Faber's *Thesaurus Eruditis Scholasticae* (1587), the title page of which runs, "A Treasure of Scholastic Knowledge for the Learned, or the Science of Teaching and Learning in an Easy, Plain, and Compendious Way: that is, from the best Latin and Greek authors. . . . including the most material content of words, of speech, of things, of exempla, and of all the things which, for both teachers and learners, can make the acquisition of knowledge easy and efficient . . ." (A3v). In his "Letter to the Reader," Faber describes his thirty-six years of teaching experience as the source of his lexicographical method. He complains about the sterility of merely grammatical teaching, and, in a passage reminiscent of Johnson's "Plan" and preface, Faber says, "Because words alone are infertile and added linguistic commentary is in itself dry, I have supplied from the Latin and Greek authors . . . whatever in them I have perceived to be elegant, learned, distinguished, witty, and charming. I have added such ornaments to the naked words and so, as it were, clothed their form and substance. Thus it is possible for the student to learn something else during the vocabulary lesson, a learned way of speech and an important and useful piece of wisdom . . ." (A3v). The similarity between Johnson's book and Faber's applies to their actual treatment of the vocabulary as well as to their prefatory commitments. Faber exemplifies and justifies his method by asking in his preface:

> Of what offense would the preceptor be guilty . . . if somewhere in the vocabulary lesson on *mundus* [world], in the midst of this great grammatical examination, he should make bold to ask wherefore this system, the beautiful structure and machinery of heaven and earth, is called κόσμος by the Greeks and by the Romans *mundus*? And of what offense would he be guilty if he should also ask if there is any truth in the opinion of Aristotle and Pliny that the world is an eternal and boundless power, never born nor ever to be dissolved? Or what line it is of the most ancient poet Orpheus that Plato remembers in the Philebus [66 c]: "In the sixth age put an end to the order [κόσμος] of song." And the preceptor should ask what κόσμος means in this place. (A3v)

The Christianity of Faber's multiple pedagogical aims is evident here, and he follows through in his treatment of "mundus" by providing from Plato's *Philebus* the quotation of Orpheus, whose theory of creation was taken by Ficino and other Christian commentators as premonitory of the Mosaic account in Genesis (Ficino 402 and n. 199). Faber enhances the opportunity for a Christian component in this vocabulary lesson by appending a sizable piece of verse about the corrupt nature of the world and the hastening apocalypse. Moreover, he carefully omits any quotation of the atheistic cosmologies of Aristotle and Pliny. Johnson's treatment of the equivalent English word, "world," suggests that his method and his basic aims are much like Faber's. Three of Johnson's first four illustrative quotations serve not only to define the word but also to teach the fundamental religious truth, perhaps prefigured in Orpheus, that God created the world: the Nicene Creed reminds Johnson's readers that One was "Begotten before all *worlds*[2]"; Hebrews adds, "God hath in these last days spoken unto us by his son, by whom he made the *worlds*[2]"; and Milton pronounces, "He the *world*[3] / Built on circumfluous waters." The Fabrian method and the religious content of this series of quotations are both pervasive in Johnson's *Dictionary*. Specifically, as later chapters will show, the divine creation of the world and its inevitable dissolution are important topics in the whole discourse that Johnson presents by means of very numerous illustrative quotations.

As his own master in lexicography Basilius Faber recognized Caelius Secundus Curione, the author of the *Forum Romanum*, first published in 1561. This title makes a suitable name also for the genre of the teaching dictionary, even though Curione is not as methodical in the preparation of his lessons as Faber. Johnson's *Dictionary* belongs to this genre and, in a sense, recovers it, because Faber's seventeenth-century editors, especially Christopher Cellarius, stripped him of his pedagogical apparatus, including his extra quotations and his prefatory material.[16] In general, the expulsion of philologically extraneous material is characteristic of the development of lexicography, and by including such a vast amount of quotation Johnson exposed himself to the same criticism that Cellarius had leveled decisively at Faber. But Johnson was not the only lexicographer who was reluctant to give up the older tradition of pedagogy. The same writer who complained to Strahan about Johnson's excessive quotation also complained about the "long moral discourses" that Scott included in his edition of Bailey's *Dictionary*; he concludes with the progressive remark that "these moral reflections are just as much out of their proper place, as the citations given by Johnson for the sake of their own beauty & not for the purpose of shewing the use & meaning of the word. No Creature, but a fool or a woman, will have recourse to Scott's Dictionary for morality or to Johnson's Dictionary for fine reading" (MS Lichfield 37, fol. 2). Had he read more carefully in Johnson, Strahan's correspondent might have complained about the adscititious morality in that work too. Although there is no hard evidence that Johnson saw a sixteenth-century edition of Faber, his *Dictionary* belongs to the tradition of the *Forum Romanum*.[17]

Like Faber's *Thesaurus*, Johnson's "Forum Britannicum" presents a symposium of writers discoursing on the whole round of learning. The audience of both books is importantly, though not exclusively, composed of students, and the teaching in both books focuses especially on fundamental points of religion and morality. This does not mean that Johnson's book is not a dictionary in the ordinary, modern sense. It is a word book and remained supremely useful in that way for all readers, not only students, for over a hundred years. That Johnson achieves more than one end in the *Dictionary* should come as no surprise. As Paul Fussell has shown, the *Dictionary* was for Johnson a summation and "an emblem of his whole writing career" (195), and, as Johnson himself says in *Rambler* 139, written when he was well into the composition of the *Dictionary*, "it is always a proof of extensive thought and accurate circumspection, to promote various purposes by the same act" (*Yale* 4: 370–71).

Although Johnson's search for the illustrative quotations that fill his book may have been partly "fortuitous and unguided" (preface, par. 28), it was also partly directed to works that would help him achieve his multiple aims. The central purpose of the *Dictionary* is philological, and the majority of Johnson's bibliographical decisions were, broadly speaking, linguistic: acknowledged masters of English are heavily quoted, while scores of lesser writers are neglected. But Johnson also made bibliographical choices that promoted his moral and educational purposes; for example, he excluded the works of the morally dangerous Hobbes and frequently cited refutations of them by John Bramhall. On a larger scale, Johnson ensured his book's overall educational character by taking a significant number of his quotations from other educational writings. The most conspicuous educational works in the *Dictionary* are those of Locke and of his disciple, Isaac Watts, but these are supplemented by numerous others, including an elementary geography book by George Abbot, *A Brief Description of the Whole Worlde*; Roger Ascham's *Schoolmaster*; two works by Richard Allestree, whom Locke perpetually recommended to students; Andrew Bourde's *Fyrst Boke of the Introduction of Knowledge*; Henry Felton's *Dissertation on Reading the Classics*, written "to a young Nobleman of sprightly Parts, and a lively Imagination" (x); William Derham's *Physico-Theology*, a book that Johnson recommended to students on other occasions;[18] Bishop Wilkins's *Mathematical Magick*;[19] Roger L'Estrange's translation of Aesop's fables, a standard work for students, equipped with morals and reflections; Milton's essay "Of

Education," the only one of Milton's prose works that Johnson cites;
Peacham's *Graphice*, as well as some of his other instructional books;
William Walker's *Syntaxis*; *English Exercises for school-boys to translate
into Latin* by J. Garretson; George Cheyne's *Philosophical Principles of
Religion: Natural and Reveal'd*, written "for the Use of Younger Students of *Philosophy*, who while they were taught the most probable
account of the *Appearances of Nature* from the Modern Discoveries,
might thereby have the *Principles of Natural Religion* insensibly instill'd
into them at the same time" (preface, par. 1); and Sir Kenelm Digby's
Of Bodies and *Of the Immortality of Man's Soul*, comprehensive texts
addressed to the author's son and meant to fulfill from exile his
parental obligation to educate him.

A good many other works cited in the *Dictionary* also contribute to
basic educational goals or have primarily educational sections, to
which Johnson was generally receptive, but the bulk of purely educational works is itself a significant portion of Johnson's bibliography,
especially when it is considered in light of the size and constitution of
Johnson's total body of sources. A majority of the 116,000 quotations
in the *Dictionary* come from a handful of predictable literary exem-
plars: Shakespeare, Dryden, Swift, Pope, Addison, Hooker, Bacon,
and the King James Bible. A numerically similar group of well-known
sermon writers, together with the reference works that Johnson cited,
account for about another quarter of the illustrative material. In
the 25 percent of the *Dictionary* that comes from less obvious, less
philologically obligatory sources, Johnson's educational intentions are
clearly visible. In a rare instance of bowdlerizing, I think, Johnson
acknowledges the moral, educational nature of his book. Under the
key word "to learn" he has Caliban say,

> You taught me language, and my profit on't
> Is, I know not how to curse: the red plague rid you
> For *learning*[2] me your language.
> *Shakesp. Tempest.*

The "not" that Johnson interpolates here (which he neither found in
Warburton's Shakespeare, nor included in his own edition of Shakespeare in 1765, nor expunged from his correction of the *Dictionary* in
1773) makes the passage a self-conscious address to the book itself
from one of its reluctant students. The *Dictionary* is a moral teacher
whose principal subject is language, but, as the passage also suggests,
it is not without a sense of humor about itself and its audience.

The *Dictionary*'s educational concerns are coherent with Johnson's overall life of writing. He very often saw his position as a writer in society as an educational position. In *Rambler* 119, for example, he once styled himself one of "those who undertake to initiate the young and ignorant in the knowledge of life" (*Yale* 4: 270). There is throughout his published work a sense of public responsibility, and he always saw this responsibility as ultimately moral. In the last *Rambler* Johnson shows which aspects of education and public service he considered most important: he takes the greatest satisfaction in recalling his emphasis upon the serious topics of religion and morality. He showed a similar commitment to the religious aspect of education when he discovered that a certain charity school in London did not (in November 1756) include religion in its course of study; as James Clifford reports in his biography of the middle years, "Johnson complained so strenuously that a teacher of religion was hired the next February" (177).

The underlying reasons for Johnson's emphasis upon these serious topics in education probably have as much to do with his concern for his own soul as with his concern for the spiritual well-being of others. He received from Locke, Bacon, and countless others the ancient doctrine that young persons are literally impressionable, even malleable. This was often the premise of a powerful conclusion. In a sermon "Of the Education of Children," John Tillotson concludes from the pliant condition of youth that "*Parents* must one Day be accountable for all their neglects of their *Children*: And so likewise shall *Ministers* and *Masters* of *Families* for their *People* and *Servants*, so far as they had the Charge of them" (*Six Sermons* 238-39). In the second sermon in his series on domestic duties, Tillotson makes the point in a way that probably came home to Johnson: "all the evil they commit ever after, will be in a great measure chargeable upon us, and will be put upon our score in the Judgment of the Great Day. It ought to make us tremble to think with what bitterness and Rage our Children and Servants will then fly in our faces, for having been the Cause of their eternal Ruin . . ." (*Six Sermons* 86).[20] Although Johnson had no children, he was the master of a household and perpetually a teacher. At about the time he finished the *Dictionary* he resolved in his diary "to instruct my family" (*Yale* 1: 57), meaning certainly his servant, Frank Barber, but also, perhaps, anyone else who came under his roof. Furthermore, he extended the duties incumbent upon him as household master to more public theaters, including his public literary performances and his conversations with the young and impressionable Boswell. Like Bacon, Johnson may well have felt that "the care of posterity is most in them that have no posterity."[21]

Some rare inside evidence that Johnson indeed modeled his public presentations for the public good, rather than for the sake of anything like self-expression, appears in Clifford's *Dictionary Johnson*: writing about a conversation that took place at Samuel Richardson's, Mrs. Chapone says, "I had the assurance to dispute with him [Johnson] on the subject of human malignity, and wondered to hear a man who by his actions shows so much benevolence, maintain that the human heart is naturally malevolent, and that all the benevolence we see in the few who are good, is acquired by reason and religion. . . . I told him I suspected him of these bad notions from some of his Ramblers. . . . To which he answered, that if he had betrayed such sentiments in the Ramblers, it was not with design, for that he believed the doctrine of human malevolence, though a true one, is not a useful one, and ought not to be published to the world" (120). In the *Dictionary*, as in the rest of his public presentations, and perhaps to a greater degree than in most of them, Johnson is conscious of his educational responsibilities. His usual sensitivity to audience and to every other aspect of genre guides his performance. Carlyle was not, therefore, completely wrong when he made his famous remark that "had Johnson left us nothing but his Dictionary, one might have traced there a great intellect, a genuine man" (see Wimsatt, *Philosophic Words* 26). But the "man" one finds in the *Dictionary*, or indeed in all of Johnson's works, is a public presentation circumscribed by the larger, less regular, and finally unknowable person who created it.

3. The Meaning of the *Dictionary*

Although as a book Johnson's *Dictionary* is partly an encyclopedia and partly an educational text, it is clearly and primarily a dictionary in the ordinary sense. Nevertheless, like any other work that Johnson admired and recommended, his book carries an important moral message. It does this chiefly by presenting quotations that, besides illustrating the meanings of words, teach fundamental points of morality. This is the same method employed by many of the educational texts included in the *Dictionary*, and Johnson often simply transfers their work to his book. In a representative case, he adduces Watts to help define a logical term and at the same time to make a moral point: "*Sorites* is when several middle terms are chosen to connect one another successively in several propositions, till the last proposition connects its predicate with the first subject. Thus, all men of revenge have their souls often uneasy; uneasy souls are a plague to themselves; now to be one's own plague is folly in the extreme." Similarly, Watts's discussion under "determinative[2]" ends with the example: "every pious man shall be happy."[22] In a few rare cases Johnson invented his own instructive examples. Under the printing terms "burgeois" and "brevier," for instance, he inserts literal illustrations by having some lines set in the respective type sizes signified by the two words. The choices he makes here are significant because he had the world of English literature open before him: in bourgeois type Johnson had printed Pope's "Laugh where we must, be candid where we can, / But vindicate the ways of God to man"; a few pages earlier we read in brevier letters Milton's equally broad moral injunction, "Nor love thy life, nor hate, but what thou liv'st, / Live well, how long or short, permit to heav'n."[23]

The broad generality of these lines and the fact that Johnson chose them above all others makes them appear as emblems for the whole meaning of the *Dictionary*, but there is a slightly more specific message that is more prevalent in Johnson's book and that he seems to have taken pains to emphasize. This message is much like the moral of the allegorical tale "The Vision of Theodore," which Johnson appended to Dodsley's educational text *The Preceptor* earlier in the same year that saw Dodsley recommend Johnson for the task of writing the English Dictionary. The allegory centers around a vision of the Mountain of Existence and the various bands of pilgrims trying to ascend it and get into heaven. The pilgrims are led first by Innocence, then by Education, and finally by Reason and Religion. Theodore follows the progress of the pilgrims up the Mountain until some of them reach the mist at the top where "*Reason* however, discerned that they were safe, but *Religion* saw that they were happy" (Dodlsey 2: 524). At last Theodore sees the demonic spectacle of the students who followed Reason without Religion: they are overcome by bad habits like avarice, ambition, sloth, despair, and the "Bowl of Intoxication." The message that Dodsley wanted at the end of his educational text is one that warns against excessive devotion to the standards of learning that the rest of his book encourages.

Although they are formally very different works, *The Preceptor* and the *Dictionary* share many educational goals, and each in its own way

contains an admonition about an irreligious devotion to learning. What
The Preceptor does in an allegorical fable, the *Dictionary* does with apt
citation. In the imperative mood of Proverbs 3.5, for example, the
Dictionary urges: "Trust in the Lord with all thine heart; and *lean*[2]
not unto thine own understanding." Similarly, Wisdom 17.12 warns,
"Fear nothing else but a betraying of *succours*[2] which reason offer-
eth." Not many of the *Dictionary*'s statements on the subject are this
extreme, but many point out the inferiority of mere reason in terms
reminiscent of Theodore's "Vision." Rogers seems to interpret the mist
at the top of the Mountain of Existence when he says, "The understanding is *dim*[2], and cannot by its natural light discover spiritual
truths" and "What *unassisted* reason could not discover, that God has
set clearly before us in the revelation of the gospel: a felicity equal to
our most enlarged desires; a state of immortal and unchangeable
glory." Under a key word Johnson adduces Dryden to make a metaphor for reason that could be a gloss for the whole "Vision":

> Dim, as the borrow'd beams of moon and stars
> To lonely, weary, wand'ring travellers,
> Is *reason*[1] to the soul: and as on high,
> Those rowling fires discover but the sky,
> Not light us here; so *reason's* glimmering ray
> Was lent, not to assure our doubtful way,
> But guide us upward to a better day.

In *Rambler* 180 Johnson speaks more directly to the vanity of those
who pin their hopes for happiness on reason or learning: "If, instead of
wandering after the meteors of philosophy which fill the world with
splendour for a while, and then sink and are forgotten, the candidates
of learning fixed their eyes upon the permanent lustre of moral and
religious truth, they would find a more certain direction to happiness"
(*Yale* 5: 186). As the motto for this *Rambler* Johnson chose a pair of
lines from the *Greek Anthology* that might also serve as an epigraph
for a great number of quotations in the *Dictionary*. He makes the
lines religious by rendering the Greek σοφός, which usually means
"learned," "wise," or "clever in practical matters," as "life and morals";
he has the ancient poet say, "On life, on morals, be thy thoughts
employ'd; / Leave to the schools their atoms and their void" (*Yale* 5:
181). An expository version of the message appears in the *Dictionary*
under "conformation": "Virtue and vice, sin and holiness, and the

conformation[2] of our hearts and lives to the duties of true religion and morality, are things of more consequence than the furniture of under-standing." No matter what the particular region of learning he burns to conquer, the student who consults the *Dictionary* is bound to find reminders of his vanity. A snippet from Pope, for example, drives the point home to the aspiring poet: "That man makes a mean figure in the eyes of reason, who is measuring syllables and *coupling*[2] rhimes, when he should be mending his own soul, and securing his own immortality." Likewise, Hooker reminds the lover of natural history: "There is a knowledge which God hath always revealed unto them in the works of nature: this they honour and esteem highly as profound wisdom, *howbeit* this wisdom saveth them not." But perhaps the greatest number of contributions to the theme are general. Tillotson puts human knowledge in perspective by saying, "That man that doth not know those things, which are of necessity for him to know, is but an ignorant man, whatever he may know *besides*[1]." In much the same tone South refers to "the grandees and giants in knowledge, who laughed at all besides themselves, as barbarous and insignificant, yet *blundered*[1], and stumbled, about their grand and principal concern." Like a surprising number of its entries, the *Dictionary*'s illustration of "reverently" regales the reader with an injunction to stop what he is doing:

> Then down with all thy boasted volumes, down;
> Only reserve the sacred one:
> Low, *reverently* low,
> Make thy stubborn knowledge bow: .
> To look to heav'n, be blind to all below.
>
> *Prior.*

In Sermon 6 Johnson discourses on the vanity of human learning in relation to religion. In so doing he seems to explain "The Vision of Theodore" and to summarize the primary theme of the *Dictionary*:

> Another common motive to pride is knowledge, a motive
> equally weak, vain and idle. . . . Learning indeed, imperfect as it
> is, may contribute to many great and noble ends, and may be
> called in to the assistance of religion; as it is too often perversely
> employed against it; it is of use to display the greatness, and
> vindicate the justice, of the Almighty; to explain the difficulties,
> and enforce the proofs, of religion. . . . But how little reason

have we to boast of our knowledge, when we only gaze and

wonder at the surfaces of things? When the wisest, and most arrogant philosopher knows not how a grain of corn is generated,
or why a stone falls to the ground? But were our knowledge far
greater than it is, let us yet remember that goodness, not knowledge, is the happiness of man! The day will come, it will come
quickly, when it shall profit us more to have subdued one proud
thought, than to have numbered the host of heaven. (*Yale* 14:
71–72)

In the *Dictionary* Johnson prints a possible source for his last sentence
when he cites Hooker in illustration of "disdainful": "There will come
a time when three words, uttered with charity and meekness, shall
receive a far more blessed reward than three thousand volumes,
written with *disdainful* sharpness of wit." Writing on "The Hermit of
Teneriffe," Richard B. Schwartz declares that Johnson's fable is "a
kind of epitome or précis of his total statement as essayist, poet,
biographer, travel writer, dramatist, and writer of sermon and parable"
(33). I merely wish to add that the *Dictionary* does not fall outside these
bounds and is thematically consistent with the rest of Johnson's works.

In general, the superiority of virtue to knowledge, the limitations of
human reason, and the need for revealed religion are important
subjects of a great many of the works that Johnson canvassed for
inclusion in the *Dictionary*. These themes are prominent in Hooker,
Raleigh, Browne, Boyle, and Locke, and their ancestry can be traced
to the wisdom literature of the Bible through such notable observers of
human ignorance and error as Cornelius Agrippa, Nicholas of Cusa,
and the third-century church father Lactantius Firmianus. But Johnson made sure his book would carry ample reminders of the vanity of
human learning by extracting numerous quotations from two works
wholly devoted to the theme: Joseph Glanvill's *Scepsis Scientifica: or,
Confest Ignorance the way to Science* and Thomas Baker's *Reflections upon
Learning; Wherein is Shewn the Insufficiency Thereof, in its several Particulars: in order to Evince the Usefulness and Necessity of Revelation.* Dryden
expresses the theme of all these works in lines used to illustrate "to
oblige" and "to spring":

> Thus man by his own strength to heav'n would soar,
> And would not be *oblig'd*[2] to God for more.
> Vain, wretched creature, how art thou misled,
> To think thy wit these godlike notions bred!

These truths are not the product of thy mind,
But dropt from heav'n, and of a nobler kind:
Reveal'd religion first inform'd thy sight,
And reason saw not, 'till faith *sprung*[2] the light.

Locke's words under "veneration" bring religious knowledge more closely into the circle of human understanding, but he gives it a highly privileged place: "Theology is the comprehension of all other knowledge, directed to its true end, *i.e.* the honour and *veneration* of the creator, and the happiness of mankind." The neo-Platonist divine Henry More perceives the same relationship: "The christian *religion*[2], rightly understood, is the deepest and choicest piece of philosophy that is"; and something like this perception is what underlies Bentley's redaction of a famous sentence in Bacon's *Essays*: "Since, by a little *smattering*[1] in learning, and great conceit of himself, he has lost his religion, may he find it again by harder study and an humbler mind."

Because religion is perpetually placed above reason and learning, it is safely seen on some occasions in terms of its inferiors. South effectively uses learning as a metaphor for religion when he says, "The truths [sic] of Christ crucified, is the Christian's philosophy, and a good life is the Christian's logick; that great instrumental *introductive* art, that must guide the mind into the former." This aspect of the relationship between reason and religion is most compactly expressed in Oxford University's pious motto, which comes from the Vulgate version of the twenty-sixth Psalm: "Dominus illuminatio mea" (the Lord is my light). Arbuthnot provides one version of this: "O truth divine! enlighten'd by thy ray, / I *grope* and guess no more, but see my way." Hosea contributes an even more radical form of the sentence: "Then shall we know, if we *follow*[5] on to know the Lord."

However, the danger of describing religion in terms of reason is that the more comprehensible vehicle of the description will seem more important than its divine subject. This danger is apparent in Tillotson's worldly exhortation to religion: "Men *stand*[65] very much *upon* the reputation of their understandings, and of all things hate to be accounted fools: the best way to avoid this imputation is to be religious." The assumption that religion is the highest form of understanding is sunk in the midst of the good social sense it makes to be pious. The danger is even greater in some of Locke's formulations. Indeed, reason tends to step out of its proper place in a modern

reading of Locke's brief statement on inspiration: "If this internal
light[2], or any proposition which we take for inspired, be conformable to the principles of reason, or to the word of God, which is attested revelation, reason warrants it." Although he probably intended nothing of the kind, Locke inaugurates the sort of eighteenth-century theology that Mark Pattison sums up in the sentence, "Reason was at first offered as the basis of faith, but gradually became its substitute" (2: 48).

By and large, however, the *Dictionary* stands in opposition to the growing rationalism that Pattison perceived in the theology of its day. One indication of this opposition is Johnson's treatment of the deist Lord Bolingbroke: Johnson defines "irony" as "a mode of speech in which the meaning is contrary to the words: as, *Bolingbroke was a holy man.*" He also attacks Bolingbroke's style under "Gallicism," and he mainly quotes him from the odd letter to Pope.[24] Other deistic writers do not appear in the *Dictionary* at all, and the best measure of the *Dictionary*'s commitment to a more conventional subordination of reason to religion is in the great body of quotation from more orthodox writers. Robert Boyle, though a true philosopher, expresses the subordination of learning to religion properly: "Though with wit and parts their possessors could never engage God to send forth his light and his truth; yet now that revelation hath disclosed them, and that he hath been pleased to make them *radiate* in his word, men may recollect those scatter'd beams, and kindling with them the topicks proper to warm our affections, enflame holy zeal." On the whole, the *Dictionary* tends to quote passages that enact Boyle's advice. The only way to show this is by presenting, gradually, in many distinct chapters, a significant selection of Johnson's approximately 116,000 illustrative quotations. But here and there in his book Johnson seems to print somewhat more direct statements of what it is all about. In his definition of "crossrow" he comes close to summing up the whole meaning of his book: he defines the word simply as "Alphabet," but then he explains that it is "so named because a cross is placed at the beginning, to shew that the end of learning is piety." The generality of the remark is significant, and the fact that it does not appear in Phillips, Bailey, Chambers, or Ainsworth suggests that its presence is due to Johnson's own extraphilological motives.

4. The Genre of Johnson's *Dictionary*

Despite its general seriousness and the overall piety of its message, the *Dictionary* also contains a certain degree of self-conscious irony. Just as the vanity of human learning is an important theme in this vast exposition of learning, the particular vanity of lexicography is a theme in this lexicon. Johnson defines "lexicographer" as "a harmless drudge," and to exemplify the eighth sense of "dull" he writes, "*to make dictionaries is* dull *work*." The entry under "Grubstreet," which is, to begin with, out of place in an appellative dictionary, includes dictionaries among the examples of this district's "mean productions." Johnson included "lich" in his book and ended his entry with a salute to his homeland: "*Salve magna parens*" (Hail, glorious mother). Likewise, before concluding his entry under "Grubstreet" he adds a salute to his literary homeland in the decent and jocular obscurity of a learned language:

> *Χαῖρ᾽ Ἰθακὴ μετ᾽ ἄεθλα, μετ᾽ ἄλγεα πικρὰ*
> *Ἀσπασίως τέον οὖδας ἱκάνομαι.*
> [Hail, Ithaca! after struggles and bitter hardships,
> I happily arrive at your border.]

In this lofty language Johnson styles himself a sort of satirical, scribbling Ulysses.[25] This combination of the lofty and the satirical, although not prevalent, is an important part of the *Dictionary*'s overall form and meaning; it is found here and there throughout the book in exemplary sentences of Johnson's own devising and, at least apparently, in illustrative quotations that satirize the lexicographer's tasks. Under "to peddle," for instance, Johnson seems to reflect on his labor when he says, "It is commonly written *piddle*: as, what *piddling* work is here." Under "to gather" and "gatherer" Johnson seems to assume the voice of Wotton in order to denigrate his work in the same vein: "I will spend this preface about those from whom I have *gathered*[2] my knowledge; for I am but a *gatherer*[1] and disposer of other mens stuff." Under "pincushion" the satire assumes the more invective second person when Congreve declares, "Thou art a retailer of phrases and dost deal in remnants of remnants, like a maker of *pincushions*." In the words of Arbuthnot, which he saw fit to cite three times, Johnson seems to lament the casualties of his piddling work: "After all the care I have taken, there may be, in such a multitude of passages, several *misquoted, misinterpreted,* and *miscalculated.*" Taking up the third person, Atterbury ridicules the same aspect of magpie lexicography: "In all that heap of quotations which he has *piled*[1] up, nothing is aimed at." But a witty retort to this accusation comes to Johnson's pen from Prior: "I had a mind to collect and digest such observations and *apophthegms,* as tend to the proof of that great assertion, All is vanity."

The notes of self-conscious irony in Johnson's *Dictionary* put it in a class of encyclopedic works that Northrop Frye identifies as Menippean satire—or the anatomy, as he later and more happily calls it (309–12). Frye's remarks on the literary form to which his own *Anatomy* is a brilliant modern contribution are unfortunately few; the many, many subspecies require longer treatment and more distinct classification. Nevertheless, his sketch of this neglected genre reveals much about the literary relations of the *Dictionary* and about Johnson's intellectual ancestry.

As Frye describes it, the "creative treatment of exhaustive erudition is the organizing principle" of the anatomy, and there are two main branches of the form: "short" and "long." Johnson's *Dictionary* performs in both kinds, and, like anatomies of every length, it sees evil and folly "as diseases of the intellect." "The short form of the Menippean satire is usually a dialogue or colloquy, in which the dramatic interest is in a conflict of ideas rather than of character. This is the favorite form of Erasmus, and is common in Voltaire." It is also present in the works of their fellow lexicographer and satirist, Samuel Johnson. Parts of *Rasselas, Irene,* Johnson's periodical essays, and "The Vanity of Human Wishes" work in this form, and so do many passages in the *Dictionary* where successive speakers seem to engage one another in an intellectual colloquy. Moreover, the subjects of the colloquies in Johnson's "Forum Britannicum" are very often the same eternal problems discussed in seminal Menippean works such as Boethius's *Consolation of Philosophy.* For example, in prose section VI of the *Consolation* Boethius says the first question of Philosophy is whether "this world is run by random and chance events, or . . . rationally directed"; the response is, "I know that God the creator watches over and directs his work" (167). A similar colloquy occurs in the *Dictionary* in illustration of the philosophically sensitive word "chance":

> As th' unthought accident is guilty
> Of what we wildly do, so we profess

Ourselves to be the slaves of *chance*[1], and flies
Of every wind that blows.

Shakes. Winter's Tale.

Chance[1] is but a mere name, and really nothing in itself;
a conception of our minds, and only a compendious way of
speaking, whereby we would express, that such effects as are
commonly attributed to *chance*, were verily produced by their
true and proper causes, but without their design to produce
them. *Bentley.*

To say a thing is a *chance*[3] or casuality, as it relates to second
causes, is not profaneness, but a great truth; as signifying no
more, than that there are some events besides the knowledge
and power of second agents. *South.*

All nature is but art, unknown to thee;
All *chance*[3] direction, which thou canst not see.

Pope.

Like Boethius, the *Dictionary* provides a pious answer to the ancient
philosophical question.

The elaborate commentary on the Shakespearean quotation provided by the other three is reminiscent of the Menippean works of
Macrobius, which find all things under the sun implicit in Vergil's
poetry. But Johnson is both more pious and more satirical than
Macrobius. A second good example of his piety in the short form of
Menippean satire occurs in illustration of the word "to misshape." The
colloquy here turns on a reference to a physicotheological debate
about the apparent uselessness and irregularity of mountains. Thomas
Burnet found mountains horrific signs of the fallen nature of the
world, but later pious naturalists attempted to show that mountains,
like every other part of God's creation, are useful and only apparently
deformed. Addison reopens the debate with an observation from his
Travels in Italy: "The Alps broken into so many steps and precipices,
form one of the most irregular, *misshapen* scenes in the world." Bentley
corrects this view with the more orthodox statement, "We ought not to
believe that the banks of the ocean are really deformed, because they
have not the form of a regular bulwark; nor that the mountains are
misshapen, because they are not exact pyramids or cones."

With equal alacrity Milton answers Spenser's dangerous abrogation

> He said, dear daughter, rightly may I rue
> The fall of famous children born of me;
>   But who can turn the stream of *destiny*[2],
>   Or break the chain of strong necessity,
> Which fast is ty'd to Jove's eternal seat?
> *Fairy Queen, b.* i.

> How can hearts, not free, be try'd whether they serve
> Willing or no, who will but what they must
> By *destiny*[2], and can no other chuse?
> *Milton's Paradise Lost.*

Here, as elsewhere, the *Dictionary* seems eager to remind its students
that freedom is a necessary condition of morality, and, although the
notion of fate is granted more reality than is chance, its reality weighs
nothing against the *Dictionary*'s very frequent assertions of human
freedom (see below, section 9.3).

Other dialogues add to the *Dictionary*'s admonition on the vanity of
human learning. Under "elevate," for example, Locke's commentary
upon Milton reminds Johnson's readers that human learning is irrelevant and trivial in comparison to the saving grace of revealed religion:

> Others apart sat on a hill retired,
> In thoughts more *elevate*[3], and reason'd high
> Of providence, foreknowledge, will and fate.
> *Milton.*

> In all that great extent, wherein the mind wanders, in those re-
> mote speculations it may seem to be *elevated*[3] with, it stirs not
> beyond sense or reflection. *Locke.*

Since they are about devils in Hell, Milton's lines are themselves, in
their own context, ironic, but Johnson makes sure their irony appears
also in the context of his book when he appends Locke's sentence to
them. A similar piece of satire on the whole human effort to reason out
the great truths of life appears appropriately in a dialogue that illustrates the meaning of "discussion." South says, "Truth cannot
be found without some labour and intention of the mind, and the
thoughts dwelling a considerable time upon the survey and *discus-*

sion[1] of each particular." But Prior rallies this sober and serious advice with the satirical retort,

> Various *discussions*[1] tear our heated brain:
> Opinions often turn; still doubts remain;
> And who indulges thought, increases pain.

Throughout the *Dictionary* Johnson often employs Prior to remind his readers of human ignorance and error. Such reminders discourage pride in learning while finding a positive blessing in our state of ignorance. This healthy sense of human fallibility prevents humility from degenerating into gloom. Prior performs his more cheerful office in response to the unusually long quotation from Dryden that Johnson positioned under the key word "life":

> When I consider *life*[2] 'tis all a *cheat*[1],
> Yet fool'd by hope men favour the deceit,
> Live on, and think to-morrow will repay;
> To-morrow's falser than the former day;
> Lies more; and when it says we shall be blest
> With some new joy, takes off what we possest.
> Strange cozenage! none would live past years again,
> Yet all hope pleasure in what yet remain;
> And from the dregs of *life* think to receive
> What the first sprightly running could not give:
> I'm tir'd of waiting for this chemick gold,
> Which fools us young, and beggars us when old.

Prior does much to lighten this burden when he adds cheerfully:

> Howe'er 'tis well that while mankind
> Through *life's*[2] perverse meanders errs,
> He can imagin'd pleasures find,
> To combat against real cares.

The precious space devoted to these lengthy illustrative quotations and their placement under such a common and important word suggest that Johnson wanted these remarks in his book for moral as well as philological purposes. In this collocation, as in his illustration of brevier type with Milton's "Nor love thy life, nor hate," Johnson appears to offer his readers fundamental wisdom that sums up the teaching in his whole encyclopedic work.

Whereas individual colloquies in the *Dictionary* represent the "short" form of Menippean satire, the whole book is an example of the "long" form. The long anatomy is exemplified by Athenaeus's *Deipno-sophists* and Macrobius's *Saturnalia*, but it derives ultimately, like the encyclopedia itself, from Varro, "who was," says Frye, "enough of a polymath to make Quintilian, if not stare and gasp, at any rate call him *vir Romanorum eruditissimus*" (311). The most important English example of the long form of Menippean satire is Burton's *Anatomy of Melancholy*, a book that Johnson loved and admired above almost all others. The most central and typical example of the species is another book that Johnson admired and partly translated; Frye could be talking about many sections of the *Dictionary* when he says, "Boethius' *Consolation of Philosophy*, with its dialogue form, its verse interludes and its pervading tone of contemplative irony, is a pure anatomy, a fact of considerable importance for the understanding of its vast influence" (312). Especially when the *Dictionary* is properly taken into account, Johnson resembles Boethius both in the piety of his universal concerns and in his treatment of many particulars. Johnson's tone is often in the range of Burton's, but he is much less compelled to drive all of his observations under a single heading. In his attitude to the "exhaustive erudition" that characterizes the whole genre of the anatomy, Johnson is closest to Boethius, turning away with equal force from the extremes of Swiftian disgust with, and Macrobian adulation of, knowledge.

Another fellow satirist to whom Johnson is importantly related is Erasmus. All in all, considering the powerful strain of Lactantian skepticism in the *Dictionary* and the great masses of knowledge through which it runs, Johnson's attitude to learning may be closest of all to what Erasmus expresses in the *Praise of Folly*, especially in the apologetic addendum, the *Letter to Martin Dorp*. Having urged Dorp to learn Greek, with malicious sincerity, Erasmus concludes (in Clarence Miller's translation): "But if you are of the opinion that the love of true holiness makes all human learning contemptible, if you think that we can reach such wisdom more quickly by transforming ourselves, as it were, into Christ, and that everything else worth knowing can be perceived more fully in the light of faith than in the books of men, I am quite willing to agree with you. On the other hand, as matters now stand, if you think you can get a true knowledge of theology without skill in languages, especially in that language in which almost all of Holy Scripture has come down to us, you are completely 'off the track'" (163). The first part of Erasmus's conclusion appears often in Johnson's other works, and it is therefore not surprising to find it prominent in the *Dictionary*.[26] To give just one example here, the citation of Henry More under "discursive" comes very close to Erasmus's particular indictment of learning: "There is a sanctity of soul and body, of more efficacy for the receiving of divine truths, than the greatest pretences to *discursive*[2] demonstration."

Despite all its various assertions of this theme,[27] however, the *Dictionary*, like Erasmus, also embodies a statement that is "on the other hand"—namely, the sheer weight of all the learning contained in the book and, in a sense, the fact of the book itself. Although Johnson continuously arranges assertions of the vanity of human learning and the fallibility of human knowledge, he nevertheless presents and encourages learning and knowledge as thoroughly as any writer of his time. Like many other anatomies, the *Dictionary* cherishes the knowledge that it derides and writes its satirical phrases over the volumes of a dream book, "a book," as Johnson described it in his preface, "in place of all other dictionaries whether appellative or technical" (par. 72).

5.   The Field of Knowledge in Johnson's *Dictionary*

"An ideal philosophy," according to Kenneth Burke, "would seek to satisfy the requirements of a perfect dictionary. It would be a calculus (matured by constant reference to the 'collective revelation' that is got by a social *body* of thought) for charting the nature of events and for clarifying all important relationships" (113n). Johnson's book, besides being an important collection of words and definitions, is a dictionary in the sense that Burke uses here, even if it is not a perfect one: it presents a "collective revelation" culled from important works of English literature, though not from the whole range of linguistic expression in English. The revelation to which Johnson constantly refers is selective as well as collective. It is not possible to write a calculus that accurately maps everything revealed in the book—some of what appears is random, and, of course, the constraints of Johnson's principal, lexicographical task do not always permit the revelation of material that he would have chosen if he were not beating the track of the alphabet. Then, the alphabetic organization itself obviously obscures any other organization of the field of knowledge that Johnson presents. Yet, even if it is not obvious, and even if it is interrupted by randomness and by the primary linguistic concerns of the book, there

is a field of knowledge in the *Dictionary*, and it is possible to describe
this field, though it may not be possible to define it.

As an encyclopedic book of quotations, the *Dictionary* both records a history of knowledge and is itself an important event in that history. In order to describe the knowledge in the *Dictionary*, it seems best to see Johnson's book after the model of the commonplace book. This is a model that some contemporary lexicographers consciously invoked in recommending their work. For example, the translators of LeClerc's version of Morery's *Great Historical Dictionary*, which Johnson used in writing some of his early biographies, praise the work in the following terms:

> *Of how great Subserviency this* Work *must needs be to the Encrease and Improvement of Humane Knowledge, will easily appear to any one that considers it as an Universal* Common-place-Book, *to which they may have* Familiar Recourse, *on all Occasions of Enquiry after whatsoever has been, or is Remarkable, either in* History, Geography or Poesy: *And with this Unspeakable Advantage, that here you may find it, at a far less Expence of Time, Money and Trouble, than ever you cou'd hitherto in any other Treatise: This* Dictionary *being a Perfect Extract, and the very Quintessence of what was writ on these Subjects before him; and he has laid them up in such Obvious Repositories, as they may be come at by anyone who understands the* Alphabet. (preface, par. 5)

The "Obvious Repositories" that Morery's translators speak of are the words in their dictionary, many of which are proper names. Johnson's *Dictionary* also is a commonplace book, although it uses a general list of English words as its "repositories" or heads for the arrangement of information.

However, there are other boundary lines in the *Dictionary*'s field of knowledge, somewhat less distinct than the divisions between the individual entries in the word list. Like most other eighteenth-century schoolbooks and encyclopedias, Johnson's book follows the main outlines of knowledge drawn by John Locke at the end of the seventeenth century. Locke describes these broad outlines, among other places, in his widely read essay "A New Method of a Common-Place-Book." First of all, he says, "If I would put any thing in my Common-Place-Book, I find out a Head to which I may refer it. Each Head ought to be some important and essential Word to the Matter in Hand" (*Works* 3: 485). Later on he makes one large division in the field of knowledge when he recommends that readers keep two commonplace books, one for each of "the two Heads, to which one may refer all our Knowledge, *viz.* Moral Philosophy and Natural." He continues, however, "You may add a third, which may be called the *Knowledge of Signs*, which relates to the Use of Words, and is of much more Extent, than meer Criticism" (*Works* 3: 488).[28] Broadly speaking, Johnson's *Dictionary* sees knowledge as divisible into Locke's three main heads—but some further division is necessary in order to present the *Dictionary*'s field of knowledge in a more distinct and useful way.

The appropriate divisions might reasonably be sought in the actual commonplace books that Locke himself kept. In fact, Locke's notebooks do contain many "heads" that work as descriptive titles for the material contained in Johnson's quotations. The Bodleian Library's MS Locke c. 25, for instance, has heads like "passions," "anguish," "love," "hope," "pain," "pleasure," "weariness," "happiness," "atheism," "mundus," "God," "Ignorance," "drink," "study," "food," "error," "folly," "imagination," and "madnesse" (fols. 24–26). On the whole, however, Locke's heads are often too detailed to be usefully applied to the field of knowledge in the *Dictionary*; he commonly uses very specific titles for his entries, preferring most of all the proper names of men, books, plants, and diseases.

It is a tantalizing but unverifiable probability that Johnson himself prepared a notebook with heads after the manner of Locke while he was in the midst of writing the *Dictionary*: the Sotheby's Sale Catalogue for 24 May 1825 lists "A Pocket Book, date in the first leaf, April 14, 1752; containing an Index apparently to a Common Place Book" (Fleeman, *Preliminary Handlist of Documents* 8). Unfortunately, this book has not been seen since the tenth day of the 1825 sale. If it were found, and if its index was filled out, the book would provide a view of the field of knowledge that Johnson perceived, and important clues to the field of knowledge that he represented in his *Dictionary*. In the absence of Johnson's own work, however, there are still some interesting places to turn. A schoolmate of Locke's named Daniel Burgess has left a commonplace book (complete with an introductory copy of Locke's "New Method") that is suggestive. Among the topics included by Burgess and prominent in Johnson's circle of knowledge are "Methodus," "Otium," "Mulieres," "Morbus," "Ignorantia," "Educatio," and "Anima Immortalis." One of the most interesting things about Burgess's collection is that he finds contributions to these topics in many of the same books that Johnson read in order to fill the

Dictionary: like Johnson, he quotes Tillotson, Bacon, Locke, Dryden, and Milton. These writers may be particularly apt to supply remarks on the round of topics covered in the *Dictionary*, but it seems likely too that the collection of heads has its own sort of durability. Burgess or Johnson probably would have found material on the same topics in whatever literature they read for extracts, and the topics describe a complete, general, Lockean education.

Another collection of heads that works fairly well as an outline for the *Dictionary* is found in Bacon's *Essays*, which are the actual source of hundreds of the *Dictionary's* most pithy sentences in the area of knowledge that Locke called "moral philosophy." Bacon himself, in *The Advancement of Learning*, called this subject "Care and Culture of the Soul." Given the number of direct infusions of Bacon in Johnson's book, and given the vast influence that Bacon's vision of knowledge exerted over the generations of writers recorded in the *Dictionary*, it is not surprising that his topics provide a good summary of the ethical part of Johnson's field of knowledge: "custom, exercise, habit, educa-tion, example, imitation, emulation, company, friends, praise, reproof, exhortation, fame, laws, books, studies" (Bacon, *Works* 2: 517). The additional heads in the titles of Bacon's *Essays*—for example, "Truth," "Death," "Unity in Religion," "Of Parents and Children," "Marriage and a Single Life," "Atheism," "Superstition," "Travel," "Wisdom," "Health," "Youth and Age," "Faction," "Vicissitude," and "Vain glory" —make them perhaps the best general outline of what is in Johnson's *Dictionary*. Bacon's apothegms and his *Centuries* of notes and queries on natural history also supplied Johnson with many short, material sentiments. Indeed, in its structure and content of knowledge, the *Dictionary* is as close to Bacon as it is to Locke. Johnson's topics are closest to Bacon's, but his overall educational program, like Locke's, is more general and less aristocratic than Bacon's.

Part of the justification for seeing the *Dictionary* as a collection of contributions to a loosely defined set of topics is that it seems likely that Johnson thought of the field of knowledge in this topical way and that he tended to extract such things from his reading. Johnson's ability to reduce passages of Shakespeare to dilations on a standard humanis-tic topic has often been observed in commentary on his edition of the plays. He used just this capability on a much grander scale in the *Dictionary*. Part of what one acquaintance meant when she talked about Johnson's capacity to "tear out the heart of [a book]" (Boswell 3: 285) was his power to see and extract its topics or key words. As I hope to show, the *Dictionary* is the greatest sustained example of Johnson's, or perhaps anyone's, powers of reading in English. In a few instances, however, Johnson's task of extracting meaningful, topical sentences was lightened by the particular books he searched for quotations. The best example is his use of what W. R. Keast identified as "a busy lexicographer's dream—a thesaurus of quotations from *Clarissa*: 'An Ample Collection of Such of the Moral and Instructive Sentiments interspersed throughout the Work, as may be presumed to be of General Use and Service' " (436).[29] Keast counts ninety-seven references to *Clarissa* in the *Dictionary* and divides them into two groups: one of relatively random pieces, and another of more material sentiments. He finds that the seventy-eight more material remarks come from the thesaurus, a book that complied particularly well with the dreams of the sort of moral, encyclopedic lexicography that Johnson tried to achieve. It seems likely too that Johnson gave his own book direct infusions of this "Collection" rather than submitting it to the laborious process of underlining and extraction. He probably used it as a dictionary, just as he used Bailey's or Chambers's. Furthermore, in light of the paucity of extant books marked up for making the *Dictionary*, one must wonder if Johnson did not use other works of this kind to supply him with quotations already reduced to "Moral and Instructive Sentiments." Such a work was available on the Bible, for example, a book called Γραφαυτάρκεια, *or the Scriptures' Sufficiency Practically Demonstrated*, long thought to be by Locke because of its adherence to his directions for the proper organization of a commonplace book.

A discovery that Johnson used other indexed commonplace books in order to fill his *Dictionary* with material sentiments would provide further justification for a division of his book into topics, but there is already a good deal of justification for this in the intellectual tradition out of which the *Dictionary* grows and to which it makes an important contribution. The humanistic tradition in which Johnson participated valued abbreviations and compressions of learning into general, manageable commonplaces. In Johnson's own immediate time, the intellectual progeny of the great early humanists were excited about making such vast stores of knowledge more accessible by arranging them under proper heads. One of Locke's great disciples, Isaac Watts, carried on the humanist's work of conquering, reducing, and organizing the field of knowledge in *The Improvement of the Mind*, an educational work that Johnson cites very often in the *Dictionary*. With true zeal for the enterprise of classification, Watts says:

It is necessary that we should as far as possible *entertain and lay up our daily new Ideas, in a regular Order*, and range the Acquisitions of our Souls under proper Heads, whether of *Divinity, Law, Physics, Mathematicks, Morality, Politicks, Trade, domestick Life, Civility, Decency*, &c. whether of *Cause, Effect, Substance, Mode, Power, Property, Body, Spirit*, &c. We should inure our Minds to Method and Order continually; and when we take in any fresh Ideas, Occurrences and Observations, we should dispose of them in their proper Places, and see how they stand and agree with the rest of our Notions on the same Subject: As a *Scholar* would dispose of a *new Book* on a proper shelf among its kindred Authours; or as an *Officer* at the Post-house in *London* disposes of every *Letter* he takes in, placing it in the Box that belongs to the proper Road or County. (240–41)

Playing postman or note-taking student with the material in Johnson's *Dictionary* is a way of recovering the encyclopedic tendency in the book that the alphabetical arrangement of the material obscures. The particular categories under which I have ranged the circle of knowledge in the *Dictionary* derive mostly from my reading of the whole book, but I have gotten encouragement and confirmation along the way from my researches into commonplace books and other topical distributions of knowledge that seemed relevant and similar.[30] The whole act of recovery itself, however, seems justified by Johnson's habits as a reader and writer and by the assumptions fostered in his intellectual milieu. The remaining chapters of this book are devoted to outlining in some detail the circle of knowledge that Johnson presents and the values he teaches. It assimilates the *Dictionary* to the rest of Johnson's writings, and it draws Johnson closer to the seventeenth-century English heritage that he claimed in the preface, as well as to the older European humanistic culture that still was strong in his intellectual blood.

1. Knowledge

1.1. The Shape of Knowledge

The circle of knowledge is too wide for the most active and diligent intellect, and while science is persued, other accomplishments are neglected; as a small garrison must leave one part of an extensive fortress naked, when an alarm calls them to another. (Rambler *180*, Yale *5: 182–83*)

As a whole, Johnson's *Dictionary* presents a general round of knowledge, but it also happens that one of the most frequently treated topics in this encyclopedia is knowledge itself. Furthermore, the *Dictionary*'s collected material on the topic of knowledge is generally consistent with the way in which the book embodies knowledge as a whole, and it is consistent also with the way in which Johnson describes knowledge in his other works. Like *Rambler* 180, the quotations in the *Dictionary* depict knowledge as retaining a sort of architectural, geometrical, or otherwise spatial unity that is unfortunately invisible or unattainable for mortals. Locke's geographical expression of knowledge and our relation to it is representative: "The horizon sets the bounds between the enlightened and dark parts of things, between what is and what is not *comprehensible* by us" (see Locke, *Essay* 47).[1]

When speakers in the *Dictionary* refer to the whole of knowledge, they usually do so with reverential awe and connect such a universal perception with divine revelation. Watts, for example, exclaims, "What a glorious entertainment and pleasure would fill and *felicitate* his spirit, if he could grasp all in a single survey!" Tillotson describes the achievement of total knowledge in terms fit only for the giants before the flood: "A man, by a vast and *imperious*[2] mind, and a heart large as the sand upon the sea-shore, could command all the knowledge of nature and art." Tillotson's image of mental magnitude as sand is nicely adjusted to the way in which the *Dictionary* generally looks at the possibilities for men to acquire complete understanding: only by gathering numerous, individually unimpressive particulars can we put

together a notion of the divine whole. Locke says it best and most
succinctly: "God has made the intellectual world *harmonious*[1] and beautiful without us; but it will never come into our heads all at once; we must bring it home piece-meal." This sounds like an endorsement of the way in which the *Dictionary* is obliged to present knowledge, although Locke is really talking about the natural world, as indicated by his words under "to glean": "In the knowledge of bodies we must be content to *glean*[2] what we can from particular experiments; since we cannot, from a discovery of their real essences, grasp at a time whole sheaves, and in bundles comprehend the nature and properties of whole species together."

The problem with this method of achieving full understanding, of course, is that there are so many particulars to gather. Matthew Hale reminds Johnson's readers of this difficulty under "complicateness" and then again under the less likely word "to get": "Although the universe, and every part thereof, are objects full of excellency, yet the multiplicity thereof is so various, that the understanding falls under a kind of despondency of *getting*[1] through so great a task." Despite the frightening multiplicity, however, the gradual acquisition of particular bits of knowledge is the only way to proceed. For one thing, the *Dictionary*'s faith in empirical examination makes it hostile to anything resembling the scholastic preference for perceiving the whole before the parts. For another, from our narrow, earthly perspective, wholes that might delight an ideal perceiver are shapeless and impenetrable. According to Hale, multiplicity causes mental despondency, but Locke finds this preferable to the stultifying appearance of imperceptibly large spheres of knowledge: "The mind frights itself with anything reflected on in gross: things, thus offered to the mind, carry the shew of nothing but difficulty in them, and are thought to be wrapped up in *impenetrable*[2] obscurity."

The sense that knowledge, although it may never be perfected, is best managed in small, compact pieces, which can be gradually assembled into wholes, is one of the deepest epistemological assumptions in the *Dictionary*, and the same sense is operative in many of Johnson's other works. For example, Rasselas's final means of escaping from the Happy Valley by thousands of small steps, rather than one great leap, may be read as an allegory for Locke's remark in the *Dictionary* that "distinct gradual growth in knowledge carries its own light with it, in every step of its progression, in an easy and orderly *train*[4]." In a way that makes it seem likely he was thinking of Locke when he wrote *Rasselas*, Johnson cites him in *Rambler* 137: "The chief art of learning, as Locke has observed, is to attempt but little at a time. The widest excursions of the mind are made by short flights frequently repeated; the most lofty fabrics of science are formed by the continued accumulation of single propositions" (*Yale* 4: 361).

This sense of the way to progress in knowledge is related to an older notion of knowledge as a progression of steps leading to ever more remote and difficult stages of understanding. Repeating a passage from Locke that appears in the *Dictionary* under "bent," Watts says, "If the mind apply itself first to easier subjects, and things near a-kin to what is already known; and then advance to the more remote and knotty parts of knowledge by slow degrees, it will be able, in this manner, to *cope*[1] *with* great difficulties, and prevail over them with amazing and happy success." Watts's Lockean notion gets its rhetorical strength from the image of knowledge as a chain, a ladder, or a pyramid that leads to the Most High. As Hooker says in the *Dictionary*, "From smaller things the minds of the hearers may go *forward* to the knowledge of greater, and climb up from the lowest to the highest things."[2] The final goal of this old noetic chain is God, but a complete expression of the old order seems to be just outside the bounds of the *Dictionary*'s treatment of knowledge. In a passage that Johnson did not quote, Bacon expresses the noetic order this way: "knowledges are as pyramids, whereof history is the basis. So of natural philosophy, the basis is natural history; the stage next the basis is physick; the stage next the vertical point is metaphysick. As for the vertical point, *Opus quod operatur Deus a principio usque ad finem*,[3] the summary law of nature, we know not whether man's enquiry can attain unto it" (*Works* 2: 472). The closest the *Dictionary* gets to this noetic pyramid is a recognition that theology is above all other sciences. Locke says, "One science is incomparably above all the rest, where it is not by corruption *narrowed*[2] into a trade, for mean or ill ends, and secular interests; I mean, theology, which contains the knowledge of God and his creatures." The spatial implication in Locke's use of "above" in this passage is the remainder of the older order of knowledge in which each particular acquisition was a step toward the highest knowledge, rather than another equally lowly building block in the noetic edifice.

The *Dictionary*'s most conspicuous reminder of the old noetic pyramid is its preference for general and fundamental pieces of knowledge, which are usually seen as located at either the base or the pinnacle of some building or concatenation of all knowledge. Speaking

about the "ground" of the episteme, Locke says, "There are fundamental truths the basis upon which a great many others rest: these are
teeming[2] truths, rich in store, with which they furnish the mind, and,
like the lights of heaven, give light and evidence to other things."
Although Watts does not speak of these truths as the earth and the sun
of the episteme, he nevertheless supports his master by ordering his
students to "gain some general and *fundamental* truths, both in philosophy, in religion, and in human life" because these "conduct our
thoughts into a thousand *inferiour*[4] and particular propositions." As
Watts's words suggest, fundamental truths in the *Dictionary* are primarily moral and ethical. Ultimately, this is so because of the profound
connection in the *Dictionary* (and throughout Johnson's works) between the general and the moral, and between the natural and the
ethical. South displays the background of Johnson's conviction that to
think generally is to think morally in a quotation used to illustrate
"particular": "These notions are universal, and what is universal must
needs proceed from some universal constant principle; the same in all
particulars[1], which can be nothing else but human nature."

Whether they are specifically described as moral or not, the "constant principles" are the most important parts of human understanding, as the elements are the most important parts of matter. Johnson
himself makes a similar analogy in *Rambler* 68: "as the chemists tell us,
that all bodies are resolvable into the same elements, and that the
boundless variety of things arises from the different proportions of
very few ingredients; so a few pains, and a few pleasures are all the
materials of human life" (*Yale* 3: 359). However, the way to arrive at
these basic truths is more often and more reliably by the study of
particulars. Hence, general knowledge has a double place in the
Dictionary's episteme: at the base and at the pinnacle of knowledge.[4]
According to Locke, whose epistemology is the prevalent one in the
Dictionary, "In particulars our knowledge begins, and so spreads itself
by degrees to *generals*[1]." This model inverts the noetic pyramid, and
turns it into a kind of telescope, but generals are still the goal of
knowledge. As Bacon has it, "The eye of the understanding is like the
eye of the sense; for as you may see great objects through small *crannies*
or holes, so you may see great axioms of nature through small and
contemptible instances."

Because of their compression and their superior value, general
observations seem to Locke and Watts like jewels. This image transforms the noetic pyramid into the kindred image of the chain of being:

general knowledge is at the top of the chain of knowledge just as jewels are atop the chain of inorganic things. Each is the most valuable item of its respective kind, and each is, because of its value, liable to be counterfeit or falsified. Locke says, "General observations drawn from particulars, are the jewels of knowledge, comprehending great store in a little room; but they are therefore to be made with the greater care and caution, lest, if we take *counterfeit*[1] for true, our shame be the greater, when our stock comes to a severe scrutiny." Watts follows with the slightly less cautious redaction, "When general observations are drawn from so many particulars as to become certain and *indubitable*, these are jewels of knowledge." Locke, Watts, and most of Johnson's readers remembered that in the Gospel according to John jewels are symbolic of moral wisdom. Both metaphorically and philosophically the *Dictionary* demonstrates a connection between the moral and the general that is a characteristic feature in all of Johnson's works.

Although the whole structure of knowledge may be unattainable, the *Dictionary* commands us to put together what fragments we can glean and to organize them in relation to one another. Its remarks about progressing to general truths are one example. Watts makes the overall point when he says, "Those who contemplate only the fragments or pieces of science, dispersed in short unconnected discourses, without relation to each other, can never survey an entire body of truth, but must always view it as deformed and *dismembered*." Glanvill finds further evidence of inevitable human ignorance: "Every science borrows from all the rest, and we cannot attain any single one without the *encyclopædy*." "The circle of knowledge is too wide for the most active and diligent intellect" (*Rambler* 180), but some structure of knowledge must be in sight.[5] Watts declares, "As much as systematical learning is decried by some vain *triflers* of the age, it is the happiest way to furnish the mind with knowledge." Arbuthnot indicates less equivocally that system is a higher form of knowledge than particular notices: "Arts and sciences consist of scattered theorems and practices, which are *handed*[5] about amongst the masters, and only revealed to the *filii artis*, 'till some great genius appears, who collects these disjointed propositions, and reduces them into a regular system."

However, these recommendations of systematic learning are balanced with warnings against it, and in its ambivalence over systematic learning, the *Dictionary* shows a good deal about where it stands in the history of knowledge. Against the recommendations of Watts, for example, must be put Locke's warning under a key word: "The systems of natural philosophy that have obtained, are to be read more to know the hypotheses, than with hopes to gain there a comprehensive, *scientifical*, and satisfactory knowledge of the works of nature." Johnson himself seems to express his *Dictionary*'s ambivalence about systematic structures of knowledge in *Rambler* 43 when he says, "The student who would build his knowledge on solid foundations, and proceed by just degrees to the pinacles of truth, is directed by the great philosopher of France to begin by doubting of his own existence" (*Yale* 3: 235). Both the beginnings and the ends of this noetic scheme are partly serious and partly ludicrous. Like the schemes that spread "o'er Bodley's dome" in "The Vanity of Human Wishes," these Babel-like pinnacles are related to Cowley's "slipp'ry tops of human state, / The gilded *pinnacles*[2] of fate" and Allestree's "tottering *pinnacle*[1], where the standing is uneasy, and the fall deadly." Doubting one's own existence is going too far in the other direction. The *Dictionary* is not as satirical about knowledge as this passage from *The Rambler* because it leaves its reader plenty of middle ground between unprovable simple knowledge and the unscalable heights; but, like this passage, the *Dictionary* transmits a mixed message about the feasibility of erecting a unified structure of knowledge.

As in Chambers's *Cyclopædia*, the most important and least controverted descriptions of knowledge in Johnson's *Dictionary* are psychological and avoid imagery in favor of logical or linguistic terms. Locke defines the key word: "*Knowledge*[1], which is the highest degree of the speculative faculties, consists in the perception of the truth of affirmative or negative propositions." In this definition knowledge is a class of perception and not something exterior to the mind or susceptible of spatial description. But as in Johnson's other writings and in Locke's work, there are in the *Dictionary* plentiful recurrences of noetic imagery. Taking the circle as a sort of standard for the spatial expression of the field of knowledge, the imagery of knowledge in the *Dictionary* falls somewhere between the conventional, organizing circle, most beautifully represented in Raphael's "School of Athens," and the altogether broken circle in the frontispiece of Chambers's *Cyclopædia* (see plates 1 and 2).[6] Chambers's frontispiece represents an ironic version of the "School of Athens": there is no organizing circle; the stage is much larger and much more populous; there are many more technical instruments present; and the figures are all anonymous rather than historical. The viewer is in a largely indeterminate expanse of buildings that are simultaneously being built and being used as

PLATE I.
The frontispiece to Chambers's Cyclopædia.

PLATE 2.
Raphael's "School of Athens," the Papal Palace, Vatican City.

classrooms for lectures in all the arts and sciences. The greats of science are represented in busts on distant balustrades: Pythagoras, Descartes, Boyle, Bacon, Kepler, Copernicus, Newton, Epicurus, Plato, Gassendi, Hooke, Hippocrates, and other founding fathers— but they are all immobile, unlike the active participants in Raphael's vision of human learning. Nor are they deified by the perspective of the etching; the eye of the beholder goes out over the rooftops into the empty sky. The scene is remarkably Godless, devoted, with one exception, to the examination of the natural objects and artifacts that are strewn all over the stage. In the midst of all these skeletons, antique coins, and hanging bunches of flora, the one nonempirical image is an archway through which can be seen part of a large library with the word "Theologia" sculpted over the top of the bookshelves. This little arch in the middle ground of the etching is all that remains of the great heavenly vault that holds together and circumscribes the field of knowledge in Raphael's "School." The *Dictionary* does more than Chambers to encircle the field of knowledge with religion, but it admits a good deal more dispersion and disintegration than Raphael or contemporary pansophists like Comenius. The *Dictionary* represents the circle of knowledge as broken into particulate, empirically gathered fragments; it encourages efforts to piece them together, but it finds that the only perspective from which the entire hidden harmony can be perceived is divine.

1.2. The Acquisition and Possession of Knowledge

The advancing day of experimental knowledge discloseth such appearances[3], *as will not lie even in any model extant.* Glanville's Scepsis Scientifica, Pref.

Experience is the true opposite of systematic knowledge, and it supplies the pressure that explodes all hypothetical systems. The *Dictionary*'s lack of confidence in system is partly a confidence in immediate experience. An aspect of this confidence is the good common sense that shows up, for example, in South's remark, "The meanest soldier, that has fought often in an *army*[1], has a truer knowledge of war, than he that has writ whole volumes, but never was in any battle." "Truer knowledge" is more immediate knowledge, as Locke also suggests in a commonsensical remark: "The ordinary

qualities observable in iron, or a diamond, that make their true
complex idea, a *smith*[1] or a jeweler commonly knows better than a philosopher." The closer the object, the truer our perception of it; falsification varies directly with distance. Denham says:

'Tis the fate of princes that no knowledge
Come pure to them, but passing through the eyes
And ears of other men, it takes a *tincture*[1]
From every channel.

But Locke is more absolute, and he equates knowledge and experience: "'Till we ourselves perceive by our own understandings, we are as much in the *dark*[3], and as void of knowledge, as before."[7]

However, just as it is unwilling to abandon systematic arrangements of knowledge, the *Dictionary* is also committed to knowledge that is somewhat less immediate than raw experience. First of all, the *Dictionary* recognizes that all the senses, even sight, are subject to error. Bacon says, for example, "The knowledge of men hitherto hath been *determined*[3] by the view or sight; so that whatsoever is invisible, either in respect of the fineness of the body itself, or the smallness of the parts, or of the subtilty of the motion, is little enquired." Our reliance on sight leads not only to neglect but also to illusion: Locke points out, "Any thing, that *moves*[1] round about in a *circle*[1], in less time than our ideas are wont to succeed one another in our minds, is not perceived to *move* but seems to be a perfect entire *circle* of that matter, or colour, and not a part of a *circle* in motion." One of Glanvill's reminders about the limitations of sense is particularly nice because it displays those limitations as an aspect of man's basic vulnerability, a subject close to the *Dictionary*'s main theme: "If the motion be very slow, we perceive it not: we have no sense of the accretive motion of plants or animals; and the sly shadow steals away upon the *dial*, and the quickest eye can discover no more but that it is gone." By joint calibration of knowledge and time Glanvill makes man's understanding as fragile as his life on earth. Moreover, such trenchant challenges to sense are frequent enough in the *Dictionary* to give an ironic ring to assertions like South's, "If sense be not certain in the reports it makes of things to the mind, there can be *naturally*[1] no such thing as certainty or knowledge."

The cure for the errors of sense is learning, the dialectical opposite that itself often requires the correction of sense. Using the word "phantasy" for what Glanvill more intelligibly calls "naked *intellection*,"

Hale points out the commonly observed truth that "the perception intellective often corrects the report of phantasy, as in the *apparent*[2] bigness of the sun, the *apparent* crookedness of the staff in air and water." In ethical matters, the merely visible is a similar form of superficiality; Shakespeare supplies an utterly irreverent epithet for the eye under "fool":

> The *fool*[1] multitude, that chuse by show,
> Not learning more than the fond eye doth teach,
> Which pry not to the interior.

The tragedy of *Othello* is partly about "the fond eye" and the extent to which one trusts the "proof optical" even in the face of surer, learned knowledge. Mere experience is a form of illiteracy, despite its apparent reliability, and it requires improvement.

Even though raw experimental knowledge is not always reliable knowledge in itself, there is little dispute in the *Dictionary* that it is the only true source of reliable knowledge. Locke's statement under "boundary" articulates the main epistemological position that Johnson presents in his book: "Sensation and reflection are the *boundaries* of our thoughts; beyond which the mind, whatever efforts it would make, is not able to advance."[8] What Locke leaves out of the picture, of course, are innate ideas. This was a very controversial exclusion, as another quotation from Locke suggests: "What censure, doubting thus of innate principles, I may deserve from men, who will be apt to call it *pulling*[7] *up* the old foundations of knowledge, I cannot tell; I persuade myself, that the way I have pursued, being conformable to truth, lays those foundations surer." In the *Dictionary* Locke certainly has the best of the controversy; the proponents of innate ideas are allowed to submit only a small minority report, and that mainly on the subject of God.

Potentially the most copious speaker for the minority was Matthew Hale. His *Primitive Origination of Mankind* is concerned to show the innate status of certain fundamental religious and moral ideas. Johnson marked out for inclusion 1149 words in his copy of Hale, but, for reasons that E. J. Thomas traces to the habits of the amanuensis concerned, only 307 of these found their way into the *Dictionary* (Thomas 129). If a higher percentage of Hale's sentences had been included, the *Dictionary* would have come close to recommending an anti-Lockean epistemology.[9] There is no strong evidence that Johnson purposely cut down on his inclusions of Hale for ideological reasons.

However, despite the fact that fragments of Hale's epistemology
appear[10] under "to characterize[2]," "to inscribe[1]," and "placable,"
and though he gets some support from Tillotson and South,[11] the
majority report belongs to Locke, even on the status of religious and
moral ideas. Locke's view is found clearly expressed under "whensoever": "Men grow first acquainted with many of these self-evident
truths, upon their being proposed; not because innate, but because the
consideration of the nature of the things, contained in those words,
would not suffer him to think otherwise, how or *whensoever* he is
brought to reflection."[12]

Under "to stamp" the *Dictionary*'s dispersed dialogue between
Locke and the few writers who uphold the validity of innate ideas
comes to a head:

> No constant reason of this can be given, but from the nature of
> man's mind, which hath this notion of a deity born with it, and
> *stamped*[4] upon it; or is of such a frame, that in the free use of
> itself it will find out God. *Tillotson.*

> Though God has given us no innate ideas of himself, though he
> has *stampt*[4] no original characters on our minds, wherein we
> may read his being; yet having furnished us with those faculties
> our minds are endowed with, he hath not left himself without
> witness. *Locke.*

If Tillotson leans a little in Locke's direction here, Locke sometimes
also bends to accommodate Tillotson's concerns. In an emotional
moment, he can even speak as though religion and morality were
innate: "Cain was so fully convinced that every one had a right to
destroy such a criminal, that he cries out, every one that findeth me
shall slay me; so plain was it *writ*[2] in the hearts of all mankind." But
usually the mind, as the *Dictionary* represents it, is a tabula rasa at
birth, and this is no impediment to religion. As Bentley says, "That
natural and indelible *signature*[1] of God, which human souls, in their
first origin, are supposed to be stampt with, we have no need of in
disputes against atheism."

Following its principal philosopher, most of the *Dictionary* rejects
innate ideas. At the same time, however, it accepts the doctrine that
knowledge is available to us primarily in the form of ideas—but since
these ideas derive from experience (and reflection) they provide a
synthesis of the dialectical extremes of raw experience and innate

ideas. Such a synthesis corrects the errors of the senses by elevating perception, but it leaves man a great distance from the objects of his perception and provides the material for many reflections on his incurable ignorance. Under the key word we find Locke's explanation of the relationship of man's knowledge to reality: "Whatsoever the mind perceives in itself, or is the immediate object of perception, thought, or understanding, that I call *idea*."[13] Locke distinguished between primary and secondary ideas, and he found that we are closer to reality in our perception of the former, but the *Dictionary* often seems to stress his insistence on our separation from the real world. The Lockean mind is like a camera that records a two-dimensional version of the world. Johnson drives this point home by citing Locke four consecutive times under the third sense of "to imprint." Bentley's general point is found under a key word in epistemology: "No sensible *qualities*[2], as light and colour, heat and sound, can be subsistent in the bodies themselves absolutely considered, without a relation to our eyes and ears, and other organs of sense: these *qualities* are only the effects of our sensation, which arise from the different motions upon our nerves from objects without, according to their various modification and position."

Although human ideas are relative to reality, we are not able to reverse that relation or even to control it. One sign of Johnson's commitment to such an epistemological position is that there is no expression of Berkeley's (or anyone's) idealism in the *Dictionary*, and several quotations seem pointedly to refute it. Johnson makes his entry under the unlikely word "glassfurnace" a more terrible refutation of Berkeley than his famous assault on the primary massiveness of a rock (Boswell 1: 471). He has Locke say, "If our dreamer pleases to try whether the glowing heat of a *glassfurnace* be barely a wandering imagination in a drowsy man's fancy, by putting his hand into it, he may perhaps be awakened into a certainty that it is something more than bare imagination." The sensation of heat is unalterably the reality we know in such a situation, yet it is not an absolute, natural reality. As Locke says elsewhere, "Another more incurable part of ignorance, which sets us more remote from a certain knowledge of the coexistence or *incoexistence* of different ideas in the same subject, is, that there is no discoverable connection between any secondary quality and those primary qualities it depends on."

Absolute reality is a sort of untouchable glassfurnace throughout the *Dictionary*, something we can neither know nor deny. Yet we are

constantly reminded of our obligation to try to know it. As Tillotson
says, "The truth of things will not *comply with* our conceits, and bend itself to our interest," and "Our belief or *disbelief* of a thing does not alter the nature of the thing." Watts's redaction of a statement from Locke (s.v. "conception[3]") reminds Johnson's students that "the nature of things are *inflexible*[3], and their natural relations unalterable: we must bring our understandings to things, and not bend things to our fancies."[14] Glanvill asks the crucial question: "Is our knowledge adequately *commensurate*[2] with the nature of things?" Making similar assumptions about our relation to reality, Watts sings a litany of exhortation: "*Conceive*[1] of things clearly and distinctly in their own natures; *conceive* of things completely in all their parts; *conceive* of things comprehensively in all their properties and relations; *conceive* of things extensively in all their kinds; *conceive* of things orderly, or in a proper method." All this advice is merely palliative, however: it can never cure our inherent ignorance of substantial reality. The *Dictionary* continually urges us to measure our conceptions against an external standard from which it assures us that we are ultimately divorced.

Quotation on the subject of epistemology in Johnson's *Dictionary* adds up to a picture of man as a solitary creature isolated from the real sources of his experience, striving weakly and fallibly to build up an adequate or commensurate simulacrum of reality from the notices of his senses. He is doomed to live in a world of shadows that are nevertheless unalterable for him, and he is under strict orders to keep on attempting to know reality as best he can. In such circumstances pride in knowledge is insupportable, and man can only hope that, although he now sees through a glass darkly, he may one day know the truth by the grace of God. The best we here can manage is a tolerable hypothesis, as Glanvill suggests: "Descartes hath here infinitely outdone all the philosophers that went before him, in giving a particular and *analytical*[2] account of the universal fabrick: yet he intends his principles but for hypotheses." In *The Language of Adam* Russell Fraser has shown that Newton's theories gave pause to some exponents of Glanvill's position, but there is little evidence of this in the *Dictionary*.

The best guess the *Dictionary* offers is a median between perception and reality; it calls this median the learned perception or the "philosophical idea" of a thing. For example, Watts combines recognition of our alienation from reality with a recommendation of greater precision: "It is a vulgar idea of the *colours*[1] of solid bodies, when we perceive them to be a red, or blue, or green tincture of the surface; but a philosophical idea, when we consider the various *colours* to be different sensations, excited in us by the refracted rays of light, reflected on our eyes in a different manner, according to the different size, or shape, or situation of the particles of which the surfaces of those bodies are composed." Dryden translates this notion into a recommendation to writers and critics:

> Th' *illiterate* writer, empirick like, applies
> To minds diseas'd unsafe chance remedies:
> The learn'd in schools, where knowledge first began,
> Studies with care th' anatomy of man;
> Sees virtue, vice, and passions in their cause,
> And fame from science, not from fortune draws.

Although Dryden here employs science as an ally of learning, the concept is really mediatory between the dialectically opposed notions of pure experience and abstract ideas or merely systematic learning.

In its primitive sense, "science" is the apotheosis of experience, as Hammond's illustrative quotation indicates: "If we conceive God's sight or *science*[1], before the creation of the world, to be extended to all and every part of the world, seeing every thing as it is, his prescience or foresight of any action of mine, or rather his *science* or sight, from all eternity, lays no necessity on any thing to come to pass, any more than my seeing the sun move hath to do in the moving of it." In the next three definitions, however, science descends to "certainty grounded on demonstration," to "art attained by precepts," and then to "any art or species of knowledge." Reading up the column of senses from bottom to top, "science" seems to be a human means of approaching divine perception, but the end is still perception, not art itself. In other words, the object is to make perception learned, but not to replace it with learning. Johnson indicates the mediatory and synthetic qualities of "science" in *Rambler* 92: "Criticism reduces those regions of literature under the dominion of science, which have hitherto known only the anarchy of ignorance, the caprices of fancy, and the tyranny of pre-scription" (*Yale* 4: 122). The triad of terms in the predicate represent, respectively, reading without perception or learning, reading without learning, and reading without perception; science is above all three of these inadequate possibilities because it provides learned perception.

Ignorance *is the curse of God,*
Knowledge *the wing wherewith we fly to heav'n.*
Shakes.

The *Dictionary* relentlessly drills into its students reminders of the inevitability of human ignorance and the vanity of human learning. However, it also makes a connection between knowledge and salvation that elevates certain kinds of knowledge and makes the desire for knowledge an aptitude for religion. In illustration of "surmise," Johnson grants Hooker a good deal of precious space to suggest such a connection: "Man coveteth what exceedeth the reach of sense, yea somewhat above the capacity of reason, somewhat divine and heavenly, which with hidden exultation it rather *surmiseth* than conceiveth; somewhat it seeketh, and what that is directly it knoweth not; yet very intentive desire thereof doth so incite it, that all other known delights and pleasures are laid aside, and they give place to the search of this but only suspected desire." Hooker suggests here a traditional identification between God and true knowledge that often appears in the illustrative quotations of the *Dictionary*. In Denham's lines the identification is more explicit than usual but no less strong: "Then the true Son of knowledge first appear'd, / And the old dark *mysterious*[1] clouds were clear'd." Not only is the search for salvation a search for knowledge, heaven itself is a place of perfect knowledge. Employing an image reminiscent of Bunyan's House of the Interpreter, Glanvill portrays spiritual pilgrimage in terms of knowledge: "The observers view but the backside of the hangings; the right one is on the other side of the grave: and our knowledge is but like those broken ends; at best a most confused *adumbration*[2]." Salvation is an apotheosis of knowledge, which reminds us of our ignorance but also elevates the general concept of knowing.

All human knowledge, however, is not equally related to its apotheosis in heaven. Tillotson makes a distinction of which the *Dictionary* as a whole is very mindful when he says, "The best knowledge is that which is of greatest use in *order*[12] to our eternal happiness." South also comes close to articulating the general theme of the *Dictionary* when he speaks of the "vanity and *uselessness* of that learning, which makes not the possessor a better man." The desire for knowledge is equally susceptible of corruption. Davies's lament (found under "root") is more smartly addressed to students than most, but it is representative of a large number of reminders that the desire for knowledge caused the fall of man:

> Why did my parents send me to the schools,
> That I with knowledge might enrich my mind?
> Since the desire to know first made men fools,
> And did corrupt the *root*[4] of all mankind.[15]

The moral appears in a quotation from Ecclesiasticus in illustration of a key word: "Be not *curious*[1] in unnecessary matters; for more things are shewn unto thee than men understand." Atterbury allegorizes the theme and lets Johnson teach morality in his treatment of an unlikely word: "He that too curiously observes the face of the heavens, by missing his *seedtime*, will lose the hopes of harvest."

All we have to do is pursue the proper sort of knowledge, it appears. Alas, this is deceptively simple because, paradoxically, the most important human knowledge tends to be beyond knowledge in the ordinary sense. Throughout the *Dictionary* the three most important areas of saving knowledge are self-knowledge, knowledge of God, and virtue. The first two are valuable because their imperfectibility humbles us; the last is really a form of acting rather than knowing. "Among the objects of knowledge," says Hale, "two especially *commend*[1] themselves to our contemplation; the knowledge of God, and the knowledge of ourselves." Tillotson stresses the absolute requirement of the first: "Whatsoever other knowledge a man may be *endued*[1] withal, he is but an ignorant person who doth not know God, the author of his being." This is impossible knowledge to pursue, as Dryden's prayer for it indicates:

> Thy throne is darkness in th' abyss of light,
> A blaze of glory that *forbids*[3] the sight!
> O teach me to believe thee thus conceal'd,
> And search no farther than thyself reveal'd.

Dryden's prayer is an appropriate response to the archetypal interrogatives in Job, which Johnson reprints under "to find": "Can'st thou by searching *find*[19] *out* God? Can'st thou *find out* the Almighty unto perfection?" When knowledge reaches God, it is either transformed into faith or it is useless for salvation. Hooker says, "It is not the deepness of their knowledge, but the *singleness* of their belief, which God accepteth." In the way it abjures searching, the knowledge of God has a greater resemblance to human ignorance than to finite forms of knowledge. Glanvill takes special care to distinguish ignorance from the knowledge of God: "'Tis here that knowledge wonders, and there is an admiration that is not the daughter of ignorance. This indeed stupidly gazeth at the unwonted effect; but the philosophic passion truly *admires*[1] and adores the supreme efficient."

Whereas the knowledge of God ends in faithful admiration, self-knowledge leads mostly to the equally beneficial virtue of humility. In both cases, the ends are the result of finding out the limitations of knowledge. Glanvill says, for example, "He that knows most of himself, knows least of his knowledge, and the exercised understanding is conscious of its *disability*[1]." Davies's introit to the altar of self-knowledge is a reminder to himself of ignorance, as if that were, paradoxically, the most important knowledge to be gained in self-examination:

> And thou, my soul, which turn'st with curious eye
> To view the beams of thine own form divine,
> Know, that thou can'st know nothing perfectly,
> While thou art clouded with this *flesh* of mine.

Jeremy Taylor, as usual, is much more blunt when he represents the scourge of self-knowledge: "No man truly knows himself, but he groweth daily more *contemptible*[1] in his own eyes." The same relations between self-knowledge, ignorance, and humble piety that appear throughout the *Dictionary* are the explicit subject of Johnson's poem "Γνῶθι Σεαυτόν," which he wrote on completing the huge revision of his own potentially hubristic book of knowledge. Self-knowledge is an antidote for pride in learning; Johnson passes the message on to his students in the words of Dryden's Persius: "*Study*[2] thyself: what rank, or what degree, / The wise Creator has ordain'd for thee."

In an illustration under "according" Sprat provides a litany designed to control religious pride, just as Watts's litany under "to conceive" (see above, p. 53) controls intellectual exuberance. Sprat says, "Our zeal, then, should be *according*[1] to knowledge. And what kind of knowledge? Without all question, first, *according* to the true, saving, evangelical knowledge. It should be *according* to the gospel, the whole gospel: not only *according* to its truths, but precepts: not only *according* to its free grace, but necessary duties: not only *according* to its mysteries, but also its commandments." The emphasis in these phrases is on the second element of knowledge, which in each case implies an action in addition to a conception. The message that active virtue is the highest form of knowledge is also implicit in the quotation from Proverbs under "slow": "He that is *slow*[5] to wrath is of great understanding."[16] Mere knowledge, even when it is knowledge of goodness, is inferior to active virtue, even when this is based on ignorance; Sidney implies as much when he describes the moral condition of Philoclea: "The sweet-minded Philoclea was in their degree of well doing, to whom the not knowing of evil serveth for a ground of virtue, and hold their inward powers in better form, with an unspotted *simplicity*, than many who rather cunningly seek to know what goodness is, than willingly take unto themselves the following of it."

The single word in the *Dictionary* that best connects knowledge and virtue is "wisdom," though even in this word the connection is not continuous. Philosophically speaking, wisdom applies to practice; a quotation from Nehemiah Grew demonstrates: "As science is properly that knowledge which relateth to the essences of things, so *wisdom* to their operations." In this philosophical sense, wisdom is amoral. Employing this sense, St. Paul says, "I would have you *wise*[1] unto that which is good, and simple concerning evil."[17] Most uses of the word recorded by Johnson, however, show the writers' interest in making morality a part of its meaning, and they often follow the distinction between cunning and wisdom in Bacon's essay "Of Cunning." Addison seems directly indebted to Bacon, for example, when he says: "These, as my guide informed me, were men of subtle tempers, and *puzzled*[2] politicks, who would supply the place of real wisdom with cunning and avarice." The important distinction is between worldly wisdom and wisdom of a more permanent sort. As Tillotson has it, we should "refer all the actions of this short and dying life to that state which shall shortly begin, but never have an end; and this will approve itself to be wisdom at last, whatever the world judge of it *now*[1]."[18]

Tillotson's words, as selected by Johnson, probably do the most to make the pious sense of "wisdom" conspicuous in the *Dictionary*.[19] In the most definitive example, Tillotson says, "Religion comprehends the knowledge of its principles, and a suitable life and practice; the first, being speculative, may be called knowledge; and the latter, because 'tis *practical*, wisdom." But he is not the source of this use of "wisdom," as he himself indicates: "According to the genius and *strain*[4] of the book of Proverbs, the words wisdom and righteousness

are used to signify all religion and virtue." In this light, we read in the
Dictionary such remarks from Proverbs as, "Wisdom is the principal
thing, therefore get wisdom; and with all thy *getting*[1] get understanding"; and "*How*[1] much better is it to get wisdom than gold? and to get
understanding rather to be chosen than silver?" Accordingly, King
Charles prays, "Make me wise by thy truth, for my own soul's
salvation, and I shall not regard the world's opinion or *diminution*[4] of
me." Addison similarly puts wisdom in place of virtue in his redaction
of the choice of Hercules, his century's favorite moral fable: "Health,
wealth, victory, and honour, are introduced; wisdom enters the last,
and so captivates with her *appearance*[10] that he gives himself up to
her."

The identification of wisdom with activity, usually virtuous activity,
was so great by 1784 that Cowper could write, "Knowledge and
Wisdom, far from being one / Have ofttimes no connection." This
appears in the *OED* (s.v. "wisdom" 1.a) and is an important part of its
definition of the word, but in Johnson's *Dictionary* the connection
Cowper mentions is mostly unbroken. The maintenance of the connection is one of the ways in which the *Dictionary* belongs to an
intellectual milieu that is centered in the seventeenth century and is
only vestigial by the end of the eighteenth. For Davies, a principal
speaker on knowledge in Johnson's "Forum," wisdom is the crown of a
noetic chain:

> As from senses reason's work doth spring,
> So many reasons understanding gain,
> And many understandings knowledge bring,
> And by much knowledge *wisdom* we obtain.

Milton also connects wisdom and knowledge and comes close to
summarizing the chief message of the whole *Dictionary*:

> Not to *know*[2] at large of things remote
> From use, obscure and subtile; but to *know*
> That which before us lies in daily *life*[11],
> Is the prime wisdom.

One of the most important qualities of wisdom as a sort of knowledge is its simplicity and general availability. Milton says, "be *lowly*[2]
wise." Like general knowledge, wisdom has a dual place at the base
and pinnacle of knowledge, and it is likewise related to the commonest,
most universal truths of nature. Hooker explains, "Wisdom, to the end

she might save many, built her house of that nature which is common unto all; she made not this or that man her *habitation*[2], but dwelt in us." This common knowledge is also the highest knowledge. Allestree appropriately describes a central book of the Bible in terms of wisdom, but his description also fits Johnson's book: "The sum of his whole book of *proverbs*[1] is an exhortation to the study of this practick wisdom." In another place, Hooker is unequivocal about the supremacy of this basic element of the natural, human constitution: "To prescribe the order of doing in all things is a peculiar prerogative, which wisdom hath, as queen or sovereign *commandress*, over all other virtues."[20]

The similarity between wisdom and general knowledge and the connection of both of these to morality are evident throughout the *Dictionary* and in Johnson's other works. Indeed, its connections with wisdom and virtue are probably what cause Johnson to be so persistently interested in the General. The shift in emphasis to particulars, toward the end of the century, both changed the conception of wisdom and, as the *OED*'s citation of Cowper suggests, separated it from knowledge altogether. This is a separation that Johnson opposed openly in the wise tales of *The Rambler*, in *Rasselas*, and in "The Vision of Theodore." In more diffuse ways, the tenor of Johnson's entire life of writing is that of presenting wisdom in general truth, and this essential quality of his work expresses itself in the *Dictionary* through the selection of a great many seventeenth-century quotations that are confident about the possibility of deriving wisdom from knowledge, as long as religion is present.

2. Ignorance

2.1. Declarations and Descriptions of Ignorance

Whatever I look upon, within the amplitude*[1] of heaven and earth,
is evidence of human ignorance.* Glanville.

Apart from limiting and modifying the subject of knowledge, the doctrine of human ignorance and error is itself an important topic in Johnson's encyclopedia. Some indication of how conventional the topic was when Johnson received it appears in the preface to Chambers's *Cyclopædia* where Chambers quotes another encyclopedist: " 'The history of mens follies,' says the inimitable Fontenelle, 'makes no small part of learning; and, unhappily for us, much of our knowledge terminates there' " (1: xxii). Fontenelle himself received the topic from a tradition of correction and emendation that is central to the whole humanist tradition. Like Joseph Scaliger in his massive *De Emendatione Temporum*, humanist editors, lexicographers, and encyclopedists were perpetually engaged in acts of correction, and they frequently wrote discourses on the prevalence of ignorance and the inevitability of error. In the broadest sense, the theme derives from Xenophanes' notion that all is illusion; it has a history in ancient literature, in the wisdom literature of the Old Testament, in the Roman satirists, and in many patristic writings, especially those of the third-century father Lactantius Firmianus. The topic is so deeply ingrained in English literature of the seventeenth century that Johnson could hardly have avoided perpetuating it, even had he wished to do so.

Johnson not only refused to avoid the topic of ignorance, however, he also seems actively to have sought it in several ways. He chose as important sources of quotations three books that are thoroughly dedicated to the topic of ignorance: Sir Thomas Browne's *Pseudodoxia Epidemica*, Thomas Baker's *Reflections upon Learning*, and Joseph Glanvill's *Scepsis Scientifica*. Secondly, Johnson cited numerous contributions to the theme from writers with more general aims, such as Locke, Hooker, and Raleigh. In a few cases Johnson seems to reveal an intention to include reminders of ignorance by the way in which he excerpts his illustrative quotations. For example, Locke's baldest statement of human ignorance in the *Dictionary* appears under "incurably," where Johnson enters, "We cannot know it is or is not, being *incurably* ignorant." In the original passage, Locke does speak, as he often does, about ignorance, but he says something much more particular and complex than Johnson's radical abridgment suggests: "how can we be sure that this or that quality is in *Gold*, when we know not what is or is not *Gold*? Since in this way of speaking nothing is *Gold*, but what partakes of an Essence, which we not knowing, cannot know where it is, or is not, and so cannot be sure, that any parcel of Matter in the World is or is not in this sense *Gold*; being incurably ignorant, whether it has or has not that which makes any thing to be called *Gold*, *i.e.* that real Essence of *Gold* whereof we have no *Idea* at all" (*Essay* 581). When Johnson came across this passage in his search for illustrative quotations, he must have seized upon the phrase "incurably ignorant" as an illustration of "incurably" that would also serve his Lactantian motives; he then extracted what he needed from the rest to make some general sense of the excerpt. Far from regretting it, as he says in the preface, I think he was here willing to let "the Philosopher desert his system" for the sake of the more general remark. The alteration is more significant in light of the evidence that Johnson usually preserved the sense of his excerpts quite successfully, even when he shortened them to save space.[1]

Among Johnson's projected works on the list he gave to Bennet Langton is a "Hymn to Ignorance" (Boswell 4: 382n). Like many of the other works on that list, this one is partially fulfilled in the *Dictionary* (see above, pp. 8–9). The hymn very frequently takes the form of an inverted "O Altitudo," typified in the illustration of "to consider" from Isaiah: "None *considereth*[1] in his heart, neither is there knowledge nor understanding." Locke's tone is similar when he considers our ignorance of the natural world: "There is not so *contemptible*[2] a plant or animal that does not confound the most enlarged understanding," and "When we consider the reasons we have to think, that what lies within our *ken* is but a small part of the universe, we shall discover an huge abyss of ignorance." Denham paints an equally sublime image of ignorance:

> Through seas of knowledge we our course advance,
> Discov'ring still new worlds of ignorance;

And these discov'ries make us all confess
That *sublunary* science is but guess.

Shakespeare employs another incomprehensibly large natural phenomenon for his metaphor of ignorance: "I say there is no darkness
but ignorance, in which thou art more *puzzled*[1] than the Egyptians in
their fog." Shakespeare's "darkness" uses the commonplace of poor
vision or obscurity as a description of ignorance. Boyle points to a
source of this commonplace while providing an ironic illustration of
"noonday": "The dimness of our intellectual eyes, Aristotle fitly
compares to those of an owl at *noonday*." This sort of darkness at noon,
as the book by that name suggests, is characteristic of ironic themes,
and ignorance is certainly one of them. The depth of the irony is
evident in Hooker's description of men living in an ignorant world:
"Men are blinded with ignorance and errour: many things may *escape*[2] them, and in many things they may be deceived." Analogies
between sight and understanding are conspicuous in the principal
Greek philosophers, but perhaps the most important source of this
aspect of the language of ignorance for the *Dictionary* is in Johnson's
illustration of "face to face" from Corinthians 1: "Now we see through
a glass darkly; but then *face to face*[2]." Donne elaborates a version of
this sentence:

> Up into the watch-tower get,
> · And see all things despoil'd of fallacies:
> Thou shalt not peep through *lattices* of eyes,
> Nor hear through labyrinths of ears, nor learn
> By circuit or collections to discern.[2]

As a description of error false vision is closely related to external
darkness and to the deceptions of internal lights like the fancy. The
ignis fatuus often represents the deceptive inner light, and this may be
the reason that Johnson included a translation of a lengthy passage
from Pieter Van Musschenbroek when he came to the definition of
"*Will*[11] with a wisp"; it is particularly remarkable that so late in the
alphabet, when he was contracting everything, he included this poetic
description of the lights' movement: ". . . Now they dilate themselves,
and now contract. Now they go on like waves, and rain as it were sparks
of fire; but they burn nothing. They follow those that run away, and fly
from those that follow them. . . ." Its suitability as an image of error
may similarly have influenced Johnson's lavish treatment of "calen-

ture," a disease that causes sailors to see mirages and jump overboard. In addition to Quincy's explanation and a couplet from Denham, Johnson prints a relatively long passage from Swift:

> So, by a *calenture* misled,
> The mariner with rapture sees,
> On the smooth ocean's azure bed,
> Enamell'd fields, and verdant trees;
> With eager haste, he longs to rove
> In that fantastick scene, and thinks
> It must be some enchanted grove;
> And in he leaps, and down he sinks.

Johnson shows his interest in the satirical value of these lines by including the last four, which are not necessary for philological purposes. The action of the passage is reminiscent of Johnson's descriptions of the aeronautic projector in *Rasselas*, and it contains one of the *Dictionary*'s most important themes.[3]

As well as being dim, illusory, and boundless, error is also complicated. As Bishop Wilkins says, "The notions of a confused knowledge are always full of perplexity and *complications*[2], and seldom in order."[4] Browne enumerates some of the folds in the tangled train of error in a passage that Johnson quoted twice: "Men rest not in false apprehensions without absurd and *inconsequent* deductions from fallacious foundations, and misapprehended mediums, erecting conclusions no way *inferible* from their premises." In another place Browne says, "Though now at the greatest distance from the beginning of errour, yet we are almost lost in its *dissemination*, whose ways are boundless, and confess no circumscription"; one of the reasons for this boundlessness is a compounding process that causes error constantly to grow, despite persistent efforts to remove it. For instance, as Browne reminds us, "Scaliger, finding a defect in the reason of Aristotle, introduceth one of no less *deficiency*[1] himself."[5] In a more abstract and psychological way, Locke sees irregular connection as the principal source of error: "In their tender years, ideas that have no natural *cohesion*[3], come to be united in their heads." Browne expresses a notion similar to Locke's, but his version depends upon a strangely mixed image of human and vegetable growth: "Such errors as are but *acorns* in our younger brows, grow oaks in our older heads, and become *inflexible*[1] to the powerful arm of reason." And South makes the confused growth of error even more repulsive: "An error in the judgment is like an *impostem* in the head, which is always noisome, and frequently mortal."

There are so many declarations of ignorance in the *Dictionary* that Johnson might have placed at the bottom of every page Thomas Burnet's rhetorical question: "Do not all men *complain*[1], even these as well as others, *of* the great ignorance of mankind?"[6] But among the beneficial effects of such complaints is that they make knowledge more possible. As Glanvill says, "It is the interest of mankind, in order to the advance of knowledge, to be sensible they have yet attained it but in poor and *diminutive* measure." A recognition of human liability to ignorance and error is important to the progress of knowledge, but the deeper point is often that the recognition of ignorance is itself, paradoxically, the highest sort of knowledge. Collier, for example, inverts the expected priority and sees the recognition of ignorance as the end of knowledge: "Learning gives us a discovery of our ignorance, and keeps us from being peremptory and *dogmatical* in our determinations." The paradigm comes from Plato's *Apology* and is delivered in the *Dictionary* by Bacon: "Socrates was pronounced by the oracle of Delphos to be the wisest man of Greece, which he would turn from himself *ironically*, saying, there could be nothing in him to verify the oracle, except this, that he was not wise, and knew it; and others were not wise, and knew it not." Hooker places Augustine in the same line of wisdom by citing his *Confessions*: "Amongst so many huge volumes, as the infinite pains of St. Augustine have brought forth, what one hath gotten greater love, commendation, and honour, than the book wherein he carefully owns his *over-sights*[2] and sincerely condemneth them?"

An understanding of ignorance is superior to any positive knowledge because it better serves religious ends. In "The Vision of Theodore" Johnson depicts the area of ignorance as a mist at the top of the Mountain of Existence; the mist is impenetrable to Reason and shows the superiority of Religion. Although it is obviously a different sort of book, the *Dictionary* also makes a point about ignorance and religion. Johnson deploys hundreds of illustrative quotations to tell his students that we are ineluctably ignorant in our present state and that this ignorance is a reminder of our dependence upon God. Ultimately, the inverted "O Altitudo" that declares ignorance has exactly the same pious end as its unironic counterpart, and a hymn to ignorance is a hymn to God's everlasting glory.

Explicable. adj. *[from* explicate.*] Explainable; possible to be explained.*

Many difficulties, scarce explicable *with any certainty, occur in the fabrick of human nature.* Hale's Origin of Mankind.

Great variety there is in compound bodies, and little many of them seem to be explicable. Boyle.

The *Dictionary* contains numerous confessions of ignorance both in its treatment of particular subjects and in its discussion of knowledge in general. In its course on law, for example, the *Dictionary* includes, among many other defamatory remarks, Baker's assertion that "no human laws are exempt from faults, since those that have been looked upon as most perfect in their *kind*[2], have been found, upon enquiry, to have so many." William Holder is the *Dictionary*'s principal lecturer on speech, and he often hastens to admit the limits of his and everyone's understanding of that subject; he says, for instance, "The motions of the tongue, by contraction and *dilatation*[1], are so easy and so subtle, that you can hardly conceive or distinguish them aright."[7] On many broader subjects our general, incurable ignorance is also remarkable. Locke gets at the root of our ignorance by arguing our divorce from "real essences"—that is, from the world of nature. This divorce leads to a primary ignorance about the whole phenomenal world and a general, inevitable vagueness in our understanding of everything. Johnson gives Locke ample space to expound this important point under the unlikely word "oddly": "The real essence of substances we know not; and therefore are so undetermined in our nominal essences, which we make ourselves, that if several men were to be asked concerning some *oddly*[2]-shaped fetus, whether it were a man or no? it is past doubt, one should meet with different answers."[8]

Locke's statement of ignorance applies not only to complex phenomena, like man, but also to the more basic attributes of reality, like quantity. We understand only a very narrow range of reality, as indicated by Locke in an illustration of the word "big": "Both in addition and division, either of space or duration, when the idea under consideration becomes very *big*[1], or very small, its precise bulk becomes very obscure and confused."[9] Locke is equally poetic in a quotation under the verb "to be": "To say a man has a clear idea of quantity, without knowing how great it *is*[1], *is* to say, he has the clear idea of the number of the sands, who knows not how many they *be*." The repetition of the verb "to be" in this passage recommends it on philological grounds, but Johnson must have run across scores of passages with similar qualifications. Locke's sentence appealed to Johnson for thematic as well as philological reasons: it provides a suitable hyperbole for the *Dictionary*'s constant reminders of human ignorance. On the specific subject of the natural world, these reminders of ignorance are perhaps best summed up in George Cheyne's words: "The best accounts of the appearances of nature in any single instance human penetration can *reach*[6], comes infinitely short of its *reality*[1] and internal constitution; for who can search out the Almighty's works to perfection?"

As Cheyne's language suggests, the accents of Job are never far removed from declarations of human ignorance about the phenomenal world. These accents are more pronounced when writers mention more obviously inexplicable aspects of the universe. As Bentley states in an illustration under "incomprehensible[1]," the universe stands according to "the arbitrary pleasure of God," and therefore its basic laws are not necessarily explicable. The prime example of an arbitrary, inexplicable cosmic law is gravity.[10] There is an important deposition by Woodward on our inability to understand gravity under "effluvium," but under "gravity" itself Johnson gives Quincy room for a long dissertation that tells us what to conclude from this specific point of our incurable ignorance. Quincy says, in part, "That quality by which all heavy bodies tend towards the centre of the earth, accelerating their motion the nearer they approach towards it, true philosophy has shewn to be unsolvable by any hypothesis, and resolved it into the immediate will of the Creator." Bentley shows further that the "true philosophy" of gravity is equivalent to a pious acknowledgment of ignorance: "Gravitation is the powerful cement which holds together this magnificent structure of the world, which stretcheth the North over the empty space, and hangeth the earth upon nothing, to transfer the words of Job from the first and real cause to the *secondary*[1]." In the *Dictionary*, as in Job, "Considerations of the divine omnipotence and infinite wisdom, and our own ignorance, are," as Taylor says, "great instruments of silencing the murmurs of *infidelity*[1]."

Among the cosmic conundrums in the *Dictionary* are light and time. The philosophers that Johnson cites are in disagreement as to whether light is matter or energy, and the difference between Johnson's definitions of the word in the first and fourth editions shows that he too was uncertain about how to classify this most common and most inexplicable phenomenon. Newton is allowed to discourse on the problem under "pression," but light remains a specific instance of human ignorance. The problem of defining time is even more widely acknowledged. About time, Locke says—remembering the answer originally given to a question about light—"The answer to one who asked what time was, *si non rogas intelligo*; that is, the more I think of time, the less I understand it; might persuade one, that time, which *reveals*[1] all other things, is itself not to be discovered." As light is invisible and yet is the medium of sight, so time is the inconceivable medium of thought. Locke describes one of the illusions consequent upon this fact: "We see, that one who fixes his thoughts very intently on one thing, so as to take but little notice of the succession of ideas that *pass*[5] in his mind, whilst he is taken up with that earnest contemplation, lets slip out of his account a good part of that duration, and thinks that time shorter than it is." Johnson's own report of some homework he did in 1719 seems to exemplify Locke's point. In his Annals Johnson writes, "In making, I think, the first exercise under Holbrook, I perceived the power of continuity of attention, of application not suffered to wander or to pause. I was writing at the kitchen windows, as I thought, alone, and turning my head saw Sally dancing. I went on without notice, and had finished almost without perceiving that any time had elapsed. This close attention I have seldom in my whole life obtained" (*Yale* 1: 20–21). It seems likely that Johnson's deep engagement with Locke later in life helped him remember this incident in this particular way. His mind, like the "mind" evinced in the *Dictionary*, is Lockean in its understanding of time and, indeed, of almost everything else.

In one respect the unsolvable problem of time coincides with another of the imponderables set forth in the *Dictionary* in order to remind us of human ignorance: a full understanding of time is impossible because time, as we know it, is a part of infinity, and infinity is inconceivable to mere mortals. Locke describes the human conception in its cosmic context in an illustration of "ocean": "Time, in general, is to duration, as place to expansion. They are so much of those boundless *oceans*[2] of eternity and immensity, as is set out and distinguished from the rest, to denote the position of finite real beings, in those uniform, infinite oceans of duration and space." Under the

key word Nehemiah Grew extends the distinction between time and its
absolute: "*Time*[1], which consisteth of parts, can be no part of infinite
duration, or of eternity; for then there would be infinite *time* past today,
which to morrow will be more than infinite. *Time* is therefore one
thing, and infinite duration is another." In two separate illustrations of
"less" Locke discourses on the disparity between human ideas of the
infinite, which depend upon multiplication of parts of time or space,
and the real thing. The general principle, however, is most economi-
cally expressed by Bentley under a key word: "*Finite* of any magnitude
holds not any proportion to infinite."

Watts is one of the many writers who make the moral uses of infinity
and other imponderables clear.[11] He says, for example, "Our disputa-
tions about vacuum or space, *incommensurable* quantities, the infinite
divisibility of matter, and eternal duration, will lead us to see the
weakness of our nature." One demonstration of the incomprehensible
vastness of infinity seems especially well suited for inclusion in the
Dictionary because it humbles the student of language as well as the
lexicographer. Hale points out, "If, instead of twenty-four letters,
there were twenty-four millions, as those twenty-four millions are a
finite number; so would all combinations thereof be finite, though not
easily *computable* by arithmetick." To beat the track of an infinite
alphabet is the lexicographer's idea of hell, and neither Jeremy Taylor
nor the sermonizer at Stephen Dedalus's retreat could conceive a
more awful and humbling idea of eternity for the student of language
and learning.

Our ignorance of any aspect of creation is evidence of South's
assertion that "Providence often disposes of things by a method
beside[3], and above the discoveries of man's reason." Our failure to
understand our own human constitution is particularly poignant,
however, and makes another common point of ignorance. Speaking
about the essential fact of human life, Swift says, "The manner
whereby the soul and body are united, and how they are distinguished,
is wholly *unaccountable*[1] to us." In the same vein, Glanvill takes
Donne's glorious image of "that subtile knot, which makes us man"
and transforms it into an emblem of ignorance: "How the purer spirit
is united to this *clod*[3], is a knot too hard for our degraded intellects to
untie." In the world imagined by the theme of ignorance, the greatest
glories of creation reveal the depths of human failure and impotence.
As Watts says, "If we arise to the world of spirits, our knowledge of

them must be *amazingly* imperfect, when there is not the least grain of sand but has too many difficulties belonging to it, for the wisest philosopher to answer."

The mysteries of religion, since they involve God, are the ultimate category of incurable ignorance. For example, Crashaw says, "How God's eternal son should be man's brother, / *Poseth*[1] his proudest intellectual power." Before such mysteries orthodoxy admits only humble acceptance and a suspension of curiosity, as Swift clearly indicates: "I do not attempt explaining the mysteries of the christian religion, since Providence intended there should be mysteries, it cannot be agreeable to piety, *orthodoxy*, or good sense to go about it." In religion above all, but in every other part of the curriculum as well, an acknowledgment of ignorance is, paradoxically, wisdom.

2.3. Pseudodoxia

Like Sir Thomas Browne's encyclopedic catalogue of errors, *Pseudodoxia Epidemica*, Johnson's *Dictionary* both displays vast stores of false opinion and seeks to explode them. These purposes are widely coincident with the purposes of lexicography because so many words are names for nonexistent things instituted in vulgar opinion. In some of his definitions Johnson makes an effort to expose the errors inherent in the vocabulary of English. He defines "microcosm," for example, in a strictly etymological way as "the little world," and then he adds, "Man is so called as being imagined, by some fanciful philosophers, to have in him something analogous to the four elements." Similarly, he provides a studiously etymological definition of "pineal"—"resembling a pineapple"—and then explains that it is "an epithet given by *Des Cartes* from the form, to the gland which he imagined the seat of the soul." Johnson's article under "shrewmouse" is more expansive and treats vulgar error with more gaiety: "A mouse of which the bite is generally supposed venomous, and to which vulgar tradition assigns such malignity, that she is said to lame the foot over which she runs. I am informed that all these reports are calumnious, and that her feet and teeth are equally harmless with those of any other little mouse. Our ancestors however looked on her with such terrour, that they are supposed to have given her name to a scolding woman, whom for her venom they call a *shrew*."

In general, Johnson affords gaiety in his treatment of only those vulgar opinions that are relatively harmless and that do not have to do with religious or moral matters. As the *Dictionary*'s entries under "ignorance" show, the King James Bible identifies ignorance with sin, but, clearly, some sorts of errors are more sacrilegious or dangerous to morality than others. Johnson is careful to disapprove of the Cartesian use of "pineal" because it is superstitious to locate the immaterial soul in a material organ. In "Of Superstition" Bacon says that "superstition is the reproach of the Deity," and, when he cites a principal source of the sin, he articulates some of Johnson's deepest feelings on the subject: a main cause of superstition is "the taking aim at divine matters by humane, which cannot but breed mixture of imaginations" (*Works* 3: 325).

Most of the pseudodoxia that the *Dictionary* seems concerned to explode involve some dangerous superstition or "mixture of imaginations." All sorts of fortune-telling come under this heading, and the *Dictionary*'s many warnings against them perform, on a much larger scale, Johnson's operation in *Rambler* 129, where, after quoting Horace on the hopeless obscurity in which the gods have hidden the decrees of fate, he comments in Christian tones on the moral sentences of the pre-Christian philosophers:

> It is not without true judgment that . . . they often warn their
> readers against enquiries into futurity, and solicitude about
> events which lie hid in causes yet unactive, and which time
> has not brought forward into the view of reason. An idle and
> thoughtless resignation to chance, without any struggle against
> calamity, or endeavour after advantage, is indeed below the dig-
> nity of a reasonable being, in whose power providence has put a
> great part even of his present happiness; but it shews an equal
> ignorance of our proper sphere, to harrass our thoughts with
> conjectures about things not yet in being. How can we regulate
> events, of which we yet know not whether they will ever hap-
> pen? And why should we think, with painful anxiety, about that
> on which our thoughts can have no influence? (*Yale* 3: 159)

Johnson's treatment in the *Dictionary* of terms related to fortune-telling is accordingly severe. "Astrology" is defined as "the practice of foretelling things by the knowledge of the stars; an art now generally exploded, as without reason." "Geomancer" is defined with equal censure as "a fortuneteller; a caster of figures; a cheat who pretends to foretell futurity by other means than the astrologer." Most of the censure, however, like most of the messages in the *Dictionary*, is delivered in the illustrative quotations. Drummond, for instance, poses two difficult problems for the adherents of astrology: "If that moment of the time of birth be of such moment, whence proceedeth the great difference of the constitutions of *twins*[1], which, tho' together born, have strange and contrary fortunes"; and "How unlikely is it, that the many almost numberless conjunctions of stars, which occur in the progress of a man's life, should not match and countervail that one *horoscope* or conjunction which is found at his birth?"[12] Allestree derisively reports that a certain astrologer "made his *almanack* give a tolerable account of the weather, by a direct inversion of the common prognosticators." More direct warnings are also frequent in the *Dictionary*, and many of these, following a tradition recorded as early as Strabo, point out the susceptibility of women and children to fortune-telling mountebanks. L'Estrange says, for example, "Among women and children, care is to be taken that they get not a *hankering* after these juggling astrologers and fortune-tellers."

Various illustrative quotations in the *Dictionary* interdict many other forms of divination besides astrology. Ornithoscopy may be the most frequently censured, but Butler ably reduces all the forms of spurious prognostication to scatomancy:

> A *flam* more senseless than the rog'ry
> Of old Aruspicy and aug'ry,
> That out of *garbages* of cattle
> Presag'd th' events of truce or battle.

As well as attacking all the individual forms of fortune-telling, the *Dictionary* also strikes often at the notion of fortune itself. Raleigh says, for instance, "Fortune is nothing else but a power *imaginary*, to which the successes of human actions and endeavours were for their variety ascribed." Under "to proscribe[1]" South exposes the atheistic basis of the collateral notion of chance, and elsewhere Watts takes on omens and the humbler notion of luck: "The child who is taught to believe any occurrence to be a good or evil omen, or any day of the week lucky, hath a wide inroad *made*[6] upon the soundness of his understanding." The whole, complex concept of fortune is impious because it locates power in an imaginary notion and derogates the omnipotence of God; it is likewise immoral because it diminishes human freedom and weakens resolve.

The most serious class of vulgar errors is closely related to the belief

in fortune and falls under the general rubric of idolatry. Johnson's
treatment of this archerror is inseparable from the *Dictionary*'s derision of Roman Catholicism. The corruptions and superstitions of papal religion are objects of scorn in Johnson's definition of "indulgence" and in the illustrative quotations from Milton, Allestree, and Atterbury. Swift issues a short broadside under "popery," and the assault is kept up in many unpredictable places, such as Atterbury's words under "to reply." Bishop Hall ridicules the notion of transubstantiation under "wafer[2]" and "multipresence," but Stillingfleet most consistently connects his attack on the Romans with the vulgar error of idolatry. Most of the quotations from Stillingfleet in the *Dictionary* come from his *Defence of the Discourse concerning the Idolatry Practiced in the Church of Rome*, and Johnson's inclusion of so much from this large volume ensured that his own book would be partly an attack on Roman idolatry. Stillingfleet's argument with the Romans turns on the distinction between *dulia* and *latria*. Johnson defines "latria" as "The highest kind of worship; distinguished by the papists from *dulia*, or inferior worship." Then he introduces Stillingfleet, who succinctly summarizes his argument: "The practice of the catholick church makes genuflections, prostrations, supplications, and other acts of *latria* to the cross." Elsewhere Stillingfleet puts idolatry of this sort firmly within the corpus of human error, citing at the same time three of its most important historians: "What sport do Tertullian, Minucius and Arnobius make with the images consecrated to divine worship? from the meanness of the matter they are made, the casualties of fire, and rottenness they are subject to, on purpose to represent the *ridiculousness* of worshipping such things." Many other speakers in the *Dictionary* add to the sport. To give just one more example, L'Estrange reports, "A man that had a great veneration for an image in his house, found that the more he prayed to it to prosper him in the world, the more he went *down the wind*[9] still."[13]

Not all the many warnings about idolatry in the *Dictionary* have to do with Roman Catholicism, however. In fact, most of them are more general. Many come from the Old Testament: for example, "*Turn*[18] ye not unto idols, nor make to yourselves molten gods. *Lev.* xix.4" and "This man that of earthly matter maketh graven images, knoweth himself to *offend*[1] above all others. *Wisd.* xiv.13." The even more general problem in idolatry concerns a distinction between matter and spirit. As it appears in Habakkuk 2.19 and under "to lay": "Wo unto him that saith to the wood, awake; to the dumb stone, arise, it shall teach: behold, it is *laid*[46] *over* with gold and silver, and there is no breath at all in the midst of it." Stillingfleet uses a commonplace to make a similar point under "harmoniously": "If we look upon the world as a musical instrument, well-tuned, and *harmoniously*[2] struck, we ought not therefore to worship the instrument, but him that makes the musick." Johnson himself knew that the tendency to idolatry was natural; it was neither limited to Roman Catholics nor likely to be spread only by them. In *Rambler* 110 he writes about the psychology of this archerror: "Incorporated minds will always feel some inclination towards exterior acts, and ritual observances. Ideas not represented by sensible objects are fleeting, variable, and evanescent" (*Yale* 4: 222). In the *Dictionary* Johnson adduces Glanvill to apply this psychology to an explanation of anthropomorphism, a form of idolatry, in religion: "Judging the infinite essence by our narrow selves, we ascribe intellections, volitions, and such like *immanent* actions, to that nature which hath nothing in common with us." Like other kinds of idolatrous superstition, this anthropomorphism involves the "mixture of imaginations" that Bacon saw as essential to the error. A struggle against the various forms that such mixture might assume is a conspicuous feature of Johnson's life and works.

Johnson is careful steadily to censure the error of idolatry, but he is more relaxed in his presentation of less harmful and more obviously foolish errors. Under "high-mettled" Garth dubs the whole pack of old wives' tales "erroneous abundance." Johnson's *Dictionary* casually alludes to such foolish notions as that chameleons eat air (s.v. "ingustable" and "to inviscate"); that ostriches eat iron ("to ingest"); that bear cubs are licked into shape ("informous"); that differences in the color of men's skins are the result of exposure to the sun ("inhabitant" and "intermigration"); the supposed bitterness of gall ("gall[1]" and "gustable"); the story taken up by Aristotle in his *Ethics* that the beaver bites off his testicles in order to escape the hunter ("divulsion"); the mysterious powers of eaglestone, which are discussed under that word by Calmet and Hill; and the belief in spontaneous generation ("equivocal[1]," "generant," "formative," and "instance[4]").

Whether or not their authors expose the falsehood of these opinions, Johnson's message about human ignorance is usually plain, and the expression of the folly makes some of the best and most Menippean reading in the *Dictionary*. A few complete examples are in order. Bentley reports that "the conceit of Anaximander was, that the first men and all animals were bred in some warm moisture, inclosed in crustaceous skins, as lobsters; and so continued 'till their *shelly* prisons, growing dry and breaking, made way for them." "The relation of a Spartan youth, that suffered a fox concealed under his robe to tear out his bowels, is *mistrusted* by men of business," Browne says in one place, and in another he suggests an emendation of the sixteenth century's greatest emendator: "That camphire begets in men an impotency unto venery, observation will hardly confirm, and we have found it fail in cocks and hens, which was a more favourable tryal than that of Scaliger, when he gave it unto a bitch that was *proud*[8]." Elsewhere, Browne's words provide a nice pseudodoxical headnote for a couplet by Pope: "Mathiolus hath a passage, that a toad communicates its venom not only by urine, but by the humidity and *slaver* of its mouth, which will not consist with truth." Pope evidently picked up this sleeveless tale when he wrote, "Of all mad creatures, if the learn'd are right, / It is the *slaver* kills, and not the bite." The learned, as so often happens in the *Dictionary*, are wrong. By means of a similarly happy arrangement of quotations under "unburied" Johnson seems to ridicule some pseudodoxical medical advice offered by Bacon: "The moss which groweth upon the skull of a dead man *unburied*, will stau[n]ch blood potently," says Bacon, but immediately thereafter and with no further philological benefits, he adds, "The hardest ingredient to come by, is the moss upon the skull of a dead man *unburied*." Bacon's persistence here is funny to an audience accustomed to reading pseudodoxia, but the joke seems to turn on Johnson's readers in a nearly Swiftian fashion in Hill's entry under "woodlouse." Hill's advice is revolting but perhaps not incredible enough, for many, to be merely funny: "Millepedes are aperient, attenuant, and detergent; and the best way of taking them is swallowing them alive, which is easily and conveniently done; and they are immediately destroyed on falling into the stomach." This may be a sick joke, but it is not an impious one, and the *Dictionary* affords much harmless humor at its contributors' and its naive readers' expense.

The recognition of error is not merely amusing, of course—it is also essential to the acquisition of knowledge. In fact, the recognition and purgation of error are as important to understanding as fresh learning. Bacon stated this in apothegm 237, and Browne repeats the lesson for Johnson's students: "Knowledge is made by *oblivion*[1], and to purchase a clear and *warrantable* body of truth, we must forget and part with much we know." Browne makes the point in more practical terms when he says, "Wise men know, that arts and learning want *expurga-*

tion[2]; and if the course of truth be permitted to itself, it cannot escape many errours." Johnson may have recalled this remark in *Rambler* 156, where he says, "the studies of mankind, all at least which, not being subject to rigorous demonstration, admit the influence of fancy and caprice, are perpetually tending to error and confusion. . . . The systems of learning therefore must be sometimes reviewed, complications analised into principles, and knowledge disentangled from opinion" (*Yale* 5: 66). For the sake of personal progress in knowledge, Locke makes a more radical suggestion: "He that has any doubt of his tenets, received without examination, ought to *put*[3] himself wholly into this state of ignorance, and throwing wholly by all his former notions, examine them with a perfect indifference." The *Dictionary* does not altogether embrace this extreme position, but it does present the recognition of ignorance in a very favorable light. As a document, the *Dictionary* both reflects a certain period in the history of knowledge and ignorance, and is an important event in that history. As part of this particular intellectual landscape, a conspicuous feature of the *Dictionary* is its concern to assert the claims of ignorance in opposition to an optimism about knowledge and reason that, for a while, posed a threat to religion. There was always, however, a threat from the opposite side of the dialectic. The many derogatory remarks in the *Dictionary* about skepticism show this, as does Bramhall's statement on the proper use of ignorance: "The *unsearchableness* of God's ways should be a bridle to restrain presumption, and not a sanctuary for spirits of error."

Despite great and demonstrable increases in knowledge, since 1755 the region of ignorance has grown even more dramatically, and ignorance rather than knowledge has probably usurped the greater part of the regions once sacred to religion. E. R. Dodds concludes his autobiography, *Missing Persons*, with a reflection on ignorance in the modern world that suggests this usurpation:

> What is all but totally missing from this record is the religious dimension. . . . to me, as to many of my generation, the age-old question "why are we here?" has ceased to be meaningful. It was meaningful once, when the earth was God's theatre and man the tragic hero of a unique and divinely conceived drama. But for a small animal bred we know not how on a third-rate planet in a fourth-rate galaxy even to ask such questions seems to me senseless; to offer confident answers, hybristic. I can

only say humbly with Erasmus, "Scientiae pars est quaedam nescire."(193)

A history of knowledge that takes sufficient account of the history of ignorance is yet to be written, and the great shifts in the moral valence of the topic are just part of what such a history should reveal.

3. Truth

3.1. The Rhetoric of Truth

The acquisition of truth is of infinite concernment: hereby *we become acquainted with the nature of things.* Watts.

Like knowledge, truth can be defined as a logical condition. Locke explains, "*Truth*[1] is the joining or separating of signs, as the things signified agree or disagree." However, most of the writers in the *Dictionary* speak of truth in terms that are less abstract and more metaphorical. These metaphors fall into a number of distinct categories, but taken together they suggest a coherent set of properties for truth.

Very often in the *Dictionary* truth is described as substance: solid, tangible, independent, and inflexible; indeed, it is frequently characterized in terms of Locke's "primary" qualities of matter. Although he is responsible for the logical, nonmetaphorical definition of truth, Locke himself frequently resorts to descriptions of it as substance. He warns, for example, "The mind by degrees loses its natural relish of real, solid truth, and is reconciled insensibly to any thing that can be but dressed up into any *feint* appearance of it." Norris likewise sees truth as ineluctable reality, though he filters the analogy through legal language: "These are standing and irrepealable truths, such as have no precarious existence, or *arbitrarious* dependance upon any will or understanding whatsoever." Johnson uses this rhetoric of truth when he speaks in his preface to Shakespeare about the "stability of truth" and the "adamant of Shakespeare" (*Yale* 7: 62, 70). In *Rambler* 74 he uses the rhetorically consistent phrase, "the coarseness of truth": "He that gives himself up to his own fancy, and converses with none but such as he hires to lull him on the down of absolute authority, to sooth him with obsequiousness, and regale him with flattery, soon grows too slothful for the labour of contest, too tender for the asperity of contradiction, and too delicate for the coarseness of truth" (*Yale* 4: 25).

Because it refers to texture, "coarseness," like so many descriptions of

truth in the *Dictionary*, invokes one of the qualities that Locke identified as primary and therefore a genuine part of the real, material world.
The irrepressible reality of truth appears again in Stillingfleet's remark
that "Truth may be smothered a long time, and *kept*[40] *under* by
violence; but it will break out at last." Despite Locke's logical definition, there is a strong tendency in the *Dictionary* to identify truth with
reality rather than to locate it in a relation between language and the
reality it expresses.

Another vehicle for representing truth in the *Dictionary* is light.
South shows how consistent this vehicle is with Locke's primary
qualities of matter by passing easily from one to the other in a single
sentence: "Our religion is a religion that dares to be understood; that
offers itself to the search of the inquisitive, the *inspection*[1] of the
severest and the most awakened reason; for, being secure of her
substantial truth and purity, she knows that for her to be seen and
looked into, is to be embraced and admired, as there needs no greater
argument for men to love the light than to see it." In the Gospel
according to John, God is light, and in James, God is the Father of
Lights, as almost all the physicotheologists in the *Dictionary* are eager
to remind us. In many of their entries, light drops out of the associative
cluster, and truth is immediately identified with God. This is apparently what happens in Norris's philosophical argument for the existence of God: "Truths must have an external existence in some
understanding; or rather, they are the same with that understanding
itself, considered as variously *exhibitive* or representative, according to
the various modes of inimitability or participation." Thomson makes
the same identification in his reference to "Socrates, / Truth's early
champion, *martyr* for his God." In another idèntification of truth and
God, Addison leaves just a hint of the vehicle of light: "Religion has
given us a more just idea of the divine nature: he whom we appeal to is
truth itself, the great *searcher*[1] of hearts. . . ." The associative cluster
of God, light, and truth is useful for representing not only the
ineluctability and reality of truth but also its wholeness and indivisibility. Under the first sense of "deduction," Johnson quotes Hooker: "all
truth, out of any truth, may be concluded," and later he gives Glanvill's
image of this proposition: "Truths hang together in a chain of mutual
dependance; you cannot draw one *link*[1] without attracting others."
The illustrative quotations from More's *Divine Dialogues* and his
Antidote against Atheism, as well as Johnson's reference to Cudworth's
"*intellectual*[5] system," show that Johnson was familiar with religious

Platonism and that he thought it a safe recommendation for the young and impressionable. Moreover, the Platonic concept of truth as whole and unified is consistent with Johnson's love of distinction and his detestation of mixture and confusion in all matters of truth and falsehood.[1]

A third class of metaphors in the *Dictionary* puts truth in a commanding position but not as high as God or the sun. Sometimes the position, like Johnson's "throne of truth" in "The Vanity," is interior. For example, South says, "Truth is a strong hold, fortified by God and nature, and diligence is properly the understanding's laying siege to it; so that it must be perpetually observing all the *avenues*[1] and *passes*[1] to it, and accordingly making its approaches."[2] South's image of strategic prominence is a military version of the more familiar geographical elevation that Johnson mistakenly attributes to Crashaw, not Donne: "On a huge hill, / *Cragged* and steep, truth stands." Johnson quotes a locus classicus for this image of truth in *Rambler* 117:

> Sed nil dulcius est, bene quam munita tenere
> Edita doctrina sapientum templa serena;
> Despicere unde queas alios, passimque videre
> Errare, atque viam palantis quaerere vitae.
>
> Lucretius, 2: 7–10.

Bacon assured these lines a place in the English history of truth by paraphrasing them in his essay "Of Truth": "no pleasure is comparable to the standing upon the vantage ground of truth: (a hill not to be commanded, and where the air is always clear and serene;) and to see the errors, and wanderings, and mists, and tempests in the vale below." Bacon goes on to add a note of Christian charity by saying, "so always that this prospect be with pity, and not with swelling or pride. Certainly, it is heaven upon earth, to have a man's mind move in charity, rest in providence, and turn upon the poles of truth" (*Works* 3: 302). In the translation that Johnson used in *Rambler* 117, Dryden calls the "templa serena" "virtue's heights," thus directly introducing a moral reading. This moral notion of absolute truth is important throughout the *Dictionary* and the rest of Johnson's works, but, like other pinnacles on Johnson's intellectual landscape, it is usually unattainable.[3] Pope's ironic account of the "huge hill, / *Cragged* and steep" is more often the story of human attempts to reach the truth: "Hills *peep*[1] o'er hills, and Alps on Alps arise." Only a divine man can "turn upon the poles of truth," but the *Dictionary* compensates for our mortal inability to achieve this by providing ways of calculating our declinations from the ideal.

3.2. Conviction

He that will not eat*[2] 'till he has a demonstration that it will nourish him, he that will not stir 'till he infallibly knows the business he goes about will succeed, will have little else to do but sit still and perish.* Locke.

If a man should forbear his food or his business, 'till he had a certainty of the safeness *of what he was going about, he must starve and die disputing.* South's Sermons.

The first degree of declination from truth is called "certainty." This degree is so close to truth that Isaac Watts sees truth itself simply as an objective version of certainty: "Certainty, according to the schools, is distinguished into objective and *subjective*: objective is when the proposition is certainly true in itself; and *subjective*, when we are certain of the truth of it." Unlike truth, however, subjective certainty requires the demonstrative proof of reason, testimony, or experience. When such proof is obtainable, knowledge is advanced to science, Johnson's second definition for which is "certainty grounded on demonstration." But Johnson's definition of "demonstration" shows how difficult it is to achieve real certainty in the intellectual world of the *Dictionary*: demonstration is "the highest degree of deducible or argumental evidence; the strongest degree of proof; such proof as not only evinces the position proved to be true, but shews the contrary position to be absurd and impossible." The exuberance of this definition is another example of the *Dictionary*'s continuous awareness of human ignorance and error. Although Glanvill may be referring specifically to theological writers, he gives us a pretty conceit on the narrowness of all human certainty, as the *Dictionary* tends to describe it: "All the certainty of those high pretenders, bating what they have of the first principles, and the word of God, may be circumscribed by as small a circle as the creed, when *brachygraphy* had confined it within the compass of a penny."

Although reason and authority deserve attention, the best way to demonstrative certainty is a heightened form of experience. Experience may be heightened by generalization, as Locke's important qualifiers "common" and "constant" indicate: he says, for example, "No definitions, no suppositions of any sect, are of *force*[3] enough to destroy constant experience," and "Common experience has justly a mighty influence on the minds of men, to make them give or *refuse*[1] credit to any thing proposed." A second enhancer of experience is immediacy. The various definitions of "intuitive" describe intuition as an immediate form of sight—"seen . . . without the intervention of reason." Locke puts this purified form of experience at the top of the ladder of "subjective certainty": "Intuitive knowledge needs no probation, nor can have any, this being the highest of all *human*[2] certainty." Watts makes a similar determination when he describes inspiration as a Lockean form of immediate experience: "*Inspiration*[3] is when an overpowering impression of any proposition is made upon the mind by God himself, that gives a convincing and indubitable evidence of the truth and divinity of it: so were the prophets and apostles *inspired.*" "Impression" is a key word in Locke's epistemology; it stands for the marks graven by experience on the mind, but only God can bypass the meanderings of thought and inscribe with the certainty of intuitive knowledge. For this reason, certainty is rare, and most human determinations must be made on more slender and more rational grounds.

As Locke and many other writers in the *Dictionary* often urge, the essence of good judgment is to proportion belief to the degree of demonstration underlying whatever is proposed. In Locke's words, "Lovers of truth, for truth's sake; there is this one *unerring*[2] mark, the not entertaining any proposition, with greater assurance than the proofs it is built upon will warrant." The only complication in this apparently simple advice is that various propositions are capable of various sorts and degrees of evidence. Tillotson implies his awareness of this complication: "When any thing is proved by as good *arguments*[1] as that thing is capable of, supposing it were [existent]; we ought not in reason to make any doubt of the existence of that thing." Despite its involvement in the train of human error, testimony,[4] for example, is not only admissible but, under certain circumstances, essential evidence of truth. Tillotson indicates one of the areas in which testimony is admissible: "Mathematical things are only capable of clear demonstration: conclusions in natural philosophy are proved by *induction*[2] of experiments, things of a *moral*[3] nature by *moral* arguments, and matters of fact by credible testimony."[5] Watts makes the point in scholastic terms: "Human testimony is not so proper to

lead[5] us into the knowledge of the essence of things, as to acquaint us
with the existence of things." The standard example is the existence of
places we have never actually seen: Tillotson says, "None can demonstrate to me, that there is such an island as Jamaica; yet, upon the
testimony of *credible* persons, I am free from doubt." But the existence
that testimony is most importantly called upon to verify is Christ's. The
quotation from Addison used in illustration of "account" is representative: "Being convinced, upon all *accounts*[12], that they had the same
reason to believe the history of our Saviour, as that of any other person
to which they themselves were not actually eyewitnesses, they were
bound, by all the rules of historical faith, and of right reason, to give
credit to this history." There are other areas in which testimony is
acceptable, but its apotheosis occurs in matters of religion that are
fundamentally beyond scientific demonstration.

Partly because less demonstrative proofs are needed in order to
show the truth of basic religious principles, the *Dictionary* spends a
good deal of energy denigrating a skeptical approach to conviction that
fails to adjust itself to the various degrees of probation possible for
various propositions. Atterbury says, for example, "The evidence they
had before them was enough, *amply*[1] enough, to convince them; but
they were resolved not to be convinced: and to those, who are resolved
not to be convinced, all motives, all arguments are equal." Several
writers see an unwillingness to be convinced as the mark of a light and
trifling mind. Bacon says, "There be that delight in *giddiness*[2], and
count it a bondage to fix a belief," and Sidney, sounding like a model
for Isaac Watts's educational texts, says, "Dametas, according to the
constitution[5] of a dull head, thinks no better way to shew himself wise
than by suspecting every thing in his way." Skepticism in general, like
other codified philosophies, is an object of scorn in the *Dictionary*.
Johnson represents the attitude of his book toward this "system" when
he defines "skeptick" as "one who doubts, or pretends to doubt of
every thing." Under a synonymous word, Glanvill shows that one can
appropriately engage or disengage skepticism: "Though I confess that
in philosophy I'm a *seeker*, yet cannot believe that a sceptick in
philosophy must be one in divinity." But the pretension of skepticism
has dangerous consequences even when it is not at first aimed at
sacred subjects. Browne implies there is always something potentially
impious in it when he refers to "sceptical infidelity" (s.v. "reserva-
tion"), and Atterbury sees it as a debilitating addiction: "The mind, by
every degree of affected unbelief, contracts more and more of a

general *indisposition*[2] towards believing." About the same time that he
entered Atterbury's sentence in the *Dictionary*, Johnson wrote the story
of Pertinax, a soul lost to the habit that Atterbury decries. In *Rambler*
95 Pertinax confesses:

> The habit of considering every proposition as alike uncertain,
> left me with no test by which any tenet could be tried; every
> opinion presented both sides with equal evidence, and my falla-
> cies began to operate upon my own mind in more important
> enquiries. It was at last the sport of my vanity to weaken the ob-
> ligations of moral duty, and efface the distinctions of good and
> evil, till I had deadened the sense of conviction, and abandoned
> my heart to the fluctuations of uncertainty, without anchor and
> without compass, without satisfaction of curiosity or peace of
> conscience; without principles of reason, or motives of action.
> (*Yale* 4: 147)

In the next paragraph, Johnson delivers the moral of this *Rambler* and
an important part of the *Dictionary*'s lesson on the vanity of human
learning: "Such is the hazard of repressing the first perceptions of
truth, of spreading for diversion the snares of sophistry, and engaging
reason against its own determinations."

Johnson's phrase "the sense of conviction" properly suggests the
way conviction shades rapidly into belief and then into faith. In each
successive shading the demonstrative evidence is less, but the subjective certainty remains the same. What must change along with the
decreasing demonstration is the possibility of demonstration in the
nature of the proposition. Hooker shows how far from certainty belief
can go: "We all know, that many things are believed, *although* they be
intricate, obscure and dark; *although* they exceed the reach and capacity of our wits; yea, *although* in this world they be no way possible to
be understood."[6] Locke's definitive remark also speaks of the disproportion between demonstration and conviction: "Faith is the assent to
any proposition, not made out by the deductions of reason, but upon
the credit of the *proposer*, as coming from God." Ordinarily, of course,
testimony is a far weaker sort of proof than demonstration. If the
absence of rational deduction is a requirement of faith, so too,
emphatically, is the absence of direct experience or intuitive knowledge. Browne makes this clear in his description of angelic life: "It is
also their felicity to have no faith; for, enjoying the *beatifical* vision in

the fruition of the object of faith, they have received the full evacuation of it."

In its treatment of certainty, conviction, belief, and faith, the *Dictionary* gives most scope to the two middle terms. Certainty is not often to be expected, and faith is probably best achieved by the unintellectual acts of prayer and charity. On one side, this distribution leaves an important space for religion safe from rational, scientific encroachment; on the other, it encourages exertions of judgment to weigh the various probabilities of things in an uncertain intellectual world.

3.3. Probability and Opinion

Discoursing of matters dubious, and many controvertible *truths, we cannot without arrogancy intreat a credulity, or implore any farther assent than the probability of our reasons and verity of our experiments.* Browne's Vulgar Errours, b. i.

In his definition of probability Johnson gives it a place on the scale of knowledge correspondent to conviction and belief: probability is "likelihood; appearance of truth; evidence arising from the preponderation of argument: it is less than moral certainty." The supplemental definition from Locke stresses the residence of this notion in the area of appearance: "*Probability* is the appearance of the agreement or disagreement of two ideas, by the intervention of proofs, whose connection is not constant; but appears for the most part to be so." A constant and real connection is indicative of truth, but the *Dictionary* rarely finds certainty or truth available to mortals. We live almost entirely in a world of shadows and probabilities, as Locke suggests: "All the light truth has, or can have, is from the clearness and validity of those proofs upon which it is received: to talk of any other light in the understanding, is to put ourselves in the dark, or in the power of the prince of *darkness*[4]." The variable lights of probabilities do not mean that truth is itself unconstant or nonexistent; they are only one more indication of human ignorance and error. South makes an important distinction when he says, "Probability does not properly make any alteration, either in the truth or *falsity*[1] of things; but only imports a different degree of their clearness or appearance to the understanding."

One indication of Locke's significance in the *Dictionary* is the number of times his important philosophical points are used in illustration of extremely common words. Johnson demonstrates the meaning of the preposition "in," for instance, with a short discourse by Locke on the proper method of determining probabilities: "However it be *in*[2] knowledge, I may truly say it [syllogism] is of no use at all *in* probabilities; for the assent there, being to be determined by the preponderancy, after a due weighing of all the proofs on both sides, nothing is so unfit to assist the mind *in* that as syllogism." Johnson's use of "preponderation" in his definition of "probability" further suggests that the determination of the probable depends upon an imprecise and relative sort of balancing rather than the strict abstract reasoning of logical deduction.[7] In the analogy between this operation of judgment and weighing there are implications of disinterestedness, justice, and a capacity for almost infinite degrees of distinction. One must not merely choose the heavier side of the argument; one must also choose a side only to the extent that it outweighs the other side. Locke drills this point into Johnson's students throughout the *Dictionary*, as when he says, for example, "If the evidence of its being, or that this is its true sense, be only on probable proofs, our assent can reach no higher than an assurance or *diffidence*, arising from the more or less apparent probability of the proofs." Hence, Taylor instructs, "Be not confident and *affirmative*[3] in an uncertain matter, but report things modestly and temperately, according to the degree of that persuasion, which is, or ought to be, begotten by the efficacy of the authority, or the reason, inducing thee." Browne gives an example of the correct behavior when he declares, "If any affirm the earth doth move, and will not believe with us it standeth still; because he hath probable reasons for it, and I no infallible sense or reason against it, I will not quarrel with his *assertion.*"

In the *Dictionary*'s Lactantian intellectual landscape the area of probability is very large. Raleigh, in fact, sees it as extending fully over the region of error: "There is no errour which hath not some appearance of probability resembling truth, which when men, who study to be singular, find out, straining reason, they then publish to the world matter of contention and *jangling*." Locke maps the *Dictionary*'s episteme with an equally strong awareness of error, but he continually urges judicious distinctions and steady acts of mind to steer a safe course. One of his most important principles is that "reason can never permit the mind to reject a greater evidence, to embrace what is less evident, nor allow it to *entertain*[7] probability in *opposition*[5] to knowledge and certainty." A mind that goes to school on the Lockean principles in Johnson's *Dictionary* will not "strain reason," like the contentious and singular writers described by Raleigh; on even the greatest matters that are subject to dispute, he will defer to the determinations of reason. Like students of Reynolds's later discourses, Johnson's faithful student will even let reason determine when it is to retreat in the face of superior evidence. As Locke says under a key word, "Whether it be a divine revelation or no, reason must *judge*[2]."

Just as the mathematical theory of probability is a way of controlling and calculating a field of events that is essentially random and arbitrary, the philosophical theory of probability tries to control a noetic field that otherwise tends toward arbitrariness. When the mind fails to observe the rational rules of probability, it falls upon its tenets as senselessly as dice produce numbers. Locke is clearly speaking about those who do not observe the laws of probability when he says, "These mens opinions are not the product of judgment, or the consequence of reason; but the effects of chance and hazard, of a mind floating at all adventures, without choice, and without *direction*[2]." Here and throughout the *Dictionary* "opinion" is the name for conviction or belief when it is uncontrolled or unadjusted to the findings of judgment. Rhetorically, opinion is just the opposite of "substantial" truth, as shown in Ben Jonson's description: "*Opinion*[1] is a light, vain, crude and *imperfect*[1] thing, settled in the imagination, but never arriving at the understanding, there to obtain the tincture of reason." Glanvill sees opinion as weightless, or at least frictionless: "The judgment being the leading power, if it be stored with *lubricious*[2] opinions instead of clearly conceived truths, and peremptorily resolved in them, the practice will be as irregular as the conceptions." Clothing is another appropriate metaphor for this insubstantial stuff, and Locke provides a model for Swift's and Carlyle's more famous uses of the analogy in a pair of nearby quotations, which when pieced together read: "They would think themselves miserable in a *patched*[1] coat, and yet they suffer their minds to appear in a pie-bald livery of coarse *patches*[1] and borrowed shreds, such as the common opinion of those they converse with clothe them in." The largely rhetorical nature of this analogy is evident in the fact that its converse never appears in the *Dictionary*. It is not possible to construct a suitable wardrobe of opinions, nor to produce them organically, like some natural sort of clothing.

On the contrary, wishes for self-creation and will itself are harmful to the search for truth and the determination of reasonable views. Hooker makes the antagonism quite clear in his contradistinction between will and knowledge: "Two principal fountains there are of human actions, knowledge and *will*[1]: which *will*, in things tending toward any end, is termed choice." The *Dictionary*'s usual word for the sort of will that interferes with knowledge is "inclination." Locke supports Hooker's sense of the antagonism between knowledge and will in a typically negative fashion when he says, "Ignorance, with an indifferency for truth, is nearer to it than opinion with *ungrounded* inclination, which is the great source of errour." Hooker's contradistinction is also at the bottom of Atterbury's remark that "the truth is, such a man understands by his *will*[1], and believes a thing true or false, merely as it agrees or disagrees with a violent inclination; and therefore, whilst that inclination lasts in its strength, he discovers nothing of the different degrees of evidence." In opposition to modern understandings of the term, "will" in these cases has little to do with freedom. In the *Dictionary*, willful inclination is described as a physical attribute that diminishes freedom as it increases error. Newton delivers the primary sense of the word when he talks about the *inclination*[1] of rays of refracted light.[8] The mindless physical quality of inclination is present in a quotation from Swift: "It seems a principle in human nature, to incline one way more than another, even in matters where we are wholly *unconcerned*[1]." Johnson tightens the connection between will and inclination by defining "will" as "choice, arbitrary determination." Such a pairing of words seems strange to minds formed after Coleridge's rejection of Hartley, but choice and inclination are not evidence of freedom and creativity in the intellectual world of the *Dictionary*: like everything connected with opinion, they are the sources of slavery. Only the truth can make one free, and, as Dryden says, "stiff in *opinion*[1], ever in the wrong." Glanvill puts it even more directly: "Obstinacy in opinions holds the dogmatist in the chains of error, without hope of *emancipation*."

The way to truth is to resist inclination and maintain instead a philosophic indifference. As Locke says, "They that do not keep up this indifferency for *all*[2] but truth, put coloured spectacles before their eyes, and look through false glasses." Indifference or disinterestedness, on the other hand, is a kind of purity, nakedness, and openness. Locke is looking for intellectual heroes when he asks for someone "who will be prevailed with to *disrobe* himself at once of all his old

opinions, and pretences to knowledge and learning, and turn himself
out stark naked in quest afresh of new notions." South is less dramatic
in his appeal, but he is looking for the same quality of disinterestedness: "Where diligence opens the door of the understanding, and
impartially keeps it, truth is sure to find both an *entrance*[1] and a
welcome too." Like the *Dictionary*'s more direct statements on the
subject, its representations of indifferency and openness favor the
validity of immediate experience. Glanvill takes the point to its extreme
when he says, "We must endeavour to *estrange*[4] our belief from every
thing which is not clearly and distinctly evidenced to our faculties."
Dennis makes a more specifically literary critical application: "Because, as he was a very natural writer, and they were without prejudice,
without prepossession, without affectation, and without the influence
of *coxcomical*, senseless cabal, they were at liberty to receive the
impressions which things naturally made on their minds."

Along with a subjective openness and simplicity, the *Dictionary*
instructs its readers to find a correspondent simplicity in the objects of
its inquiries. As usual, Watts gives the most straightforward instruction: "Contemplate things first in their own simple natures, and
afterwards view them in *composition*[4] with other things." On this point
Watts receives the backing of no less an authority than Newton: "The
investigation of difficult things, by the method of analysis, ought ever
to precede the method of *composition*[2]."[9] The end of any analysis is
the collection of simples that compose the object or, paradigmatically,
its origin. "In all sorts of reasoning," says Locke, "the connexion and
dependance[3] of ideas should be followed, 'till the mind is brought to
the source on which it bottoms." Hooker provides one possible source
for these analytical assumptions: "A common received error is never
utterly overthrown, till such times as we go from signs unto causes,
and shew some manifest root or fountain thereof common unto all,
whereby it may clearly appear how it came to pass that so many have
been *overseen*." Like the indifferent mind, the analyzed object has a sort
of harmony, wholeness, and calm. South gives a representative image
of the mind working toward such harmony and simultaneously achieving a calmness for itself: "The mind casts and turns itself restlessly
from one thing to another, 'till at length it brings all the ends of a long
and various *hypothesis* together; sees how one part coheres with another, and so clears off all the appearing contrarieties that seemed to
lie *cross*[6], and make[s] the whole intelligible."

In *Rambler* 158 Johnson expressed his very high esteem for analytical and synthetic methods: "To proceed from one truth to another, and connect distant propositions by regular consequences, is the great prerogative of man" (*Yale* 5: 78). But neither in the *Rambler* nor in the *Dictionary* does Johnson fail to recognize that the real state of things often resists our logical designs. As Watts says, "There are a multitude of human actions, which have so many *complicated*[1] circumstances, aspects, and situations, with regard to time and place, persons and things, that it is impossible for anyone to pass a right judgment concerning them, without entering into most of these circumstances." In a work so full of reminders of human limitations and ignorance, it goes without saying that such entrances are not always possible. It is likewise impossible always to strip oneself bare of opinions and preconceptions in order to make a perfectly open, Lockean inquiry— nor does the *Dictionary* recommend this without qualification. For all that the *Dictionary* says about the value of naked inquiry and the importance of eschewing opinion, the book itself is a storehouse of opinion, testimony, and predigested learning. The *Dictionary* is in part the embodiment of a love of learning and other forms of testimony that Johnson expresses more directly in *Rambler* 154, where he discusses method in the following way:

> The direction of Aristotle to those that study politicks, is, first to examine and understand what has been written by the an-cients upon government; then to cast their eyes round upon the world, and consider by what causes the prosperity of communi-ties is visibly influenced, and why some are worse, and others better administered.
>
> The same method must be pursued by him who hopes to be-come eminent in any other part of knowledge. The first task is to search books, the next to contemplate nature. He must first possess himself of the intellectual treasures which the diligence of former ages has accumulated, and then endeavour to en-crease them by his own collections. (*Yale* 5: 54–55)

Johnson goes on in this *Rambler* to make his famous remark that "the mental disease of the present generation, is impatience of study, contempt of the great masters of ancient wisdom, and a disposition to rely wholly upon unassisted genius and natural sagacity" (55). The "present generation" was formed in part, however, on the method-ological recommendations of Locke and his followers that Johnson plentifully transmits in his own great educational text. This is a contradiction not to be resolved, and, as it stands, it reveals something

essential about Johnson's whole mentality. The concourse of method-
ologies in the *Dictionary*, which embodies a love of testimonial learning
and, at the same time, warns continually against it, accurately reflects
Johnson's own complex way of thinking. To see the *Dictionary*, with all
its inconsistencies and counterpoints, as a record of Johnson's mind
does no injustice to a thinker who was not systematic by any account.
Like the *Dictionary*, the contents of Johnson's mind are probably best
organized around topics, and the topics best seen as containing but not
resolving their subtopics. The various complexes of knowledge have
points and structures in common, but they are not united by organic
filaments, nor are they monadistic representations of the whole or of
each other. In such an episteme, point and aphorism are not altogether
subordinate to an overarching method. A place to stand is just as
important as a way of proceeding.

The modern prejudice for overall unity and consistency got a boost
from Coleridge's strictures against the contradictory evaluations in
Johnson's preface to Shakespeare. Though it is easy today to defend
the preface, it is still very difficult to appreciate on its own terms an
essentially classical mind, like Johnson's, that does not flow in a
continuous stream but rather, as South describes it, "plants this
reasoning and that argument, this consequence and that distinction,
like so many intellectual *batteries*[2], till at length it forces a way and
passage into the obstinate, inclosed truth." The *Dictionary*, like many
other great anatomies in literature, represents just such a discontinuous but powerful act of mind.

4. Mind

4.1. Soul

To Animate. . . . 1. To quicken; to make alive; to give life to: as, the soul animates *the body; man must have been* animated *by a higher power.*

The soul in the body is but a subordinate efficient, and vicarious *and instrumental in the hands of the Almighty, being but his substitute in the regiment of the body.* Hale.

In Johnson's *Dictionary* "mind" assembles a group of meanings that were prevalent in the early seventeenth century. Whereas Locke and some of his followers achieve superior positions of authority on "truth" and "knowledge," in the case of "mind" writers as early as Hooker, Milton, and Raleigh are not comparably superseded. The reason for this seems to be Johnson's unwillingness to give up a connection between mind and soul that was prevalent in the earlier writers and that continued to be useful as evidence of the existence of God. Johnson remands explanation of the complexities of "mind" to Raleigh, just as he remands certain technical terms to Harris or Chambers and many key epistemological and logical words to Locke. The length of Raleigh's quotation is itself an important recommendation of the connection it affirms between mind and soul:

This word being often used for the soul giving life, is attributed abusively to madmen, when we say that they are of a distracted *mind*[1], instead of a broken understanding: which word, *mind*, we use also for opinion; as, I am of this or that *mind*: and sometimes for mens conditions or virtues; as, he is of an honest *mind*, or a man of a just *mind*: sometimes for affection; as, I do this for my *mind's* sake: sometimes for the knowledge of principles, which we have without discourse: oftentimes for spirits, angels, and intelligences: but as it is used in the proper signification, including both the understanding agent and possible, it

is described to be a pure, simple, substantial act, not depending
upon matter, but having relation to that which is intelligible, as
to his first object: or more at large thus; a part or particle of the
soul, whereby it doth understand, not depending upon matter,
nor needing any organ, free from passion coming from without,
and apt to be dissevered as eternal from that which is mortal.

Raleigh's strong connection between mind and soul wins full assent
from almost every speaker in the *Dictionary* except Locke.[1] It is
Bentley, however, who offers the greatest number of relevant assertions. His argument runs this way: (1) "There is something in our
composition, that thinks and apprehends, and reflects and deliberates,
determines and doubts, consents and denies; that wills and *demurs*[3],
and resolves and chuses, and rejects"; (2) "These powers of *cogitation*[1], and volition and sensation, are neither inherent in matter as
such, nor acquirable to matter by any motion and modification of it";
(3) "Sense and perception must necessarily proceed from some *incorporeal* substance within us"; (4) ". . . they proceed from some *cogitative*[1] substance, which we call spirit and soul." Watts glosses the last
part of the argument when he says, "When we know cogitation is the
prime attribute of a spirit, we infer its immateriality, and thence its
immortality." Locke objects, "It is an opinion that the soul always
thinks[1]," and "Defining the soul to be a substance that always thinks,
can serve but to make many men suspect, that they have no souls at all,
since they find a good part of their lives *pass*[25] *away* without
thinking." But in this one case at least, Locke's is the minority report.
Johnson seems to agree with the consensus of opinion in the *Dictionary*
when he urges us to control our mental powers in *Rambler* 8: "That the
soul always exerts her peculiar powers, with greater or less force, is
very probable, though the common occasions of our present condition
require but a small part of that incessant cogitation. . . . Lest a power
so restless should be either unprofitably, or hurtfully employed, and
the superfluities of intellect run to waste, it is no vain speculation to
consider how we may govern our thoughts, restrain them from irregular motions, or confine them from boundless dissipation" (*Yale* 3: 41).[2]
    The same writers who see cogitation as evidence of our incorporeal
and immortal souls are also careful to distinguish soul from everything
in our mentality that might be explained in material terms or might
have a material location. The *Dictionary* insists that the cogitative
rational soul of man is categorically different from the "sensible soul"

in animals and also from the human power of sensation. Davies, for example, makes this distinction: "Sense outside knows, the soul thro' all things sees: / Sense, *circumstance*[3]; she doth the substance view."[3] Likewise, Watts separates body and sense from soul and thought: "As we learn what belongs to the body by the evidence of sense, so we learn what belongs to the soul by an inward consciousness, which may be called a sort of internal *feeling*[3]."

Although it is often identified with mind, the soul is neither an agent nor an object of mere sense, and it has no definite place in the body; to think otherwise is a sort of idolatry. In terms reminiscent of those Johnson uses in *Rambler* 110 (see above, p. 94), Glanville warns: "That the soul and angels have nothing to do with grosser locality is generally opinioned; but who is it that retains not a great part of the *imposture*, by allowing them a definitive *ubi*, which is still but imagination." The various bodily loci that have been imagined for the soul include the pineal gland, the blood, and the brain. Johnson refers to the pseudo-doxical belief in the first under "pineal" (see above, p. 70). Of the second, a location favored by the ancients, Davies says, "If she doth then the subtil sense excel, / How *gross*[6] are they that drown her in the blood." But the brain is the fanciful location that gets the most attention in the *Dictionary*, and because of its involvement in this piece of pseudodoxia it becomes an object of general ridicule. Glanvill looks at the brain as a "quagmire" with a "*clammy*" consistency utterly unsuitable for supporting the motion of thought, and Collier is even more derogatory: "The brain has a very unpromising aspect for thinking: it looks like an odd sort of bog for fancy to *paddle*[2] in." The brain is doubly fit for the *Dictionary*'s satirical purposes because it is not only a false location for the cogitative soul but also symbolizes the vain, mortal intellect. Prior strikes idolatry and the vanity of human learning with a single blow when he says:

Why shou'd all honour then be ta'en
From the lower parts to load the brain:
When other limbs we plainly see,
Each in his way, as *brisk*[1] as he?

The difference between the soul and the body is absolute, and the fact that the two should be united during earthly existence is one of the mysteries of life that will always be beyond human understanding (see above, p. 69). Collier, for instance, says, "[Man] is compounded of two very different ingredients, spirit and matter; but how such *unallied*[2]

and disproportioned substances should act upon each other, no man's
learning yet could tell him." Johnson himself assents to an absolute distinction between body and soul in his definition of "life" as "1. Union and co-operation of soul with body" and in his definition of "trance" as "an extasy; a state in which the soul is rapt into visions of future or distant things; a temporary absence of the soul from the body." The union of soul and body is an important item in the catalogue of human ignorance, but it also serves, like the rest of God's creation, to prove the wisdom, power, and glory of God. In some quotations the proof is startlingly direct because the soul is described as being in direct communication with the divine world. Raleigh says, for example, "Our souls, piercing through the impurity of flesh, behold the highest heavens, and thence bring knowledge to contemplate the *everduring* glory and termless joy." Davies describes the soul as "being like those *spirits*[2] which God's bright face do see, / Or like himself whose image once she was"; but this is going almost too far, and Davies demurs, "Though now, alas! she scarce his shadow be." Bentley takes up Davies's caution and argues against the hubristic notion that the soul participates in God's eternity. Johnson affords Bentley a good deal of leeway for this effort under "potentiality" and "potentially[1]." Bentley asserts of souls that "their eternity consists only in an endless capacity of continuance without ever ceasing to be in a boundless futurity," but they did not always exist. In another place Bentley concludes, "No man in his *wits*[7] can seriously think that his own soul hath existed from all eternity." Like everything else in the universe, souls are creatures of God. As long as that subordination is remembered, souls serve as well as, or better than, the rest of creation as evidence of God's glory. Hence Addison says piously, "With what astonishment and veneration may we look into our own souls, where there are such *hidden* stores of virtue and knowledge, such inexhausted sources of perfection?" This physicotheological approach to the soul is carried on in the examination of its particular faculties—reason, understanding, judgment, memory, and imagination. But the pure wonder of Addison's remark requires the general word "soul," which, of all the words in the *Dictionary*, comes closest to uniting the human and the divine.

> *Life and sense,*
> *Fancy and* understanding*[1]: whence the soul*
> *Reason receives, and reason is her being.*
>   Milton.

> *Reason is nothing but the faculty of* deducing*[2] unknown truths*
> *from principles already known.* Locke.

> *Reason is the great distinction of human nature, the faculty by which*
> *we approach to some degree of association with celestial intelligences.*
> *(*Rambler *162, Yale 5: 95)*

Despite the great variety of usages it records, the *Dictionary* generally charts the language of mind chronologically in a progression from spiritual to logical language. The progression, however, has a coda or tail that points it back toward its spiritual beginnings: this final emphasis is supplied by Johnson's placement of older quotations in conspicuous places and by the reactions of some nearly contemporary writers to the possible impieties of using a logical language to describe the operations of the soul. The pattern is perhaps most visible in the usages of the words "reason" and "understanding," which vary from near identity with the immortal soul in the quotation by Milton illustrating "understanding[1]" to the more logical description by Locke under "to deduce[2]." Johnson shows his sympathy with the older identification in *Rambler* 162 and throughout the *Dictionary*. There is never, however, a strong antagonism between the two views because the language of mind remains sufficiently loosely defined to permit the spiritual and logical interpretations to shift around among a variety of words without any loss of meaning. One of the most common shifts available is between reason and understanding. If "reason" is required to carry a logical meaning, "understanding" is ready to carry the spiritual sense. For example, for the sixth definition of "reason" Johnson gives "ratiocination, discursive power"; he then quotes Davies, who uses "understanding" as an alternate name for the soul:

> When she rates things and moves from ground to ground,
> The name of *reason*[6] she obtains by this;

But when by *reason* she the truth hath found,
And standeth fixt, she *understanding*[1] is.

Whether a substitution is needed or not, however, the spiritual sense of "reason" frequently reappears to foil its logical and progressive sense. Using "discourse" and "reason" as a pair, Hamlet provides a very revealing instance in which the progressive meaning of reason fails to emerge—like himself—from the older, spiritual order to which it is connected:

> Sure he that made us with such large discourse,
> Looking before and after, gave us not
> That capability and godlike reason,
> To rust in us *unus'd*[1].

In his composition of the entry for "reason" Johnson shows a similar recusance. He defines the word progressively as "the power by which man deduces one proposition from another, or proceeds from premises to consequences; the rational faculty." But his illustrations recur to the older, more thoroughly spiritual senses of the word that connect it with moral truth. This is most evidently the case in Hooker's statement that "*reason*[1] is the director of man's will, discovering in action what is good; for the laws of well-doing are the dictates of right *reason*." Swift also uses the modification of "right" to express reason complete with its moral and religious connotations: "It would be well, if people would not lay so much weight on their own *reason*[1] in matters of religion, as to think every thing impossible and absurd, which they cannot conceive: how often do we contradict the right rules of *reason* in the whole course of our lives? *reason* itself is true and just, but the *reason* of every particular man is weak and wavering, perpetually swayed and turn'd by his interests, his passions and his vices." By combining his Lactantian strictures with a confidence in general reason, Swift comes close in this little sermon to summing up the message of the *Dictionary*.

When illustrative quotations in the *Dictionary* distinguish a ratiocinative reason, they often do so without abandoning the moral sense by shifting to the terms "wit" and "will." The best example is Davies's lines under the key word:

> Will puts in practice what the *wit*[1] deviseth:
> Will ever acts, and *wit* contemplates still:

And as from *wit* the power of wisdom riseth,
All other virtues daughters are of will.
Will is the prince, and *wit* the counsellor,
Which doth for common good in council sit;
And when *wit* is resolv'd, will lends her power
To execute what is advis'd by *wit*.

In Locke's treatment of "will" he is again at odds with the prevailing tendency of the *Dictionary*. Like his definition of "reason," his definition of "will" removes the moral and religious implications. He says simply, "*Will*[1] is the power, which the mind has to order the consideration of any idea, or the forbearing to consider it, or to prefer the motion of any part of the body to its rest, and vice versa." Despite his progressive language, however, Locke is in concert with the *Dictionary*'s interest in distinguishing the mind's human and merely logical determinations from true, revealed religion. According to South, "Reason is a weak, diminutive light, compared to revelation; but it ought to be no *disparagement*[3] to a star that it is not a sun."[4] Since Locke is the least inclined to use reason as a metonymic for the whole soul, he is, in a way, most free to contrast reason unfavorably to revelation. He says, for example, "When the spirit brings light into our minds, it *dispels* darkness: we see it, as we do that of the sun at noon, and need not the twilight of reason to shew it." In another place, he shows how his logical and progressive definitions of psychological terms allow him both to praise reason and to denigrate its merely human, and therefore inevitably fallible, character; in this combination of praise and denigration he is closer to the mainstream of the *Dictionary* than in his attempt to write a progressive language of mind. He says typically, "Reason elevates our thoughts as *high*[2] as the stars, and leads us through the vast spaces of this mighty fabrick; yet it comes far short of the real extent of even corporeal being."

Next below reason, though sometimes confused with it, is the faculty of judgment. In the *Dictionary*'s language of mind, "judgment" is in the process of splitting off from "reason": whereas the older writers tend to equate the two terms, the newer ones distinguish them. The terms are used almost synonomously in Shakespeare's lament, "O *judgment*[1]! thou art fled to brutish beasts, / And men have lost their reason." But Locke's illustration of the same sense of the same word defines the arena of judgment more narrowly and more closely according to Johnson's definition: "The faculty, which God has given man to supply the want of certain knowledge, is *judgment*[1], whereby the mind takes any proposition to be true or false, without perceiving a demonstrative evidence in the proofs." Whereas "reason" is a power of deducing and proceeding, "judgment" is "the power of discerning relations between one term or one proposition and another." In its progressive sense, judgment has to do with the large area of probability and relative value, and it leaves reason in command of truth and moral certainty. This newer apportionment of responsibility is evident in the contrast between quotations from Browne and Locke under "to resign": both writers censure blind approval of opinion, but Browne speaks of "whoever shall *resign*[2] their reason," whereas Locke refers to "those, who always *resign*[2] their judgment to the last man they heard or read."

Judgment proper has little to do with the divine nature of the soul; it is confined to the materials of experience, and it operates upon them in a largely mechanical fashion. Locke calls judging "*balancing*[4] an account," and Dryden refers similarly to the "*poize*[3] of judgment." The mechanism of judgment is primarily analytical, as Locke indicates in a distinction that all students of the eighteenth century will recognize: "*Wit*[2] lying most in the assemblage of ideas, and putting those together with quickness and variety, wherein can be found any resemblance, or congruity, thereby to make up pleasant pictures in the fancy. Judgment, on the contrary, lies in separating carefully one from another, ideas, wherein can be found the least difference, thereby to avoid being misled by similitude." Despite its lowliness in comparison to reason and its largely mechanical operation, judgment gets perhaps the greatest attention in the *Dictionary*'s discussion of mind because it is the most improvable faculty, the faculty that best protects one against deception, and the most active faculty in a field of knowledge that is founded upon experience.

In order to operate at all, however, the judgment requires a supply of intellectual materials. "Memory," says Locke, "is the storehouse of our ideas. For the narrow mind of man, not being capable of having many ideas *under*[23] view at once, it was necessary to have a repository to lay them up." For followers of Locke, like Watts and Johnson, who are especially concerned with education, memory is of the utmost importance. Under "to collect" Johnson reprints Watts's admonition that "'tis memory alone that enriches the mind, by preserving what our labour and industry daily *collect*[1]." In the sentences that precede this in *The Improvement of the Mind*, Watts says, "So necessary and so excellent a Faculty is the *Memory* of Man, that all other Abilities of the Mind borrow from hence their Beauty and Perfection; for the other Capacities of the Soul are almost useless without this. To what Purpose are all our Labours in Knowledge and Wisdom, if we want Memory to preserve and use what we have acquired? What signify all other intellectual or spiritual Improvements, if they are lost as soon as they are obtain'd?" (246). One sign of Watts's enthusiasm is his reference to mind as "soul," its highest denomination. Although Johnson does not reprint this part of the passage, he captures Watts's enthusiasm about memory under "to stamp": "What an unspeakable happiness would it be to a man engaged in the pursuit of knowledge, if he had but a power of *stamping*[4] his best sentiments upon his memory in indelible characters?"[5]

In the *Dictionary*'s most progressive psychological language, memory has the place of honor that romantic theorists like Coleridge reserve for the imagination. Memory gives depth to the mirror of the mind and stability to perception, but this estimation depends upon the increased scope of judgment as an active comparative faculty distinct from reason. In quotations that only distinguish between memory and the higher faculties, memory is just a lifeless warehouse of stuff. Glanvill displays the older, less distinct view: "'Tis better to own a judgment, though but with a *curta suppellex* of coherent notions, than a memory, like a sepulchre, furnished with a load of broken and *discarnate* bones." However, both in his definitions and in his distribution of quotations Johnson seems mostly to back the progressive view of memory, and he cites many more recommendations than derogations of it. One of the nicest recommendations is a brief homiletical tale by Robert South, quoted in illustration of "failure." This is a quintessential entry in Johnson's *Dictionary* because it serves at once the religious purposes of the memento mori, the educational purpose of inculcating the importance of memory, and the philological purpose of defining the word. Furthermore, it contains the not distasteful sort of black humor that Johnson seems to have found most entertaining: "He that, being subject to an apoplexy, used still to carry his remedy about him; but upon a time shifting his cloaths, and not taking that with him, chanced upon that very day to be surprised with a fit: he owed his death to a mere accident, to a little inadvertency and *failure*[1] of memory."

Unlike "memory" and "judgment"—but like "mind"—"fancy" and "imagination" are defined primarily by older writers in the *Dictionary*, and their meanings are very unprogressive. But whereas it is the

elevation of "mind" that keeps it tied to an older, less logical order, it is
the depression of "fancy" and "imagination" that holds them back.
The focus of Johnson's presentation of these notions is in the works of
Bacon and Milton, and, generally, the *Dictionary* remains strikingly
close to Hobbes's famous delimitation of imagination as "decaying
sense." Glanvill comes close to Hobbes's dictum, for example, when
he says, "Our simple apprehension of corporal objects, if present, is
sense; if absent, *imagination*[1]: when we would perceive a material
object, our fancies present us with its idea." Bacon gives the concept
somewhat greater scope, but, like Hobbes, he connects imagination
with an exalted conception of memory: "*Imagination*[1] I understand to
be the representation of an individual thought. *Imagination* is of three
kinds: joined with the belief of that which is to come; joined with the
memory of that which is past; and of things present, or as if they were
present: for I comprehend in this *imagination* feigned and at pleasure,
as if one should imagine such a man to be in the vestments of a pope,
or to have wings." Here, as is usual in the *Dictionary*, fancy is an
inferior version of experience that is at least once removed from reality.
Locke sums up the inferiority of fancy under the verbal form of the
word, and at the same time he issues one of the *Dictionary*'s many
warnings about the deceitfulness of language: "If our search has
reached no farther than simile and metaphor, we rather *fancy* than
know, and are not yet penetrated into the inside and reality of the thing;
but content ourselves with what our imaginations furnish us with."

   In the illustrative quotations in the *Dictionary* there is rarely any
distinction between the imagination and the fancy, though the former
is a little more likely to be used philosophically and the latter, with its
resemblance to "phantasy" (see Hale under "apparent[2]"), appears
more often in Lactantian contexts. The suppressed progress of these
terms may result from a commitment to controlling the faculties they
represent. Worried, like Johnson, about the dangers of the imagination, Locke did not advance the theory of fancy or the semantics of
"imagination" much farther than does the passage from *Paradise Lost*
that Johnson adduces in illustration of the key word:

> In the soul
> Are many lesser faculties, that serve
> Reason as chief: among these *fancy*[1] next
> Her office holds; of all external things,
> Which the five watchful senses represent,

She forms imaginations, airy shapes,
Which reason joining, or disjoining, frames
All what we affirm, or what deny, and call
Our knowledge, or opinion.

The rest of Milton's description, which contains more admonition, is found under "to misjoin," and Dryden gives an equally monitory version under "mob":

Dreams are but interludes, which fancy makes,
When monarch reason sleeps, this mimick wakes;
Compounds a medley of disjointed things,
A court of cobblers, and a *mob* of kings.

In literary critical contexts, however, Dryden provides some rare praise of fancy and imagination, and along with his praise goes a greater distinction between the two terms than the *Dictionary* usually recognizes. He says, for example, "The *quickness*[2] of the imagination is seen in the invention, the fertility in the fancy, and the accuracy in the expression."[6] Addison's famous essays on the imagination in *The Spectator* supply another group of laudatory remarks, but most of these are similarly restricted by their connection to art; the following illustration of "to call" is representative: "By the pleasures of the imagination or fancy, I mean such as arise from visible objects, when we *call*[2] up their ideas into our minds by paintings, statues, or descriptions." Only a few of Addison's remarks about the pleasures of the imagination are more general, and there is some evidence that Johnson does not fully approve them. For Johnson, Addison is describing a kind of enthusiasm when he says, "By imagination a man in a *dungeon* is capable of entertaining himself with scenes and landskapes, more beautiful than any that can be found in the whole compass of nature." Johnson's second definition of enthusiasm is "heat of imagination; violence of passion; confidence of opinion"; this definition qualifies Addison's praise of the imagination, and Johnson commonly makes its extension to areas outside of art seem risky at best.

Outside of art, fancy gets more commendation in association with memory than with sense, and in this connection its highest exaltation in the *Dictionary* comes from Nehemiah Grew: "The fancy may be so strong, as to *presentiate* upon one theatre, all that ever it took notice of in times past: the power of fancy, in *presentiating* any one thing that is past, being no less wonderful, than having that power, it should also

acquire the perfection to *presentiate* them all." But Johnson omits the
greater part of Grew's extensive praise of fancy, which is part of his
generally ecstatic observation of God's wisdom, power, and glory in the
formation of human physiognomy. Johnson excludes Grew's excessive
panegyrics on fancy just as decisively as he excludes his hymns to the
"harmonic vibration" that wisely was made an accompaniment to
coition; there is no place in the *Dictionary* for Grew's "Schemes of
phancy," which give each man his peculiar genius, or for his strange
idea that propagation begins in the fancy where are formed "Rude
Draughts of the Sperme Animals" (*Cosmologia Sacra* 47). At times,
Grew seems to think of fancy as the general, inarticulate force behind
all human action, but Johnson usually admits only those of his remarks
that also recognize the limitations or dangers of fancy. Hence, for
example, Grew says, "In the disquisition of truth, a ready fancy is of
great use: provided that *collation*[2] doth its office." Similarly, he warns
readers against the seduction of one of fancy's activities: "The conceptions of things are placed in their several degrees of similitude; as in
several proportions, one to another: in which harmonious *chimes*[4],
the voice of reason is often drowned." In a typical instance, Johnson
does not allow Grew the philologically complete, "As virtue is seated
fundamentally in the intellect, so *perfectively* in the fancy," without the
important resultative clause, "so that virtue is the force of reason in the
conduct of our actions and passions to a good end."

The precise reasoning behind Johnson's selection of illustrative
quotations is impossible to determine, but some things, like Grew's
harmonics of coition, are clearly inadmissible, and many others seem
excluded as a matter of course. Among these are remarks that might
appear to sanction idolatry, to increase dependence upon fate and
chance, or to challenge the proper polity of the soul, in which the
supremacy of reason is the most important point. Watts is close to the
center of the *Dictionary*'s didactic presentation of mind when he
declares, "Happy souls! who *keep*[14] such a sacred dominion over
their inferior and animal powers, that the sensitive tumults never rise
to disturb the superior and better operations of the reasoning mind."
Dryden articulates part of the rationale for teaching in the *Dictionary*
when he says, "*Science*[3] perfects genius, and moderates that fury of
the fancy which cannot contain itself within the bounds of reason." As
a fragment of science, a rule can have its uses in this important
enterprise, as Wotton indicates: "To leave as little as I may unto fancy,
which is wild and irregular, I will *propound*[1] a rule."

The benefits of maintaining a proper intellectual polity are both worldly and eternal. South says, for instance, "When the supreme faculties move regularly, the inferior passions and affections following, there arises a serenity and complacency upon the whole soul, infinitely beyond the greatest bodily pleasures, the highest *quintessence*[2] and elixir of worldly delights." Burnet also contributes to the exaltation of the pleasures of reason: "There is no *chase*[1] more pleasant, methinks, than to drive a thought, by good conduct, from one end of the world to another, and never to lose sight of it till it fall into eternity." Burnet's remark is especially meet for an instructional work like Johnson's because it finds a high, moral equivalent for the frivolous and much desired pleasures of the hunt.[7]

Although he steadily inculcates the need for proper mental government, Johnson is never thoroughly optimistic, either in the *Dictionary* or elsewhere, about the prospects of achieving it. The problem is, as Locke puts it, "There is nothing more resty and ungovernable than our thoughts: they will not be directed what objects to pursue, nor be *taken*[85] *off* from those they have once fixed on; but run away with a man in pursuit of those ideas they have in view, let him do what he can." In *Rambler* 43 Johnson recognizes the impossibility of ordering the mind with absolute propriety: "it cannot be denied that every difference in the structure of the mind has its advantages and its wants; and that failures and defects, being inseparable from humanity, however the powers of understanding be extended or contracted, there will on one side or the other always be an avenue to error and miscarriage" (*Yale* 3: 233). All of the *Dictionary*'s advice on controlling the mind is likewise played out against a general recognition of its near impossibility. Still, Johnson's book mingles a Lactantian sense of inevitable error with the hopefulness appropriate to a book addressed to a youthful audience. Johnson uses pessimism for the hopeful purposes of instruction and warning, and even in its treatment of the imagination the *Dictionary* is more affirmative than the tradition in which it is rooted. Bacon's statement in *Valerius Terminus* is one document against which the pessimism of the *Dictionary* should be measured:

> That the mind of man, as it is not a vessel of that content or re-
> ceipt to comprehend knowledge without helps and supplies, so
> again it is not sincere, but of an ill and corrupt tincture. Of the
> inherent and profound errors and superstitions in the nature of
> the mind, and of the four sorts of idols or false appearances

that offer themselves to the understanding in the inquisition of
knowledge; that is to say, the idols of the tribe, the idols of the
palace, the idols of the cave, and the idols of the theatre; That
these four, have added to the incapacity of the mind, and the
vanity and malignity of the affections, leave nothing but impotency and confusion. (*Works* 1: Appendix 90)

The center of the *Dictionary*'s treatment of mind is somewhere
between this pessimism and the sort of enthusiasm about the mind
evident in Addison's remarks on the pleasures of the imagination. It is
impossible to say precisely what the *Dictionary* asserts about mind or
any other subject. It is, after all, a gathering of opinions that retain a
good deal of heterogeneity, and it is very far from presenting a
coherent philosophical system on any of its subjects. But, though they
may be rough in places, there are boundaries around all the *Dictionary*'s topics. As in the intellectual world that Robert Frost conceives in
one of his poems, in the spaces of meaning that the *Dictionary*
represents "There Are Roughly Zones," and there must have been
some care on Johnson's part to preserve them in his progress through
the language.

5. Education

5.1. Learning

A sound mind in a sound body is a short but full description of a happy state in this world: he that has these two has little more to wish for, and he that wants either of them will be but little the better for[1] any thing else. Locke.

Education is a particular topic of discussion in Johnson's *Dictionary*, but, in its broadest sense, education is also the subject of the whole book. As James Axtell has correctly defined it, a work of education takes responsibility for the transmission of the whole culture that supports and underlies the work itself (Locke, *Educational Writings* ix). In this large effort, as well as in many particular points of education, Johnson's work is best compared to Locke's. Fundamentally, the *Dictionary* reiterates with a difference Locke's unoriginal but highly influential view that "'tis Vertue then, direct Vertue which is the hard and valuable part to be aimed at in Education. . . . All other Considerations and Accomplishments should give way and be postpon'd to this. This is the solid and substantial good, which Tutors should not only read Lectures, and talk of; but the Labour, and the Art of Education should furnish the Mind with, and fasten there, and never cease till the young Man had a true relish of it, and placed his Strength, his Glory, and his Pleasure in it" (*Educational Writings* 170).

The difference in Johnson's presentation is not in the primary ends of education but in the ancillary and subordinate elements. Beneath virtue Locke listed, in order of importance, three other aspects of education: wisdom, breeding, and learning. These are important for Johnson too, but the words have somewhat different meanings for him, and their order of importance is different. For Johnson, wisdom has more to do with religion and less to do with practical, worldly matters than it has for Locke. As a fundamental religious conviction—the fear of the Lord—wisdom is equal in importance to virtue. Johnson locates the worldly part of wisdom in breeding, and he depresses Locke's

emphasis upon both of these parts of education. In *Rambler* 98 Johnson
indicates that he understood Locke's conception of the notion when he declares, "Wisdom and virtue are by no means sufficient without the supplemental laws of good-breeding to secure freedom from degenerating to rudeness, or self-esteem from swelling into insolence" (*Yale* 4: 161). This high praise is consistent with Locke's definition of breeding in terms of the golden rule: "Not to think meanly of our selves, and not to think meanly of others" (*Educational Writings* 245). However, in practice, advice on breeding was dependent upon social position and was generally addressed only to the four or five percent of the population who comprised the upper classes of early eighteenth-century England. Because Johnson, to an even greater extent than Locke, wished to write a general education, he made the category of breeding less conspicuous in the *Dictionary*, thus leaving more room for the more general matter of virtue.

But perhaps the most interesting difference between Locke and Johnson is in their respective treatments of learning. In the *Dictionary* and elsewhere Johnson fully agrees with Locke's view that virtue is more important in education than learning. However, he puts more emphasis on learning than does Locke, and he thinks of it in a broader sense. In his introduction to Locke's *Educational Writings* James Axtell sees Locke's work as a successful rebellion against the current state of university education: "The acknowledged primary function of the university at this time," writes Axtell, "was the preservation, refinement, and communication to future generations of the knowledge of the past" (38). Education had dwindled down to a nearly exclusive concentration on classical texts, and Locke essayed to restore a classical emphasis upon education as training and nurture to make men capable and virtuous. "With Locke," continues Axtell, "the emphasis of education ceased to be placed on brain-stuffing and was firmly transferred to the *process* for the formation of character, of *habits*—a word always on his tongue—of mind and body" (58). As Axtell's opposition of "brain" and "mind" suggests, Locke was trying to reassert the claims of the whole soul in a cultural atmosphere that had come to accept the mechanics of humanistic scholarship as an end rather than a means to education. In this effort Locke repudiates the claims of learning, which meant for him and for Johnson the knowledge of the classical languages. When Johnson says, "The mental disease of the present generation, is impatience of study . . . and a disposition to rely wholly upon unassisted genius" (*Yale* 5: 55), he suggests that Locke may have succeeded all too well in his effort to reassert the dignity of the independent, active mind, unhampered by the rules and constraints of learning. Johnson's best expression of this dissatisfaction with the Lockean demotion of learning is the *Dictionary*. Although Johnson's book reprints a high percentage of Locke's remarks on education and generally vindicates his view of the aims of education, it nevertheless attempts to stop the pendulum of educational theory from swinging too far in the direction of Stoic training and to set it going back a little in the direction of Alexandrian learning.

5.1.1. The Ancients

He was not only a professed imitator of Horace, but a learned plagiary in all the others; you track *him everywhere in their snow.* Dryden.

A conspicuous sign of Johnson's effort to reform educational theory is the presence of classical learning and literature on virtually every page of the *Dictionary*. The most pervasive evidence appears in the forms of translation and imitation. Horace, for example, is a prominent figure in Johnson's book not only because he is cited in Latin in the epigraph but also because Johnson includes in his illustrative quotations much of the Earl of Roscommon's version of the *Ars Poetica*, King's admiring parody *The Art of Cookery*, some of Pope's *Imitations*, and many, many writers' paraphrases of famous Horatian remarks.[1] Other translations quoted in the *Dictionary* include Addison's Ovid; Chapman's Homer; Creech's Juvenal and Manilius; Dryden's Vergil, Homer, Ovid, Lucretius, and Juvenal; Garth's Ovid; May's Vergil; Pope's Homer (with his and Broome's notes); Pope's Statius; Tate's Juvenal; and West's Pindar. And in addition to all this, there are the imitations, like Johnson's own of Juvenal, and the countless casual translations of classical writers that fill the volumes of the seventeenth-century English writers whom Johnson most frequently cites.

The presence of so much translation is particularly significant in light of Johnson's statement in the preface that "the great pest of speech is frequency of translation" (par. 90). Johnson evidently exempts translations of the classics from this censure, as he exempts the King James Version of the Bible, and Sandys's and Sternhold's Psalms, because of their cultural and literary importance. The same sort of

exemption operates in favor of Fairfax's Tasso, Dryden's Chaucer,
Camden's *Britannia*, and the translation of Calmet's *Dictionary of the Bible.* Johnson's cultural prejudice comes out more clearly later in the same paragraph of the preface when he expresses his desire to "stop the licence of translatours, whose idleness and ignorance, if it be suffered to proceed, will reduce us to babble a dialect of *France*"—and indeed the only French author translated in the *Dictionary* is Du Fresnoy. It appears that Johnson was not so much against translation as he was determined to present English culture as a ramification of the classical and biblical literatures.

Nevertheless, the *Dictionary* is not a polemical advocate of classical culture, and its commitment to ancient learning is easily overestimated in an age that has let this commitment dwindle away to almost nothing. Considering the possibilities in a book that quotes heavily from Bentley, Swift, Temple, Dryden, and Wotton, there is very little in the *Dictionary* of the famous debate over the relative merits of the ancients and the moderns. Under an appropriate word Temple is permitted a moment on his hobbyhorse: "Whoever converses much among old books, will be something hard to please among *new*[2]." Dryden's Crites has his say under "to track," and Denham reiterates his main point under "to outshine," but most recommendations of the ancients are less connected to denigration of the moderns. Locke's words sum up the attitude in the *Dictionary* when he cites a classical author as authority for dismissing the whole debate between the ancients and the moderns: "Another partiality is a fantastical and wild attributing all knowledge to the ancients or the moderns: this *raving*[3] *upon* antiquity, in matter of poetry, Horace has wittily exposed in one of his satires."

The *Dictionary*'s recommendation of ancient learning is subordinate both to Locke's ideal of impartial inquiry and, of course, to religion. Felton shows the nature of the subordination when he says, "In comparison of these divine writers, the noblest wits of the heathen world are *low*[15] and dull." More commonly, however, Johnson's illustrations show the superiority of religion to classical learning by using the ancients for the higher purposes of Christianity. Addison, for example, argues that "the *preeminence*[1] of christianity to any other religious scheme which preceded it, appears from this, that the most eminent among the Pagan philosophers disclaimed many of those superstitious follies which are condemned by revealed religion." Accordingly, the highest praise of the ancients is that they believed in

Christian fundamentals. Thomson calls Socrates "truth's early champion, *martyr* for his God," and Raleigh says, "Pindarus the poet, and *one*[1] of the wisest, acknowledged also one God the most high, to be the father and creator of all things." With a more sweeping gesture, Stillingfleet declares, "Plato, and the *rest* of the philosophers, acknowledged the unity, power, wisdom, goodness, and providence of the supreme God." Similarly, Dryden vindicates the worth of Juvenal when he reports, "The bishop of Salisbury recommended the tenth satire of Juvenal, in his *pastoral*[2] letter, to the serious perusal of the divines of his diocese."

When all the necessary qualifications have been made, however, and when true religion has been given its due, the fact remains that the names of classical figures are highly conspicuous in the *Dictionary*. One cannot read far in the *Dictionary* without encountering the names of Aristotle, Vergil, and Homer. Also prominent are Cicero, Caesar, Horace, Seneca, Juvenal, Plato, and Pindar. Some of the many others that crop up here and there are Claudius, Caligula, Dionysius, Antony, Octavius, Lucan, Agrippa, Lucretius, Hiero, Demosthenes, Hesiod, Pythagoras, Titus, Vespasian, Plutarch, Vitruvius, Ptolemy, Sophocles, Euripides, Aristides, Galen, Xerxes, Archimedes, Anacreon, Themistocles, Theseus, Philo, Casselius, Anaxagoras, Solon, Prodicus, Telegonus, and Cato. The literature in the *Dictionary* shows a familiarity and conversation with the classics such as Johnson reveals when he quotes from memory the first line of Pitt's *Aeneid* to illustrate "first[1]" and the first line of Lauderdale's *Aeneid* to illustrate "warriour." Although they are English words, "first" and "warriour" are, for Johnson and the whole culture his book represents, closely associated with Vergil. Many other words in the *Dictionary* evoke a similar readiness to recur to the ancients. For example, Johnson defines "victor" as "conquerer; vanquisher; he that gains the advantage in any contest," but he goes on, "*Victor* is seldom used with a genitive, and never but with regard to some single action or person. We rarely say Alexander was *victor* of Darius, though we say he was *victor* at Arbela; we never say he was *victor* of Persia." Examples of allusions to antiquity in the *Dictionary* could be multiplied ad infinitum, but the point is simply that in the *Dictionary* the willing student finds a census of noteworthy ancients and enough information about them to stimulate curiosity and to testify to their importance.

It has traditionally been thought that Johnson gave English a direct infusion of antiquity by cataloguing a great many Latinate words and by writing such English himself in his definitions. However, Sledd and

Kolb concluded thirty years ago that "too much has been made of the Latinity of [Johnson's] word-list and definitions" (*Dr. Johnson's Dictionary* 45). Somewhat more recently E. L. McAdam, Jr., has located Johnson's attitude toward "inkhorn words" midway between Bailey's permissiveness and Chambers's outrage ("Inkhorn Words before Dr. Johnson"). Such comparisons with his immediate predecessors in lexicography are useful in making a fair estimate of the extent to which Johnson makes English incline to Latin. Despite the complaints of Thomas Edwards about "monsters" in the *Dictionary*, Johnson has fewer of them than either Bailey or Phillips. Furthermore, Johnson tried harder than earlier general lexicographers to pay attention to the Germanic roots of English: he uses Hickes's work on Icelandic; he heeds Edward Lye's emendations of Junius; and he consults Verstegan's Gothic scholarship. Johnson's history of the language does something to elevate the importance of the Teutonic element in English, and his word list promotes interest in Old English by including some of its productive morphemes, such as "ric" and "lich." Under "many" he takes up valuable space with a list of the twenty Saxonic variations of the word, and under "to stain" there is a little Welsh, which philologers of his day expected to figure more prominently in the "native" roots of English than it does. Though it is in itself a very small point, it seems representative of Johnson's reluctance to Latinize English that he rejects the diphthong "æ" as a letter "of very frequent use in the Latin language, which seems not properly to have any place in the English; since the *æ* of the Saxons has been long out of use, being changed to *e* simple, to which, in words frequently occuring, the *æ* of the Romans is, in the same manner, altered, as in *equator*, *equinoctial*, and even in *Eneas*."

In his etymological notes Johnson gives some of the best evidence of his wish to see English as a language independent of Latin, but at the same time he shows his own tendency to recur to learned languages in order to explain his native tongue. He distinguishes himself from relatively naive philologists when he gives the derivation of "oak" as "ac, æc, Saxon" and ridicules the attempts of Junius and Skinner to link this word, like so many others, to classical originals:

> *Oak.* n.s. [ac, æc, Saxon; which, says *Skinner*, to shew how easy
> it is to play the fool, under a shew of literature and deep re-
> searches, I will, for the diversion of my reader, derive from

οἶκος, a house; the oak being the best timber for building. *Skinner* seems to have had *Junius* in his thoughts, who on this very word has shewn his usual fondness for Greek etymology, by a derivation more ridiculous than that by which *Skinner* has ridiculed him. *Ac* or *Oak*, says the grave critick, signified among the Saxons, like *robur* among the Latins, not only an *oak* but *strength*, and may be well enough derived, *non incommode deduci potest*, from ἀλκὴ, strength; by taking the first three letters and then sinking the λ, as is not uncommon.]

Similarly, he is contemptuous of Junius's "idleness of conjecture" when he derives "to quaff" from κναφίζειν. Johnson insists reasonably on the nearer French word "coeffer." However, under "match" he rejects Skinner's correct conjecture of the Saxon "maca," and substitutes the Latin "mico." Under "to peep" Johnson himself indulges "idleness of conjecture," and in such cases his thoughts, like Junius's, run to Latin:

> To peep. v.n. [This word has no etymology, except that of *Skinner*, who derives it from *ophessen*, Dutch, *to lift up*; and of *Casaubon*, who derives it from ὀπιπευτήρ, a spy; perhaps it may come from *pip*, *pipio*, Latin, to cry as young birds: when the chickens first broke the shell and cried, they were said to begin to *pip* or *peep*; and the word that expressed the act of crying, was by mistake applied to the act of appearing that was at the same time: this is offered till something better may be found.]

Johnson also makes etymological conjectures on the bases of Old English, onomatopoeia, and eponymy, but his inclination is always to Latin. His entry under "to ferry" is representative of his whole approach in the etymological notes: he correctly offers a Saxon etymon and a German cognate, rejects a misguided attempt to find a Latin original, but errs equally in his own recurrence to Latin: "*faran*, to pass, Saxon; *fahr*, German, a passage. *Skinner* imagines that this whole family of words may be deduced from the Latin *veho*. I do not love Latin originals; but if such must be sought, may not these words be more naturally derived from *ferri*, to be carried?" Modern philology observes the consonant shift and derives "to ferry" from Latin "per" and Greek περί.

Like other lexicographers, Johnson thought the roots of English were Teutonic and classical. He distinguishes himself from earlier

dictionary-makers by his enlightened attention to the Teutonic roots,
but he is tied, like his predecessors, to his own training in the classics, and he usually relies upon that training when in doubt. About the same combination of philological enlightenment and habitual recurrence to the classical languages is also evident in Johnson's word list and in his definitions. The tension between his predilection for Latin and his awareness that English is a separate language appears representatively in his treatment of "to pretend." He defines the word as "to hold out, to stretch forward," but then he adds, with reference to the illustrative quotation from Dryden, "This is mere Latinity, and not used"; however, the "merely" Latin definition of the word is its first definition. In many other instances, Johnson gives the Latin meaning first without criticizing the example and often, as in the case of "ardour," without providing any example at all. By so often listing the Latin meaning as the primary meaning of his words he makes English seem a ramification of Latin much more persuasively than by his inclusion of Latinate "monsters."[2]

Furthermore, Johnson's explanations of most grammatical and rhetorical terms suggest that language means for him primarily Latin and sometimes Greek. In his introductory "Grammar" he opposed this identification by choosing as his model the English grammar of John Wallis, the first grammar to recognize the injustice of explaining English in terms designed for the explanation of Latin—but inside the *Dictionary* grammar is usually classical grammar. "Aptote," "diptote," "heteroclite," and "case" are a few of the grammatical terms that Johnson characteristically treats as though they were universally applicable to all languages rather than specific to the classical languages or especially useful in describing them. His continuous attention to the classical languages in his thoughts on language is even more explicit in the examples he gives of "dialect": "Attic, Doric, Ionic, Æolic." The fourth definition of "to govern" is grammatical, and, typically, the only instance is "*amo governs* the accusative case." Under the word "grammar" itself, Johnson adduces an example from Dryden that again shows that grammar means primarily Latin grammar: "*Varium & mutabile semper femina*, is the sharpest satire that ever was made on woman; for the adjectives are neuter, and animal must be understood to make them *grammar*[2]."

Most of Johnson's explanations of grammar come from Clarke's Latin grammar; Smith's *Classical Rhetoric* is the main source for explanations of rhetorical terms. Equally revealing are the examples of rhetoric that Johnson comes up with on his own to fill out his entries under the appropriate terms. His example of asyndeton is *"veni, vidi, vici,"* and the same passage occurs to him when he defines "polysyndeton" and looks for an English instance: "polysyndeton" is "a figure of rhetorick by which the copulative is often repeated: as, I came, *and* saw *and* overcame." He manages a simple English example of a palindrome, but the Latin example is more elaborate and significant: "palindrome" is "a word or sentence which is the same read backward or forwards: as, *madam*; or this sentence, *Subi dura a rudibus.*"[3] Even a rhetorical category with a particularly Teutonic name finds in Johnson's book a classical explanation. Under "spell" he writes: "1. A charm consisting of some words of occult power. Thus Horace uses *words*: *Sunt* verba & voces *quibus hunc lenire dolorem possis.*"[4]

In his original "Scheme" for the *English Dictionary* Johnson made a suggestion that, if adopted, would have bound his book even more completely to European Latin learning. Contemplating the difficulty of explaining such common, simple, and unanalyzable words as "bright," "sweet," "salt," and "bitter," he suggested, "It may be doubted whether it be not necessary to give the interpretation of the principal words in some other Language, which would much facilitate the use of the Dictionary to foreigners and might perhaps contribute to its sale in other Countries, and would not be without advantages to the English themselves" (*Adam Library* 2, "Scheme" fol. 12). As a general practice the idea was abandoned before Johnson began writing, but many vestiges of it appear in the *Dictionary*, and these show that the "other language" he had in mind is only Greek on the few occasions when it is not Latin. One very large group of words with a close but veiled connection to Latin are the 523 that he borrowed or translated from Robert Ainsworth's Latin-English, English-Latin *Thesaurus*. Johnson used Ainsworth by looking up words in the English-Latin section and then either translating Ainsworth's Latin definition or using Ainsworth's own translation of the key word in the other section of his *Thesaurus*. In either case Johnson's definition takes a sharp detour through Latin. For example, under "to feaze" in Ainsworth Johnson finds, "*To feaze one*, Flagello, 1. verbero; virgis aliquem cædere"; into his own book he translates the definition of "to feaze[2]" as "to beat; to whip with rods." The depth of the tincture taken in Johnson's translations of Ainsworth's Latin varies, but many of Johnson's definitions display their classic colors unmixed and original. His fifth definition of "dignity," for example, is "maxims, general principles, κυριαί δοξαί." In his third definition of "revolution" he finds it convenient to express the notion "par excellence" in Greek: revolution means "Change in the state of a government or country. It is used among us κατ᾽ ἐξοχὴν, for the change produced by the admission of king William and queen Mary." Classical phrases often enter Johnson's definitions when something extra is needed, as, for instance, in his treatment of "necessaries": "Things not only convenient but needful; things not to be left out of daily use. *Quibus doleat natura negatis.*"[5] Similarly, he defines "erelong" satisfactorily as "before a long time had elapsed," but he must add, "*Nec longum tempus.*" "Scourge[2]," "feat," and "frontispiece" likewise get Latin additions, but the addition under "consummate" better displays the sort of irritable reaching for something more perfect that often impels Johnson to write Latin: "consummate" is not only "complete; perfect; finished," it is also "*omnibus numeris absolutus.*"[6]

Probably because Johnson thinks of grammar primarily in classical terms, his definitions of English words or morphemes that operate syntactically often tend to include Latin or Greek. In explaining "amiss," for example, he describes "miss" as "the English particle, which shews any thing, like the Greek παρά, to be wrong." Similarly, under "Godward" he writes, "To *Godward* is toward God. So we read, *Hac Arethusa tenus*, for *hactenus Arethusa.*" The syntactical complications of "that" drive Johnson to Latin when he arrives at the sixth sense: "When *this* and *that*[6] relate to foregoing words, *this* is referred like *hic* or *cecy* to the latter, and *that* like *ille* or *cela* to the former" (also see "hither[3]"). Because it involves reference to a special grammatical function, he also reverts to Latin in his definition of "to irk": "This word is used only impersonally, *it* irks *me; mihi pæne est*, it gives me pain; or, I am weary of it. Thus the authors of the Accidence say, *tædet*, it *irketh.*" A desire to express this sentiment may have extended Johnson's treatment of "to irk" into Latin—however, whether or not his bosom returned an echo to the meaning he had in hand, his inclusion of so much classical language in his definitions of grammatical functions shows that when he thinks of the way language works, Johnson thinks of Latin and Greek.

They are not common, but Johnson's direct citations of classical authors are his boldest inclusions of classical culture. Like practically all the writers he used as sources of quotations, he adduces classical quotations in his book in order to add weight or point to important sentiments. Whether the quotations come in along with the English selected for illustrative purposes or are additions of his own, they tacitly recommend the ancients and learning. Examination of the books Johnson marked and gave to his amanuenses for collecting quotations shows that he made an effort to exclude most of the Latin that appears in them (the work of such exclusion is probably what made him reluctant to mark out more passages than he did in Burton's *Anatomy*[7]); there is, therefore, reason to believe that the classical quotations he did admit often had some special qualification. In many cases I find the Latin quotations in the *Dictionary* to be especially pointed versions of some of its general concerns; this seems to be a qualification for admission. Bacon's recommendation of study found under "to blanch," seems, for example, to meet this qualification and to win entry despite its Latinity: "*Optimi consiliarii mortui;*[8] books will speak plain, when counsellors *blanch*." South is likewise permitted a warning about laziness under a word that generally evoked a powerful response from Johnson: "The sot cried, *Utinam hoc esset laborare,*[9] while he lay *lazing* and lolling upon his couch." Among the *Dictionary's* many other exhortations to Johnson's students about the necessity for hard work, one of the best is by Browne, which he points with a quotation from the Vulgate: "It were some extenuation of the curse, if *insudore vultus tui* [by the sweat of your brow] were confinable unto corporal *exercitations*[1]." Under "requisite," Dryden's redaction of a classical saying makes a point about happiness, another important topic in the *Dictionary*: "*Res non parta labore, sed relicta* [wealth gained by inheritance rather than labor], was thought by a poet to be one of the *requisites* to a happy life." In another place Johnson retains a little Latin with a religious message from Camden: "The succeeding kings coined *rose-nobles* and double *rose-nobles*, the great sovereigns with the same inscription, *Jesus autem transiens per medium eorum ibat.*"[10] An even more general theme, the vanity of human wishes, gets support from one of its most famous classical expositors in a quotation from Addison: "A cabinet of medals Juvenal calls, very *humourously*[1], *concisum argentum in titulos faciesque minutas.*"[11]

The degree of deliberation behind Johnson's inclusion of Latin quotations from his sources is impossible to determine absolutely, but on a number of occasions throughout the *Dictionary* he clearly went out of his way and took up valuable space with Latin and Greek quotations. These quotations, being purely gratuitous in the English *Dictionary*, must be taken to reveal a good deal about what Johnson meant to communicate in his book. For example, personal feeling and public ideals combine forcefully in the remark on freedom found in the etymological note under "caitiff": "*cattivo*, Ital. a slave; whence it came to signify a bad man, with some implication of meanness; as *knave* in English, and *fur* in Latin; so certainly does slavery destroy virtue. Ἥμισυ τῆς ἀρετῆς ἀποαίνυται δούλιον ἦμαρ. Homer.[12] A slave and a scoundrel are signified by the same words in many languages." Johnson's personal passion for freedom and his conviction that it is necessary to any conception of morality are elements of the *Dictionary*'s total meaning; the points are simply more overt here than elsewhere, and, as often is the case, a classical quotation is part of the form such overtness takes. Another example appears under the second sense of "to rest." Johnson defines the sense as "to sleep the final sleep; to die"; then, seizing the opportunity to express the fundamental belief that eternal life is the reward of virtue, he quotes Callimachus:

$$ἱερὸν ὕπνὸν$$
$$κοιμᾶται· θνῄσκειν μὴ λέγε τοὺς ἀγαθούς.^{13}$$

The topic of death again stimulates Johnson to quote a classical source under the twelfth definition of "measure":

Limit; boundary. In the same sense is

$$Μέτρον$$
$$Τρεῖς ἐτίων δεκάδας τριάδιας [sic] δύο, μέτρον ἔθηκαν$$
$$Ἡμετέρης Βιοτῆς μάντιες αἰθέριοι.$$
$$Ἀρκοῦμαι τούτοισιν.^{14}$$

Johnson makes the same association in this definition that he makes in the last *Idler* between any end and the final end; his sense of analogy is always strong, but he seems to have an especially great aptitude for that mental activity when the analogon is death. Moreover, such somber reflections often suggest to him the somber expressions of a learned language.

In a book that tries, in Walker's words, to "temper all discourses of *philology* with interspersions of morality," the tongue itself will have been constrained to moral employment. Thus Johnson took many quotations from Allestree's *The Government of the Tongue*, but he also found occasion for reinforcing the point with Latin quotations. To explain "amice" Johnson adduces both Du Cange, the great lexicographer of Medieval Latin, and Jacobus Pancratius Bruno, the reviser of Castello's *Dictionary*. Du Cange places this clerical garment in the order of those that are worn over it and sufficiently explains the word for aspiring divines, an important part of Johnson's audience; but the added quotation from Bruno, the only one from him in the *Dictionary*, provides the more general lesson on the government of the tongue: "*Amictus quo collum stringitur, & pectus tegitur, castitatem interioris hominis designat; tegit enim cor, ne vanitates cogitet, stringet autem collum, ne inde ad linguam transeat mendacium.*"[15] To some extent, warnings about gluttony also come in under the government of the tongue, and there are plenty of these also in the *Dictionary*. One of the neatest appears under "phenicopter," which Johnson describes by means of an epigram from Martial: "*Dat mihi penna rubens nomen sed lingua gulosis / Nostra sapit; quid si garrula lingua foret?*"[16]

In many entries Johnson's movement between English and Latin or Greek examples is very casual and provides a model for conversation with the learned languages without pressing any of the *Dictionary*'s major themes. The etymology of "poetress," for example, brings Persius to Johnson's mind: "from *poetris*, Lat. whence *poetridas picas* in Persius."[17] "Napkin" carries an association with Vergil's *Georgics* 4.377: "from *nap*; which etymology is oddly favoured by *Virgil, Tonsisque ferunt mantilia* [sic] *villis;*[18] *naperia*, Italian." Under "green" Johnson directs his readers' attention to Sappho: "Pale; sickly: from whence we call the maid's disease the *green* sickness, or *chlorosis*. Like it is Sappho's χλωροτέρη ποίας."[19] When he comes to the tenth sense of "to drop" Johnson casually wanders into an unacknowledged citation of *Metamorphoses* 5.461: "To bedrop; to speckle; to variegate with spots. *Variis stellatus corpora* guttis."[20] In other entries the casual excursion into Latin or Greek may be stimulated by a wish to speak in the decent obscurity of learned language; "hoiden," for example, is "*fæmina levioris famæ*"[21] in the etymological note. Under the third sense of "gold" Johnson briefly mentions beauty in Greek and follows it with a Horatian recommendation of virtue: "It is used for any thing pleasing or valuable; so among the ancients Χρυσῆ ἀφροδίτη;[22] and *animamq; moresque* aureos *educit in astra.*"[23] Under "cork," Horace's *Odes* 3.8 gives dignity to a recommendation of libation, although the *Dictionary* in general is against drinking. The citation seems to mark time for Johnson in his long pull through the alphabet; in these lines Horace speaks of celebrating the kalends of March, and it is pleasant to imagine that Johnson entered them on that day:

hic dies anno redeunte festus
corticem astrictum pice dimovebit
amphoræ fumum bibere institutæ
consule Tullo.[24]

A more sober recommendation gains dignity by appearing in Latin, as pharmacological prescriptions still often do, under "to comfort": "*Salvia comfortat nervos. Schol. Sal.*" Under "sage" itself Johnson reveals the source of this prescription and adduces from it a higher recommendation of the herb: sage is "a plant of which the school of *Salernum* thought so highly, that they left this verse: *Cur moriatur homo cui* salvia *crescit in horto.*"[25]

A variety of reasons seem to motivate Johnson's many other excursions into Latin and Greek throughout the *Dictionary.* An interest in adding celebrity to English names other than those of Bacon, Hooker, Milton, and Boyle may stimulate his use of Matthaeus Westmonasteriensis to mention Lady Godiva under the second sense of "to trick" and his citation of Fortunatus's verses about Hilperic at the battle of Poitiers under "ric." Some extra Latin and a word of Greek may get into the etymological note on "copy" because of Johnson's solicitude for his amanuenses: in Latin he defends a derivation from *copia.* Junius's further suggestion of κόπος, labor, as the source of "copy" is not akin to Johnson's, but the ingenious reason is much the same as Johnson's Latin justification: "because, says he, to copy another's writing is very painful and laborious." Whatever other purposes they serve, Johnson's Latin and Greek quotations always build up his recommendation of the learned languages and lend weight to the side of learning, as opposed to practice, in the ever-unsettled dialectic between the two that composes the ideal of liberal education.

Johnson also found more explicit ways to recommend the learned languages. His reading in Felton's *On Reading the Classics* provided him with many illustrative quotations that make just such a recommendation. It also seems that he sought quotations from his other sources that praise classical learning or exhort or cajole students into acquiring it. Under "sonnet" Johnson made the unusual decision to exemplify rather than merely explain the word; the result is one of the longest passages of poetry in the *Dictionary*, and it seems clear that the poem's defense of classical learning qualifies it for this special inclusion every bit as much as its exemplification of the form in which it is written. Johnson's entry under "sonnet" reads:

1. A short poem consisting of fourteen lines, of which the rhymes are adjusted by a particular rule. It is not very suitable to the English language, and has not been used by any man of eminence since *Milton*.

A book was writ of late call'd Tetrachordon,
And woven close, both matter, form, and stile;
The subject new: it walk'd the town a-while,
    Numb'ring good intellects, now seldom por'd on:
    Cries the stall-reader, Bless us, what a word on
A title-page is this! and some in file
Stand spelling false, while one might walk to Mile-
End-green. Why is it harder, sirs, than Gordon,
Colkitto, or Macdonnel, or Galasp?
    Those rugged names to our like mouths grow sleek,
    That would have made Quintilian stare and gasp:
    Thy age like ours, soul of sir John Cheek,
Hated not learning worse than toad or asp,
When thou taught'st Cambridge and king Edward Greek.

5.1.2. Grammar, Rhetoric, Logic, and Philosophy

[*Science*] *5. One of the seven liberal arts, grammar, rhetorick, logick, arithmetick, musick, geometry, astronomy.*

> *Good sense, which only is the gift of heav'n*
> *And though no* science[5], *fairly worth the sev'n.*
> Pope.

Though unlearned[1] *men well enough understood the words white and black, yet there were philosophers found, who had subtlety enough to prove that white was black.* Locke.

Although it gets widespread support from Johnson's frequent allusions to classical languages, learning also encounters some stiff opposition in the *Dictionary*. This opposition comes largely from two quarters: the Lockean notion that devotion to learning is a form of illiberality in education and, secondly, the *Dictionary*'s pious recognition of the vanity of all human learning. On the subjects of grammar, rhetoric, and logic, three of the seven liberal arts, the contest over the

usefulness and desirability of learning is especially even. Johnson
implicitly sides with those in favor of the liberal arts by devoting so
much space to them. Moreover, in a couple of interesting instances, he
seems more explicitly to demonstrate his partiality for grammar and
logic by converting Locke's criticisms of these studies into recommendations of them. Under "to involve" Johnson reports Locke as saying,
"Syllogism is of necessary use, even to the lovers of truth, to shew
them the fallacies that are often concealed in florid, witty, or *involved*[6]
discourses"—but in book 4, chapter 17 of the *Essay concerning Human
Understanding* Locke says, "Indeed Syllogism is thought to be of
necessary use. . . . But that this is a mistake will appear, if we consider
. . . the Reason why sometimes Men, who sincerely aim at Truth, are
imposed upon by such loose, and as they are called Rhetorical Discourses . . ." (*Essay* 675–76). Clearly, Johnson makes Locke seem to
speak for the usefulness of logic when, in fact, he was attacking it. In
another citation, Johnson draws from Locke a recommendation of
grammar that is very different from what he intended when he has
Locke say, "The grammar of a language is sometimes to be carefully studied *by*[1] a grown man." The passage from which this remark comes is in section 167 of *Some Thoughts concerning Education*:
". . . particularly in Learning of Languages there is least Occasion for
poseing of Children. For Languages, being to be learn'd by Roate,
Custom, and Memory, are then spoken in greatest Perfection, when all
Rules of Grammar are utterly forgotten. I grant the Grammar of a
Language is some times very carefully to be studied; but it is only to be
studied by a grown Man, when he applies himself to the Understanding of any Language critically, which is seldom the Business of any but
profess'd Scholars" (*Educational Writings* 273). Locke's pleas for usefulness and common sense are antithetical to the cause of learning,
and by reversing Locke's meaning Johnson seems to show where his
own sympathies lie in the larger educational debate.

Yet Locke is certainly permitted to have his say and to make his
argument against rhetoric, logic, grammar, and conventional, classical
learning in general. Under "to exercise," for instance, Locke is allowed
to make the point that Johnson deflected in the excerpt he took to
illustrate "to involve": "Reason," says Locke, "by its own penetration,
where it is strong and *exercised*[3], usually sees quicker and clearer
without syllogism." He reiterates under "to brandish[2]," and he states
his understanding of the way knowledge is prior to learning under a
key word in the language of logic: "A man knows first, and then he is

able to prove *syllogistically*; so that syllogism comes after knowledge, when a man has no need of it." His point about syllogism is a moment in one of Locke's most important general arguments about education. Johnson gives Locke's direct statement of the argument a prominent place: "Till a man can judge whether they be truths or no, his understanding is but little improved: and thus men of much reading are greatly *learned*[3], but may be little knowing." However, this remark has more to do with the larger topic of the vanity of human learning than with logic, and from that broader position Locke's argument about logic receives most of its support in the *Dictionary*. Thomas Baker reminds us, for example, "We ought not to value ourselves upon our ability, in giving subtile rules, and finding out *logical*[1] arguments, since it would be more perfection not to want them." This is a reminder of human frailty because, as Baker says elsewhere, "God who sees all things intuitively, neither stands in *need*[2] of logic, nor uses it."

The *Dictionary* also contains many unequivocal, explicit recommendations of logic. Watts says, for instance, "Logick is to teach us the right use of our reason, or *intellectual*[2] powers"; "Logick helps us to *strip*[6] off the outward disguise of things, and to behold and judge of them in their own nature"; and "Logick *renders*[8] its daily service to wisdom and virtue." There is an even larger implicit recommendation of logic in the *Dictionary*'s attention to logical terms. By defining the nomenclature of logic under words like "induction" and "sorites" Watts contributes to the *Dictionary*'s considerable instruction in the subject, and numerous other writers explain particular aspects of logic in their illustrative quotations.[26] Altogether, the *Dictionary*'s brief lessons in logic by such respected writers as Hooker, Atterbury, and Watts build a recommendation of the subject solid enough to stand against the reservations of Locke.

Johnson's implicit recommendation of grammar and other parts of philological learning is even stronger than that of logic, but perhaps on account of this strength philology is obliged to weather the most persistent satire. Many of the derisive remarks about grammar are light-hearted and seem to belong primarily to the *Dictionary*'s lively, ironic self-deprecation, as when Shakespeare jocularly says, "Thou hast most traitorously corrupted the youth of the realm in erecting a *grammar school*." [27] But Locke's censures of grammar are more serious than those Johnson adduces from Shakespeare; they indict grammar, and learning in general, by denigrating the study of Latin: "The

ordinary way of learning Latin in a *grammar school* I cannot encourage"; "Under whose care soever a child is put to be taught, during the
tender and *flexible*[3] years of his life, it should be one who thinks Latin and language the least part of education."[28] Locke's concern is to move the attention in education from words to things, and he lodges his most trenchant attack on grammar by suggesting that it is irrelevant to real knowledge: "Men, speaking language according to the *grammar*[1] rules of that language, do yet speak improperly of things." In some other writers too, grammar is sometimes a name for irrelevant, empty knowledge, but in such remarks the specific educational recommendation yields to a broader theme. For instance, when Sidney denigrates grammar, he reiterates the principal theme of the *Dictionary*: one may teach grammar, he suggests, but only with "the beauty of virtue still being set before their eyes, and that taught them with far more diligent care than *grammatical*[1] rules."

Locke's objections to grammar apply in a higher degree to rhetoric, and he uses rhetoric as his example par excellence of the distinction he perceives between learning and real knowledge. Johnson reprints an important statement of Locke's argument under "to fend": "The dexterous management of terms, and being able to *fend* and prove with them, passes for a great part of learning; but it is learning distinct from knowledge." The distinction is far from original with Locke; Johnson takes one model for it from Ecclesiasticus 21.7: "An eloquent man is known far and near; but a man of understanding knoweth when he *slippeth*[6]." Elsewhere Locke states an even more familiar argument against rhetoric: "All the art[s] of rhetorick, besides order and clearness, are for nothing else but to *insinuate*[4] wrong ideas, move the passions, and thereby mislead the judgment." Though it involves a denigration of rhetoric, Locke's statement here is perhaps primarily devoted to the *Dictionary*'s universal insistence on the rule of reason over the passions.

Under a word very important to the culture represented in the *Dictionary* a quotation from Swift provides more moderate instruction on the use of rhetoric: "If your arguments be *rational*[2], offer them in as moving a manner as the nature of the subject will admit; but beware of letting the pathetick part swallow up the *rational*." Given its large inclusion of rhetorical terms and examples, the *Dictionary*'s total statement on the subject of rhetoric seems very close to what Swift says here. When the subject is sufficiently valuable, some authors go farther than Swift and give a warrant to all the pathos that rhetoric can muster. Hammond, for example, reports, "A popular orator may represent vices in so formidable appearances, and set out each virtue in so amiable a form, that the covetous person shall scatter most liberally his beloved idol, wealth, and the *rageful* person shall find a calm." The ultimate defense of rhetoric, however, must be attributed to South: "Christ had not only an infinite power to work miracles, but also an equal wisdom to know the just force and measure of every argument, to persuade, and *withal*[1] to look through and through all the dark corners of the soul of man, and to discern what prevails upon them, and what does not." When goodness employs rhetoric, the more the better, and the art itself is redeemed.

South's ultimate orator was unschooled in rhetoric, however, and, as Dryden imagines, the greatest writer needed no training: "Shakespeare was naturally learned: he needed not the *spectacles*[3] of books to read nature; he looked inwards and found her there." These and other examples suggest a view of learning as an artificial aid to insight that can easily become an impediment when it attracts too much attention to itself. Prior versifies the divorce that learning can effect between the system of discourse it creates and the reality it is supposed to explain:

> He who reading on the heart,
> When all his *quodlibets* of art
> Could not expound its pulse and heat,
> Swore, he had never felt it beat.

Although the *Dictionary*'s implicit recommendations of all the parts of learning, including grammar, rhetoric, and logic, far outweigh its satires of them, its reminders about the importance of practical, empirical knowledge are ingredient in its essential meaning as a pious and partly satirical book of knowledge. Under the key word "literature," which Johnson defines as "learning," Addison expresses the *Dictionary*'s serious critique of learning as well as its overall recommendation of it: "When men of learning are acted by a knowledge of the world, they give a reputation to *literature*, and convince the world of its usefulness."

The *Dictionary* applies the same standard of usefulness to other learned subjects. On the particular subjects of scholastic philosophy, metaphysics, and philosophy in general one finds the same qualified recommendation that appears in Johnson's treatment of grammar, rhetoric, and logic. The "school" is rarely mentioned without satire in the *Dictionary*'s illustrative quotations.[29] Oldham says, for example,

"In the schools / They *poach*[1] for sense, and hunt for idle rules," and
Rowe adds:

> Let him with pedants hunt for praise in books,
> *Pore* out his life amongst the lazy gownmen,
> Grow old and vainly proud in fancy'd knowledge.

Nevertheless, Johnson recognizes in his preface that he depends upon scholastic distinctions throughout his whole book, and he trains his students in them on almost every page: "The nice and subtle ramifications of meaning were not easily avoided by a mind intent upon accuracy, and convinced of the necessity of disentangling combinations, and separating similitudes. Many of the distinctions which to common readers appear useless and idle, will be found real and important by men versed in the school philosophy, without which no dictionary ever shall be accurately compiled, or skilfully examined" (par. 74). Because it is embedded in so many definitions, the implicit recommendation of scholastic philosophy outweighs the frequent satire it endures from writers like Oldham, Rowe, and Swift. The *Dictionary* in fact does just what Swift deplores when he says:

> Nature's fair *table-book*, our tender souls,
> We scrawl all o'er with old and empty rules,
> Stale memorandums of the schools.

In the face of all the derision leveled at metaphysics in the *Dictionary*, Watts makes much the same defense that Johnson makes of scholastic thinking: "Metaphysicks are so necessary to a distinct conception, solid judgment, and just reasoning on many subjects, that those who ridicule it, will be supposed to make their wit and *banter* a refuge and excuse for their own laziness." When it is condemned, on the other hand, metaphysics is the type of useless or abstract philosophy, and it is just as likely to be called by that general name. Atterbury provides an example under a form of the key word: "Acquaintance with God is not a speculative knowledge, built on abstracted reasonings about his nature and essence, such as *philosophical*[2] minds often busy themselves in, without reaping from thence any advantage towards regulating their passions, but practical knowledge." Johnson's receptivity to illustrative quotations that deride philosophy is even more evident in a selection from Shakespeare that does nothing to explain the word it supposedly helps to define:

Hang up *philosophy*[1];
Unless *philosophy* can make a Juliet,
Displant a town, reverse a prince's doom,
It helps not.

Although Juliet is arguably not the highest or most universal of these ends, learning must be useful to other ends in order to be valuable in the intellectual world of the *Dictionary*.

Bacon's verb is crucial when he says, "*Studies*[4] serve for delight in privateness and retiring, for ornament in discourse, and for ability in the judgment and disposition of business." Study that does not lead to practice is so frequently ridiculed in the *Dictionary* that Addison might have been commenting on a reading of Johnson's sources when he said, "Nothing is more easy than to represent as *impertinencies*[4] any parts of learning, that have no immediate relation to the happiness or convenience of mankind." Lest Addison's statement be taken as a rebuke to facile criticism of learning, an adjacent quotation from Watts certifies that "there are many subtle *impertinencies*[4] learnt in the schools, and many painful trifles. . . ." When Denham satirizes the lives of the learned, he focuses mainly on the production of useless learning:

Yet vainly most their age in study spend;
No *end*[3] of writing books, and to no end.

Because the most important uses are moral and religious, learning that neglects these subjects is a prime target of the *Dictionary*'s satirical remarks. Allestree, for example, sees a direct relation between the decay of piety and the overrefinement of learning: "Divisions *grow*[7] upon us, by neglect of practick duties: as every age degenerated from primitive piety, they advanced in nice enquiries." Speaking about individuals rather than society, Brerewood alludes to charity as one of the "virtues which rarely cohabit with the swelling *windiness*[3] of much knowledge. . . ."

The tragedy of learned lives, as Baker points out, is that "whilst they have busied themselves in various learning, they have been wanting in the one *main*[1] thing." The *Dictionary* takes care to warn its students against this disaster; the need to make learning useful by reference to something higher is a constant theme in Johnson's illustrative quotations. The something higher is always a form of practice, or experience, and the highest sorts of these are moral and religious. Although

Bacon does not mention "the one *main*[1] thing," his words under "without" are a slogan for a great deal of what the *Dictionary* says: "Wise men use studies; for they teach not their own use; but that is a wisdom *without*[1] them, and above them, won by observation." Johnson himself characterizes the instrumental nature of learning in his interesting explanation of "analogy": "1. Resemblance between things with regard to some circumstances or effects; as, *learning* is said to *enlighten* the mind; that is, it is to the mind what light is to the eye, by enabling it to discover that which was hidden before." This example shows that Johnson had the topic of learning on his mind as he composed the *Dictionary*, and it suggests the very high yet instrumental place he assigned to learning in his thinking. Learning is not the thing itself, but it is an extremely important medium. It yields only to some kinds of direct experience and to religious revelation, in which, according to Oxford University's motto, *Dominus illuminatio mea.*

5.1.3. Specific Uses and Abuses of Learning

Readers, who are in the flower of their youth, should labour at those accomplishments which may set off their persons when their bloom is gone, and to lay*[43] in timely provisions for manhood and old age.* Addison's Guardian.

In the larger project of education learning is both an important help and, frequently, a hindrance. The *Dictionary* spells out these benefits and liabilities in great detail. In a number of cases the uses of learning are expressed metaphorically, and these metaphors are interesting because they show something about the precise place of learning in the larger project it serves. Hammond describes learning, or a branch of it, as a secondary agricultural instrument—one that sharpens the tilling device—when he says, "Literature is the grindstone to sharpen the *coulters*, to whet their natural faculties." More directly but in the same vein, Wotton speaks about the "*manurement*" of wits. Shifting from the initial production to the preparation of food, Shakespeare describes learning as one of many seasonings: "Is not discourse, manhood, learning, gentleness, virtue and liberality, the spice and *salt*[1] that seasons a man?" The quotations illustrating such simple words often contribute more to the subject of education than to the explanation of the word they illustrate, thus providing some of the best evidence that Johnson intended his book to be an educational work.

As learning in general is useful to education, various kinds of learning have particular uses in forming the products of education. Digby says, "A complete brave man must know solidly the main end he is in the world for; and withal how to *serve*[14] *himself* of the divine's high contemplations, of the metaphysician's subtile speculations, and of the natural philosopher's minute observations." But Bacon is probably the writer in the *Dictionary* who is most adept at distinguishing the effects of the various parts of learning on the product. He determines, for example, that "histories make men wise, poets *witty*[2], the mathematick subtil," and, in general, that "reading makes a full man, conference a ready man, and writing an exact man; and therefore, if a man write little, he had need have a great memory; if he *confer* little, he had need have a present wit; and if he read little, he had need have much cunning, to seem to know that he doth not." Elsewhere Bacon sees education as a sort of medical art, and different branches of learning as prescriptions for health: "If he be not apt to beat over matters, and to call up one thing, to prove and illustrate another, let him study the lawyer's *cases*[7]: so every defect of the mind may have a special receipt." Watts follows in Bacon's pedagogical tradition, saying, for instance, "Narrowness of mind should be cured by reading histories of past ages, and of nations and countries, *distant*[1] from our own," and "Academical disputation gives vigour and briskness to the mind thus exercised, and relieves the *languor* of private study and meditation." Providing another "receipt" for intellectual health, Bacon says, "After long enquiry of things immerse in matter, interpose some subject which is immateriate or less *materiate*, such as this of sounds, to the end that the intellect may be rectified, and become not partial." Most of the *Dictionary*'s teaching on sound comes from Bacon's inquiries, and while this remark justifies their inclusion in a general educational text, it also suggests the values of symmetry and wholeness that other educators often express by means of an architectural analogy. Wotton sounds like the collective voice of the *Dictionary* when he says, "I was encouraged to assay how I could build a man; for there is a moral as well as a natural or artificial *compilement*, and of better materials." Addison employs the same analogy in a warning about superfluous intellectual attainments: "Nature seems to have designed the head as the *cupola* to the most glorious of her works; and when we load it with supernumerary ornaments, we destroy the symmetry of the human figure."

The difference between Wotton's blueprint and Addison's warning is significant: in one case education is primarily addition, whereas in the other it also involves subtraction. The same difference appears in a comparison between Wotton's or Hooker's use of magnetism as an analogy for education and Locke's view of it as the removal of a bias. Hooker's analogy is found under "to inure"; Wotton's is in two places: "If iron will acquire by mere continuance an habitual inclination to the site it held, how much more may education, being a constant plight and *inurement*, induce by custom good habits *into*[1] a reasonable creature." Locke, on the other hand, stresses the power of education to remove inclination: "Few of Adam's children are not born with some biass, which it is the business of education either to take off, or *counterbalance*." Likewise, when Addison compares education to a practical art, he finds one that depends upon subtraction: "An human soul without education is like marble in the quarry, which shews none of its beauties 'till the skill of the polisher *fetches*[6] out the colours."[30] This vacillation between the cumulative and excoriative powers of learning and education is typical of the *Dictionary*'s attitude to the whole field of knowledge and ignorance. Like Dryden's dialogue in *Of Dramatic Poesy*, or like many of Pierre Bayle's entries in his dictionary,[31] Johnson's *Dictionary* locates truth in alternative views and in a pattern of successive opposition.

In a wonderful section of his *Anatomy*, Robert Burton discourses on "the love of study in excess" as one of the causes of melancholy. Unfortunately, Johnson did not mark out passages from this section for inclusion in the *Dictionary*;[32] however, versions of most of Burton's remarks come into Johnson's book from a variety of other sources. Besides encouraging pride and impeding the true moral and religious ends of education, learning also tends to depress the spirits and ruin the bodies of its enthusiastic devotees. Boyle speaks of a student who "*distempered*[2] himself one night with long and hard study"; under "draught[2]," Johnson prints more of Boyle's description, and it appears that the distemperature brought on by immoderate study led to a recurrence of alcoholism. A quotation from Acts 26.24 describes an equally disastrous result: "Festus said with a loud voice, Paul, thou art *beside*[5] *thyself*: much learning doth make thee mad." On three separate occasions Johnson transmits Isaac Walton's predictable prescription for treating the melancholy of excessive study: "Angling was, after tedious study, a rest to his mind, a *cheerer* of his spirits, a *diverter* of sadness, a *calmer* of unquiet thoughts, a moderator of passions, a procurer of contentedness." The part of Walton's statement that the *Dictionary* reiterates again and again, however, is not the cure but the description of the disease caused by devotion to learning. While he was entering many descriptions of such distemperature in the *Dictionary* Johnson also probed the psychology of it in *The Rambler*. In number 74, for instance, he observes, "It sometimes happens that too close an attention to minute exactness, or a too rigorous habit of examining every thing by the standard of perfection, vitiates the temper, rather than improves the understanding, and teaches the mind to discern faults with unhappy penetration. . . . Knowledge and genius are often enemies to quiet, by suggesting ideas of excellence, which men and the performances of men cannot attain" (*Yale* 4: 27). Prior shows us the light-hearted way out of such depression:

> If to be sad is to be wise,
> I do most *heartily*[2] despise
> Whatever Socrates has said,
> Or Tully writ, or Wanley read.

The physical problems suffered by the votaries of learning also concerned Johnson in *The Rambler*; in number 48 he warns his learned readers about these in appropriately learned terms: "Those who lose their health in an irregular and impetuous persuit of literary accomplishments are yet less to be excused; for they ought to know that the body is not forced beyond its strength, but with the loss of more vigour than is proportionate to the effect produced. . . . They whose endeavour is mental excellence, will learn perhaps too late, how much it is endangered by diseases of the body, and find that knowledge may easily be lost in the starts of melancholy, the flights of impatience, and the peevishness of decrepitude" (*Yale* 3: 263). The elegance of Johnson's quasi-Newtonian formula is entirely his own, but he might have learned the warning it conveys from a great many of his sources in the *Dictionary*. Watts, for example, says, "If persons devote themselves to science, they should be well assured of a *solid*[5] and strong constitution of body, to bear the fatigue." Thomas Browne gives an ironic parable on the theme when he refers to a learner who "*emaciated* and pined away in the too anxious enquiry of the sea's reciprocation,

although not drowned therein." The same symptoms appear in the
addressee of an illustration from Dryden: "Thou art pale in mighty
studies grown, / To make the Stoick *institutes*[2] thy own." In the
context of the *Dictionary*, Shakespeare sounds as though he is speaking
about a student when he describes the condition of King Henry IV in
his final illness:

> The incessant care and labour of his mind
> Hath wrought the *mure*, that should confine it in,
> So thin, that life looks through and will break out.

Some of the more specific ailments brought on by study are the
subjects of many other quotations. Bacon, for instance, warns that
"curious printing in small volumes, and reading of small letters, do
hurt the *eye*[1] by contraction." Glanvill mentions *dizziness*, and Addison corroborates both Bacon's and Glanvill's findings under "bad[4]."
There is a tendency toward satire of the learned in many of these
warnings, but in none is it so explicit as in the illustration of "bum[1],"
which is attributed to "W———n":

> The learned Sydenham does not doubt,
> But profound thought will bring the gout;
> And that with *bum*[1] on couch we lie,
> Because our reason's soar'd too high.

This is a cruel joke because the gout was a cause of Sydenham's early
death, as Johnson well knew. In his brief "Life of Sydenham" (1742)
Johnson finds a less crude irony in the death of the precocious
physician, though he attributes it to the same cause as W———n: "It
is a melancholy reflection, that they who have obtained the highest
reputation, by preserving or restoring the health of others, have often
been hurried away before the natural decline of life, or have passed
many of their years under the torments of those distempers, which
they profess to relieve. In this number was Sydenham, whose health
began to fail in the fifty second year of his age, by the frequent attacks
of the gout . . ."(Fleeman, *Early Biographical Writings of Dr. Johnson*
194). In the *Dictionary* Dr. Harvey authorizes W———n's notion that
study can cause diseases like the gout, if not gout itself: "A *sedentary*[1]
life, appropriate to all students, crushes the bowels; and, for want of
stirring the body, suffers the spirits to lie dormant."[33] On two other
occasions Harvey issues the general warning that appears so frequently

in the *Dictionary*: "Moderate *labour*[3] of the body conduces to the preservation of health, and curing many *initial*[2] diseases; but toil of the mind destroys health, and generates maladies." Johnson probably recognized that the humoral theory behind this advice was vague and superannuated, but Harvey's subject is so relevant to Johnson's audience, and he contributes so materially to establishing the vanity of human learning, that his remarks are welcome again and again.

One of the oldest warnings about learning is that excessive attention to it disqualifies one for practical affairs. In the *Gorgias* Callicles tells Socrates that philosophy is an appropriate pastime for a few years of youth but an improper and debilitating activity for a grown man. E. R. Dodds points out that Callicles adapts this speech from the *Antiope* of Euripides, and he finds important parallels in Isocrates (*Gorgias* 272–73). English versions of this speech abound, and fragments of many of them appear in the *Dictionary*. "Oft it *falls*[24] out," says Sidney, "that while one thinks too much of his doing, he leaves to do the effect of his thinking," and "They might talk of book-learning what they would; but, for his part, he never saw more unseaty fellows than great *clerks*[2] were." "Unseaty" is a metaphor from the eminently practical activity of horseback riding, and refers to those with no knack for it. Another word for the excessively studious is "musty," as Addison shows: "Xantippe, being married to a bookish man who has no knowledge of the world, is forced to take his affairs into her own hands, and to spirit him up now and then, that he may not grow *musty*[4] and unfit for conversation." Perhaps the harshest Calliclean speech comes from Pope; his image is horrific enough to send even the most devoted reader of the *Dictionary* out into the street:

> The *bookful* blockhead, ignorantly read,
> With loads of learned lumber in his head,
> With his own tongue still edifies his ears,
> And always list'ning to himself appears.

The *Dictionary* does not, of course, recommend abstention from books; the whole work is one long, implicit recommendation of them. But, like *Rambler* 137, the *Dictionary* forces on its readers the reminder that " 'Books,' says Bacon, 'can never teach the use of books.' The student must learn by commerce with mankind to reduce his speculations to practice, and accommodate his knowledge to the purposes of life" (*Yale* 4: 363). Dr. South gives specific advice to this end in a commonplace that Johnson probably loved: "I look upon your city as

the best place of *improvement*[4]: from the school we go to the
university, but from the universities to London."

The satirical warnings about learning in the *Dictionary* often blend easily into satire of the learned themselves. Scholars, poets, philosophers, and all bookish people belong to the class of the learned in the *Dictionary*, and one of the degrading characteristics of this class is poverty. Ben Jonson laments this state of affairs: "The time was when men were had in price for learning; now letters only make men vile. He is upbraidingly called a poet, as if it were a contemptible *nickname*." Under a key word Bishop Wilkins adds, "This same *scholar's*[2] fate, *res angusta domi*,[34] hinders the promoting of learning." L'Estrange makes roughly the same point but with more levity when he says, "Words *butter*[1] no parsnips."[35] For Ayliffe the poverty of scholars leads to a conclusion concerning probate: "If any person has been at expence about the funeral of a scholar, he may retain his books for the *reimbursement*." For a number of other writers in the *Dictionary* the poverty of their class is lamentable, but at the same time it contributes to their honor. Philips eulogizes Spenser:

> Thus tender Spenser liv'd, with mean repast
> Content, depress'd with penury, and *pin'd*[1]
> In foreign realm: yet not debas'd his verse.

Dr. Littleton waxes lyrical on the subject and provides Johnson with yet another salute to his Grubstreet brethren:

> Insidious, restless, watchful *spider*,
> Fear no officious damsel's broom;
> Extend thy artful fabrick wider,
> And spread thy banners round my room:
> While I thy curious fabrick stare at,
> And think on hapless poet's fate,
> Like thee confin'd to noisome garret,
> And rudely banish'd rooms of state.

A fine anecdote from Bacon also finds some honor, if not romance, in the poverty of the learned: "Diogenes was asked, in a *kind*[6] of scorn, what was the matter that philosophers haunted rich men, and not rich men philosophers? He answered, because the one knew what they wanted, the other did not."

Wit can sometimes transform the shameful and laughable poverty of scholars into a badge of honor, but their dirtiness and uncouth manners are intractably ironic. In this fashion Pope depicts the scholar: "With sharpen'd sight pale antiquaries *pore*, / Th' inscription value, but the rust adore." Swift's irony may cut the speaker of the following lines, but that does not save from slander his scholarly subject:

> Though Artemisia talks by fits,
> Of councils, classicks, fathers, wits;
> Reads Malbranche, Boyle, and Locke:
> Yet in some things, methinks, she fails,
> 'Twere well, if she would pair her nails,
> And wear a cleaner *smock*[1].

Typically, the *Dictionary* represents the learned as stupidly unaware of their follies or impudent in their presentation of them. The effrontery of a representative scholar attracts Baker's attention: "Isidore's collection was the great and bold *stroke*[6], which in its main parts has been discovered to be an impudent forgery." Johnson himself apparently carved a similarly satirical remark about scholars out of Locke's *Conduct* by omitting the initial qualification "some" and printing the flat statement, "Men of study and thought, that reason right, and are lovers of truth, do make no great *advances*[3] in their discoveries of it" (*Works* 3: 391). The most amusing story about the ineffectuality of learning against stupidity comes from Bacon: "A company of scholars, going to catch conies, carried one with them which had not much wit, and gave in charge, that if he saw any, he should be silent for fear of scaring them; but he no sooner espied a company of *rabbits*, but he cried aloud, *ecce multi cuniculi* [Here are many rabbits!] which he had no sooner said, but the conies ran to their burrows; and he being checked by them for it, answered, who would have thought that the *rabbits* understood Latin?" It is some evidence of Johnson's continuous concern with the topic of the vanity of learning that he was able to make a contribution to it under such an unlikely word as "rabbit."

Humility may not cure the learned of stupidity or impotence, but it makes them socially and morally acceptable. Learned pride is utterly insufferable. The *Dictionary* attacks the vanity of all learning, but, among the various sects of philosophers, those most frequently accused of intellectual pride are the Stoics. The Stoic school is representative of arrogant learning, as Milton suggests:

Others in virtue plac'd felicity:
The stoic last in *philosophick*[1] pride
By him call'd virtue; and his virtuous man,
Wise, perfect in himself, and all possessing.

Perhaps the most damnable result of the Stoic's philosophic pride is his pretense of self-sufficiency. Such a pretense classes him with the unlucky students in "The Vision of Theodore" who pledge themselves to Reason without becoming votaries of Religion. As a warning for students Tillotson provides the testimony of a great Stoic that reason is inadequate without the assistance of religion: "Lipsius was a great *studier* of the the Stoical philosophy: upon his death-bed his friend told him, that he needed not use arguments to persuade him to patience, the philosophy which he had studied would furnish him; he answers him, Lord Jesus, give me Christian patience." In the extreme, the arrogance of Stoic self-sufficiency claims an immunity from worldly suffering that would rival the consolations of faith in God's eternal kingdom. Tillotson exposes the inferiority of this rival position under "measure": "Our religion sets before us not the example of a stupid stoick, who had, by obstinate principles, hardened himself against all pain beyond the common *measures*[6] of humanity, but an example of a man like ourselves." Stoic consolation succeeds only with the loss of humanity, but more often the *Dictionary* shows that it does not really succeed. Tillotson's fight against Stoicism is further found under two very common words: "Some of the philosophers have run so far back *for*[25] arguments of comfort against pain, as to doubt whether there were any such thing; and yet, for all that, when any great evil has been upon them, they would *cry*[6] out as loud as other men."[36]

Tillotson's sentence could serve as a text for chapter 18 of *Rasselas* in which "The Prince Finds a Wise and Happy Man," whose happiness and philosophical training desert him utterly when he suffers the loss of his daughter. Some of the outrage Johnson expressed at Soame Jenyns's sophistical denial of evil also pertains to the Stoics.[37] However, both the *Rambler* and the *Dictionary* are full of Stoic advice and contain plenty of Stoic tags. To give just one example from the *Dictionary*, Taylor urges us to "reduce desires to narrow *scantlings*[3] and small proportions." Such advice is admirable as long as it is understood as merely palliative. Swift shows how to understand Stoicism regarded as a cure: "The stoical *scheme*[2] of supplying our wants by lopping of our desires, is like cutting off our feet when we want shoes." As usual in the *Dictionary*, learning topples when vanity imagines it as a self-sufficient scheme for curing earthly pain without humble deference to a compassionate God.

5.2. Teachers and Pupils

Taught, or untaught*[1], the dunce is still the same;*
Yet still the wretched master bears the blame.

Dryden.

Few pedagogues *but curse the barren chair,*
Like him who hang'd himself for mere despair
And poverty.

Dryden.

The learned men for whom the *Dictionary* has the greatest sympathy are teachers. They suffer from the same ridiculous impecuniousness and have most of the same foibles as other scholars, but they are more praiseworthy. The main reason for this is that teaching goes beyond mere learning and centers on the more important aspects of education: religion and morals. Johnson defines "tutor" as "one who has the care of another's learning and morals; a teacher or instructor." Accordingly, South exalts the teacher over the ruler: "He that governs well, leads the blind, but he that teaches, gives him eyes; and it is a glorious thing to have been the *repairer* of a decayed intellect . . . to be a *subworker* to grace, in freeing it from some of the inconveniences of original sin." When Locke describes the job of a teacher, he leaves learning out of it altogether: "The great work of a *governour*[4] is to fashion the carriage, and form the mind; to settle in his *pupil*[2] good habits, and the principles of virtue and wisdom." This is extreme, and as an educational work the *Dictionary* tries to correct Locke's demotion of learning. It is a kind of correction, for example, when Ben Jonson is quoted ridiculing a shallow teacher who cares for breeding rather than learning:

For his mind I do not care,
That's a toy that I could spare:
Let his title be but great,
His clothes rich, and *band*[4] fit neat.

Another kind of correction is Watts's addition of learning to the

qualities in a tutor that Locke most highly recommended: "He should have so much of a natural *candour* and sweetness, mixed with all the improvement of learning, as might convey knowledge with a sort of gentle insinuation." Even with such corrections, however, the majority of important charges to teachers in the *Dictionary* stress the formation of proper habits, morals, and religion rather than learning. The teacher's influence in these areas is what makes him valuable and less susceptible to attack than other men of learning. Taylor charges tutors to "secure their religion, *season*[4] their younger years with prudent and pious principles." Milton emphasizes the same point when he advises that "to season them, and win them early to the love of virtue and true labour, ere any flattering *seducement* or vain principle seize them wandering, some easy and delightful book of education should be read to them." Despite his attempts to reintroduce learning and depress breeding in education, Johnson did not wish to tamper with the fundamental notion of the teacher's duty that Locke articulates: "Virtue is the solid good, which tutors should not only read *lectures*[1] and talk of, but the labour and art of education should furnish the mind with, and fasten there."

Part of the *Dictionary*'s sympathy for teachers comes out in terms of advertisements for education both public and private. In the context of the *Dictionary* Spenser's exhortation is general, though he originally made it specifically about Ireland: "Every parish should keep a petty schoolmaster, which should bring up children in the first *elements*[6] of letters." Under the famously defined "pension" Johnson continues his attack on "state hirelings" by adducing Addison to contrast their worth unfavorably with the worth of public schools: "A charity bestowed on the education of her young subjects has more merit than a thousand *pensions* to those of a higher fortune."[38] Elsewhere, Swift makes the opinion a flat command: "Erect publick schools, provided with the best and ablest masters and *mistresses*[4]." The justification for such development can only be the moral rather than the intellectual value of education, and South expresses this in the highest possible terms: "There are so many young persons, upon the well and ill *principling*[1] of whom next under God, depends the happiness or misery of this church and state."

Seeing heads of households as those responsible for education, the *Dictionary* directs many of its advertisements to them. Dryden persuasively recalls a golden age when this responsibility was taken seriously:

Time was, a sober Englishman would *knock*[1]
His servants up, and rise by five o'clock;
Instruct his family in ev'ry rule,
And send his wife to church, his son to school.

As Mrs. Barker also suggests (s.v. "life[5]"), parents should shoulder some of the grave responsibility of education themselves, but the *Dictionary* usually stresses the need for professional assistance. Wotton says, for example, "If any think education, because it is *conversant*[3] *about* children, to be but a private and domestick duty, he has been ignorantly bred himself." Wotton catalogues the follies that have diverted parents from properly discharging their duty: "Sometimes the possibility of preferment prevailing with the credulous, expectation of less expence with the covetous, opinion of ease with the fond, and assurance of remoteness with the unkind parents, have *moved*[4] them without discretion, to engage their children in adventures of learning, by whose return they have received but small contentment." Locke specifically addresses the folly of covetousness in education when he says, "If you can get a good tutor, you will never repent the charge; but will always have the satisfaction to think it the money, of all other, the best *laid*[47] *out.*" The only thing worse than a bad teacher is none at all. Ben Jonson completes the logic of the *Dictionary's* advertising for teachers when he says, "Very few men are wise by their own counsel, or learned by their own teaching; for he that was only taught by himself had a fool to his *master*[11]."

Another way in which the *Dictionary* expresses sympathy for teachers is by printing a few indulgent and humorously irresponsible justifications of corporal punishment. Swift provides the jubilant "The schoolmaster's joy is to *flog*," and the more subtle remark that,

> *Bastings* heavy, dry, obtuse,
> Only dulness can produce;
> While a little gentle jerking
> Sets the spirits all aworking.

Ascham declares, "The best schoolmaster of our time, was the greatest *beater*[2]." (This is an interesting quotation because the remark does not represent Ascham's own view: a character in *The Schoolmaster* makes the assertion, and the rest of the book is written in reaction against it.) Indulgences such as these aside, the *Dictionary's* attitude toward corporal punishment is generally condemnatory. However,

Locke, who was against beating, excepted cases of what he calls
"obstinacy"—he thought that children might attempt to gain mastery over their parents or tutors, and if they succeeded, all hope of achieving the basic aims of education would be lost. The exceptional case is argued under "to master": "Obstinacy and wilful neglects must be *mastered*[2], even though it cost blows." Exemplification appears under an equally appropriate word: "If a child cries for any unwholsome fruit, you may purchase his quiet by giving him a less hurtful *sweetmeat*: this may preserve his health, but spoils his mind."[39] Locke's exception is broadly expressed in the *Dictionary*, and Johnson even used it in defense of a schoolmaster accused of cruelty, for whom Boswell took a brief (Boswell 2: 184). Collier is one of the many who echo and exaggerate Locke's position in the *Dictionary*: "To the young if you give any tolerable *quarter*[7], you indulge them in their idleness, and ruin them." In this simple form, however, the sentiment is as old as Ecclesiasticus: "Children being haughty, through *disdain* and want of nurture, do stain the nobility of their kindred."

Despite all these warnings, and some deference to the frustrations of teachers, the steadiest recommendation in the *Dictionary*, as in Locke and Ascham, is for patience and gentleness. Locke says, for example, "There is no virtue children should be excited to, nor fault they should be *kept*[28] from, which they may not be convinced of by reasons." Besides being unreasoning, corporal punishment is usually impractical. The Lockean mind is a limited space that will not accommodate punishment and education at the same time: "Passionate words or blows from the tutor, fill the child's mind with terrour and *affrightment*[1]; which immediately takes it wholly up, and leaves no room for other impression." Without explaining the psychology of it, Ascham and South both authorize Locke's opinion: "If the child miss either in forgetting a word, or *misordering* the sentence, I would not have the master frown" (Ascham); "Nor is the *dulness*[1] of the scholar to extinguish, but rather to inflame the charity of the teacher" (South). Another argument against corporal punishment is that it is a species of tyranny that either stimulates rebellion or destroys the noble love of freedom. Locke's discussion of the first possibility is found under an appropriate word: "*Command*[2] and force may often create, but can never cure, an aversion; and whatever any one is brought to by compulsion, he will leave as soon as he can."[40] To Locke's authority on this point Johnson adds Milton's: "The main skill and *groundwork*[2] will be to temper them such lectures and explanations, upon every opportunity, as may lead and draw them in willing obedience." Milton's ideal student and, I think, Johnson's maintains his freedom as he achieves obedience; like Milton's pious man, he can, but does not, rebel.

Another important reason for opposing rough tutorial treatment is the prevalent view that education depends to a great extent upon imitation. Locke makes the point: "Passionate chiding carries rough language with it, and the names that parents and *preceptors* give children, they will not be ashamed to bestow on others." The depth of Locke's conviction that education works through imitation is the source of his obsession with the potentially damaging effects of vulgar, foul-mouthed, or dishonest servants. This obsession is what finally determines him in favor of private rather than public education: "A father that breeds his son at home, can keep him better from the *taint*[3] of servants than abroad."[41] Quotations from Swift's *Advice to Servants* sometimes make sport of Locke's concern over the corrupting influence of household help, but the underlying principle is taken very seriously throughout the *Dictionary*.[42] Locke says, "He, that will have his son have a *respect*[3] for him, must have a great reverence for his son," and L'Estrange echoes, "Tutors should behave reverently before their *pupils*[2]." Spenser says, "Doctrine is much more profitable and *gracious*[3] by example than by rule," and Rogers adds, "Example not only teaches us our duty, but convinces us of the *possibility* of our imitation." Atterbury makes an important application of this convic- tion: "He that talks deceitfully for truth, must hurt it more by his example, than he *promotes*[1] it by his arguments." In *Rambler* 50 Johnson seems to be distilling the *Dictionary*'s many quotations on the importance of imitation in education when he writes, "the teacher gains few proselytes by instruction which his own behaviour contra- dicts; and young men miss the benefit of counsel, because they are not very ready to believe that those who fall below them in practice, can much excel them in theory. Thus the progress of knowledge is retarded, the world is kept long in the same state, and every new race is to gain the prudence of their predecessors by committing and redress- ing the same miscarriages" (*Yale* 3: 271).

It is probable that the wide acceptance of Locke's educational views in early eighteenth-century England contributed to Johnson's failure as a schoolmaster. Parents who believed with Locke that "politeness of manners, and knowledge of the world, should principally be *looked*[12] after in a tutor" must have seen the awkward and provincial young

Johnson as a poor risk. When he wrote *The Rambler* and the *Dictionary*,

Johnson corrected Locke's extreme emphasis on breeding in education, but he did not argue with Locke's convictions about the importance of imitation in teaching. Yet this importance is so often expressed
in terms of danger and awesome responsibility that one suspects
Johnson was happy enough to have failed as a tutor. Dryden says, for
example, "The scholar believes there is no man under the *cope*[3] of
heaven, who is so knowing as his master." Locke takes it even one step
further: "Nor is it a small power it gives one man over another, to have
the authority to be the *dictator*[3] of principles, and teacher of unques-
tionable truths." Because of this power, Allestree warns, "the vice of
professors exceeds the *destructiveness* of the most hostile assaults, as
intestine treachery is more ruinous than foreign violence." Allestree's
simile becomes an analogy in the hands of other writers in the
Dictionary, and the responsibility of tutors epitomizes the grave burden
on everyone in a position of authority over the young. Because he
excerpted so many remarks on the theme, it is reasonable to think that
Johnson often reflected on the responsibilities inherent in the pedagogical position he assumes in the *Dictionary* and in many of his other
works. Johnson's consciousness of the dangers inherent in such a
position has an effect on his public utterances that should never be
forgotten by students of his writing or of writing about him. Johnson
knew that the risks he ran involved himself as well as his tutees. What
1 Samuel 3.13 says about parents Johnson could easily have read
analogically as applicable to all those responsible for educating the
young: "I will judge his house for ever, because his sons *made*[7]
themselves vile, and he restrained them not." More plainly directed to
the teacher is the equally monitory illustration from Shakespeare
under the important pedagogical word "to train":

> We did *train*[3] him on,
> And his corruption being ta'en from us,
> We as the spring of all shall pay for all.

Atterbury again reminds teachers of their grave responsibility when
he says, "The force of education is so great, that we may *mould*[1] the
minds and manners of the young into what shape we please, and give
the impressions of such *habits*[4] as shall ever afterwards remain." As
Atterbury's language suggests, education is powerful not only because
of its own force but also because children are so responsive to its
pressure. Indeed, the malleability or flexibility of children seems to be

their most characteristic feature, as far as the *Dictionary* is concerned. Locke again sets the standard: "His son, being then very *little*[2], I considered only as wax, to be moulded as one pleases." The soft, wax- or paper-like impressionability of children also invites a description of education in terms of inscription, especially among contemporaries and followers of Locke, who tended to identify words and ideas. Atterbury, for example, exhorts teachers to "imprint upon their minds, by proper arguments and reflections, a *lively*[4] persuasion of the certainty of a future state." Watts shows similar assumptions in his remark about some childhood learning: "Those impressions were made when the brain was more susceptive of them: they have been *deeply*[1] engraven at the proper season, and therefore they remain." In his preface to *The Fables of Aesop* (1692), from which Johnson quotes widely in the *Dictionary*, Roger L'Estrange redacts the most famous of Locke's epistemological metaphors: "Children *are but* Blank Paper, *ready Indifferently for any Impression, Good or Bad (for they take All upon Credit) and it is much in the Power of the first Comer, to Write Saint, or Devil upon't, which of the Two He pleases*" (A1r). I have not found this particular passage from L'Estrange in the *Dictionary*, but it supplies the underpinning for many of his contributions. For example, in a quota- tion under "ahead," he says, "It is mightily the fault of parents, guardians, tutors, and governours, that so many men miscarry. They suffer them at first to run *ahead*[2], and, when perverse inclinations are advanced into habits, there is no dealing with them."

Pre-Lockean writers in the *Dictionary* often express the suscepti- bility of youthful minds in horticultural or architectural terms. As Bacon has it, "A man's nature *runs*[34] either to herbs or weeds; therefore let him seasonably water the one, and destroy the other." In another instance Bacon articulates the assumption behind this admo- nition with a metaphor that could come from either gardening or building: "The late learners cannot so well take the *ply*[1], except it be in some minds that have not suffered themselves to fix, but have kept themselves open and prepared to receive continual amendment." Dryden likewise mixes the natural and the artificial:

> Children, like tender osiers, take the bow;
> And as they first are fashion'd, always *grow*[3].[43]

In some rare cases the educator has a power over his charges that is more demiurgic than that of a gardener or architect. Milton, for example, urges teachers to "*infuse*[2] into their young breasts such an

ingenuous[1] and noble ardour, as would not fail to make many of them
renowned." Especially after Locke, however, more mechanical and
practical analogies prevail in the *Dictionary*'s expression of the teacher's operation on the young and impressionable. But the operation
retains its great influence no matter what the terms in which it is
expressed. Philips, for example, finds Milton's grander language appropriate, even as he describes the ideal teacher in terms that are not
incompatible with Locke's:

> He generous thoughts instills
> Of true nobility; forms their *ductile*[3] minds
> To human virtues.

Unfortunately for teachers, the minds of all students are not equally
impressionable, and not all pupils are equally docible or ductile. In the
Dictionary's portrayal of students, Milton is the exception that proves
the rule. He declares:

> When I was yet a child, no *childish*[2] play
> To me was pleasing; all my mind was set
> Serious to learn and know.

The besetting sin of most other students who appear in Johnson's
illustrative quotations is laziness. Shakespeare's satirical image of the
student is characteristic:

> The whining school-boy, with his satchel,
> And shining morning face, creeping like snail
> *Unwillingly* to school.

Butler presents Jacques' schoolboy at college with a couple of quick
strokes: "Tir'd with dispute, and speaking Latin, / As well as *bast-
ing*[1], and bear bating." Swift's agreement with these earlier satirists is
limited to an observation on wealthy students, but the point is generally
applicable: "It may be the disposition of young *nobles*[1], that they
expect the accomplishments of a good education without the least
expence of time or study."

The overall concurrence on this point among the speakers in
Johnson's *Dictionary* is deducible from the sort of advice they give to
students: almost all of it has to do with self-discipline. Some of this
advice takes the humble form of the helpful hint, as when Dryden
suggests, "The *morning* is the proper part of the day for study." Watts
makes a more general suggestion about scheduling studies: "When

you have fixed proper hours for particular studies, keep to them, not with a superstitious *preciseness*, but with some good degrees of a regular constancy." Bacon's counsel is subtler and more philosophical: "In studies, whatsoever a man commandeth upon himself, let him *set*[12] hours for it; but whatsoever is agreeable to his nature, let him take no care for any *set* times: for his thoughts will fly to it of themselves, so as the spaces of other business or studies will suffice." In stronger words, Watts urges upon his young readers what Johnson himself so often urged upon his audiences and himself: "Once a day, especially in the early years of life and study, *call*[4] yourselves to an account, what new ideas, what new proposition or truth, you have gained."

Rather than giving advice on how to achieve good study habits, a number of quotations in the *Dictionary* make the more fundamental point that discipline and diligence are required in studies. Perhaps the most basic form of discipline is attention, and quotations from Locke and Watts collaborate to drive home its importance. "By *attention* the ideas, that offer themselves, are taken notice of, and, as it were, registered in the memory," says Locke; Watts adds, "*Attention* is a very necessary thing; truth doth not always strike the soul at first sight." South describes a very high degree of attention and implicitly recommends it: "Diligence is a steady, constant and *pertinacious*[2] study, that naturally leads the soul into the knowledge of that, which at first seemed locked up from it." If the *Dictionary* were a book directed to aspiring military men, the illustration of "pertinacious" might have been arranged to promote military valor—but the *Dictionary*'s primary direction is to students, and this makes study the right choice for a field on which to describe pertinacity. Elsewhere South speaks about the necessity of discipline in the most important area of study, but his remark applies to all studies: "The knowledge of what is good and what is evil, what ought and what ought not to be done, is a thing too large to be *compassed*[5], and too hard to be mastered, without brains and study, parts and contemplation." The notion that any success depends upon two complementary and opposing qualities, like "brains and study," is deeply rooted in the whole culture of the *Dictionary*. However, the notion so often informs some advice on study itself that even when it appears in other terms, it seems directed to the student. Hence, even Johnson's quotation of an anonymous and proverbial couplet must be read as another attempt to instill diligence in his audience of students:

He that will a good *edge*[1] win
Must forge thick, and grind thin.

Like most other valuable qualities, as the *Dictionary* sees them, eagerness to study is either too great or too little in most students, and both extremes lead to the same frustration. The more numerous students are those identified by Locke who "*depress*[3] their own minds, *despond*[1] at the first difficulty, and conclude that the making any progress in knowledge is above their capacities."[44] Teachers must take this liability into consideration, and above all, as Watts has it, "not be too hasty to *plunge*[4] their enquiries at once into the depths of knowledge." Watts's advice grows out of one of Locke's educational principles: "The surest way for a learner is, not to advance by *jumps*[1] and large strides; let that, which he sets himself to learn next, be as nearly *conjoined*[3] with what he knows already, as is possible." This principle was also known to Milton, whose warning based upon it is used in illustration of the unlikely word "shallows": "Having but newly left those grammatick flats and *shallows*, where they stuck unreasonably, to learn a few words with lamentable construction, and now on the sudden transported, to be tost with their unballasted wits in fathomless and unquiet deeps of controversy, they do grow into hatred of learning." Pope condenses the whole thought into a couplet:

Full in the midst of Euclid dip at once,
And *petrify* a genius to a dunce.

The fear of surprising difficulty halts the progress of some students, but others are stopped by their equally painful eagerness to surmount all. Dryden reports, "It has happened to young men of the greatest wit to waste their spirits with anxiety and pain, so far as to *doze* upon their work with too much eagerness of doing well." Gibson describes the earlier symptoms of excessive scholarly zeal when he says, "Some have been seen to bite their pen, scratch their head, *bend*[7] *their brows*, bite their lips, beat the board, and tear their paper." In the *Dictionary*, as in Johnson's other works, extremes tend to fill up the space that should intervene between them (as when, for example, Rasselas concludes that one marries either too early or too late); thus, a sense of imminent success is as destructive to the student as a conviction of inevitable failure. The only way to succeed on this intellectual landscape is by a gradual conversion of the painful into the pleasant. Addison alludes to the changing historiography of his time when he describes this rare achievement: "I have heard one of the greatest genius's this age *has*[20] produced, who *had* been trained up in all the polite studies of antiquity, assure me, upon his being obliged to search into records, that he at last took an incredible pleasure in it." However, the student who expects pleasure at once is doomed to suffer in the intellectual world of the *Dictionary*. In this world of generally antagonistic opposites Dryden's sketch of the confident student is ironic: "Encouraged with success, he *invades*[1] the province of philosophy." Johnson sums up the *Dictionary*'s description of the student's situation in *Rambler* 25, where he advises the middle course between discouragement and overconfidence: "False hopes and false terrors are equally to be avoided. Every man, who proposes to grow eminent by learning, should carry in his mind, at once, the difficulty of excellence, and the force of industry; and remember that fame is not conferred but as the recompense of labour, and that labour, vigorously continued, has not often failed of its reward" (*Yale* 3: 140).

5.3. Extracurricular Activities

5.3.1. Conversation

In thy discourse[2]*, if thou desire to please,*
All such is courteous, useful, new, or witty;
Usefulness come by labour, wit by ease,
Courtesy grows in court, news in the city.
                                    Herbert.

The second definition of "discourse" is "conversation," and on either side of Herbert's advice Johnson prints commendations of the practice: one from Bacon and the other from Dryden. The three entries together fairly represent what the *Dictionary* as a whole says on the topic. The importance of conversation to a complete education is the subject of numerous quotations. Dryden is unequivocal about its particular importance to the aspiring poet: "Knowledge of men and manners, the freedom of habitudes, and *conversation*[3] with the best *company*[3] of both sexes is necessary." Conversation, like travel, palliates our irremediable human isolation, and foreigners are therefore especially helpful interlocutors. As Watts points out, "Conversation with foreigners enlarges our minds, and sets them free from many

prejudices we are ready to *imbibe*[2] concerning them." The contact
between heterogeneous speakers results in beneficial friction and has
some of the figurative coarseness of the *Dictionary*'s conception of
truth. Howell expresses it dramatically: "As fire *breaks*[20] *out* of flint
by percussion, so wisdom and truth issueth out of the agitation of
argument." Rogers also finds an essential, material quality in talk:
"What we hear in conversation has this general advantage over *set*
discourses, that in the latter we are apt to attend more to the beauty
and elegance of the composure than to the matter delivered." The
public nature of truth and its requirement of a public soil are parts of
Johnson's credo; as he puts it in *Rambler* 168, "The seeds of knowledge
may be planted in solitude, but must be cultivated in publick" (*Yale* 5:
129).

Like other forms of public expression, however, conversation is an
art that must be practiced and improved. Addison says, "Method is not
less requisite in *ordinary*[2] conversation, than in writing." To the
Dictionary's very extensive advice to ministers, Swift contributes, "If
the clergy would a little study the arts of conversation, they might be
welcome at every *party*[6], where there was the least regard for
politeness or good sense." Without the application of improving arts,
conversation is risky at best. In his treatise on *The Improvement of the
Mind* Watts points out that "the Errors of Conversation are almost
infinite" (147), and various writers in the *Dictionary* enumerate the
common mistakes. The dangers appear to come from the extremes of
formality and immorality. L'Estrange's discussion of the former is
found under "blind[1]," and his point receives a nicely satirical illustration in Swift's presentation of a company of formal bores: "One can
revive a languishing conversation by a sudden surprising sentence;
another is more dexterous in seconding; a third can fill the *gap*[6] with
laughing." But the greatest danger of conversation is not boredom;
parents educating their children must consider, as Locke warns, that
"conversation will add to their knowledge, but be too apt to *take*[75]
from their virtue." Rogers's words under "maxim" show that Locke's
warning is part of the received wisdom presented in the *Dictionary*:
"That the temper, the sentiments, the morality of men, is influenced
by the example and disposition of those they converse with, is a
reflexion which has long since passed into proverbs, and been ranked
among the standing *maxims* of human wisdom."[45] On this point, as on
many others, Jeremy Taylor is the strictest speaker in the *Dictionary*; he
commands, "Entertain no long discourse with any; but, if you can,

bring[17] *in* something to season it with religion." Few sentences in the *Dictionary* are this nearly Carthusian, but the book clearly tells us that, even though it is informative and desirable, conversation, like every branch of learning, must serve the ends of morality and religion.

5.3.2. Travel

Travel*[2] in the younger sort is a part of education; in the elder a part of experience.* Bacon's Essays, No. 18.

No eighteenth-century British education was complete without the grand tour, and the *Dictionary* both recommends this educational experience and does its best to supply some of its benefits for those with insufficient means. Travel broadens the mind, as Watts says: "Nothing tends so much to enlarge the mind as *travelling*[3], that is, making a visit to other towns, cities, or countries, beside those in which we were born and educated." Wotton finds that travel is useful even to those who might command half the world to come in train before them: "It was said that the prince himself had, by the sight of foreign courts, and observations on the different natures of people, and rules of government, much excited and awaked his spirits, and *corroborated*[2] his judgment." Bacon indicates something about the proper placement of travel in one's education when he says, "He that travelleth into a country before he hath some *entrance*[5] into the language, goeth to school, and not to travel." In another place, Bacon makes a true observation that implicitly establishes a preference for one mode of transportation over another: "In sea-voyages, where there is nothing to be seen but sky and sea, men make *diaries*; but in land-travel, wherein so much is to be observed, they omit it." Bacon's remark on modes of conveyance must have appealed to Johnson. On the other hand, many of Ascham's remarks on the proper goal of travel probably seemed like bad advice to Johnson, who appears accordingly to have tailored them to his own predilections. Ascham spends a sizable portion of *The Schoolmaster* on the dangers to young people who travel to Italy; his theme is, "*Italy* now, is not that *Italy*, that it was wont to be: and therefore now not so fit a Place, as some do count it, for young men to fetch either Wisdom, or Honesty from thence" (75). But in the *Dictionary* Italy is the cynosure of all travelers' eyes, and Ascham's warnings are generally excised from his remarks on the subject. For

example, Johnson quotes Ascham as saying, "Divers worthy gentlemen
of England, all the Syren songs of Italy could never *untwine*[3] from the mast of God's word," and leaves out the adversative sentence, "But I know as many or more, and some sometime my dear Friends, (for whose sake I hate going into that Country the more) who parting out of *England* fervent in the Love of Christ's Doctrine, and well furnished with the Fear of God, returned out of *Italy* worse transformed than ever was any in *Circe's* Court" (Ascham 78–79).[46] In another instance, Johnson admits a slightly derogatory remark about travel, but he carefully excludes Italy, which was the focus of Ascham's attack; Johnson admits, "This book, advisedly read and diligently followed but one year at home, would do a young gentleman more good, I *wis*, than three years travel abroad," but he leaves out the final phrase of Ascham's sentence: "in *Italy*" (Ascham 65).[47]

Johnson took positive steps to ensure that his book would include a recommendation of travel in Italy, the most important of these being a wide inclusion of illustrative quotations from Addison's *Travels in Italy*. In many cases Addison supplies vignettes of Italy that both fire the reader's wish to go there and provide a substitute for those too poor or busy to travel. Under "to float," for example, one finds: "Venice looks, at a distance, like a great town half *floated* by a deluge." Elsewhere one glimpses another famous spot: "The bay of Naples is the most delightful one that I ever saw: it lies in almost a round figure of about thirty miles in the *diameter*." Addison mentions many provincial places, but the bulk of his attention goes to Rome, and he fixes the educational quality of his remarks by relating his observations to classical learning. Over and over he proves his statement, "A man that is in Rome can scarce see an object, that does not call to mind a *piece*[2] of a Latin poet or historian." To give one example of many, Addison says, "The brazen figure of the consul, with the ring on his finger, *reminded* me of Juvenal's majoris pondera gemmae [the weight of a mighty gem— *Satires* 1.29]." Addison breaks into verse to describe the overall effect on him of seeing Rome:

> Immortal glories in my mind revive,
> When Rome's exalted beauties I descry,
> *Magnificent*[1] in piles of ruin lie.

And Addison provides Johnson Italian venues when he imagines the riches in the "*bed*[5] of the Tiber" and glimpses an ancient manuscript

of Vergil in a Florentine library with a "printed *catalogue*." Such tantalizing prospects must have added to Johnson's great desire to visit Italy
and contributed to his deep disappointment when his scheduled trip
with the Thrales fell through. With the classical world visible through
the cerements of crumbling statuary, Rome appears to have been the
student's equivalent of a trip to the Celestial City.

In the *Dictionary*, China appears in quotations from Temple and
references to Kircher; America is explored by Ray, Raleigh, and Ellis;
Abbot describes the South Seas; and Broome mentions Zante—
following Johnson's principle that "the love of knowledge . . . [is]
gratified by the recital of adventures, and accounts of foreign countries" (*Yale* 3: 107). But Rome is the principal object of travel in the
Dictionary, as it was in Johnson's imagination and in the minds of all
other eighteenth-century votaries of learning.

5.4. Religion and Morality

> Acquaint[*1*] yourselves with things ancient and modern, natural,
> civil, and religious, domestic and national; things of your own and
> foreign countries; and, above all, be well acquainted with God and
> yourselves. . . . . Watts.

Despite the breadth of its curriculum, the ends of education in
the *Dictionary* are always in view. The discontinuous form of the
Dictionary facilitates this by permitting the juxtaposition of religious
information and moral exhortation next to every other sort of educational contribution. The most tendentious use of the form, however,
appears in the persistent illustration of key educational words with
religious and moral sentences. Johnson's entry under "to instruct" is
representative:

> 1. To teach; to form by precept; to inform authoritatively; to
> educate; to institute; to direct.
>
> Out of heaven he made thee to hear his voice, that he might *in-
> struct* thee. *Deut.* iv.6
>
> His God doth *instruct* him to discretion, and doth teach him.
> *Isa.* xxviii.26

They that were *instructed* in the songs of the Lord were two
hundred fourscore and eight. 1 *Chron.* xxv.7

These are the things wherein Solomon was *instructed* for building of the house of God. 2 *Chron.* iii.3

Only at this point does Johnson admit instruction from a source other
than God; the instructors in the remaining four examples are a holy
prophet, an angel, an oracle, and a mother. Although the definition of
the word "to instruct" does not specify religious instruction, the
illustrative quotations make clear that this is the most important sense
of the term. Likewise, under "instructor" Johnson lists Christ and
other supernal teachers before such sublunary teachers as poetry are
permitted to appear.

Characteristically, the first illustration of "to teach" is "The Lord
will *teach*[1] us of his ways, and we will walk in his paths" (Isaiah 2.3).
Johnson lists the preterite of the verb separately and gives only two
illustrations: "All thy children shall be *taught* of the Lord" (Isaiah
54.13), and "How hast thou satisfy'd me, *taught* to live" (Milton).
Hooker's definitive illustration of the word "education" similarly
displays Johnson's primary intention, though here, strictly speaking,
the ends are moral rather than religious: "*Education* and instruction are
the means, the one by use, the other by precept, to make our natural
faculty of reason both the better and the sooner to judge rightly
between truth and error, good and evil." Swift is equally certain of the
universal ends of education; he adds, "All nations have agreed in the
necessity of a strict *education*, which consisted in the observance of
moral duties."[48] The linking of educational definitions with religious
and moral illustrations is an important feature of the *Dictionary's*
meaning. Moreover, it is a product of Johnson's composition of the
Dictionary just as much as the same linking in other writers represents
their acts of composition. Addison's sentence under "tincture" displays in its small compass the same connection between education and
religion that Johnson perpetually makes in the larger, more heterogeneous stylistic units of the *Dictionary*: "Few in the next generation who
will not write and read, and have an early *tincture*[1] of religion."

Viewing the *Dictionary* from a distance, so that only its most prominent features are visible, one sees an educational project united with
religious and moral intentions. On 3 April 1753, the day he began the
second volume of the *Dictionary*, Johnson wrote a prayer that shows

how strongly and personally he felt about the connection between literary and religious work. In this frequently quoted prayer Johnson beseeches God for help in "this labour & in the Whole task of my present state" (*Yale* 1: 50; and see below, p. 265). In his other prayers on studies, all of which are generically related to Bacon's "Student's Prayer" (Bacon, *Works* 4: 488; below, p. 237), Johnson ascribes to God his literary power and vows to use that power for the glory of God—but the moral responsibilities are doubled when the literary work in question is educational. On another occasion during the composition of the *Dictionary* Johnson wrote a prayer begging God's assistance in his literary efforts, and here he takes account of his religious responsibility to others. The prayer was written specifically for the inauguration of *The Rambler*, but it applies with equal propriety to the *Dictionary*: "Almighty God, the giver of all good things, without whose help all Labour is ineffectual, and without whose grace all wisdom is folly, grant, I beseech Thee, that in this my undertaking thy Holy Spirit may not be witheld from me, but that I may promote thy glory, and the Salvation both of myself and others . . ." (*Yale* 1: 43). Johnson was perpetually an instructor, and his salvation often seems dependent upon the quality of the influence he exerts over others, especially the young and impressionable. Where his pedagogical role is most clearly defined, as in *The Preceptor*, *The Rambler*, and the *Dictionary*, Johnson's efforts to teach morality and religion are correspondingly most powerful and most persistent.

6. Language

6.1. A World of Words

The business of our redemption is to rub over the defaced copy of the creation, to reprint God's image upon the soul, and to set forth nature in a second and a fairer edition*[2]*. South.

One aspect of the *Dictionary*'s generic self-consciousness is its tendency to describe things in terms of its own ontological category. The *Dictionary* is a book of words, and thus it frequently depicts the world as composed of linguistic or literary elements. Ordinary objects sometimes take linguistic form, as when Shakespeare makes the philologically unilluminating exclamation: "But his neat cookery!——— / He cut our roots in *characters*[2]." More ingeniously, Addison turns a clock into an instrument of linguistic communication: "He tells us that the two friends, being each of them possessed of one of these needles, made a kind of *dial-plate*, inscribing it with the four and twenty letters, in the same manner as the hours of the day are marked upon the ordinary *dial-plate*." There is enough of this metamorphosis, at times, to suggest that the lexicographer, or his reader, may be falling prey to an imaginative disorder brought on by excessive work, like the dreamer in Frost's "After Apple Picking." To anyone beating the track of Johnson's alphabet the most awesome example is Chambers's diabolical choice of material in his illustration of a mathematical term: "*Combination*[5] is used in mathematicks, to denote the variation or alteration of any number of quantities, letters, sounds, or the like, in all the different manners possible. Thus the number of possible changes or *combinations* of the twenty-four letters of the alphabet, taken first two by two, then three by three, &c. amount to 1,391,724,288,-887,252,999,425,128,493,402,200."

The inclination to refer all other subjects to language is a feature of many of the books upon which Johnson most often relied. For Locke, Chambers, Watts, and others, language was not merely a branch of knowledge but an ingredient element in the whole body of under- *153* standing. For Johnson, undoubtedly the most influential examination of the close relation between language and knowledge was Locke's *Essay concerning Human Understanding.* All over the *Dictionary* Johnson prints the ramifications of Locke's acknowledgment, "When I began to *examine*[5] the extent and certainty of our knowledge, I found it had a near connexion with words." However, Johnson may also have received from other lexicographers the sense that language is practically coextensive with knowledge. Thirty years before the appearance of Locke's *Essay* Edward Phillips wrote in the preface to his *New Worlde of English Words*:

> The very Summe and Comprehension of all Learning in General, is chiefly reducible into these two grand Heads, *Words* and *Things*; and though the latter of these two be, by all men, not without just cause, acknowledged the more solid and substantial part of Learning; yet since, on the other side, it cannot be denyed but that without *Language* (which is as it were the *vehiculum* or conveyancer of all good Arts) *things* cannot well be expressed or published to the World, it must be necessarily granted, that the one is little lesse necessary, and an inseparable concomitant of the other. . . . (par. 1)

When Chambers passes on to Johnson this basic humanistic wisdom, it has clearly been altered by faithful reading of Locke. Nevertheless, the central idea and its application to lexicography remain intact:

> It is confessed, that all our knowledge, in its origin, is no other than sense; whence it should follow, that one being has no natural advantage over another, in its disposition for knowledge, other than what it has in the superior number, extent, or acuteness of its senses.
>
> It is, then, to language that we are chiefly indebted for what we call *science.* By means of language our ideas and notices, though things in their own nature merely personal, and adapted only to private use, are extended to others, to improve their stock. And thus, by a kind of second sense, a man gets perceptions of the objects that are perceived by all mankind; and is present, as it were by proxy, to things at all distances from him. . . .
>
> [In a dictionary] every word is supposed to stand for some point, article, or relation of knowledge. . . . [Nouns are] no

other than a representation of the works of nature and art, as
they exist in a kind of still life. . . . The whole compass of
words, in all their cases, is supposed equivalent to the whole
system of possible science. . . . The business of knowledge,
then, is cantoned out among the body of words. . . . (*Cyclopædia*
1: viii–xii)

In a famous passage of his preface Johnson says he is "not yet so lost in
lexicography, as to forget that *words are the daughters of earth, and that
things are the sons of heaven.* Language is only the instrument of science,
and words are but the signs of ideas . . ." (par. 17). Part of what
lexicography means in this passage and throughout Johnson's *Dictionary* is the identification of language and knowledge. Though Johnson
may be skeptical about this meaning of lexicography, he is profoundly
influenced by it.

The *Dictionary* expresses this identity in one direction by being itself
an encyclopedic round of knowledge as well as a word book; it
expresses the identity in the other direction by describing much of the
encyclopedia in terms of the linguistic order it explicitly records.
Perhaps the best example of this is the subject of religion, because
religion is the most important part of knowledge. Divines with an
ancillary interest in linguistics help Johnson describe their subject in
terms of language. Robert South is the most useful in this respect; his
sermons continually describe candidates for salvation as readers and
editors (see the epigraph to this chapter), God as a supernatural writer,
Adam as a natural scholar, and Eden as a place of easy learning.
Johnson quotes South some two thousand times in the *Dictionary*, and
a good number of these quotations continue the theme and the
terminology of the example found under "to decipher": "Assurance is
writ in a private character, not to be read, nor understood, but by the
conscience, to which the spirit of God has vouchsafed to *decipher*[1] it."
Jeremy Taylor, another divine with linguistic interests,[1] also contributes to this way of speaking about religious matters "Our most
considerable actions are always present, like *capital*[6] letters to an
aged and dim eye." Such remarks moralize the language of literary
publication much as the pious verses Johnson chose to set in bourgeois
and brevier type (see "burgeois[2]" and "brevier"; above, p. 20).

A conception of the world as God's book is a prominent feature of
the rhetoric of physicotheology so frequently cited in the *Dictionary*.
For example, Locke says, "The works of nature, and the words of

revelation, *display*[2] truth to mankind in characters so visible, that those, who are not quite blind, may read." A quotation from Raleigh is more revelatory: "The Almighty, whose hieroglyphical characters are the unnumbered stars, sun and moon, written on these large volumes of the *firmament*." Bentley makes God a more personal epigraphist when he exclaims, "There are books extant which the atheist must allow of as proper evidence; even the mighty volumes of visible nature, and the everlasting *tables*[5] of right reason; wherein if they do not wilfully shut their eyes, they may read their own folly written by the finger of God in a much plainer and more terrible sentence, than Belshazzar's was by the hand upon the wall." Elsewhere, Bentley combines his use of the analogy with one of the *Dictionary*'s many aspersions of Hobbes: "If a man should affirm, that an ape casually meeting with pen, ink and paper, and falling to *scribble*, did happen to write exactly the Leviathan of Hobbes, would an atheist believe such a story? And yet he can easily digest things as incredible as that."[2]

Many of the relations between language and religious truth are metaphorical, but the connection between language and morality is just as often literal and substantive. In the intellectual world of the *Dictionary* language is ingredient in all kinds of thought, but it is essential to moral thought. As Locke points out, "In moral ideas, we have no sensible marks that resemble them, whereby we can set them down: we have nothing but words to *express*[3] them by." Consequently, "good and evil commonly operate upon the mind of man, by respective names or *appellations*, by which they are notified and conveyed to the mind," and "the generality of men are wholly governed by names, in matters of good and evil; so far as these qualities relate to, and *affect*[1], the actions of men." Language is the medium of morality, and for this reason the sins of speech often appear to be the most immoral deeds in the *Dictionary*. South says, "Men more easily pardon ill things done, than ill things said; such a peculiar rancour and venom do they leave behind in men's minds, and so much more *poisonously* and incurably does the serpent bite with his tongue than his teeth." The greatest sin of speech is lying; as South describes it in a sermon delivered in 1688, it is the archetypal sin. Ultimately, "Christ saves the world, by un-deceiving it" (*Twelve Sermons* [1692] 605), and "all deception in the course of life, is, indeed, nothing else but a lie reduced to practice and *falsehood*[1] passing from words to things." In moral matters, the symbolic action of language maintains a priority over real action; on the basis of this priority South issues numerous warnings about the "*bewitchery*, or fascination in words" and "that besotting *intoxication* which verbal magick brings upon the mind": "Such an enchantment is there in words, and so fine a thing does it seem to some, to be ruined plausibly, and to be ushered to their destruction with panegyric and acclamation."[3]

The field of knowledge in the *Dictionary* is of such a nature that whatever contributes to knowledge also brings in error and ignorance. This seems to be especially true of language. One large group of quotations is dedicated to reminding students that language in itself is an empty, vain thing and not knowledge at all. Milton's warning about the vanity of linguistic learning, found under an appropriate word, makes an important contribution to the *Dictionary*'s achievement of its self-conscious, satirical mode: "Though a linguist should pride himself to have all the tongues that Babel cleft the world into, yet if he had not studied the solid things in them as well as the words and *lexicons*, yet he were nothing so much to be esteemed a learned man as any yeoman competently wise in his mother dialect only." Swift's satirical description of the postgraduate under "cadence" equally discourages the attention to mere words that dictionaries encourage: "He hath a confused remembrance of words since he left the university; he hath lost half their meaning, and puts them together with no regard, except to their *cadence*[4]." The whole weight of Locke's theory of language is behind this sobering image of learned stupidity, and Locke's warnings, though less frightening than Swift's, are more solid. In a hundred different ways the *Dictionary* issues again and again Locke's principal warning about vanity in learning: "They who would *advance*[2] in knowledge, and not deceive and swell themselves with a little articulated air, should not take words for real entities in nature, till they can frame clear and distinct ideas of those entities."[4]

In religion, as in every area of knowledge, the *Dictionary* ironically finds that language is a frequent source of confusion and an aspect of man's intellect that shows he is fallen. Under "to confound" Locke twice expresses the representative view that there is an Edenic level of harmony and clarity, which is unfortunately, though perhaps inevitably, clouded by words: "I am yet to think, that men find their simple ideas agree, though, in discourse, they *confound*[3] one another with different names." Again, he says, "They who strip not ideas from the marks men use for them, but *confound*[2] them with words, must have endless dispute." But such nakedness of ideas cannot be achieved by mortals, as Watts suggests in one of his lamentations on human error: "If we could conceive of things as angels and *unbodied*[1] spirits do, without involving them in those clouds language throws upon them, we should seldom be in danger of such mistakes as are perpetually committed."

The problem is in the relation between words and ideas. Watts explains, under a word that recalls the Fall: "Here is our great *infelicity*, that, when single words signify complex ideas, one word can never distinctly manifest all the parts of a complex idea." Moreover, most words do signify complex ideas, as Johnson recognizes in the preface where he says, "names, therefore, have often many ideas, but few ideas have many names" (par. 48). There are as many ideas as there are distinct sensations, and the language we use to describe them is a collection of packages containing bunches of impressions. But the contents of the packages are always concealed from the hearer, who must take them on faith or on the bond of their title. The difficulty is that the relationship between the title, or outward word, and what it contains is unreliable. In one sense, then, all the errors of language are versions of the gross error of equivocation. Browne explains this fallacy with a broadly comic example: "There is a fallacy of equivocation from a society in name, inferring an *identity* in nature: by this fallacy was he deceived that drank aqua-fortis for strong water."[5] In his modern treatise on verbal error, Benjamin Whorf adduces a similarly disastrous case involving limestone explosions. Locke shows that equivocation can also cause errors with less immediate but ultimately more terrible consequences: "A verbal concordance leads not always to texts of the same meaning; and one may observe, how apt that is to *jumble* together passages of scripture, and thereby disturb the true meaning of holy scripture." The essential problem of equivocation is further compounded by the different collections of ideas that different individuals bundle up with the same words. Locke complains, "What precise collection of simple ideas, modesty or frugality [for example] stand for, in another's use, is not so *certainly*[1] known." Pointing to the same problem, Cheyne writes what might be the text expounded by *Rasselas*, chapter 22, "The Happiness of a Life Led according to Nature": "There is nothing made a more common subject of discourse than nature and it's laws; and yet few agree in their *notions*[1] about these words." Johnson himself sums up a whole body of quotation in his *Dictionary* when he writes in *Rambler* 202: "Among those who have endeavoured to promote learning, and rectify judgment, it has been long customary to complain of the abuse of words, which are often admitted to signify things so different, that, instead of assisting the

understanding as vehicles of knowledge, they produce error, dissen-
tion, and perplexity, because what is affirmed in one sense, is received
in another" (*Yale* 5: 287).

As with the other effects of the Fall, the treatment of linguistic
frailty, and particularly of equivocation, cannot be curative; at best, it is
palliative. The cure is simply stated, though impossible to achieve; in
Watts's words, "If one *single*[2] word were to express but one simple
idea, and nothing else, there would be scarce any mistake." Unfortunately, as Locke points out, "If every particular idea that we take in,
should have a distinct *name*[2], *names* must be endless." Watts suggests
a more practicable solution, but Johnson tacitly indicates that it too is
impossible by printing it ironically under the tenth sense of "sense":
"When a word has been used in two or three *senses*[10], and has made a
great inroad for error, drop one or two of those *senses*, and leave it only
one remaining, and affix the other *senses* or ideas to other words."
Obviously, Johnson thinks a faithful lexicographer cannot follow such
advice. Yet there is evidence in the *Dictionary* that Johnson was
sympathetic to the ideals presented in Watts's and Locke's linguistic
theory. It is likely that Johnson's effort to improve the English art of
definition was fueled, in part, by the importance that Locke attached to
it. Remarks like the one that illustrates "contest" must have spurred
Johnson on: "A definition is the only way whereby the meaning of
words can be known, without leaving room for *contest* about it."
Perhaps the most striking aspect of Johnson's definitions is the many
senses into which he divides them, which seems to be a response to the
dangers of equivocation that worry so many of Johnson's sources.
Hooker, for one, articulates a plausible reason for Johnson's great
efforts at distinction throughout all parts and every revision of the
Dictionary: "The mixture of those things by speech, which by nature
are divided, is the mother of all error: to take away therefore that error,
which confusion breedeth, *distinction*[7] is requisite."

Another prominent feature of the *Dictionary* is also explicable in
terms of the wish to avoid equivocation; as he suggests in the preface,
Johnson provides illustrative quotations in order to compensate for the
deficiencies in all definitions, even those as carefully ramified as his.
Stillingfleet presents the principle: "Words of different significations,
taken in general, are of an *equivocal*[1] sense; but being considered
with all their particular circumstances, they have their sense restrained." Stillingfleet's point is exemplified by William Holder in his
discussion of a highly equivocal word: "*But*, if I ask you what I mean by

that word, you will answer, I mean this or that thing, you cannot tell which; but if I join it with the words in construction and sense, as, but I will not, a but of wine, *but* and boundary, the ram will but, shoot at but, the meaning of it will be as ready to you as any other word." Like the preface (par. 50), the *Dictionary* as a whole recognizes the inevitability of equivocation, but Johnson tries hard to palliate what cannot be cured and to represent English as a larger, more fully distinct collection of terms than any previous lexicographer had perceived. If every numbered sense in Johnson's *Dictionary* were a different word, the language would approach the ideal that Locke and Watts suggest. If, further, every illustration within each sense were a different word, the language would achieve the ideal—but Johnson was far too realistic and too empirically minded to undertake such a project. Like Locke, Johnson knew that "one cannot attempt the perfect *reforming* the languages of the world, without rendering himself ridiculous." Johnson's knowledge of this fact is as firm as his opposing commitment to defining and distinguishing more thoroughly than any earlier recorder of English, and in the opposition between such knowledge and such a commitment the *Dictionary* is largely made.

Alas, far from trying to clear up the inevitable confusions of language, many men contribute to the problem by means of conscious linguistic abuse, and Johnson's sources complain about this aggravating abuse and describe some of its kinds. All such abuses are conscious exploitations of frailties inherent in the language. Johnson distinguishes a pair of linguistic abuses that stem from the primary frailty of language when he defines "amphibology": "Discourse of uncertain meaning. It is distinguished from *equivocation*, which means the double signification of a single word; as, *noli regem occidere, timere bonum est*, is *amphibology*; *captare lepores*, meaning by *lepores*, either hares or jests, is *equivocation*."[6] The recourse to Latin is characteristic of Johnson's treatment of grammatical, rhetorical, and other linguistic terms, but the illustrative quotation from Browne shows why Johnson found it important to discuss these two terms: "Now the fallacies, whereby men deceive others, and are deceived themselves, the ancients have divided into verbal and real; of the verbal, and such as conclude from mistakes of the word, there are but two worthy our notation; the fallacy of equivocation and *amphibology*."

Whether or not they recognize it as amphibology, numerous writers in the *Dictionary* condemn conscious attempts to make "discourse of uncertain meaning." Bacon describes the conditions that generate the offense in a sentence that itself comes close to offending: "When they *know*[2] within themselves they speak of that they do not well *know*, they would nevertheless seem to others to *know* of that which they may not well speak." Swift is far more blunt when he complains about the "vexation and *impertinence*[3] of pedants, who affect to talk in a language not to be understood." As Bacon (under the third sense of "plebeian") and Swift (under "nineteen") suggest, the unintelligible quality of learned discourse usually derives from the use of obscure terms. Locke is the most vocal assailant of this simplest but most pervasive sort of linguistic abuse. Like Bacon, he seems particularly concerned to guard against the attractions of verbal deceit. He says, for example, "Subtilty, in those who make profession to teach or defend truth, hath passed for a virtue: a virtue indeed, which, consisting for the most part in nothing but the fallacious and *illusory* use of obscure or deceitful terms, is only fit to make men more conceited in their ignorance"; and "There is no such way to give defence to absurd doctrines, as to guard them round about with legions of obscure and undefined words; which yet makes these retreats more like the dens of robbers, or holes of *foxes*[1], than the *fortresses* of fair warriors."[7]

If there are only two main varieties of linguistic abuse, amphibology may be said to cover the whole range of obscurity, and equivocation the area of ambiguity. Watts helps with the distinction: "As words signifying the same thing are called synonymous, so equivocal words, or those which signify several things, are called *homonymous*, or ambiguous; and when persons use such ambiguous words, with a design to deceive, it is called equivocation." In this area too, Locke is the loudest plaintiff, and his accusations often assume the language of civil law: "He that designedly uses ambiguities, ought to be looked on as an *enemy*[4] to truth and knowledge"; "He that uses the same words sometimes in one, and sometimes in another signification, ought to pass, in the schools, for as fair a man, as he does, in the market and *exchange*[7], who sells several things under the same name." What makes linguistic abuse so serious is Locke's theory of language, in which words are nearly identified with knowledge because they are its only means of storage and communication: "Language being the conduit whereby men convey their knowledge, he that makes an ill use of it, though he does not *corrupt*[2] the fountains of knowledge, which are in things, yet he stops the pipes."

The legal and civic analogies in many of Locke's complaints are motivated in part by a view of language as a God-given social instrument. Locke expresses an aspect of this basic conception of language when he says, "God having designed man for a sociable creature, made him not only with an inclination and under the necessity to have *fellowship*[1] with those of his own kind, but furnished him also with .language, which was to be the great instrument and cementer of society." South explains further, under two words akin to "fellowship": "By words men come to know one another's minds; by these they *covenant*[1] and *confederate*." Holder, the linguistics expert of the *Dictionary*, fundamentally agrees with this view, though he speaks more philosophically: "We may define *language*[1], if we consider it more materially, to be letters, forming and producing words and sentences; but if we consider it according to the design thereof, then *language* is apt signs for communication of thoughts." Under a word for which Johnson must have found innumerable illustrative quotations Holder corroborates the view of Locke and Watts that language is a divine gift for the purpose of communication: "The chief of all signs which the Almighty endued man with, is humane voice, and the several modifications thereof by the organs of speech, *viz.* the letters of the alphabet, form'd by the several motions of the mouth."

Locke is so sure that communication is the end of speech that he considers any other use either deceitful or nugatory: "Words are made to declare something; where they are, by those who pretend to instruct, otherwise used, they conceal indeed something; but that which they conceal, is *nothing*[4] but the ignorance, error, or sophistry of the talker, for there is, in truth, *nothing* else under them." Making similar assumptions, Felton identifies a disproportion between words and sense as a type of literary failure: "There is another extreme in obscure writers, which some empty *conceited*[2] heads are apt to run into, out of a prodigality of words, and a want of sense." What, in particular, this might mean appears in Broome's opinion that "an author who should *introduce*[2] a sport of words upon the stage, would meet with small applause." When Johnson criticizes Shakespeare's fondness for puns and quibbles in that famous portion of his preface to the *Works*, he agrees with the unanimous opinion of the *Dictionary* on the subject of verbal play. On this point the culture of the *Dictionary* is at loggerheads with the Romantic and post-Romantic mind, as an interesting pair of quotations under "pun" in *Webster's III* suggests: " 'never knew an enemy to ~s who was not an ill-natured man'—Charles Lamb; 'any man who would make such an execrable ~ would not scruple to pick my pocket'—John Dennis."

The turning point in cultural history, as the history of lexicography represents it, is in Charles Richardson's *New Dictionary of the English Language*, which was influenced by Tookean and Coleridgean linguistics. Richardson affords the word "pun" fairly lengthy and dignified treatment, reflecting Coleridge's erstwhile design to write an "Apology for Paranomasy, alias Punning" (*Notebooks* 3: 3762). Johnson's treatment, on the other hand, is brief and implicitly dismissive; he reveals his and his whole book's attitude towards word play in his etymological speculation: "can *pun* mean an empty sound, like that of a mortar beaten, as *clench*, the old word for *pun*, seems only a corruption of *clink*?" What supports this philologically groundless suggestion is a philosophy rather than a history of language. South states the philosophical position in a radical form when he says, "Words abstracted from their proper sense and signification, lose the nature of words, and are only *equivocally*[1] so called." Locke forestalls one of the objections that a Romantic linguist might raise when he says, "All negative or privative words *relate* to positive ideas, and signify their absence"; elsewhere, he reiterates the point that words are essentially instruments of direct, positive signification: "Words being but empty sounds, any farther than they are signs of our ideas, we cannot but assent to them, as they *correspond*[1] to those ideas we have. . . ." All the creative power of words is excluded on this theory, as is any sense of them as independent symbols that can be expressive of mental states. Excluded too is all the indeterminateness, the "play," and the "space" so important to Romantic and post-Romantic theories of language. In the *Dictionary* linguistic indeterminateness is mere equivocation; linguistic independence is mere emptiness. As Holder says definitively, "Speaking is a sensible expression of the notions of the mind by discriminations of utterance of voice, used as signs, having by consent several determinate *significancies*[1]."

6.2. The Growth and Reformation of English

In the first establishments of speech there was an implicit[2] *compact, founded upon common consent, that such and such words should be signs, whereby they would express their thoughts one to another.* South.

Although Johnson admits some references to language as a divine gift, and even though he himself once refers to the "antediluvian" language (see "sack"), the *Dictionary* most often describes the origins of language as civil and legal. Least of all is there any concession to the Romantic notion that language is natural and somehow coessential with the knowledge it conveys. Language is separate, civil, and conventional, according to nearly everyone who says anything on the subject in the *Dictionary*. Judge Hale is one of many who stress the legal quality of language and denigrate the natural: "Although it is as natural to mankind, to express their desires *vocally*, as it is for brutes to use their natural vocal signs; yet the forming of languages into this or that fashion, is a business of institution." William Holder explains that "languages arise, when, by institution and agreement, such a *composure*[2] of letters, *i.e.* such a word, is intended to signify such a certain thing." As usual, Locke is definitive on the subject: "Words having naturally no signification, the idea must be learned by those who would *exchange*[2] thoughts, and hold intelligible discourse with others."

The most obvious sort of natural signification is a correspondence between sound and sense, and when they reject such a correspondence, the writers in the *Dictionary* usually imply assent to Locke's position on semantics. For example, Watts says, "On the word *bishop*, in French *evêque*, I would observe, that there is no natural connexion between the sacred office and the letters or sound; for *evêque*, and *bishop*, signify the same office, though there is not one letter alike in them." In light of modern phonology or the knowledge of the Old French word "ebisque," Watts's example is unfortunate—but the principle is reasonable, and Bramhall makes more fortunate use of it in part of his debate with Hobbes: "His grammatical argument, grounded upon the derivation of spontaneous from *sponte*, weighs nothing: we have learned in logick, that *conjugates* are sometimes in name only, and not in deed." When Johnson speaks in propria persona in his etymological remarks, he usually affirms the Lockean position that meaning is conventional rather than natural. As he does in the *Life* of Pope, however, and in *Ramblers* 92 and 94, he sensibly admits some exceptions in which the sound of a word naturally carries its sense. Johnson's strictures against the relations between sound and sense are so forceful that it is hard to recall that he also said, "Every language has many words formed in imitation of the noises which they signify" (*Yale* 4: 138). His etymological notes in the *Dictionary* contain about the same proportion of concession that he expresses in the *Rambler* and the

Lives. He says, for example, that "shrill" is "a word supposed to be made *per onomatopœiam*, in imitation of the thing expressed," and he concedes that the word "indeed . . . images [the thing expressed] very happily." "Mum" requires him to confess that "of this word I know not the original," and he adds, "it may be observed, that when it is pronounced it leaves the lips closed." Tentative as these remarks are, they are exceptions to Johnson's general rule of regarding meaning as entirely conventional.

A counterconventional standard of meaning, to which Johnson is much more receptive than he is to natural sounds, is etymology. Though he knows his primary law must be usage, he makes many efforts to push the English language in the direction of its etymological foundations. Even when they are regarded as civil rather than natural, the original meanings of words maintain a priority over the subsequent ramifications wrought by use. In the preface Johnson calls the earliest meanings of words "primitive" and their later meanings "remote" or "accidental" (par. 49). This opposition of "primitive" and "accidental" approximates the Romantic opposition between the natural and the contrived, but Johnson's "nature," like Pope's or Dryden's, is itself something artificial or methodical. His conception of a word resembles his conception of other human institutions, such as laws and civilizations: in all he was inclined to oppose change and favor precedents. His predilection for primitive meaning shows up in a number of ways throughout his treatment of the vocabulary. For one thing, he often gives an etymological definition first, even when his researches have not turned up an example of its usage in that sense: hence, he first defines "ardour" as "heat" and appends no illustrative quotation. Furthermore, he often strains his definitions in order to include the etymology of the word in question: "trivial," for example, is "1. Vile; worthless; vulgar; such as may be picked up in the highway"; "mountebank" is "1. A doctor that mounts a bench in the market, and boasts his infallible remedies and cures"; "seminary" is "5. Breeding place; place of education, from whence scholars are transplanted into life." A similar unwillingness to deviate from etymology in his definitions occasionally appears in remarks that Johnson appended to words whose meaning required extensive analysis. Under number 27 of "to break" he comments, "It is to be observed of this extensive and perplexed *verb*, that, in all its significations, whether *active* or *neutral*, it has some reference to its primitive meaning, by implying either detriment, suddenness, or violence." Similarly, after sense number 64 of "to fall" he enters, "This is one of those general words of which it is very difficult to ascertain or detail the full signification. It retains in most of its senses some part of its primitive meaning, and implies either literally or figuratively descent, violence, or suddenness. . . ." On a few other occasions Johnson announces his predilection for etymology as a source and test of meaning. Under the third meaning of "to prejudice" he writes, "This sense, as in the noun, is often improperly extended to meanings that have no relation to the original sense; who can read with patience of an ingredient that *prejudices* a medicine?" He makes a similar equation of meaning and etymology in his definition of "to riddle": "To solve; to unriddle. There is something of whimsical analogy between the two senses of the word *riddle*: as, we say, *to* sift *a question*: but their derivations differ." The fact that their derivations differ is what makes the analogy between their meanings whimsical, as though an etymological similarity were required to establish a semantic congruence.

Etymological meanings, especially those based on Latin and Greek, are often in the *Dictionary* equivalent to what Locke calls "the philosophical use of words"; this use alone "conveys the precise notions of things, which the mind may *rest*[8] upon, and be satisfied with, in its search after knowledge."[8] Johnson's predilection for these meanings represents a tendency to follow through on the wishes of such linguistic projectors as Wilkins and Comenius. Wimsatt has sufficiently catalogued Johnson's interest in "philosophic words," and he correctly describes its tendency when he says, "the vocabulary of 'hard' [philosophic] words is a kind of basic English, like the language of integers and particles proposed by Bishop Wilkins" (*Philosophic Words* 110). How hard Johnson pushed to drive English back to basics is difficult to gauge, but his force is continuously counteracted by his loyalty to the ultimate, public standard of usage. The illustrative quotations under "etymology" itself undercut the faith in it that the *Dictionary* sometimes expresses. None of the writers quoted sees etymology as a guarantee of either meaning or dignity in words, but Collier is the most negative: "When words are restrained, by common usage, to a particular sense, to run up to *etymology*[1], and construe them by dictionary, is wretchedly ridiculous." Collier makes it sound as if etymology were the science or philosophy that lexicography expounds, and, no doubt, Johnson thought there was some truth in this. Still, Watts's remark under "little" expresses the *Dictionary*'s primary linguistic credo: "The received definition of names should be changed as *little*[1] as possible."

Johnson's attitude toward reform, his commitment to usage, and his predilection for the standard of etymology all come out in his orthography at least as clearly as they do in his definitions. In his "Grammar" prefatory to the *Dictionary* Johnson provides a largely satirical history of orthographical reform, which concludes, "We have since [Bishop Wilkins] had no general reformers; but some ingenious men have endeavoured to deserve well of their country, by writing *honor* and *labor* for *honour* and *labour*, *red* for *read* in the preter-tense, *sais* for *says*, *repete* for *repeat*, *explane* for *explain*, or *declame* for *declaim*. Of these it may be said, that as they have done no good, they have done little harm; both because they have innovated little, and because few have followed them." Although Johnson's sources include many spelling reformers— Wilkins, Milton, Holder, and Wallis, for example—their reformations are generally excluded. When they are mentioned, they are generally rejected. Johnson's treatment of "least" exemplifies his handling of proposed reforms: "Least. *adj.* the superlative of *little*. [læst, Saxon. This word *Wallis* would persuade us to write *lest*, that it may be analogous to *less*; but surely the profit is not worth the change.]" The principle of analogy is reasonable, but it yields to common usage and the wish for stability.

As Holder says, "It is not to be imagined that the incongruous alphabets and abuses of writing can ever be *justled* out of their possession of all libraries." Yet Johnson chafes at the corruptions of usage and does not forbear to wish for the stability of more analogical and etymological formations. In the etymological note under "righteous," for example, he enters, "rihtwise, Saxon; whence *rightwise* in old authours, and *rightwisely* in bishop *Fisher*: so much are words corrupted by pronunciation." In the case of "show," which Johnson and many other writers spelled inconsistently, he had an opportunity to apply linguistic principles; in the absence of a settled custom, he applies a principle of pronunciation but backs it up with an etymology: "This word is frequently written *shew*; but since it is always pronounced and often written *show*, which is favoured likewise by the Dutch *schowen*, I have adjusted the orthography to the pronunciation." Principles can only be applied when custom does not intervene, but they are nevertheless desirable. A new word, in which custom is not well established, gives Johnson more warrant to act on his etymological principles; of "phiz" he says, "This word is formed by a ridiculous contraction from *physiognomy*, and should therefore, if it be written at all, be written *phyz*." An older word, however, can, at most, bring regret for the ignorance of logical principles in common usage: "Pander. n.s. [This word is derived from *Pandarus*, the pimp in the story of *Troilus and Cressida*; it was therefore originally written *pandar*, till its etymology was forgotten.]" The mixture of Johnson's commitment to usage and his wish for something more rational comes out nicely in a long explanation of "latter," where he uses the words of Horace to soothe his impatience with the caprices of usage and to reiterate his basic lexicographical commitment:

> This is the comparative of *late*, though universally written with *tt*, contrary to analogy, and to our own practice in the superlative *latest*. When the thing of which the comparison is made is mentioned, we use *later*; as, *this fruit is* later *than the rest*; but *latter* when no comparison is expressed; as, *those are* latter *fruits*.
>
> ———*Volet usus*
> *Quem penes arbitrium est, & vis, & norma loquendi.*[9]

Throughout the *Dictionary*'s whole body of quotations and comments, as well as in famous passages of the preface, Johnson expresses a conviction that linguistic change is inevitable and inevitably bad. An aspect of this general conviction is the belief that the classical languages are purer and better than their modern progeny. Johnson defines "barbarism" as "A form of speech contrary to the purity and exactness of any language," but the illustrative quotation from Dryden insists that "purity and exactness" are primarily qualities of the ancient languages: "The language is as near approaching to it, as our modern *barbarism*[1] will allow; which is all that can be expected from any now extant." Johnson seems to recall Dryden's remark in *Rambler* 169 when he says, "It has often been enquired, why, notwithstanding the advances of latter ages in science, and the assistance which the infusion of so many new ideas has given us, we still fall below the antients in the art of composition. Some part of their superiority may be justly ascribed to the graces of their language, from which the most polished of the present European tongues, are nothing more than barbarous degenerations" (*Yale* 5: 132). More of Dryden's statement appears under "inferiority," and the *Dictionary* in general accords with the evaluation of Camden: "Because the Greek and Latin have ever *born*[20] away the prerogative from all other tongues, they shall serve as touchstones to make our trials by." As the accolade "touchstone" suggests, the praise of the classical languages often centers on their constancy, although this is due largely to accidents of political and cultural history rather than to something inherent in the language itself. Under "to last" Bacon praises Latin as "the universal language,"[10] and the supreme praise of Latin is the moral of an old story that Locke has the honor of repeating under the key word: "Augustus himself could not make a new *Latin* word."

Latin and Greek are praised for various other qualities, but the most important of these is another form of linguistic conservatism: Dryden says, "Latin often expresses that in one word, which either the *barbarity*[3] or narrowness of modern tongues cannot supply in more."[11] Like practically all other linguistic works before those written by Otto Jespersen at the very end of the nineteenth century, Johnson's *Dictionary* generally regards the greater copiousness of English as inferior to the succinctness of Latin. Wotton expresses this antiprogressive view when he says, "Languages, for the most part, in terms of art and erudition, retain their original poverty, and rather grow rich and abundant in *complimental* phrases, and such froth." Felton recognizes that "languages, like our bodies, are in a perpetual *flux*[2], and stand in need of recruits to supply the place of those words that are continually *falling*[51] through disuse"—but, like bodies, languages are perpetually losing energy as they expand. King puts the recognition of the need for linguistic addition in the satirical light implied by Wotton's judgment: "New things produce new words, and thus *Monteth* / Has by one vessel sav'd his name from death"; to be the eponymous creator of "a vessel in which glasses are washed" is not a glorious form of immortality, and most other sources of linguistic addition are seen in an equally derogatory way.

War, like commerce, produces much linguistic innovation, and it is just as dangerous to the purity of language. Addison is alarmed when he declares, "The present war has so *adulterated*[2] our tongue with strange words, that it would be impossible for one of our great grandfathers to know what his posterity have been doing." Under "insomuch" Spenser points out that conquest and linguistic change go hand in hand, and elsewhere Camden uses a historical example to draw attention to the linguistic and political change that English culture has traditionally feared the most: "They misliked nothing more in king Edward the Confessor than that he was *Frenchified*; and accounted the desire of foreign language then to be a *foretoken* of bringing in foreign powers, which indeed happened."

According to the *Dictionary*, the advancement of English depends upon acts of conservation and restoration that strengthen the connection between the modern language and its ancient foundations. For this sort of conservative advancement the *Dictionary* campaigns with some vigor. In the preface Johnson calls Swift's "Proposal for Correcting, Improving and Ascertaining the English Tongue" a "petty treatise" (par. 88), but he quotes a good portion of it in the *Dictionary*. Though Swift puts it more optimistically than the body of the *Dictionary* can justify, he speaks for part of its effort when he says, "What I have most at *heart*[9] is, that some method should be thought on for ascertaining and fixing our language." Swift speaks even more optimistically under "advancement[1]," and Prior, for one, reiterates the call for "some that with care true eloquence shall teach / And to just *idioms* fix our doubtful speech." In the preface Johnson more realistically wishes that the language might be "less apt to decay" (par. 17), but his dream, though later and fainter, is fundamentally the same as Swift's and Prior's; they all wished English to have more of the compression and stability of Latin.

The first job of any program to make the language as stable as Latin is to prevent further innovation. Under "to explode" Swift makes a characteristically satirical proposal that would put an end to the whole business: "Provided that no word, which a society shall give a sanction to, be afterwards antiquated and *exploded*[1], they shall receive whatever new ones they may find occasion for." Elsewhere Swift is more direct, attacking "*dunces* of figure" who "introduce and multiply *cant*[4] words." Johnson generally cooperates with Swift's aims by excluding most (but not all) cant expressions from the *Dictionary*, by centering his empirical researches on an earlier period of English, and by excluding, for the most part, contemporary authors. Linguistic innovation is defensible only on the grounds of renovation or restoration. As Ben Jonson says, "Words borrowed of antiquity, have the authority of years, and out of their *intermission*[3] do win to themselves a kind of grace-like newness." In the same vein Dryden is quoted thrice: "*Obsolete* words may be *laudably* revived, when they are more sounding, or more significant than those in *practice*[2]." Both Dryden's and Jonson's remarks recall the lines from Horace's Epistles (2.2.110–18) that Johnson took for the epigraph of the whole *Dictionary*: in the Loeb translation the last four lines run, "Terms long lost in darkness the good poet will unearth for the people's use and bring into the light—picturesque terms which, though once spoken by a Cato and a Cathegus of old, now lie low through unseemly neglect and dreary

age" (Fairclough). Swift also repeats the gist of the epigraph when he
says, "Many words deserve to be thrown out of our language, and not a few antiquated to be restored, on account of their *energy*[4] and sound."

There are a few occasions in the *Dictionary* when Johnson explicitly recommends or supports innovation. He defines "pictorial," for example, as "produced by a painter" and adds, "A word not adopted by other writers [than Browne], but elegant and useful." "Impartible" and "to vade" receive similar commendations. His strongest vote for an addition to English is his editorial comment under the third sense of "to imbibe": "To drench; to soak. This sense, though unusual, perhaps unexampled, is necessary in the English, unless the word *imbue* be adopted, which our writers seem not willing to receive." In all these cases analogical formation and Latin heritage seem necessary, but they are not sufficient criteria for inclusion; usefulness is also necessary, and this is a reminder that Johnson, like Locke, valued language primarily for its power to convey knowledge.

Neither Horace's nor the *Dictionary's* opinion on the use of old words and aureate words is simplistic. Even though they are sometimes allowed, both revival for its own sake and the anglicization of Latin words are steadily censured as forms of innovation. Locke refers to the writers who brought the most Latin into English only to belittle them: "Those few names that the schools *forged*[2], and put into the mouths of their scholars, could never yet get admittance into common use, or obtain the licence of publick approbation." Pope similarly derides a simplistic love of archaism:

> Some by old words to fame have made pretence:
> Such labour'd nothings, in so strange a style,
> Amaze th' unlearn'd, and make the *learned*[1] smile.

Under another relevant word Johnson displays Dryden's censure of Milton for "*antiquated* words, and the perpetual harshness of their sound." Johnson censures the Latinizing puns in Milton's use of "pontifical[4]" and "pernicious[2]," and Dryden himself is not exempt from such criticism. For instance, Johnson gives the etymological meaning of "to pretend" in the analogically correct first place; he defines the word as "to hold out; to stretch forward"—but before the illustration from Dryden he says, "This is mere Latinity, and not used."

One of the longest quotations in the *Dictionary* is Dryden's defense of his use of "to falsify" to mean "to pierce" in "His crest is rash'd away, his ample shield / Is *falsify'd*[4], and round with jav'lins fill'd." Not even Dryden's adduction of the Horatian rule—"*si græco fonte cadant* [sic]"[12]—can save him from Johnson's final judgment: "Dryden, with all this effort, was not able to naturalise the new signification, which I have never seen copied, except once by some obscure nameless writer, and which indeed deserves not to be received." Most other attempts at innovation by naturalization meet the same fate in the *Dictionary*, but not all foreign languages are equal. It may be that Dryden's attempt fails more thoroughly because his immediate precedent is the Italian "falsare," rather than something more directly "*græco fonte.*" Predictably, attempts to naturalize French words meet with the harshest opposition in Johnson's editorial comments. He prefaces one of Dryden's uses of "to renounce" with the remark that "the following passage is a mere Gallicism; *renoncer a* [sic] *mon sang.*" Johnson similarly criticizes Samuel Daniel's use of "to comport" to mean "to bear, to endure": "This is a Gallick signification, not adopted among us." He reveals his basic attitude toward adoptions from the French under "souvenance": "A French word which with many more is now happily disused."[13]

About a classical author's archaisms Ben Jonson complains, "Lucretius is *scabrous*[2] and rough in these: he seeks them, as some do Chaucerisms with us, which were better expunged." Spenser was regarded by the authors quoted in the *Dictionary* as the prime example of a writer who followed Lucretius in this respect. The debate on the validity of his usage mirrors the larger debate on the desirability of using antiquated language. Spenser's editor, Hughes, defends his author: "He tries to restore to their rightful heritage such good old English words as have been long time out of use, almost *disherited.*"[14] But Ben Jonson passes a judgment on Spenser that receives ample support in the *Dictionary* as a whole: "Spenser, in *affecting*[7] the ancients, writ no language; yet I would have him read for his matter, but as Virgil read Ennius." Johnson's behavior in the *Dictionary* suggests a compromise between Hughes's and Ben Jonson's opinions—much of Spenser's archaic language appears, but far from all of it.

Inclusion and exclusion of words are the most decisive demonstrations of linguistic theory in the *Dictionary*. However, in his widespread editorial comments Johnson reveals in a more dramatic way his complicated combination of reformational hopes and fidelity to the

standard of usage. One manner in which he campaigns openly for
reform is by opposing addition of prefixes that are logically redundant;
such prefixes diminish the strength of the root to which they are
attached, and by opposing them he tries to press English back toward
its roots, just as he does in his etymologically oriented definitions.
Under "to disannul" he comments, "This word is formed contrary to
analogy by those who not knowing the meaning of the word *annul*,
intended to form a negative sense by the needless use of the negative
particle. It ought therefore to be rejected as ungrammatical and
barbarous." The ignorant users of "disannul" are Hooker, Bacon,
Sandys, and Herbert, the weight of whose authority may have forced
Johnson to include the word—but his remark shows that he has
linguistic ideals that are independent of usage. In order to further his
wish that English might be "less apt to decay" he again expresses his
ideals in the face of awesome authority in his entry under "to dis-
sever": "In this word the particle *dis* makes no change in the signification, and therefore the word, though supported by great authorities,
ought to be ejected from our language"; quotations follow from
Sidney, Raleigh, Shakespeare, and Pope. Johnson has similarly lofty
opponents when he objects to the pleonasms in "unrip," "unloose,"
and "intermutual."[15] Under "hence" he nicely phrases what he is
trying to protect with objections of this kind: "*From hence*[8] is a vitious
expression, which crept into use even among good authors, as the
original force of the word *hence* was gradually forgotten."

Johnson is also trying to preserve the "original force" of words and
yet be true to the task of recording language when he brands unanalogical usages as, for example, "barbarous," "harsh," or "improper."[16] His editorial comments are always more discursive than a
modern dictionary's asterisk or other typographical symbol, and they
are quite various. As the third definition of "blush" he gives "sudden
appearance," but he warns, with some diffidence, that this is "a
signification that seems barbarous, yet used by good writers [e.g.
Locke]." Likewise, he censures the intransitive use of "to ponder" with
"on"; even though it is exemplified by Shakespeare and Dryden,
Johnson says, "This is an improper use of the word" (he prefers the
etymologically tighter transitive sense, which he defines as "to weigh
mentally"). Sometimes a more widespread impropriety stimulates
Johnson to write against it at greater length. Under "precarious" he
says, "No word is more unskilfully used than this with its derivatives. It

is used for *uncertain* in all its senses; but it only means uncertain, as dependent on others: thus there are authors who mention the *precariousness* of an *account*, of the *weather*, of a *die*."

The strength of Johnson's response to improper and innovative usage varies a good deal, and it is not always easy to tell why. When he censures the eighth sense of "would," however, he is clearly attending to linguistic reform for the sake of the higher purpose such reform might serve. Before entering illustrations from Shakespeare, Milton, Bacon, Daniel, Jonson, Allestree, and Dryden, Johnson says: "[would] has the signification of I wish, or I pray; this, I believe is improper; and formed by a gradual corruption of the phrase, *would God*; which originally imported, *that God would, might God will, might God decree*; from this phrase ill understood came, *would to God*; thence, *I would to God*: And thence *I would*, or elliptically, *would* come to signify, *I wish*: and so it is used even in good authours, but ought not to be imitated." In combination with his concern for the purity of religion, Johnson's interest in preserving the original import of words is especially strong. The same combination of motives appears to drive his violent response to the second sense of a word that was originally very important in the language of spirit: the second sense of "immaterial" is "unimportant, without weight, impertinent, without relation." This is so inimical to the first sense that Johnson raises his voice to say, "This sense has crept into the conversation and writings of barbarians; but ought to be utterly rejected." The editors of the *OED* cite Johnson's remark under their sense 4 of "immaterial," and they object, "it is, however, the opposite of material in the sense of 'important' found from 1528 onwards" (Johnson himself lists this sense of "material" and illustrates it amply). But, to a much greater extent than the *OED*, Johnson's lexicography served a standard that is not purely historical, and that standard roused him to greater action when it converged with his highest aim: to present meaning, especially religious meaning.

7. The Arts of Writing, Reading, and Speaking

7.1. Writing

I have laboured to refine our language to grammatical purity, and to clear it from colloquial barbarisms, licentious idioms, and irregular combinations. Something, perhaps, I have added to the elegance of its construction, and something to the harmony of its cadence. When common words were less pleasing to the ear, or less distinct in the significa-tion, I have familiarized the terms of philosophy by applying them to popular ideas, but have rarely admitted any word not authorized by for-mer writers; for I believe that whoever knows the English tongue in its present extent, will be able to express his thoughts without further help from other nations. (Rambler 208, Yale 5: 318–19)

Like Dodsley's *Preceptor* and other educational works of the time, the *Dictionary* gives the basic skills of reading, writing, and speaking a prominent place in its curriculum. The *Dictionary* is a very good writing teacher by Johnson's standards because he thought of English writing as mostly a matter of diction. He suggests this by defining "diction" as "stile; language; expression" and by giving very short shrift to syntax in his prefatory "Grammar."[1] Johnson's remarks in the last *Rambler* show that he believed some of the aims of writing and lexicography to be identical. This is only possible because everything he says about language in the passage, except "elegance of . . . construction" and "harmony of . . . cadence," is a matter of diction. The *Dictionary* teaches these two elements of writing implicitly in its illustrative quotations, but it teaches all the rest explicitly in its definitions, distinctions, inclusions, and exclusions.

The most explicit teaching of all occurs in Johnson's editorial comments on the vocabulary. By identifying the classes to which the words belong, as well as clarifying their meanings, these comments help his reading and writing students to choose words and meanings that are stylistically and semantically proper. His treatment of "ambassadour" provides an example of how he could use his distinctions to describe the various habits of a word: "*Ambassador* [sic] is, in popular language, the general name of a messenger from a sovereign power, and sometimes, ludicrously, from common persons. In the juridical and formal language, it signifies particularly a minister of the highest rank residing in another country, and it is distinguished from an *envoy*, who is of less dignity." Johnson perceives a number of special languages sharing the same morphemes but making them into different words, which need separate treatment. His sense of these distinctions is acute, as a typical remark under "path" should suggest: "In conversation it is used of a narrow way to be passed on foot; but in solemn language means any passage." The remarkable thing here is not the perception that the word has very different meanings but the conviction that these meanings belong so distinctly to different types of speech. The fact that lexicography has generally adopted Johnson's method should not diminish the remarkability of his interest and his power in making such discriminations.

A brief catalogue of Johnson's editorial remarks displays the great variety of special languages he perceived within the general body of English: "backslide" is "only used by divines"; "bamboozle" is a "cant word not used in pure or in grave writings"; "bawbling" is "not now in use, except in conversation"; "bawcock" is "a familiar word"; "bemused" is "a word of contempt"; "bethump" is one of a great many that Johnson brands "ludicrous"; "bounce[3]" in "low language" means "a threat"; "chimney-corner" belongs to "proverbial language"; "cudden" is "a low bad word"; "dab[4]" is "not used in writing"; "darkling" is "a word merely poetical"; "dishing" is "a cant term among artificers"; "earthly[4]" is "a female hyperbole"; "enceinte" is "a military term not yet naturalised"; "eschew" is "a word almost obsolete"; the eighth sense of "to expose" is "a colloquial abuse of the word"; "fixidity" is merely "a word of *Boyle*"; "fren" is "an old word wholly forgotten"; "frightfully[2]" is merely "a woman's word"; "grannam" is "only used in burlesque works"; "gules" is "a barbarous term of heraldry"; and "shine[2]" is one of many words that seem to fall between categories: "It is a word, though not unanalogical, yet ungraceful, and little used."

On the basis of Johnson's editorial comments and his word list, it is possible to make some generalizations about his conception of English diction, and, roughly, to chart his notion of diction against the one presented by J. A. H. Murray and the other editors of the *OED*. Murray says, "The English Vocabulary contains a nucleus or central mass of many thousand words whose 'Anglicity' is unquestioned; some of them are only literary, some of them only colloquial, the great majority at once literary and colloquial,—they are the *Common Words* of the language. But they are linked on every side with other words which are less and less entitled to this appellation, and which pertain ever more and more distinctly to the domain of local dialect, of the slang and cant of 'sets' and classes, of the peculiar technicalities of trades and processes, of the scientific terminology common to all civilized nations, of the actual languages of other lands and peoples." Murray then inserts a diagram "as an attempt to express to the eye the aspect in which the Vocabulary is here presented" (*OED* 1: xxvii):

In terms of this diagram, Johnson locates the center of English to the west and north of Murray: both in the direction of the "Scientific" and "Technical" as opposed to the "Foreign" and "Dialectal," and in the direction of the "Literary" as opposed to the "Colloquial." Moreover, Johnson sees the central area of "Common Words" as more tightly focused, and he finds more ways than does Murray for a word to diverge from the center of pure "Anglicity."

The testimony of Johnson's sources in the *Dictionary* generally supports his own decisions about diction, although it is not systematic or entirely coherent. Dryden makes a fine encomiastic phrase for the ideal of diction: "There appears in every part of his *diction*, or expression, a kind of noble and bold purity." Roscommon phrases the ideal of "bold purity" as a combination of the common and the unusual in an entry that Johnson made at least twice: "You gain your *point*[17], if your industrious art / Can make *unusual* words easy and plain." Felton explains the diction for which a writer should strive: "That peculiar turn, that the words should appear new, yet not *unusual*, but very proper to his auditors." As it is on so many other topics, however, the advice of the *Dictionary* on diction is mostly monitory. Felton warns, "In English I would have all Gallicism avoided, that our tongue may be *sincere*[3], and that we may keep to our own language." With the same concern for national purity, Hughes decries the "rags from other languages" used as ineffectual aids "to salve[2]" "our mother-tongue." Addison watches for incursions from the south—the "Colloquial" in Murray's diagram: "Since phrases used in conversation contract meanness by passing through the mouths of the vulgar, a poet should guard himself against *idiomatick* ways of speaking." Although the *Dictionary* has a predilection for philosophic words, it is not extreme in its advocacy of this or any other uncommon language. Accordingly, Watts warns us about "terms and phrases that are *latinized*, scholastick, and hard to be understood," and Dryden says, "The proprieties and delicacies of the English are known to few: 'tis impossible even for a good wit to understand and practise them, without the help of a liberal education and long reading; in *short*, without wearing off the rust which he contracted while he was laying in a stock of learning." "Learning" means Latin, and Dryden's remark is a reminder that Johnson's standard, though it might drift a little in the direction of Latinate philosophical language, is still a pure Anglicity.

Like virtually every other subject in the *Dictionary*, diction has its moral aspect, and many of the warnings about it concern its possible immorality. As Watts points out, "Among words which signify the same principal ideas, some are clean and decent, others unclean; some *chaste*[3], others obscene ... some are kind, others are *affronting* and reproachful, because of the secondary idea which custom has affixed to them." Roscommon makes the fullest condemnation of immoral language under an appropriate word: "Immodest words admit of no defence; / For want of *decency*[3] is want of sense." Addison shows that

learning to avoid such language is an important part of the whole
project of education: "It was one of the first distinctions of a wellbred
man to express every thing obscene in modest terms and *distant*[5]
phrases, while the clown clothed those ideas in plain homely terms that
are the most obvious and natural." As in the cases of "cudden,"
"bounce," and "bawcock," Johnson is careful to brand immodest
words as "low," "mean," "bad," or "familiar." But, like J. A. H. Murray,
he includes very few of the really indecent words, and so passes the
most definitive judgment of all upon them.[2]

However, although the two areas often converge, the use of immodest language is less often a transgression of morality than of civility and
politeness. These latter ideals, though clearly less important than
morality, are also defended by Johnson's sources. For example, Boyle
lends his considerable authority to the recommendation of civility
when he says, "Manage disputes with civility; whence some readers
will be assisted to discern a difference betwixt *bluntness*[2] of speech
and strength of reason." Johnson is far from equating civility and
virtue, but the *Dictionary* does represent them as compatible. Addison
expresses this general relation in terms of writing: "Compositions of
this nature, when thus restrained, shew that wisdom and virtue are far
from being *inconsistent* with politeness and good humour."

One of the most interesting incivilities against which the *Dictionary*
warns is what Addison, following the Port Royal rhetoricians, calls
"egotism." As Johnson explains it, "egotism" is "the fault committed in
writing by the frequent repetition of the word *ego*, or *I*; too frequent
mention of a man's self, in writing or conversation." The *OED* puts the
first use of the modern, psychological meaning at 1800, and for the
second it provides a sentence from Coleridge's *Shakespearian Criticism*,
which shows that the psychological sense entered literary critical
language in the second decade of the nineteenth century. The way this
word changes its meaning from the rhetorical to the psychological is
representative of a general change in the conception of writing that
took place about 1800. Whereas Coleridge finds self-expression essential to writing, the *Dictionary* regards excessive reference to the self
as incivility. Warnings about this fault appear in the illustrations of the
word and its derivatives. Addison says, for example, "A tribe of *egotists*,
for whom I have always had a mortal aversion, are the authors of
memoirs, who are never mentioned in any works but their own." I
think it is significant that Johnson does not list "egoist," which had
been used in philosophical senses by this time; it suggests that his

interest in the basic educational subject of writing is steadier than his interest in metaphysics, which inspired the philosophical word. Warnings about the incivility of egotistical writing are not dependent upon the Port Royal terminology, however, as Bacon demonstrates: "Prefaces, *excusations*, and other speeches of reference to the person, though they seem to proceed of modesty, they are bravery."

Letter writing is a literary activity in which civility is especially important. Like *The Preceptor*, the *Dictionary* teaches this art by example, but it chooses as obvious models the letters of Pope and his correspondents,[3] rather than the translations of Pliny and Cicero that appear in *The Preceptor*. The inclusion of Pope's explicit advice on epistolary style is somewhat ironic, however, in light of Johnson's censure in the *Life*. Pope says just what Johnson did not for an instant believe: "The letters, every judge will see, were by no means efforts of the genius, but *emanations*[2] of the heart." Implicitly, Pope's letters and those written to him recommend civility and polish in writing. Swift perhaps goes overboard in his attempt to be politely diffident: "While I have any ability to hold a commerce with you, I will never be silent; and this chancing to be a day that I can hold a pen, I will *drag*[2] it as long as I am able." But usually the letters are less parodically polite. There is a solid challenge to Pope's epistolary supremacy from Richardson, though his letters are almost invariably signed "Clarissa" or "Pamela"; these are as clearly contrived as Pope's, but, given the admitted fiction, they are more modest and, of course, more full of moral instruction. As in everything of a linguistic nature, what really matters to Johnson in writing is the meaning. Civility is consistent with virtuous meaning but not sufficient to it.

The ideals of civility and sense converge in the *Dictionary*'s recommendation of stylistic plainness, and it is perhaps the strength of these convergent ideals that makes this recommendation so conspicuous throughout Johnson's book. The point is always that words are best when they are invisible vehicles of meaning, and the naiveté of this view troubles few of the writers who urge plainness and simplicity. Boyle, for example, hopes "judicious men . . . shall *agree*[6] to write clearly . . . to write nothing, or books that may teach us something." Others in the *Dictionary* show that plainness is the standard of every branch of writing: William Wake says, "*Plainness*[3] and freedom, an epistolary stile required," and Atterbury, on a totally different genre, "An inscription in the ancient way, plain, *pompous*, yet modest, will be best." Swift applies the standard by calling especially for plainness in

sermons. He complains that "several clergymen, otherwise little fond
of obscure terms, are, in their sermons, very *liberal*[3] of all those
which they find in *ecclesiastical* writers, as if it were our duty to
understand them." Grade book in hand, he reports, "I have taken a list
of several hundred words in a sermon of a new *beginner*[2], which not
one hearer could possibly understand."

Most of the stylistic advice in the *Dictionary* is about proprieties of
diction and the proper adjustment of figurative language. Syntactical
units like the sentence get less attention, and most of that attention is
from prerevolutionary writers who stress an ideal of compression and
significance that is usually compatible with the ends of plainness.
Ascham demands "firm *fastness*[4]," and Hooker points out that "the
necessity of shortness causeth men to cut off impertinent discourses,
and to *comprise* much matter in few words." Ben Jonson warns against
following this advice so zealously that "the language is thin, *flagging*[3],
poor, starved, scarce covering the bone, and shews like stones in a
sack," but he also warns against the "*vast*[2], and gaping, swelling, and
irregular." His ideal is a Horatian via media: "As we should take care
that our stile in writing be neither *dry*[6] nor empty, we should look
again it be not winding or wanton with far-fetched descriptions: either
is a vice." One way of "winding" away from "firm fastness" is by the
excessive use of particles, which Felton warns against in a droll
fashion: "Deliver us from the nauseous repetition of As and So, which
some *so*[20] *so* writers, I may call them so, are continually sounding in
our ears."

Like its considerations of diction, the *Dictionary*'s views on the
proper organization of compositions derive from Johnson's commitment to a belief that language is primarily a vehicle of communication
that best serves its users when it draws no attention to itself. The ideal
organization of a composition follows exactly the organization of its
subject, as Locke suggests: "In the *divisions*[6] I have made, I have
endeavoured, the best I could, to govern myself by the diversity of
matter." Watts teaches Locke's method, and he censures artificial or a
priori modes of organization: "Some persons have disturbed the order
of nature, and abused their readers by an affectation of *dichotomies*,
trichotomies, sevens, twelves, &c. Let the nature of the subject,
considered together with the design which you have in view, always
determine the number of parts into which you divide it." The *Dictionary*'s writing instructors put a good deal of emphasis on point, or what
modern composition instructors often call "focus." Bacon stresses the

importance of focus at the same time that he warns against wordiness: "*Iterations* are commonly loss of time; but there is no such gain of time, as to iterate often the state of the question; for it chaseth away many a frivolous speech." Locke represents a large part of the *Dictionary*'s instruction on writing when he urges us to "*keep*[1] in our minds, what we are considering."

Because the *Dictionary*'s requirements for proper organization are consistent with its other stylistic recommendations, Addison can explain proper order in terms of plainness: "The man who does not know how to *methodise* his thoughts, has always a barren superfluity of words; the fruit is lost amidst the exuberance of leaves." Likewise, Hooker can describe the proper order in terms of the *Dictionary*'s espousal of Ciceronian sentence structure or "firm fastness": "I have endeavoured, throughout this discourse, that every former part might give strength unto all that follow, and every latter bring some *light*[6] unto all before." In all its advice on writing the *Dictionary* speaks of the subject as one that can be improved, if not mastered, by care and attention. The written is always something consciously designed, neatly put together, and trimmed of all the flourishes and excesses that exuberance or laziness might allow to creep in. Spontaneous, overflowing writing appears only as an object of censure or as a joke. No one who reads very far in Johnson's *Dictionary* can fail to see that Prior's description of writing as a sort of fortune is totally ironic and depends upon an assumption that things really are just the opposite of the way he describes them:

> Writing is but just like dice,
> And lucky *mains*[5] make people wise:
> That jumbled words, if fortune throw them,
> Shall, well as Dryden, form a poem.

7.2. Reading

> All Hail, *ye books, my true, my real friends,*
> *Whose conversation pleases and improves.*
> Walsh.

Johnson's *Dictionary* is, in one sense, a grand invitation to its readers to engage in what Wimsatt calls "the vast program of best

books" that Johnson read in order to find his illustrative quotations. In
fact, in the "Plan" of the *Dictionary* Johnson refers to the sources of his illustrative quotations as "books which he [Johnson's reader] finds himself invited to read . . ." (*Works*, Oxford 5: 18). Something of Johnson's own exceedingly rich life of reading appears in the *Dictionary*, and he teaches the basic subject of reading primarily by example. Furthermore, he conceived of the *Dictionary*, in part, as an aid to readers of the English works he draws upon (*Letters* 1: 56). However, he provides more specific help with a few select authors: sections of Hanmer's glossary to Shakespeare appear, as do entries from Hughes's glossary to Spenser. Likewise, Broome's and Pope's notes gloss Pope's Homer. Perhaps the most specific act of assistance that Johnson performs relates to the Bible: not only does he print large sections of Locke's *Essay for the Understanding of St. Paul's Epistles*, he also translates into the *English Dictionary* many passages from Calmet's *Dictionary of the Bible* (see Wimsatt, *Philosophic Words* 151). Although Johnson sometimes used passages from Musschenbroek and other European scientists, Calmet's is by far the most widely quoted foreign reference work.[4] Locke expresses the need for Calmet in a quotation from his essay on Paul: "Expressions now out of use, *allusions* to customs lost to us, and various particularities, must needs continue several passages in the dark." Johnson imported Calmet to throw light on such passages, and he was so impressed with the importance of the task that he once planned a commentary on the Common Prayer to be modeled on Calmet's *Dictionary* (see above, p. 9).

The five thousand or so quotations from the King James Version are the *Dictionary*'s most powerful recommendation of the Bible, but many of Johnson's other sources testify to its importance. The Bible is the quintessential book, and even a small part of it is said to hold all the wisdom of merely human works; as Hooker has it, "The *choice*[5] and flower of all things profitable in other books, the psalms do both more briefly contain and more *movingly* also express." Turning to an equally pithy section of the Old Testament, Rogers contends, "More true *political*[1] wisdom may be learned from this single book of proverbs, than from a thousand of Machiavel." The wonders of the New Testament are even greater than those of the Old: as Hooker says, ". . . things there *prefigured*, are here performed." The divine subject of the New Testament is large enough to swallow not only the Old Testament but the whole world; such is the testimony of John 21.25: "There are many other things which Jesus did, the which, if they should be written every one, I suppose that even the world itself could not *contain*[2] the books that should be written." Perhaps more surprising than such testimony is the extraordinary literary and linguistic privilege that the King James Bible enjoys. Swift speaks of it (s.v. "perpetually") as a "standard for language," and also says, "No translation our own country ever yet produced, hath come up to that of the Old and New Testament; and I am persuaded, that the *translators* of the Bible were masters of an English style much fitter for that work than any we see in our present writings. . . ." Felton also puts translation of the Bible in a class of its own: "the same *punctualness* which debaseth other writings, preserveth the spirit and majesty of the sacred text." Given Johnson's remark that "the great pest of speech is frequency of translation" (preface, par. 90), and given the *Dictionary's* general defensiveness about foreign impurities, Addison's comment on the language of the Bible is perhaps the most remarkable of all: "Our language has received innumerable elegancies and improvements from that *infusion* of Hebraisms, which are derived to it out of the poetical passages in holy writ." The King James Bible is a great linguistic achievement, but its extremely privileged place in the *Dictionary* depends upon the divine matter it contains. Making this exception is consistent not only with Johnson's religious sense of the immeasurable superiority of divine, as against human, things—it also accords with his predilection for meaning, as against form, in books and all other linguistic productions.

The primary exhortations and invitations to reading are implicit in Johnson's choice of his sources, but he also prints ample explicit encouragement in his illustrative quotations. One of the great reasons for reading is that it permits us to learn about the past and to converse with the dead. Collier says, "By reading, a man does, as it were, *antedate*[1] his life, and makes himself contemporary with the ages past." Bacon may provide a source for Collier's sentiment when he says, "*Optimi consiliarii mortui*; books will speak plain, when counsellors *blanch*."[5] Even when books are not supernaturally lively, reading them can be very beneficial. Jeremy Taylor finds the very occupation of following words on the page useful, at least in a negative sense: "Since man cannot at the same time *attend*[1] to two objects, if you employ your spirit upon a book or a bodily labour, you have no room left for sensual temptation." Watts seems to be evaluating some literary genres on this basis when he says, "Histories engage the soul by sensible occurrences; as also voyages, *travels*[5], and accounts of countries."

Although the Bible provides the most serious moral and religious reading, the *Dictionary* seems to validate an analogy between the Bible and all other reading matter, which is common in such Protestant literature as Milton's "Areopagitica." In the way it has been excerpted the following illustration from Hooker seems to make such an analogical exaltation of reading: "Wherefore should any man think, but that reading itself is one of the ordinary means, whereby it pleaseth God, of his gracious goodness, to instil that celestial *verity*[2], which being but so received, is nevertheless effectual to save souls." Though Hooker is speaking of the Bible, his language, at least in the context of the *Dictionary*, makes this remark a recommendation of the general religious value of reading.[6] Its analogical value probably contributed to John Wesley's zeal for reading: he encouraged his ministers, no matter what else they were doing, to read five hours a day, and he put together a dictionary to assist the less learned among them with hard words (Starnes and Noyes, 172–78). Although Johnson does not cite John Wesley, he does quote some poetry written by his brother Charles, and, in the way it recommends and facilitates reading, the *Dictionary* bears some resemblance to a Wesleyan project.

Unlike Wesley, however, the *Dictionary* is occasionally satirical and skeptical about reading, just as it is about learning in general. Much of the skepticism about reading comes from Locke, who constantly points out that we must do something with our reading to make it valuable: "Reading furnishes the mind only with materials of knowledge, it is thinking makes what we read *ours*[2]: it is not enough to cram ourselves with a great load of collections, unless we chew them over again, they will not give us strength." Watts glosses this remark under "to cram[2]," and elsewhere he makes the same point with a little character sketch that is very like Johnson's manner in several *Ramblers* and *Idlers*: "Vario spends whole mornings in running over *loose*[9] and unconnected pages, and with fresh curiosity is ever glancing over new words and ideas, and yet treasures up but little knowledge."[7] In one sense, it is the passivity of books that is the problem, and the *Dictionary* sometimes seems a spokesman for Plato's King Thamous in lamenting the inferiority of books to living teachers. As Watts says, "*Books*[1] are a sort of dumb teachers; they cannot answer sudden questions, or explain present doubts: this is properly the work of a living instructor." The greatest commendations of books make them out to be living persons, as when Walsh says to them, "*All Hail.*"

In keeping with its Lockean philosophy of language, the *Dictionary* views reading, ideally, as a process of discarding the medium of the text and getting at the mind of the author who created it. As Locke says, "Till we from an author's words *paint*[3] his very thoughts in our minds, we do not understand him." Addison is less hortatory, but he also implies that the meaning is the essential thing in books when he says, "No body writes a book without meaning something, though he may not have the faculty of writing *consequentially*, and expressing his meaning." Modern theories of language reject such a dichotomy between thought and language, but it is assumed by most of the *Dictionary*'s reading teachers. Dryden, for example, says: "*Thought*[3], if translated truly, cannot be lost in another language; but the words that convey it to our apprehension, which are the image and ornament of that *thought*, may be so ill-chosen as to make it appear unhandsome." The tendency to center textual attention on language, so popular today, is a subject of ridicule in a couplet of Pope's that Johnson deploys in two strategic places: "Others for *language*[3] all their care *express*[3], / And value books, as women men, for dress." Like so many of the *Dictionary*'s deepest strains, the emphasis on meaning has a precedent in Bacon. In his explanation of "the first distemper of learning, when men study words, and not matter," Bacon connects proper attention with manliness and, like Pope, sees the incorrect as effeminate: "the excess of this is so justly contemptible, that as *Hercules*, when he saw the image of *Adonis*, *Venus* minion, in a temple, said in disdain, *Nil sacri es*; so there is none of *Hercules'* followers in learning, that is, the more severe and laborious sort of enquirers into truth, but will despise those delicacies and affectations, as indeed capable of no divineness" (*Works* 2: 427–28). A steady attention to meaning is what Boswell means when he calls Johnson's criticism "manly." Had he remembered the passage from Bacon, Boswell would have found a more suitable arena than politics in which to clothe the "Hercules of Toryism" in mythological garb.

To some extent, the *Dictionary* recognizes the affective qualities of texts, and it even encourages some cultivation of their appreciation. Dryden says, "You never *cool*[2] while you read Homer," and Addison seems to advise teachers concerning their pupils when he says, "If upon reading the admired passages in such authors, he finds a *coldness*[2] and indifference in his thoughts, he ought to conclude, that he himself wants the faculty of discovering them." But the important part of reading is to carry away something more lasting. With a simple analogy Herbert supplies one model for the more acquisitive kind of

reading that the *Dictionary* generally recommends: "Pick out of tales
the mirth, but not the sin. / He *pares* his apple, that will cleanly feed."
Watts's program for acquisition is much more sophisticated; he advises
students to turn their reading into magazines of knowledge: "If a book
has no *index*[3], or good table of contents, 'tis very useful to make one
as you are reading it; and in your *index* to take notice only of parts new
to you." This thought is close to the underlying spirit of lexicography in
Renaissance Europe. J. A. Comenius's ideal of Pansophia required the
indexical reduction of all books, so their real contributions could be
extracted, and Ephraim Chambers suggested something like this in his
proposal for a second edition of his *Cyclopædia*. Morery, Watts, and
Johnson are three of the many writers who carried forth this ideal,
which implies a conception of books as repositories of overlapping but
uncoordinate knowledge rather than as unique performances or demonstrations of particular points of view. The *Dictionary* preserves this
conception of reading in its illustrative quotations, but Johnson would
have acted more directly to perpetuate it if he had succeeded in his
plan to set up a universal review called *The Bibliothèque*, which was to
have reduced and abstracted for popular consumption in England all
the important books produced in Europe. Johnson tried to establish
The Bibliothèque right after he finished the *Dictionary*; the ideal of both
projects comes out of the same Renaissance dream.

7.3. Speech

> *As language was at its beginning merely oral, all words of necessary or*
> *common use were spoken before they were written; and while they*
> *were unfixed by any visible signs, must have been spoken with great*
> *diversity, as we now observe those who cannot read to catch sounds*
> *imperfectly, and utter them negligently. (Preface, par. 7)*

Although he recognizes that the origins of language are oral,
Johnson generally records only written language, and he opposes what
in the preface he calls "the corruptions of oral utterance." In his
editorial remarks he brands "merely oral" language as "only used in
conversation," and often his prejudice against mere speech comes out
even more clearly. Of "roundabout," for instance, he says, "This word
is used as an adjective, though it is only an adverb united to a
substantive by a colloquial licence of language, which ought not to

have been admitted into books."[8] Johnson's sources generally agree that speech is inferior to writing because it is so liable to change. Denham's derogatory remark is representative: "There are certain garbs and *modes*[5] of speaking, which vary with the times; the fashion of our clothes being not more subject to alteration than that of our speech." Writers who wish English were less liable to change often campaign against the corruptions of speech. Swift and Addison, for example, both attack the English habit of swallowing the ends of words: Addison says, "this humour of speaking no more than we must, has so miserably *curtailed*[1] some of our words; and, in familiar writings and conversations, they often lose all but their first syllables"; for Swift, "this disposition to shorten our words, by retrenching the vowels, is nothing else but a tendency to *lapse*[1] into the barbarity of those northern nations from whom we are descended, and whose languages labour all under the same defect."

The seventeenth century's low opinion of speech is, in part, a correlative of its acquiescence in what Hooker calls the "tyranny of the eye." An extreme form of this appears in linguistic projects, like Wilkins's, that try to purify language of sound by replacing the alphabet with more directly symbolic characters. But the deep predilection for the visible comes out even in writers, like Bacon, who set out to redress the ignorance of sound. Bacon describes speech sounds as "articulate *figurations*[1] of the air," and he says, "We behold the species of eloquence in our minds, the *effigies* or actual image of which we seek in the organs of our hearing."

In his illustrative quotations Johnson transmits this predilection for the visual and the written; he even promulgates it in his word list and in his editorial comments. However, following Bacon's lead, he also tries to include information on sound in his encyclopedia, and he prints a good deal of William Holder's landmark work *Elements of Speech*. In the *New Atlantis* Bacon dreamed of "sound-houses" for acoustic experimentation (*Works* 3: 256), and in the *Natural History* he inquires into sounds because it is "a virtue which may be called incorporeal and immateriate" (*Works* 3: 61). Johnson prints part of Bacon's recommendation under "materiate," and he includes one of his observations on the obscure subject of speech under "heed": "Speech must come by hearing and learning; and birds give more *heed*[4], and mark words more than beasts." Bacon may very well have given Holder his initiative when he recommended inquiry into "the motions of the tongue, lips, throat, palate, etc. which go to the making of the several

alphabetical letters" (*Works* 3: 45); but it is Holder who supplies the
Dictionary with its most interesting entries on this basic linguistic
subject. The following entry is representative: "In all the vowels the
passage of the mouth is open and free, without any appulse of an organ
of speech to another: but in all *consonants* there is an appulse of the
organs, sometimes (if you abstract the *consonants* from the vowels)
wholly precluding all sound; and, in all of them, more or less checking
and abetting it." The advance Holder makes over Bacon is evident
under "guttural," where Johnson prints a remark from each, in the
usual chronological order: "The Hebrews have assigned which letters
are labial, which dental, and which *guttural*" (Bacon); "In attempting to
pronounce the nasals, and some of the vowels spiritally, the throat is
brought to labour, and makes that which we call a *guttural* pronunciation" (Holder).

The *Dictionary* is very far from fomenting a phonological revolution.
From a modern point of view, Johnson sees language narrowly as visual
and written, but the presence of Holder is both a practical and
a theoretical corrective. Along with the information on phonology,
Holder supplies an apology for oral language. He says no more than
Johnson's preface when he remarks, "The original of these signs for
communication is found in *viva voce*, in *spoken* language," but origination, in this matter, counts more for Holder than it does for Johnson.
Hence, he says, "Language properly is that of the tongue directed to
the ear by speaking; written language is *tralatitiously* so called, because
it is made to represent to the eye the same words which are pronounced." Most of Holder's entries do not derogate writing, but they
do often give exclusive praise to oral language: "There is nothing
comparable to the variety of instructive *expressions*[1], by speech,
wherewith a man alone is endowed, as with an instrument suitable to
the excellency of his soul, for the communication of his thoughts."
Johnson does not include all of Holder's work; he does not, for
instance, admit much, if any, of his notion that there is a natural
alphabet of thirty-six letters derived from the possible motions of the
mouth. Yet, because there are exclusions, Johnson's inclusion of
Holder's apologetics indicates a willingness to entertain a speech-
centered view of language, which is fundamentally opposed to what the
Dictionary generally teaches.

On the subject of formal speech, however, the *Dictionary* sticks
firmly to Johnson's primary conviction that the written form of language is superior to the spoken. Living speech in the *Dictionary* tends

to be slippery and light or trivializing. South says, "Though wit and learning are certain and habitual perfections of the mind, yet the *declaration*[1] of them, which alone brings the repute, is subject to a thousand hazards." Ascham goes further and points out that an aptitude for speech can lead to an arrested development of the "habitual perfections of the mind": "Quick inventers, and fair ready speakers, being *boldened* with their present abilities, to say more, and perchance better too, at the sudden, for that present, than any other can do, use less help of diligence and study." Swift finds the antagonism between learning and speech total when he says, "The common *fluency*[2] of speech in many men, and most women, is owing to a scarcity of matter. . . ."

Because there is an inverse relation between volubility and meaning, brevity is one of the most highly regarded qualities of speech. Pope allegorizes the point memorably:

> *Distrustful*[3] sense with modest caution speaks;
> It still looks home, and short excursions makes;
> But rattling nonsense in full vollies breaks.

At one point, Johnson includes Bacon's words recalling a beautiful image of the relation between thought and speech, which ennobles the expansiveness of speech even though it uses visual terms to do so: "Themistocles said to the king of Persia, that speech was like cloth of Arras, opened and put abroad, whereby the imagery appears in figures; whereas in thought they lie but as in *packs*[1]." But this is rare; generally, the humanistic ideal of "sententious density," which favors writing, puts a premium on curt, unexpansive speech. As Bacon says, "Short speeches fly abroad like darts, and are thought to be shot out of secret intentions; but as for large discourses, they are *flat*[8] things, and not so much noted."

Naturally, a sense that speech tends to diminish and adulterate the force of thought lowers the value of formal rhetorical training. When rhetoric is valued at all, its ideal is the antirhetorical goal of plain sense, or, at most, the less naive art that hides its artifice: *ars est celare artem. Hudibras* supplies one statement of this attitude toward formal speech in Johnson's illustration of an appropriately common word:

> When with greatest art he spoke,
> You'd think he talk'd like other *folk*[1];

> For all a rhetorician's rules
> Teach nothing but to name his tools.

Elsewhere rhetoric comes in for even harsher treatment. Locke is one of its most terrible adversaries: "Consider what the learning of *disputation*[1] is," says Locke, "and how they are employed for the advantage of themselves or others, whose business is only the vain ostentation of sounds."

Despite Locke's important criticism, however, the *Dictionary* is somewhat ambivalent about rhetoric (see above, section 5.1.2). As Watts asserts, exercises in formal speech are good training for the mind: "Academical disputation gives vigour and briskness to the mind thus exercised, and relieves the *languor* of private study and meditation." Yet even in academic circumstances there is some question about the advisability of formal speech. The question often centers on the practice that Swift notes under a relevant word: "It is usual for masters to make their boys *declaim* on both sides of an argument." In one quotation Swift seems to applaud the practice: "Nothing can better improve political school-boys than the art of making plausible or *implausible harangues* against the very opinion for which they resolve to determine"—but in the *Dictionary*, as in Swift's writing, the word "political" is often subject to ironical interpretation, and Locke provides the opinion to which Swift's recommendation may actually be pointing: "The custom of arguing on any side, even against our persuasions, dims the understanding, and makes it by degrees lose the faculty of *discerning* between truth and falsehood." Swinging back, away from Locke's radical stand on rhetoric, Johnson recommends in *Rambler* 90 what Locke condemns in the *Dictionary*, but he does so with large reservations. In one place his language acknowledges a certain frivolity in the recommendation: "The loose sparkles of thoughtless wit may give new light to the mind, and the gay contention for paradoxical positions rectify the opinions" (*Yale* 4: 108). Five *Ramblers* on, in the story of Pertinax, Johnson puts stricter limitations on the practice of paradoxical disputation in his portrait of the depravity that arises from considering all truth as subject to academical or rhetorical manipulation. Watts could very well have supplied Johnson with his theme: "Let not obvious and known truths, or some of the most plain and certain propositions be *bandied*[3] about in disputation." In the *Dictionary*, as in all of Johnson's other works, truth is more important than the considerably invigorating pleasures afforded by disputation or any other display of language.

Whether it is formal or informal, however, speech is regarded by the *Dictionary* as the most unreliable and dangerous use of language; accordingly, moral admonitions about all sorts of speech abound in the illustrative quotations. *The Government of the Tongue* is the greatest single source of these admonitions, and, plausibly, Johnson chose Allestree's work as a particularly appropriate source of quotations in a word book that designs to facilitate speech without multiplying sin. Under a key word in the language of education, Allestree sums up his message with a short anecdote: "A primitive Christian, that coming to a friend to teach him a psalm, began, I said I will look to my ways, that I offend not with my tongue; upon which he stop'd his *tutor*, saying, this is enough if I learn it." Throughout the *Dictionary* Allestree is given ample scope to articulate the message that he phrases proverbially as, "A wholesome tongue is a tree of life; *perverseness*[1] therein is a breach in the spirit." Moreover, he gets support from many other writers both in detailing the varieties of verbal sin and in exhorting students carefully to control their speech.

Mere looseness is the simplest, but not the least serious, error of the tongue. John Ray explains the error with reference to the wisdom literature of the Bible: "Why *loquacity* is to be avoided, the wise man gives sufficient reason for, In the multitude of words there wanteth not sin." Loquacity is a stock attribute of women in many of the *Dictionary*'s characterizations of "the sex," but a serious concern about the sin, like Allestree's, blasts this prejudice: "We call this *talkativeness* a feminine vice; but he that shall appropriate loquacity to women, may perhaps sometimes need to light Diogenes's candle to seek a man."[9] Ben Jonson also remarks the universality of the sin when he recalls the Homeric image of human teeth as a wall set to protect us from what might escape our mouths: "There was a wall or *parapet* of teeth set in our mouth to restrain the petulancy of our words." Like other mortal sins, loquacity can be described as the arch-sin. Milton suggests as much when Samson speaks under the key word:

> Let me here
> Expiate, if possible, my crime,
> Shameful *garrulity*[1].

In a much lower literary form Addison describes excessive speech as the cause of a dramatic spiritual and physical degradation:

The *raven* once in snowy plumes was drest,
White as the whitest dove's unsully'd breast,
His tongue, his prating tongue, had chang'd him quite,
To sooty *blackness*[1] from the purest white.

The mortal sinfulness of verbal excess may surprise the reader living in a world where the air waves never stop vibrating with words, but less surprising are the *Dictionary*'s prohibitions against irreverence. The commandment itself appears under "to take": "Thou shalt not *take*[65] the name of the Lord in vain." The prophet Daniel extends the reach of sacrilege: "Every people, nation, and language, which speak any thing *amiss*[6] against the God of Shadrach, Meshach, and Abednego, shall be cut in pieces, and their houses shall be made a dunghill; because there is no other God that can deliver after this sort." Johnson himself echoes the injunction in his monitory definition of "swearer" as "a wretch who obtests the great name wantonly and profanely," and Herbert solidifies the point with a plain image:

> Lust and wine plead a pleasure, avarice a gain;
> But the cheap *swearer* through his open sluice
> Lets his soul run for nought.

In corollary terms, Allestree agrees with Herbert: "To dip our tongues in gall, to have nothing in our mouth but the *extract*[1] and exhalation of our inward bitterness, is no great sensuality."

It is particularly important to beware of profanity in the company of impressionable people. Ben Jonson warns, "The younger part of mankind might be *beat*[16] off from the belief of the most important points even of natural religion, by the impudent jests of a profane wit." Richardson says, with wonderful bluntness, "A man who is gross in a woman's company, ought to be *knocked*[3] *down* with a club." Servants are also impressionable, and Taylor warns that "masters must correct their servants with gentleness, prudence, and mercy; not with upbraiding and *disgraceful* language, but with such only as may express and reprove the fault, and amend the person." The *Dictionary* treats every variety of foul speech as if it were a species of blasphemy, and most of its warnings cover the whole range of bad talk. Another danger of such violations is their surprising permanence. Allestree says, "I wish all words of this sort might vanish in that breath that utters them; that as they resemble the wind in fury and *impetuousness*, so they might in transientness"; but he knows that "though we think our words vanish with the breath that utters them, yet they become records in God's court, and are laid up in his *archives*, as witnesses either for or against us." What we say indelibly imprints our souls, just as deeds permanently mark the portrait of Dorian Gray or the soul in Plato's *Gorgias*. Hence, Allestree recurs to the higher mode of printed language to describe the end of governing speech as making our spiritual "copy [i.e., soul] as worth transcribing as we can" (*Government of the Tongue* 222).

Besides adding up in spiritual terms, sins of speech also have a permanent effect on one's place in earthly society. Ecclesiasticus names some verbal abuses along with physical assault as the things that cannot be forgiven: "There may be a reconciliation, except for upbraiding, or pride, or *disclosing*[3] of secrets, or a treacherous wound; for from these things every friend will depart." Allestree says, "The most eminent sin is the spreading of *defamatory* reports," and Watts agrees: "Leave all noisy *contests*, all immodest clamours, *brawling*[1] language, and especially all personal scandal and scurrility to the meanest part of the vulgar world." Defamation is a sin that requires willing hearers, and, because listening is a sort of complicity, refusing to listen is a virtue. Taylor teaches the virtuous way to respond to slanderous talk and displays one of the many moral uses of the proposition that man is perpetually liable to error: "The truly virtuous do not easily credit evil that is told them of their neighbours; for if others may do amiss, then may these also speak amiss: man is *frail*[2], and prone to evil, and therefore may soon fail in words." Indeed, the social value of stemming the spread of slander is so great that Addison finds "if we look into communities and *divisions*[4] of men, we observe that it is the *discreet*[1] man, not the witty, nor the learned, nor the brave, who guides the conversation, and gives measures to society."

Another great social sin of speech is deceit. Job provides a motto for the government of tongue that covers just about every error when he says, "My lips shall not speak wickedness, nor my tongue utter *deceit*[1]." The intentional lie is a form of social violence, like slander, as South indicates: "Whoever sees a man, who would have *beguiled*[1], and imposed upon him, by making him believe a lie, he may truly say, that is the man who would have ruined me." A quotation from Hakewill under "disconformity" extends the meaning of lying to include the results of "errour and mistake," as well as "malice and forgery." In this extended sense, lying is a sin to which the learned are especially prone, and many of Johnson's admonitions about it converge with his general warning on the vanity of human learning. Allestree

declares, "The government of the tongue is a piece of morality which
sober nature dictates, which yet our greatest scholars have *unlearnt*."

"The grand uses of speech," says Allestree, are "the Glorifying of
God, and the benefiting of men" (*Government of the Tongue* 6). Hooker
expresses half the view succinctly when he says, "Words, be they never
so few, are too many, when they benefit not the *hearer*"; the other half
of Allestree's remark is obvious throughout the *Dictionary*. Religion is
the highest use of all things, but use, even in its lower forms, is the
standard for judging all language in the *Dictionary*, and it applies most
strictly to speech. Relaxations of the standard are rare, but even
Allestree concedes that "something of speech is to be indulged to
common civility, more to intimacies and endearments, and a *compe-
tency*[1] to those recreative discourses which maintain the chearful-
ness of society."[10] The *Dictionary* has other ways of liberalizing its
views; one of the book's grand qualities is the way it presents its topics
in various degrees of seriousness ranging from the solemn to the
ludicrous. Some such multiplicity is a quality of much great literature;
Shakespeare achieves it by using subplots and minor characters whose
trials echo those of the central figures. The basis of the *Dictionary*'s
multiplicity is a consistency of topic, rather than of plot; therefore,
recognizing that there are consistent topics in the *Dictionary* is essential
to appreciating the full range of the book's literary performance. Once
seen, the topics make relevant and interesting a vast number of
quotations that otherwise seem random and meaningless. For example, the perception that the government of the tongue is a generally
solemn topic in the *Dictionary* heightens the humor of Shakespeare's
ludicrous contribution to it: "Tongue, I must put you into a *butter-
woman's* mouth, and buy myself another of Bajezet's mute, if you
prattle me into these perils." By means of such humor Johnson
alleviates the basic solemnity upon which the humor depends, but
solemnity is never far off; the serious and tragic version of this
humorous remark appears under "snare": "A fool's mouth is his
destruction, and his lips are the *snare*[2] of his soul. *Prov.* xviii.7."

8. Arts and Sciences

8.1. Critics and Criticism

The art of criticism is reckoned by some as a distinct part of philology; but it is in truth nothing else, but a more exact and accurate knowledge or skill in the other parts of it, and a readiness to apply that knowledge upon all occasions. . . . (Watts)

Studies, called philological, *are history, language, grammar, rhetorick, poesy and criticism.* Watts.

Johnson vindicates Watts's definition of criticism as philological accuracy and readiness by adding critical commentary to his lexicographical work of recording usage. Partly because he is the author most frequently cited in the *Dictionary*, Shakespeare draws the most critical commentary. When Johnson censures Sharp's improper use of "precariousness," he calls his *Surgery* "a book, otherwise elegantly written"—but Shakespeare needs no such apology; of "to pluck," for instance, Johnson writes, "It is very generally and licentiously used, particularly by *Shakespeare*." More extended criticism is also common. For example, Johnson's entry under the third sense of "perilous" reads just like a passage from a critical edition of Shakespeare, but with the order of the parts inverted. First we get the note: "Perilous. . . . 3. Smart; witty. In this sense it is, I think, only applied to children, and probably obtained its signification from the notion, that children eminent for wit, do not live; a witty boy was therefore a *perilous* boy, or a boy in danger. It is vulgarly *parlous*." After the note, the passage that occasioned it appears; Leontes is speaking about the doomed Mamillius in *The Winter's Tale*:

> 'Tis a *per'lous*[3] boy,
> Bold, quick, ingenious, forward, capable;
> He's all the mother's from the top to toe.

A more complicated piece of philological criticism occurs in the entry
on "intrenchant." Here Johnson begins, "This word, which is, I
believe, found only in *Shakespeare*, is thus explained by one of his
editors: The *intrenchant* air means the air which suddenly encroaches
and closes upon the space left by any body which had passed through
it. *Hanmer.*" Next he provides his comment on the comment: "I believe
Shakespeare intended rather to express the idea of indivisibility or in-
vulnerableness, and derived *intrenchant*, from *in* privative, and *trencher*,
to cut; *intrenchant* is indeed properly *not cutting*, rather than *not to be cut*;
but this is not the only instance in which *Shakespeare* confounds words
of active and passive signification." After the variorum commentary
Johnson provides the resultant definition and the passage from *The
Tempest* that stimulated his efforts: "intrenchant" means "not to be
divided; not to be wounded; indivisible," as in "As easy may'st thou the
intrenchant air / With thy keen sword impress, as make me bleed." The
fact that Johnson chose not to gloss either of these passages in his
edition of Shakespeare suggests that he proceeded in an ad hoc way on
both critical projects, rising to comment where he felt stimulated to do
so, rather than on a regular principle. If this is so, Johnson's procedure,
as well as his productions, justifies Watts's definition of criticism as a
"readiness to apply [philological] knowledge."

Among the other great writers who sometimes rouse Johnson's
philological readiness are Pope, Milton, and Dryden. Under the
seventh sense of "square," Johnson writes:

> A *square* number is when another called its root can be exactly
> found, which multiplied by itself produces the square. The fol-
> lowing example is not accurate.
>
> > Advance thy golden mountains to the skies,
> > On the broad base of fifty thousand rise;
> > Add one round hundred, and if that's not fair,
> > Add fifty more, and bring it to a *square*[7].
> > > *Pope.*

It is pleasant to think of Johnson attempting the square root of 50,150
and finding Pope inaccurate. Milton in his greatness more frequently
draws Johnson's fire. Under "globous," for example, Johnson combines an orthographical distinction with a nice critical comment on
Milton's prosody: "When the accent is intended to be on the last

syllable, the word should be written *globose*, when on the first *globous*: I have transferred hither a passage of *Milton*, in which this rule has been neglected." He interposes the definition, "spherical, round," and prints from Milton:

> Wide over all the plain, and wider far
> Than all this *globose* earth in plain outspread,
> Such are the courts of God![1]

As in his *Life* of Dryden, in the *Dictionary* Johnson is critical of Dryden's nautical terminology. To give one example, he says, "*Mackerel-Gale* seems to be, in Dryden's cant, a strong breeze, such, I suppose, as is desired to bring *mackerel* fresh to market." The passage requiring the gloss is "They put up every sail, / The wind was fair, but blew a *mackerel-gale*."

Although Johnson often criticizes the language of great authors, he does record it; his criticisms are frequent and loud almost in direct proportion to the frequency of quotation and the recommendation that such frequency implies. He provides an explanation of his practice when he says in *Rambler* 93, "The faults of a writer of acknowledged excellence are more dangerous, because the influence of his example is more extensive" (*Yale* 4: 134).[2] In the *Dictionary* Watts makes a similar observation: "When a poet, an orator, or a painter has performed admirably, we sometimes mistake his blunders for beauties, and are so *ignorantly* fond as to copy after them." Johnson demonstrates exactly how such a train of error gets started in his entry under "to moralize."

> 2. In *Spenser* it seems to mean, to furnish with manners or examples.
>
> Fierce warres and faithful loves shall *moralize*[2] my song.
> *Fairy Queen, b.* i.
>
> 3. In *Prior*, who imitates the foregoing line, it has a sense not easily discovered, if indeed it has any sense.
>
> High as their trumpets tune his lyre he strung,
> And with his prince's arms he *moraliz'd*[3] his song.

Of course Johnson's response to such language is visible only because he is sufficiently committed to historical lexicography to record strange and unanalogical usages even when he disapproves of them. His commitment to recording usage is especially visible, for

example, under the third sense of "overwrought," where he suggests that Shakespeare actually wrote "overraught," but the "mistake" keeps its place. Likewise, "plesh" keeps its place though Johnson thinks it "a word used by *Spenser* instead of *plash*, for the convenience of rhyme." Johnson is conservative about his presentation of the important English texts, and the advisors on critical commentary whom the *Dictionary* quotes recommend similar restraint. Bacon's belief that "most corrected copies are commonly the least correct" (*Works* 2: 504) is part of the *Dictionary*'s critical credo.[3] Johnson does not use heavily corrected editions of authors, and the proportion of usages that he comments upon is not great, despite the substantial amount of commentary in the book as a whole. Moreover, many illustrative quotations ridicule critical commentary, and encourage editorial conservatism by means of satire. Typically satirical is Felton's reference to "all those heaps of comments, which are *piled*[1] so high upon authors, that it is difficult sometimes to clear the text from the rubbish." Locke expresses the same point of view: "Commentators and scholiasts, those copious *expositors* of places, pour out a vain overflow of learning on passages plain and easy." As well as being copious where they should not be, the commentators most often sketched in the *Dictionary* are curt where they should be copious. Donne makes critical evasiveness a commonplace when he says, "Slily as any *commenter* goes by / Hard words or sense." Pope uses the commonplace in the previous entry: "No *commentator* can more slily pass / O'er a learn'd unintelligible place."

The satire on commentators is fed by a much broader stream of satire on critics of all kinds. This broader satire is, in turn, a tributary of the larger satire on the vanity of all human learning, which is one of the most conspicuous topics in the *Dictionary*. To the extent that it is a part of this larger theme, the satire on criticism should not be seen as especially derogatory to this art per se. The *Dictionary* works hard at promoting good criticism, but the satirical is the most memorable aspect of the whole treatment of the topic. In a remark that Johnson retails in *Rambler* 16, Swift puts critics in the distinctly inferior position that they occupy throughout the *Dictionary*'s satire on them: "It has been *humourously*[1] said, that some have fished the very *jakes* for papers left there by men of wit." Bacon puts critics down in much the same fashion when he reports: "Sir Henry Wotton used to say, that criticks were like *brushers* of noblemens cloaths." In other quotations the secondariness of critics is attributed to their failure as writers. Addison says, for example, "I never knew one who made it his *business*[4] to lash the faults of other writers, that was not guilty of greater himself," and "As there are none who are more ambitious of fame, than those who are coiners in poetry, it is very natural for such as have not succeeded in it to *depreciate*[2] the works of those who have." The failure of the writer is the genesis of the poor critic with all his cant. Addison suggests a source of Johnson's Dick Minim when he says, "A few general rules, with a certain *cant*[2] of words, has sometimes set up an illiterate heavy writer, for a most judicious and formidable critick."[4]

When Addison says, "If by his manner of writing he is heavy and *tasteless*[4], I throw aside his criticisms," he reiterates one of the *Dictionary*'s criteria for good criticism. Pope says it best in the most famous redaction of Horace's principle: "Let those teach others, who themselves *excel*; / And censure freely, who have written well." Elsewhere Addison invokes another Horatian critical principle: "The candour which Horace shews, is that which distinguishes a critick from a *caviller*; he declares, that he is not offended at those little faults, which may be imputed to inadvertency." Under "conformable[4]" Addison is again quoted articulating this principle in a positive way; nevertheless, like so much of what the *Dictionary* values, the Horatian position is more often supported in negative terms. For example, Broome warns that "critics form a general character from the observation of particular errors, taken in their own *oblique*[1] or imperfect views; which is as unjust, as to make a judgment of the beauty of a man's body, from the shade it casts in such and such a position." Watts makes the warning a command, but his syntax is still negative: "Where an author has many beauties consistent with virtue, piety, and truth, let not little *criticks*[1] exalt themselves, and shower down their ill-nature." Watts's remark is representative, and the *Dictionary* generally vindicates Thomas Baker's judgment that "Criticism is at a low Ebb. . . . as it is usually practis'd, [it] is little more than an Art of finding Faults, and those commonly little ones too, and such as are of small Importance to the Scope and Design of an Author" (*Reflections upon Learning* 226–27).

However, just as the most conspicuous authors in the *Dictionary* are the most frequent objects of criticism, so too the frequency with which critical evaluation is criticized is one sign of its importance. For all its liability to error, evaluation is the proper task of criticism. Johnson's

first definition of "critick" is "a man skilled in the art of judging
literature; a man able to distinguish the faults and beauties of writing."
In *The Rambler* he shows that he saw evaluative criticism in moral
terms: "To scatter praise or blame without regard to justice, is to
destroy the distinction of good and evil" (*Yale* 4: 355). In the *Dictionary*
Pope is one of many writers who rationalize the need for censure in
less lofty but nearly as moral terms: "Bad writers are not ridiculed,
because ridicule ought to be a pleasure; but to undeceive and vindicate
the honest and *unpretending* part of mankind from imposition." Allestree adds to the apology for critical evaluation with an amusing tale
about a martyr for the cause: "Philoxenus, for despising some dull
poetry of Dionysius, was condemned to dig in the quarries; from
whence being *remanded*, at his return Dionysius produced some other
of his verses, which as soon as Philoxenus had read, he made no reply,
but, calling to the waiters, said, carry me again to the quarries." The
tale entertains us, but the moral is serious. Johnson phrased it in the
highest terms in *Rambler* 93: "The duty of criticism is neither to
depreciate, nor dignify by partial representations, but to hold out the
light of reason, whatever it may discover; and to promulgate the
determinations of truth, whatever she shall dictate" (*Yale* 4: 134).

The severity with which the *Dictionary* warns against bad criticism of
all kinds derives in part from a wish to validate and dignify the
profession of literature. As early as his satirical *Compleat Vindication of
the Licensers of the Stage* (1739) Johnson displayed a loyalty to the
professional class whose dignity and independence he did the most to
promote in the *Lives of the Poets*. In the *Dictionary* he attempts to make
the study and practice of literature more estimable by moving it in the
direction of science and away from opinion. As he phrases it in *Rambler*
92: "Criticism reduces those regions of literature under the dominion
of science, which have hitherto known only the anarchy of ignorance,
the caprices of fancy, and the tyranny of prescription" (*Yale* 4: 122).

"The tyranny of prescription" is the obstruction to science that the
Dictionary does the most to clear, although there is a general consensus
that rules are required to make arts and sciences. Dryden says, for
example, "without rules there can be no art, any more than there can
be a house without a *door*[1] to conduct you in." South adds definitively, "*Art*[1] is properly an habitual knowledge of certain rules and
maxims, by which a man is governed and directed in his actions."[5]
Johnson's own definition of "drama" also shows his agreement that
rules are required, though the phraseology in which he recommends

them is purposely loose: a drama is "a poem accommodated to action; a poem in which the action is not related, but represented; and in which therefore such rules are to be observed as make the representation probable." Against this background of agreement that rules are necessary, a host of writers show the inadequacy of many specific rules, and chief among these are the unities of time and place. In one quotation, Dryden pays some heed to the unity of time even as he surmounts it: "I prefer in our countryman the noble poem of Palemon and Arcite, which is perhaps not much inferior to the Ilias, only it *takes*[109] *up* seven years" (much too long according to theorists of the unities). But in another place he is more determined to sweep away the "tyranny of prescription": "Chronology at best is but a *cobweb*[2] law. . . ." Swift reiterates, "Laws are like *cobwebs*[2], which may catch small flies; but let wasps and hornets break through." Under the key word itself, Dryden conducts a little dialogue with himself that epitomizes the *Dictionary*'s attitude toward critical rules. First he says, "This little treatise will furnish you with infallible *rules*[3] of judging truly," but this is a dream that is immediately replaced with more realistic advice to the critic:

> Know'st with an equal hand to hold the scale;
> See'st where the reasons pinch, and where they fail,
> And where exceptions o'er the general *rule*[3] prevail.

This approximates Johnson's own opinion of critical rules in *Rambler* 176: "The eye of the intellect, like that of the body, is not equally perfect in all, nor equally adapted in any to all objects; the end of criticism is to supply its defects; rules are the instruments of mental vision, which may indeed assist our faculties when properly used, but produce confusion and obscurity by unskilful application" (*Yale* 5: 166–67). Rules are merely instruments; the science of criticism must supply a total vision of its field of inquiry.

More than anyone else, Dryden is the literary critic of the *Dictionary*, and he beautifully depicts criticism in a condition of partially integrated science: "An heroick play ought to be an imitation of an heroick poem, and consequently love and valour ought to be the subject of it: both these Sir William Davenant began to shadow; but it was so as discoverers draw their maps, with *headlands*[1] and promontories." Although they do not map out the whole field, definitions such as Dryden's provide one way of regularizing the art of criticism, and if properly correlated, they might rise to theory and even to science. As

though in obedience to such a conviction, Johnson often expands the
scope of his own definitions to include a larger piece of the literary landscape than the one he is specifically concerned to delineate. Under "satire," for instance, he says, "Proper *satire* is distinguished, by the generality of the reflections, from a *lampoon* which is aimed against a particular person." Likewise, he distinguishes metaphor (q.v.) from simile by reference to his example, "the spring *awakes* the flowers" : "A metaphor is a simile comprized in a word; the spring putting in action the powers of vegetation, which were torpid in the *winter*, as the powers of a sleeping animal are excited by awaking him." Johnson's definitions of evaluative terms are also sometimes suggestive of a larger view, as when he fixes "neat[1]" very nicely as "elegant, but without dignity." Other crucial definitions come in from his sources. Dryden contributes in many places; he says, for example, "The definition of *wit*[3] is only this; that it is a propriety of thoughts and words; or, in other terms, thoughts and words elegantly adapted to the subject." Elsewhere, Dryden amplifies his definition and tells us its source: "Wit is not the *jerk*[1] or sting of an epigram, nor the seeming contradiction of a poor antithesis; neither is it so much the morality of a grave sentence, affected by Lucan, but more sparingly used by Virgil." The critical definitions in the *Dictionary*, though often suggestive, do not add up to a single theory. They truly point in that direction, however, and they provide a quasi-scientific model because the best of them involve collateral critical terminology and are derived from the object of study itself. As Dryden says, obviously alluding to Vergil, "I drew my *definition*[1] of poetical wit from my particular consideration of him; for propriety of thoughts and words are only to be found in him; and where they are proper, they will be delightful." The principles of science, as Johnson and all other readers of Bacon know, must be derived ab intra. Definitions so derived come closer to science than the unities, even though such external rules are apparently more coherent and regular.

Besides its loosely correlative body of definitions, the *Dictionary* also offers, as a potentially unifying principle in criticism, the Reader, bearer of the judgment of the ages. With a tacit allusion to Longinus, Addison gives the reader a prominent place in the *Dictionary*'s critical language: "Although in *poetry*[1] it be necessary that the unities of time, place and action should be explained, there is still something that gives a greatness of mind to the reader, which few of the criticks have considered."[6] Dryden's statement of the point sounds more Johnsonian; he says, "The readers are the jury to decide according to the merits of the cause, or to bring it to another *hearing*[3] before some other court." The problem with this location of critical weight is, as Dryden perceives, that "the liking or disliking of the people gives the play the *denomination* of good or bad; but does not really make or constitute it such." Again like Johnson, Dryden solves the problem by submitting the opinion of the audience to the alembic of time: "Time is the surest judge of truth: I am not vain enough to think I have left no faults in this, which that *touchstone*[2] will not discover."

Although the *Dictionary* expresses many good intentions and clears away some intervening obstructions, it does not advance the science of criticism much beyond the point to which Aristotle brought it in the fourth century B.C. Like Aristotle the *Dictionary* sees plot or argument as the central structural element in literature; imitation of nature as its primary cause; and moral improvement as the function of art. In every one of these areas the *Dictionary* presents literature in a manner somewhat different from Aristotle's, but the elements of the presentation are much the same. Under the fourth sense of "fable" Addison says, "The first thing to be considerd in an epick poem is the *fable*[4], which is perfect or imperfect, according as the action, which it relates, is more or less so." Dryden is equally dependent upon Aristotle when he says, "The *argument*[3] of the work, that is, its principal action, the œconomy and disposition of it, are the things which distinguish copies from originals." Pope defines "plot" in Aristotelian terms: "The causes and designs of an action, are the *beginning*[5]; the effects of these causes, and the difficulties that are met with in the execution of these designs, are the middle; and the unravelling and resolution of these difficulties, are the end." Johnson's own definition is looser but it seems influenced by Pope's phraseology and is also clearly Aristotelian: the fifth sense of "plot" is "an intrigue; an affair complicated, involved and embarrassed; the story of a play, comprising an artful involution of affairs, unravelled at last by some unexpected means."

Like Pope's elaboration of the Aristotelian notion that plot is the soul of poetry, the *Dictionary*'s treatment of Aristotle's dictum that art is an imitation of nature suggests possibilities of science in literary criticism. However, the nature that matters the most in the *Dictionary*'s critical language is the secondary nature that Dryden describes as a learned acquisition, something permanent and unchanging. The Drydenian writer is like a physician who understands the general structure of the human body even though it is invisible to the uninitiated (s.v.

"illiterate"; see above, p. 54). On the other hand, Rymer speaks up for
the "empiricks" under "collegiate," and Collier suggests a synthesis when he says, "He that would be a master, must draw by the *life*[8] as well as copy from originals, and join theory and experience together." These and other quotations try to give direct imitation some added weight, but the balance is in favor of seeing nature as most readily and importantly available in the best books. The epigram for this view is Pope's "*Nature*[10] and Homer were he found the same,"[7] but Dryden is actually the more extreme expositor of the position: "The ancient pieces are beautiful, because they resemble the *beauties*[2] of nature; and nature will ever be beautiful, which resembles those *beauties* of antiquity."[8] Locating nature in the greatest art fixes nature and gives imitative art a firmer, more scientific foundation. Johnson's own notion of general nature moves away from the Platonism implicit in Dryden's use of "beauties,"[9] but he made no changes that weakened the potential for increased critical science in Dryden's formulations. A remark in *Rambler* 36 is representative of Johnson's concern for seeing the object of poetry as firm and unchanging: "Poetry has to do rather with the passions of men, which are uniform, than their customs, which are changeable" (*Yale* 3: 199–200). What Johnson corrects in Dryden's Platonistic solutions to the problem of nature are the optimism and the related interest in the beautiful. Beauty and its correlates are scantily represented in the *Dictionary*'s critical language. One of these correlates is liveliness, an important qualifier of "imitation" for Dryden: "Since a true knowledge of nature gives us pleasure, a lively *imitation*[1] of it, either in poetry or painting, must produce a much greater; for both these arts are not only true *imitations* of nature, but of the best nature." Johnson demonstrates both his reliance on Dryden and the sort of change he wishes to make in his master's vision when he edits Dryden's definition of a play; for Dryden's "just and lively image" Johnson offers "a *play*[3] ought to be a just image of human nature, representing its humours and the changes of fortune to which it is subject, for the delight and instruction of mankind." He again omitted "lively" in the fourth edition; now whether he did so consciously or through a failure of memory, the omission is significant: it suggests a wish to settle the object of imitative art a little more squarely in empirical reality. Yet his reliance on Dryden throughout the *Dictionary* as well as in his own formulation of general nature shows that the stabilizing aims of Dryden's definition were consistent with Johnson's steadiest hopes for the science of criticism.

Finally, literature and criticism, like other subjects in the *Dictionary*, justify their place in the curriculum by adding to the store of useful knowledge, and the most useful knowledge is, always, moral. As an apologist for its own field of study, the *Dictionary* makes a strong effort to describe literature as fundamentally moral and religious. Milton directs, "To say, or to do ought with memory and imitation, no purpose or respect should sooner move us, than *simply*[3] the love of God and of mankind." Dryden hints that the structure of literature is moral by calling the moral "the *groundwork*[3]" of a poem or the "design" of "an *heroick*[3] poem." If they do not succeed in making the moral appear structural, the *Dictionary*'s critics of epic nevertheless see moral truth as the inmost part of the most important literary kind. Broome's allegorical reading of Homer is representative. He says, alluding to the Circe episode, for instance, "Homer intended to teach, that pleasure and sensuality *debase*[1] men into beasts." Speaking more generally, Broome affirms that "Homer continually *inculcates* morality, and piety to the gods," and "Homer introduces the best instructions, in the midst of the plainest *narrations*." Many other writers quoted in the *Dictionary* follow Broome's method in reading Homer. Matthew Hale, for instance, supplies a religious reading of *Iliad* 8: "The moral of that *poetical* fiction, that the uppermost link of all the series of subordinate causes is fastened to Jupiter's chair, signifies that almighty God governs and directs subordinate causes and effects." Spenser not only notices the moral nature of Homer, he asserts that it is the precedent for his own essentially moral epic: "I have followed all the ancient poets historical: first, Homer, who, in the person of Agamemnon, *ensampled* a good governor and a virtuous man." Other genres follow epic in their essential morality. Garth says Ovid's "story of Deucalion and Pyrrha teaches, that piety and innocence cannot miss of the divine protection, and that the only loss *irreparable* is that of our probity." Under "comedy" Pope extends the moral outlook even to that more frivolous genre, directing that "in every scene some moral let it teach."

In the *Dictionary* it sometimes seems that the main difference between literature and reality is moral. For example, Addison says, "Men of learning who take to business, discharge it with greater honesty than men of the world; because the former in reading have been used to find virtue extolled and vice *stigmatized*, while the latter have seen vice triumphant and virtue discountenanced." When Swift makes the same point, however, he reveals the important truth that literature is not inevitably moral but requires critical precepts to make it so: "Observe the *distributive*[1] justice of the authors, which is constantly applied to the punishment of virtue, and the reward of vice, directly opposite to the rules of their best criticks." Criticism makes literature moral by precept, by interpretation, and also by censorship. Though each of these activities is necessary, they all unavoidably obstruct the growth of critical science by treating literature as a vehicle of moral meaning rather than an integral object of study. The damaging separation between literature and its value is most evident in recommendations of critical censorship. Dryden advises, "Supposing verses are never so beautiful, yet if they contain any thing that *shocks*[2] religion or good manners, they are *Versus inopes rerum nugæquæ* [sic] *canoræ*."[10] Given the closeness of "beauty" and nature in Dryden's critical definitions, this statement does serious damage to the integrity of his literary outlook.

As the epigraph to *Rambler* 60 Johnson chose Horace's famous defense of fiction: *Quid sit pulchrum, quid turpe, quid utile, quid non, / Plenius et melius Chrysippo et Crantore dicit.*[11] This is the motto for much of the *Dictionary*'s apology for poetry, but criticism that adopts these disjunctive terms denies itself the possibility of science by imposing a category of judgment that is finally ab extra and by separating content from form. Gay laughs at writers or readers who "Morals snatch from Plutarch's tattered page, / A *mildew'd* Bacon, or Stagyra's sage"; the more deeply involved the moral, the better the work that contains it. But, despite Dryden's use of words like "groundwork" and "design," the *Dictionary* does not succeed in making morality a structural part of literature. It will not trust literature that far. As Denham says, "Musæus first, then Orpheus *civilize* / Mankind, and gave the world their deities," but the errors sown thereby are almost as great as the benefits, and a corrective, externally validated, censorious, interpretative, and therefore unscientific criticism is still required.

8.2. Poetry and Poets

> *Be dumb you beggars of the rhyming trade,*
> *Geld your loose wits, and let your muse be* spay'd.
> Cleavel*[and]*.

Johnson included the word "Grubstreet" in his book and signified his own vocational identification with that locale by printing beneath the word a salute to the archetypal homeland of Ithaca (see above, p. 26). A vast number of quotations in the *Dictionary* support Johnson's overtly comic gesture, and the whole book expresses an attitude toward the profession of writing that developed in the furious competitiveness of the Grub Street wars. As Pat Rogers has shown, the vituperative attacks on poor poets stem from an eagerness to trim the ranks and raise the dignity of professional writing. The *Dictionary* both records the satirical poetry and prose dedicated to this social movement, and is itself an important event in the movement.

Part of the evidence that selection and thinning are aimed at in Grub Street satire is its perpetual derision of profusion and excess. Dryden complains that "a multitude of writers daily *pester*[1] the world with their insufferable stuff." The complaint is not limited to the eighteenth century, as Browne suggests: "Authors *presumably* writing by common places, wherein, for many years, promiscuously amassing all that make for their subject, break forth at last into useless rhapsodies." Even earlier, Drayton notices the compulsive loquacity of those who abandon themselves to the creation of romances:

> Old Chaucer doth of Topas tell,
> Mad Rabelais of Pantegruel,
> A later third of Dowsabell,
>   With such poor *trifles* playing:
> Others the like have labour'd at,
> Some of this thing, and some of that,
> And many of they know not what,
>   But that they must be saying.

Spenser's Poet, and the *Dictionary*'s, attempts to be noble by scorning "the *rakehelly* rout of our ragged rhimers, which without learning boast, without judgment jangle, and without reason rage and foam."

To guard against prolific vacuity and the consequent degradation of all books, the *Dictionary* reminds writers that by publishing they necessarily expose themselves to harsh and unrelenting criticism. Johnson himself summarizes the theme in *Rambler* 93: "he that writes may be considered as a kind of general challenger, whom every one has a right to attack" (*Yale* 4: 133–34). Prior provides what might be Johnson's specific source: "An author is in the condition of a *culprit*; the publick are his judges. . . ." The theme, however, is common. Pope is the model literary defendant when he deposes, "I omitted no means in my power, to be informed of my errours; and I expect not to be excused in any negligence on account of youth, want of leisure, or any other

idle *allegations*[3]." Johnson may have had this model performance in mind when he restated the general principle in the last *Rambler*: "The supplications of an author never yet reprieved him a moment from oblivion" (*Yale* 5: 317). Some of the *Dictionary*'s reminders that writing provokes criticism are clearly designed to expose vanity and terrify imposters. Dryden says, "No man is so bold, rash, and *overweening* of his own works, as an ill painter and a bad poet," and, more sharply:

> All authors *to* their own defects are *blind*[2];
> Hads't thou, but Janus like, a face behind,
> To see the people, what splay mouths they make;
> To mark their fingers, pointed at thy back.

Prior teaches the young author what to expect from the world in a quotation illustrating an unlikely word: "Rough satires, sly remarks, ill-natur'd speeches, / Are always aim'd at poets that wear *breeches*[1]."

Although an anonymous multitude of bad writers is most often the object of the *Dictionary*'s satire, Johnson does not forbear to include attacks on particular poets. A few of the finest are these:

> Flow, Welsted! flow, like thine inspirer, *beer*;
> Tho' stale, not ripe; tho' thin, yet never clear;
> So sweetly mawkish, and so smoothly dull;
> Heady, not strong; and foaming, tho' not full.
>
> *Pope.*

> By long experience Durfey may no doubt
> *Insnare*[1] a gudgeon, or perhaps a trout;
> Though Dryden once exclaim'd in partial spite;
> He fish'd!—because the man attempts to write.
>
> *Fenton.*

> Holmes, whose name shall live in *epic* song,
> While music numbers, or while verse has feet.
>
> *Dryden.*

Johnson seems himself to assist in scourging Rymer by carefully signing the author's name to the frank remark, "You know I am not *cut*[21] *out* for writing a treatise, nor have a genius to pen any thing exactly." With this instrument of satire the *Dictionary* mainly assaults Swift. Johnson quotes heavily from Swift's "Verses on the Death of Dean Swift," but without the context of mock footnotes and other apparatus the satire seems to fall on Swift himself, and the signature suggests the "driveller" that Johnson cruelly lamented in "The Vanity of Human Wishes":

> Now Curl his shop from rubbish drains;
> Three genuine tomes of Swift's remains:
> And then, to make them pass the *glibber*[2],
> Revis'd by Tibbald, Moore, and Cibber.
>
> *Swift.*

Johnson also makes Swift satirize himself by connecting his name with most of the scatological words in the *Dictionary*. To give just one example besides Swift's deathless remark, "I got the *hemmorhoids*," there is this illustration of "goldfinder," which ludicrously means one that empties jakes:

> His empty paunch that he might fill;
> He suck'd his vittels through a quill;
> Untouch'd it pass'd between his grinders,
> Or 't had been happy for *goldfinders*.
>
> *Swift.*

The proverbial poverty of writers appears in the *Dictionary* both as a warning to mediocre practitioners of the trade and, sometimes, as a badge of honor among members of the brotherhood. Unlike Andrew Marvell's great satire of Richard Fleckno, the *Dictionary* mingles compassion in its depiction of the poet's poor circumstances. Swift, for instance, is not thoroughly ironic when he laments,

> Ah! where must needy poet seek for aid
> When dust and rain at once his coat invade;
> His only coat! where dust confus'd with rain
> Roughens the *nap*[2], and leaves a mingled stain.

Pope's version of Swift's "needy poet" is more monitory:

> The needy poet sticks to all he meets,
> *Coach'd*, carted, trod upon; now loose, now fast,
> And carry'd off in some dog's tail at last.

But a quotation from Dryden in illustration of "far[4]" is one of many entries in the *Dictionary* that curse the "foes of virtuous poetry" who "point at the tatter'd coat and ragged shoe." Addison sees an ugly

aspect of writing for gain when he points out, "Our Grubstreet
biographers watch for the death of a great man, like so many undertak-
ers, on purpose to make a penny of him." But this is good-natured
satire, and elsewhere Addison's satire is even friendlier: "I cannot tell
how the poets will succeed in the explication of *coins*[1], to which they
are generally very great strangers." Nothing in the *Dictionary* matches
Johnson's greatest elegiac rehearsal of literary impecuniousness—
"Toil, envy, want, the patron, and the jail"—but Swift provides a
possible source for the endearing though ironic mythology concerning
the habitations of poets that Johnson published in *Rambler* 117 at about
the same time that he composed his entry under "garret":

> On earth the god of wealth was made
> Sole patron of the building trade;
> Leaving the arts the spacious air,
> With license to build castles there:
> And 'tis conceiv'd their old pretence,
> To lodge in *garrets*[1], comes from thence.

The pseudo-classical system of patronage was the old regime that
Grub Street overthrew in its struggle for independence and dignity,
and the *Dictionary* records and contributes to revolutionary attacks on
the old order. Some of Johnson's own contributions are blatant and
well known, as, for example, his tendentious definition of "patron" as
"one who countenances, supports or protects. Commonly a wretch
who supports with insolence, and is paid with flattery." Royal patronage
receives equally harsh treatment in the famous definition of "pension":
"An allowance made to any one without an equivalent. In England it is
generally understood to mean pay given to a state hireling for treason
to his country." In the preface Johnson is against the formation of an
English Academy for the improvement of the language because he
could "never wish to see dependance multiplied" (par. 90), and he is
proud that he completed his book "without any patronage of the great"
(par. 94). Partly because of the justly renowned letter to Chesterfield,
these overtly hostile gestures have often been remarked, but they are
supported by a numerous and largely unnoticed host of illustrative
quotations throughout the *Dictionary*.

Although "patron" itself is illustrated by Prior's praise of an unusually good patron, Dorset, some of the other relevant words include
more characteristic contributions to the topic. "Unpensioned" draws

from Johnson a freedom-loving definition, "Not kept in dependence by a pension," and a strong illustration from Pope, a great hero in his class's fight for independence:

> Could pension'd Boileau lash in honest strain
> Flatt'rers and bigots, ev'n in Louis' reign;
> And I not strip the gilding off a knave,
> Unplac'd, *unpension'd*, no man's heir or slave?[12]

Allestree is quoted under another key word in the language of patronage with an observation representative of the *Dictionary*'s outlook: "How eagerly do some men propagate every little *encomium* their parasites make of them." Johnson defines a related word with monitory force: "to flatter" is "to sooth with praises; to please with blandishments; to gratify with servile obsequiousness; to gain by false compliments." The illustration from Proverbs vindicates the tone of Johnson's definition: "He that *flattereth* his neighbour, spreadeth a net for his feet." Dr. Thomas Newton, the editor of the edition of Milton that Johnson probably used, rounds out the entry with a remark from his dedication of *Paradise Lost* to the Earl of Bath: "I scorn to *flatter* you or any man." In a more surprising place Pope matches this proud poet's boast:

> When I flatter, let my dirty leaves
> Cloath spice, line trunks, or, flutt'ring in a rowe,
> *Befringe* the rails of Bedlam and Soho.

As freedom is noble, servility is base, and both parties in the relationship of patron and poet are pilloried throughout Johnson's book. A "favourite" is one who has achieved the first place in the chain of dependence, and Johnson's definition spells out his attitude towards such slaves: "2. One chosen as a companion by his superiour; a mean wretch whose whole business is by any means to please." The illustrative quotations serve as warnings to master and servant alike: "The great man down, you mark, his *fav'rite*[2] flies; / The poor advanc'd, makes friends of enemies" (Shakespeare); "Nothing is more vigilant, nothing more jealous than a *favourite*[2], especially towards the waining time, and suspect of satiety" (Wotton). Johnson's contempt seems to come out again in propria persona when he defines "minion" correctly but with philologically supernumerary energy: "A favourite; a darling; a low dependant; one who pleases rather than benefits. A word of contempt, or of slight and familiar kindness." Under an appropriate word Swift provides an image of the sort of creature that Johnson hopes his young students, with all their learning, will never become: "Certain gentlemen of the gown, whose aukward, spruce, prim, sneering, and *smirking* countenances have got good preferment by force of cringing." Obedience to the only proper master obviates the need for such miserable behavior and points up its immorality; South declares, "I need salute no great man's threshold, *sneak*[2] to none of his friends to speak a good word for me to my conscience."

The *Dictionary* hates servile traitors to the writing profession who flatter the rich, and it delights in mocking the attempts of the rich to achieve high status in the republic of letters by dint of monetary force. Addison contributes to the mockery with a philologically unhelpful anecdote: "I know a friend, who has converted the essays of a man of quality, into a kind of fringe for his *candlesticks*." In four lines that Johnson quotes at least three times in the *Dictionary* Swift explains that the trappings of wealth cannot purchase literary quality:

> For not the *desk* with silver nails,
> Nor *bureau* of expence,
> Nor standish well *japan'd*[1], avails
> To writing of good sense.

Pope also warns the rich to suspect their apparent success in letters when he complains about the venality of critical judgment:

> What *woeful*[3] stuff this madrigal would be,
> In some starv'd hackney-sonneteer, or me?
> But let a lord once own the happy lines,
> How the wit brightens! how the style refines!

Patronage is not only servile, immoral, and professionally compromising, it is also—what may be worse—undependable. *Rambler* 163 facetiously but pointedly proposes that the punishment of Tantalus in the infernal region "was perhaps originally suggested to some poet by the conduct of his patron, by the daily contemplation of splendor which he never must partake, by fruitless attempts to catch at interdicted happiness, and by the sudden evanescence of his reward, when he thought his labours almost at an end" (*Yale* 5: 102). In the *Dictionary* South's sermons provide versions of this theme that might have informed Johnson's appropriation of the mythological image; South says, for example, "For the preferments of the world, he that would reckon up all the accidents that they depend upon, may as well undertake to *count*[1] the sands, or to sum up infinity"; and, "Thou spendest thy time in waiting upon such a great one, and thy estate in *presenting*[6] him; and, after all, hast no other reward, but sometimes to be smiled upon, and always to be smiled at." Shakepeare makes a more wonderful image of the wish for preferment:

> He that depends
> Upon your favours, swims with fins of lead,
> And *hews*[3] down oaks with rushes.

The greatest hero of his class, Pope, fixes the image of the old regime for his faithful, free progeny, including Johnson, when he decries "Patrons, who sneak from living worth to dead, / With-hold the pension, and *set*[60] *up* the head." Johnson's "tardy bust" in "The Vanity" perpetuates this specific image, but his whole *Dictionary* vindicates the theme.

In the social order of the *Dictionary* poetry and learning are the true measures of nobility, and the best way for kings to ennoble themselves is by true patronage. Peacham confers honors when he declares, "That thrice *renowned* and learned French king, finding Petrarch's tomb without any inscription, wrote one himself; saying, shame it was, that he who sung his mistress's praise seven years before her death, should twelve years want an epitaph." Elsewhere, Peacham again links great poets and great rulers: "Every child knoweth how dear the works of Homer were to Alexander, Virgil to Augustus, Ausonius to Gratian, who made him *proconsul*, Chaucer to Richard II. and Gower to Henry IV." However, only the *Dictionary*'s later writers make it possible to read Peacham's remarks as elevations of the royal rather than of the poetic personages here. Dryden is the key figure; he appropriates the language of genealogy to poetic tradition and therefore claims nobility for his vocational family: "Milton was the poetical son of Spenser, and Mr. Waller of Fairfax; for we have our lineal descents and *clans*[1] as well as other families." The giants before the flood in this lineal descent are the Elizabethans, and their progeny pay them proper homage throughout the *Dictionary*. Peacham says, "Queen Elizabeth's time was a golden age for a world of *refined*[2] wits, who honoured poesy with their pens." Denham's compliment is even higher: "By Shakespeare's, Johnson's, Fletcher's lines, / Our stage's lustre Rome's

outshines[2]." A combination of famous quotations under "sock" also
elevates the Elizabethan giants, though it does so at the expense of
their Restoration epigones:

> Then to the well-trod stage anon,
> If Johnson's learned *sock*[2] be on,
> Or sweetest Shakespeare, fancy's child,
> Warble his native wood-notes wild.
>
>

Milton.

> Great Fletcher never treads in buskins here,
> Nor greater Johnson dares in *socks*[2] appear;
> But gentle Simkin just reception finds
> Amidst the monument of vanish'd minds.
>
>

Dryden.

Dryden's genealogical studies conclude in himself, and the *Dictionary's* very considerable quotation of his works does much to vindicate his claim, but Dryden's heir and the Poet of the *Dictionary* is Pope. Berkeley supplies some relevant testimony in a letter to Pope: "The imagination of a poet is a thing so nice and delicate, that it is no easy matter to find out images capable of giving pleasure to one of the *few*[1], who, in any age, have come up to that character." In another place Johnson prints a pair of quotations that dances out (as Kenneth Burke might say) the success of Pope and the failure of Swift in the contention for the poetic throne:

> Then at the last, an only *couplet*[1] fraught
> With some unmeaning thing they call a thought;
> A needless Alexandrine ends the song,
> That, like a wounded snake, drags it[s] slow length along.
>
>

Pope.

> In Pope I cannot read a line,
> But with a sigh I wish it mine;
> When he can in one *couplet*[1] fix
> More sense than I can do in six,
> It gives me such a jealous fit,
> I cry, pox take him and his wit.
>
>

Swift.

At the end of this scene Pope rises in the character of a poet to join those already canonized, and Swift leaves the stage cursing like Malvolio.

Pope is an especially appropriate choice for the *Dictionary*'s bays because one of his qualities is a gift for hard work and study. He is quoted under a key word in the *Dictionary*'s lexicon of advice to aspiring poets with an account of his rarest gift: "I writ, because it amused me; I *corrected*[2], because it was as pleasant to me to *correct* as to write." Along with a penchant for correction Pope combines a respect for learning that the *Dictionary* eagerly makes an essential aspect of writing. Addison satirizes the poet who hopes to succeed on mere imagination by describing him as a sort of superstitious fool: "The writer, resolved to try his fortune, fasted all day, and, that he might be sure of dreaming upon something at night, procured an handsome slice of *bridecake*, which he placed very conveniently under his pillow." Addison suggests a more sober method: "Authors, who have *drawn*[40] *off* the spirits of their thoughts, should lie still for some time, 'till their minds have gathered fresh strength, and by reading, reflection, and conversation, laid in a new stock of elegancies, sentiments, and images of nature." This suggestion closely resembles the answer Johnson is said to have made to the king when His Majesty discovered him in the royal library and asked him what he was planning to write: Johnson replied, "he had pretty well told the world what he knew, and must now read to acquire more knowledge" (Boswell 2: 35). In keeping with its overall educational program, the *Dictionary* consistently maintains that learning is an important qualification for writing. Sometimes learning means, in Addison's phrase, "a good *cargo* of Latin and Greek," but more often it is the whole range of study. Dryden puts it best when he describes the qualifications for the highest station in the poetic world: "He is the only *proper*[5] of all others for an Epic poem, who, to his natural endowments of a large invention, a ripe judgment, and a strong memory, has joined the knowledge of the liberal arts." Part of Johnson's first definition of "liberal" is "not low in birth"; the phrase entails an appropriation of class to learning that Dryden's illustration, like Johnson's whole book, transfers to qualified writers.

8.3. The Fine Arts

8.3.1. Music

Tully says, there consisteth in the practice of singing and playing*[10]*
on instruments great knowledge, and the most excellent instruction,
which rectifies and orders our manners, and allays the heat of anger.
Peacham.

It is possible, in some instances, to read the *Dictionary*'s inclusions and omissions as a record of Johnson's experiences, interests,
and areas of ignorance. All matters concerned with printing, writing,
and education, for example, are well covered in the *Dictionary*'s word
list and in its illustrative quotations. The fine arts, on the other hand,
are more scantily covered, and much of their nomenclature is omitted
or poorly defined. In a copy of the *Dictionary* once owned by Samuel
Dyer—now in the British Library—someone marked many of Johnson's failures to record musical terminology or to define it accurately. A
representative case is the word "tune," which Johnson does not define
at all; he leaves that task up to Locke, even though Locke's definition is
not, in this case, distinguished: "*Tune*[1] is a diversity of notes put
together." The illustration of "tune" from Bacon speaks of music as an
appeal to the passions: "*Tunes*[1] and airs have in themselves some
affinity with the affections; as merry *tunes*, doleful *tunes*, solemn *tunes*,
tunes inclining mens minds to pity, warlike *tunes*; so that *tunes* have a
predisposition to the motions of the spirits." Like Peacham's citation of
Cicero in the epigraph to this section, Bacon's association between
music and the passions adds value to the study of music, but it does not
promote for it a higher, more intellectual sort of consideration. The
Dictionary is always upgrading poetry, but Davies is explicit about the
lower place of music when he describes it as a primitive prototype of
language: "And though this sense first *gentle*[3] musick found, / Her
proper object is the speech of men."

Naturally, the *Dictionary* respects holy music, but the tunes themselves are said to be primarily for the relatively primitive worshiper.
Hooker says, "To this purpose were those harmonious tunes of psalms
devised for us, that they, which are either in years but young, or
touching perfection of virtue as yet not grown to *ripeness*[3], might,
when they think they sing, learn." The great apologists for music in the

Dictionary are Peacham and Milton. Like Milton, Shakespeare describes music chiefly as a form of relaxation:

> Know the cause why musick was *ordain'd*[1];
> Was it not to refresh the mind of man
> After his studies, or his usual pain?

Peacham makes higher claims for music, but he speaks infrequently and often justifies his subject in terms of other arts. These justifications are helpful to Johnson: they often assist the entry of musical words that he might otherwise have neglected, but they also tend to reinforce the emphasis of his book on literary culture. Peacham saves "revert" by defining it in terms of the more familiar subject of rhetoric: "Hath not musick her figures the same with rhetorick? what is a *revert* but her antistrophe?" However, this is a Johnson's-*Dictionary* definition of the term—one that shows where Johnson's predilections lie.

8.3.2. Painting and Architecture

Painting and poesy are two sisters so like, that they lend[3] *to each other their name and office: one is called a dumb poesy, and the other a speaking picture.* Dryden's Dufresnoy.

In Johnson's implicit ordering of the arts, painting is higher than music: quotations concerning it are much more prominent, and its terminology is more comprehensively included. Johnson ensured this by taking a great many quotations from Dryden's translation of Du Fresnoy's *De Arte Graphica*. However, most of the quotations from Du Fresnoy actually come from Dryden's prefatory "Parallel betwixt Painting and Poetry," and these tend to discuss painting in terms of the art Dryden and Johnson knew best. For example, Dryden says, "To make a sketch, or a more perfect model of a picture, is, in the language of poets, to *draw*[52] up the scenary of a play." The normal language for Dryden and for the *Dictionary* in general is the language of literary description. The way this language tends to predominate in discussions even of the sister art is again evident in Dryden's words under "beautiful": "The principal and most important parts of painting, is to know what is most *beautiful* in nature, and most proper for that art; that which is the most *beautiful*, is the most noble subject: so, in poetry, tragedy is more *beautiful* than comedy, because the persons are greater whom the poet instructs, and consequently the instructions of more

benefit to mankind." As in the Horatian formula *ut pictura poesis*, poetry is most often the principal subject in the *Dictionary*'s analogies between the arts.

There are a few remarks by Dryden in the *Dictionary* that pertain solely to painting. Under "pleasingly" and "to perfectionate," for instance, Dryden formulates principles of imitation for painting. Furthermore, his translation of Du Fresnoy helps a little to elevate the dignity of painting by discussing its history and suggesting something of its royal lineage. One of the best contributions to this effort is under "mass": "The whole knowledge of groupes, of the lights and shadows, and of those *masses*[4] which Titian calls a bunch of grapes, is, in the prints of Rubens, exposed clearly to the sight." This has little of the force and design of Dryden's similar remarks on literary lineage, but it is a start for painting that music lacks altogether.

Visual art gets further support in the *Dictionary* by figuring much more prominently than does music in the plans of the educational theorists whom Johnson most often quotes. Locke does not stress its importance, but he does recommend for the student "so much insight into perspective, and skill in *drawing*[6], as will enable him to represent tolerably on paper any thing he sees. . . ." Locke's greater use for pictures in education has little to do with the fine art of drawing; most importantly, for Locke, pictures take the place of verbal definitions of words. In a representative passage he says, "[One] has a clearer idea from a little print than from a long definition; and so he would have of *strigil* and *sistrum*, if, instead of *currycomb* and cymbal, he could see stamped in the margin small pictures of these instruments." Quotations like this one from Locke's *Education* are commonplace on the title pages of dictionaries with prints, but Johnson's *Dictionary*, though it contains Locke's advice, offers no illustrations. With the rare exception of some printer's terms,[13] the space and money devoted to pictures in competing dictionaries, like Bailey's, went into illustrative quotations in Johnson's book. In this unusual departure from Locke's guidance, as in its infrequent attention to the fine arts, the *Dictionary* is obedient to its fundamentally literary nature.

Some specific instructional advice on drawing comes into the *Dictionary* from Peacham's *Graphice*, but even this is turned, in many cases, to literary uses. We learn how to shade the *ankle-bone* and draw a few other basic lines, but Johnson's Peacham is generally concerned with more allegorical subjects that make drawing narrative, articulate, and therefore literary. In the many instructions he adapts from Spenser, Peacham makes drawing serve poetry in another way. He says, for instance, "Dissimulation is expressed by a lady wearing a vizard of two faces, in her right-hand a *magpie*, which Spenser described looking through a lattice." As *The Preceptor*'s lessons indicate, the passions were considered among the most important subjects for the young artist to try. Peacham's adaptations of Spenser set just such assignments for Johnson's drawing students, but they also supply an allegorical literary interpretation. In the three entries under "forelock," none of which is from Peacham, the *Dictionary* demonstrates the use of such interpretation:

> Tell her the joyous time will not be staid,
> Unless she do him by the *forelock* take.
> *Spenser, Sonnet* 70.

> Zeal and duty are not slow,
> But on occasion's *forelock* watchful wait.
> *Milt. Parad. Reg.*

Time is painted with a lock before, and bald behind, signifying thereby that we must take time by the *forelock*; for, when it is once past, there is no recalling it. *Swift*.

Emblematic poetry like this is the closest the *Dictionary* gets to including pictures; a verbal picture is the kind of drawing it prefers.

Wotton's *Elements of Architecture* supplies the *Dictionary* with some information germane to that art, but the contributions are rare, and, like contributions to other arts, they are usually subordinate to some other end. In one of the longest quotations from his work, for instance, Wotton sounds as if he is talking about the construction of a play rather than an estate: "I make haste to the casting and comparting of the whole work, being indeed the very *definitive* sum of this art, to distribute usefully and gracefully a well chosen plot." Under "pillar" Wotton supplies a brief but proper description, yet many important architectural terms go unrecorded. The *Dictionary* is sporadic in its omissions in this area and probably represents the state of Johnson's own interests. "Corinthian" gets elaborate treatment from Harris's *Lexicon*, but neither "Doric" nor "Ionic" is listed at all. Johnson's predilections come out pretty clearly under "column," where he devotes most attention to the word's meaning in printing and least to its meaning in architecture. Two of the most frequent sources of architectural terminology in the *Dictionary* are Dryden's literary criticism and

Addison's *Travels in Italy*. In one case, architecture serves clearly as a vehicle for the more important theme of information about writing, and in the other, architecture is simply a conduit for Addison's admiration of Roman civilization. Such subordination shows the lowly place reserved for the fine arts in general throughout Johnson's curriculum.

8.4. The Professions of the Gown

Johnson's third definition of "gown" is "The long habit of a man dedicated to acts of peace, as divinity, medicine, law." The first definition of "doctor" is "One that has taken the highest degree in the faculties of divinity, law, or physick." The *Dictionary* recognizes these three professions above all others, and it supplies some preparation for them while serving the more immediate and important aims of lexicography and basic education. Yet visible and separable from its most prominent aims is the *Dictionary*'s largely satirical characterization of the three professions.

8.4.1. Medicine

A painter became a physician; whereupon one said to him, you have done well; for before the faults of your work were seen, but now they are unseen[1]. Bacon.

Quincy, Hill, Sharp, and Wiseman fill the *Dictionary* with a good deal of genuine medical knowledge and quite a full measure of medical terminology—lexicography, especially the encyclopedic branch of it that Johnson pursues, requires this much. But more obscure and less optimistic intentions lead to the admission of much satire on medical practice. Temple dismisses the whole art when he says, "It is best to leave nature to her *course*[14], who is the sovereign physician in most diseases." Baker does as much by declaring that medicine is not a science but merely a display of shifting fashions: "At *one*[3] time they keep their patients so warm, as almost to stifle them, and all of a sudden the cold regimen is in vogue." South is more vituperative, describing doctors as sophisticated murderers: "When he intends to bereave the world of an illustrious person, he may cast him upon a bold *self*[8]-opinioned physician, worse than his distemper, who shall make a shift to cure him into his grave." The *Dictionary*'s warnings about the danger of physicians are a long-standing part of the cultural wisdom it transmits, as a passage from Mark 5.26 suggests: "A woman *suffered*[1] many things of physicians, and spent all she had." There may be a proper way for physicians to treat patients; unfortunately, like other viae mediae in Johnson's book, it is difficult to locate. Bacon is representative when he describes the extremes that even honest physicians use to torture their patients: "Physicians are some of them so conformable to the humour of the patient, as they press not the true cure of the disease; and some *other*[2] are so regular in proceeding according to art, as they respect not the condition of the patient."

8.4.2. Divinity

If others may glory *in their birth, why may not me, whose parents were called by God to attend on him at his altar?* Atter*[bury]*.

The overwhelming majority of theological material in the *Dictionary* is made up of unsophisticated reminders of religious fundamentals (see below, chapter 9). Religion is the most important subject in Johnson's curriculum, but the learned science of divinity gets no more specific treatment than does medicine, natural history, or any of a number of other subjects. Indeed, there is some debate in the *Dictionary* as to whether or not learning is essential to the primary duties of a divine. Under "to pitch[2]" Hooker says there is "no need to mention the learning of a fit, or the unfitness of an ignorant minister," but elsewhere he acknowledges that there is a fundamental level of religious truth that does not require special learning: "If all the clergy were as learned as themselves are that most complain of *ignorance*[1] in others, yet our book of common prayer might remain the same." Swift is the writer who most often warns the prospective divines among Johnson's readers against misplaced learning, with statements like the following: "A *divine*[1] has nothing to say to the wisest congregation, which he may not express in a manner to be understood by the meanest among them." He concludes that "in preaching, no men succeed better than those who trust entirely to the stock or *fund*[1] of their reason, advanced indeed, but not overlaid by commerce with books." This is close to the *Dictionary*'s overall view, but South and

Atterbury, among others, guard against a drastic diminution of respect for learning among the clergy. South deplores a recent decline in standards when he says, "The ignorant took heart to enter upon this great calling, and instead of their cutting their way to it through the knowledge of the tongues, the fathers and councils, they have taken another and a shorter *cut*[8]." Atterbury is the greatest champion of the clergy in the *Dictionary*, and part of his class pride is involved in learning. He addresses his tribe, "Ye are the sons of a clergy, whose *undissembled*[2] and unlimited veneration for the holy scriptures, hath not hindered them from paying an inferiour, but profound regard to the best interpreters of it, the primitive writers." The extent to which this is a proud reclamation of distinction appears in its contrast to the warning about pride in learning that Richardson makes to the clergy and that the *Dictionary* transmits to all: "A good clergyman must love and *venerate* the gospel that he teaches, and prefer it to all other learning."

An issue related to the place of learning in the clerical life is the question of whether sermons should be read or spoken extempore. South and Swift are antagonists in this debate. South says, "The *extemporizing* faculty is never more out of its element than in the pulpit," and Swift counters, "I cannot *get*[11] *over* the prejudice of taking some little offence at the clergy, for perpetually reading their sermons." An examination of Johnson's marked copy of South's sermons shows that South would surely have had the best of this debate if Johnson had not intervened. South devoted two entire sermons to a campaign against extempore addresses from the pulpit, but these two alone Johnson omitted to mark for illustrative quotations, although he heavily marked the other sermons in the volume. In his own sermons Johnson follows the homiletical rather than the extempore tradition, as James Gray and Jean Hagstrom have shown (*Yale* 14: xli–xlii). The *Dictionary* is full of such carefully prepared works and implicitly recommends them, but it appears that Johnson was unwilling to enlist his book in an internecine ecclesiastical debate. Such an unwillingness to take sides in intramural religious disputes is characteristic of all of Johnson's religious pronouncements, but he seems to have taken special care to avoid such presumption in the *Dictionary*. The reason for this, I think, is that he intended his book to present a general, largely noncontroversial round of education, such as that provided in *The Preceptor*.

Part of the reason Atterbury speaks proudly about his tribe is that he wished to elevate their social standing and improve their worldly reputation. Johnson allows Atterbury to carry on his campaign to some extent, quoting his declarations that "St. Chrysostom, as great a lover and *recommender* of the solitary state as he was, declares it to be no proper school for those who are to be leaders of Christ's flock," and that "the clergy have gained some insight into men and things, and a *competent*[3] knowledge of the world." Added social prominence, however, brings added risks and responsibilities, and Rogers makes this point very clearly: "The *ministers*[3] of the gospel are especially required to shine as lights in the world, because the distinction of their station renders their conduct more observable; and the presumption of their knowledge, and the dignity of their office, gives a peculiar force and authority to their example." In another important place, South and Dryden team up to remind prospective divines of their first responsibility: "Many," says South, "while they have preached Christ in their *sermons*, have read a lecture of atheism in their practice." Dryden adds, "His preaching much, but more his practice wrought; / A living *sermon* of the truths he taught."

Johnson's extremely high consciousness of this particular duty may be what kept him from a clerical life and even from theological dispute. The *Dictionary*'s advice to the clergy makes the obligation of proper social conduct too strict for Johnson's habitual irregularity and too profound in its consequences for Johnson's feverish sense of how much would be expected of him on Judgment Day. Collier puts the responsibility of the divine in terms that I think Johnson must have found awesome when he defines an ecclesiastical word with a debased social significance: "I thought the English of *curate* had been an ecclesiastical hireling.—No such matter; the proper import of the word signifies one who has the cure of souls."

8.4.3. Law

Is the law evil, because some lawyers *in their office swerve from it?* Whitgift.

Civil law and history are studies which a gentleman should not barely touch*[3] at, but constantly dwell upon.* Locke.

The *Dictionary* honors the law as an institution essential to government and as a study of importance to every citizen, but it treats the practitioners of the law—jurymen, judges, and lawyers—with severity and suspicion. Apparently examining their products, Swift declares, "The inns of court must be the worst instituted *seminaries*[5] in any Christian country." Milton analyzes the problem further in an appropriate place: "Some are allured to law, not on the contemplation of equity, but on the promising and pleasing thoughts of litigious terms, *fat*[3] contentions, and flowing fees." Pope notices that lawyers are well placed for illicit profit, and at the same time he contributes to a small stream of rough but sympathetic humor that the *Dictionary* seems to pour out for its amanuenses: "Alas, the small *discredit* of a bribe, / Scarce hurts the lawyer but undoes the scribe."[14] A more famous couplet by Pope is used to illustrate a key word in the language of professional law: "The hungry judges soon the sentence sign / And wretches hang that *jurymen* may dine." Another of Pope's satires on the practice of law derives from Donne, as the *Dictionary* shows. Donne says, "In parchment then, large as the fields, he draws / Assurances, big as *gloss'd*[1] civil laws"—while nearby, Pope bears witness to his theft:

> Indentures, cov'nants, articles they draw,
> Large as the fields themselves, and larger far
> Than civil codes with all their *glosses*[1] are.

Frequently in the pages of the *Dictionary* lawyers and judges are made to pay for their abuses by serving as the butts of humorous tales. Addison reports, "When Innocent XI. desired the marquis of Carpio to furnish thirty thousand *head*[4] of swine, he could not spare them; but thirty thousand lawyers he had at his service." Swift retails an account of grimly poetic justice: "An Eastern king put a judge to death for an iniquitous sentence; and ordered his hide to be stuffed into a *cushion*, and placed upon the tribunal, for the son to sit on." Bacon's apothegm is less violent though more damning: "A poor blind man was accounted cunning in prognosticating weather: Epsom, a lawyer, said in scorn, Tell me, *father*[3], when doth the sun change? The old man answered, when such a wicked lawyer as you goeth to heaven." These lashings are funny and may even suggest a degree of camaraderie, but Shakespeare provides the motto for their serious side when he observes, "*Plate*[2] sin with gold, / And the strong lance of justice hurtless breaks."

Civil law is important in itself as a foundation of society, but it has added significance in the *Dictionary* due to its relations with divine and natural law. For the honor of originating society, law competes with poetry. For example, Atterbury points out, "We, who see men under the awe of justice, cannot conceive, what savage creatures they would be without it; and much *beholden* we are *to* that wise contrivance." Bacon also notes the pioneering work of law in mapping society when he declares, "The mislayer of a merstone is to blame; but the unjust judge is the capital *remover* of landmarks, when he defineth amiss." The origins of civil law, however, are in a nature that is not merely savage but already invested with order. South perceives that "all the laws of nations were but a *paraphrase* upon this standing rectitude of nature. . . ." Likewise Hooker: "Out of the precepts of the law of nature, as of certain, common, and *undemonstrable* principles, man's reason doth necessarily proceed unto certain more particular determinations: which particular determinations being found out according unto the reason of man, they have the names of human laws." In another sense, civil law is an expression of divine law and an imperfect version of it; Bacon suggests such a relation when he argues that something "is lawful, both, *by*[9] the laws of nature and nations, and *by* the law divine, which is the perfection of the other two."

Even without the intermediary support of natural law, the *Dictionary* finds ways of affirming an underlying connection between civil law and religion. The *Dictionary* represents society in general as dependent upon religion, and Bentley uses a connection between law and religion as a step in his contribution to the argument: "What government can be imagined, without judicial proceedings? and what methods of judicature, without a religious oath, which supposes an omniscient being, as conscious to its falsehood or truth, and a *revenger*[2] of perjury." Hooker is less logical in his construction but maintains equal conviction: "So natural is the union of religion with justice, that we may boldly *deem* there is neither, where both are not." Atterbury's language makes the point implicitly when he says, "A just and wise magistrate is a *blessing*[3] as extensive as the community to which he belongs: a *blessing* which includes all other *blessings* whatsoever that relate to this life." Under the important word in legal language "chancellor," Johnson takes the unusual step of printing gratuitously some Latin verses from "*Nigel de Wetekre* to the Bishop of Ely, chancellor to Richard I," thus helping to affirm the connection between civil law and piety:

Quæsitus regni tibi cancellarius *Angli,*
   Primus solliciti mente petendus erit.
Hic est, qui regni leges cancellat iniquas,
   Et mandata pii principis æqua facit.[15]

Like every other subject in the *Dictionary*, law is most important when it serves pious ends, and like every other part of learning, it is inevitably prone to error. Baker declares the inadequacy of law just as he declares the inadequacy of every other department of human language and learning: "No human laws are exempt from faults, since those that have been looked upon as most perfect in their *kind*[2], have been found, upon enquiry, to have so many." Hooker also finds that "laws are many times full of *imperfections*; and that which is supposed *behooveful* unto men, proveth oftentimes most pernicious." Dryden brings out the satirical humor that often accompanies Lactantian observations of human learning:

> The man who laugh'd but once to see an ass
> Mumbling to make the cross-grain'd thistles pass,
> Might laugh again, to see a jury chaw
> The *prickles* of unpalatable law.

One sign of the imperfection of laws is their perpetual mutability; as Hooker says, "Laws, that have been approved, may be again *repealed*[2], and disputed against by the authors themselves." Dryden describes the process of change as more regular but no less likely: "Statutes are silently *repealed*[2], when the reason ceases for which they were enacted." A legal system is like a language, as Johnson recognizes in the "Plan" (*Works*, Oxford 5: 16), and observations of legal mutability often sound like Johnson's lamentations of verbal corruption. The impossible ideal is stated by Spenser: "Laws ought to be like stony tables, plain, *steadfast*[1], and immoveable." But the body of quotation in the *Dictionary* is no more sanguine about the possibility of realizing this ideal than is Johnson's preface about its wish that "signs might be permanent, like the things which they denote" (par. 17). Indeed the vanity of wishes for the permanence of earthly things is a theme that pervades the *Dictionary*'s accounts of every human endeavor.

9. Fundamentals

One of the many intellectual desiderata that Bacon established for the following generation was an answer to the question of "what points of religion are fundamental, and what perfective, being matter of farther building and perfection upon one and the same foundation" (*Works* 2: 542). The scholar who tried most vigorously to advance learning in this area was Henry Hammond, an Oxford theologian who suffered during the interregnum but survived to produce many heavy volumes. Johnson admired Hammond and evidently purchased copies of his *Works* for young men going into orders (*Johnsonian Miscellanies* 2: 19). Likewise, he recommends Hammond to all readers of the *Dictionary* by quoting widely from his *Practical Catechism* and from his *Fundamentals*, the book in which he most specifically and comprehensively addresses Bacon's question. Hammond's *Fundamentals* is the backbone of the *Dictionary*'s treatment of this essential part of its whole curriculum, but many other authors strengthen it and flesh it out with extensive contributions of their own.

Hammond was apostolic about the need to distinguish between the fundamental and the perfective parts of religion; his fervor reflects his experience of the divisive religious controversies of his day, but he expresses it in terms consistent with the *Dictionary*'s timeless, Lactantian reminders of the vanity of human learning.[1] Like other Lactantian writers, Hammond's perennial foe is opinion. Typically he decries "that great scandal in the church of God, at which so many myriads of *solifidians* have stumbled, and fallen *irreversibly*, by conceiving heaven a reward for true opinions." All writers in the *Dictionary* agree with Hammond that the fundamentals of religion are easy to understand, incontrovertible, and readily available in the most obvious sources. Theological disputes have no effect on fundamentals; in fact, as John Stephens ingeniously suggests, such disputes strengthen their solidity: "A difference in their sentiments as to particular questions, is no *valid*[2] argument against the general truth believed by them, but rather a clearer and more solid proof of it." Attempts to go beyond "general truth" in religion are merely vain, and Swift's discouragement of them is representative of the *Dictionary*'s attitude: "Men should consider, that raising *difficulties*[5] concerning the mysteries in religion, cannot make them more wise, learned, or virtuous." Similarly, Hooker finds that everything necessary to religion is "*expressly* set down in Scripture," and the most important things are in the most prominent places: "The decalogue of Moses declareth *summarily* those things which we ought to do; the prayer of our Lord, whatsoever we should request or desire." Consequently, as Rogers says, "All the great lines of our duty are clear and *obvious*[3]. . . ."

9.1. Faith, Hope, and Charity

> *That God will forgive, may, indeed, be established as the first and fundamental truth of religion; for though the knowledge of his existence is the origin of philosophy, yet, without the belief of his mercy, it would have little influence upon our moral conduct.* (Rambler *110*, Yale *4: 221*)

The only points of faith that matter are reducible to an incontrovertible rule, while all other points of theology are opinions circulating perpetually in and out of favor: "The rule of faith is alone unmoveable and *unreformable*; to wit, of believing in one only God omnipotent, creator of the world, and in his son Jesus Christ, born of the virgin Mary." A Christian life must be built on this rule before there can be any hope of salvation; but there is a second half of Hammond's fundamental religion: "Two notions of fundamentals may be conceived, one signifying that whereon our eternal bliss is immediately *superstructed*, the other whereon our obedience to the faith of Christ is founded" (see Hammond, *Works* 1: 462). The other half of fundamental religion is active obedience or good works. This comes out very plainly in Hammond's attack on a Protestant doctrine: "He that is so sure of his particular election, as to resolve he can never fall, if he commit those acts, against which scripture is plain, must necessarily resolve, that nothing but the removing his fundamental error can *rescue* him from the superstructive." The bipartite conception of religious fundamentals appears frequently in the *Dictionary*, often in sublime, gnomic statements. Tillotson says, "To fear the Lord, and depart from evil, are *phrases*[2] which the scripture useth to express the sum of religion," which is a comment on Ecclesiastes 12.13: "Fear God, and keep his commandments, for this is the *whole* of man." Rogers employs two sets of the fundamental binary pair, but the message is the same: "He who feareth God, and worketh righteousness, and perseveres in the faith and duties of our religion, shall certainly be *saved*[2]."

Johnson's own bipartite sense of fundamentals comes out in his definition of the key word "religion" as "virtue, as founded upon reverence of God, and expectation of future rewards and punishments." Faith in God has the priority in fundamentals, but it is useless without hope, which entails the other primary Christian virtues. Hooker teaches: "Not that God doth require nothing unto happiness at the hands of men, saving only a *naked*[4] belief, for hope and charity we may not exclude; but that without belief all other things are as nothing, and it is the ground of those other divine virtues." Hope is even more prominent in Johnson's expressions of fundamentals, as *Rambler* 110 shows (see the epigraph above). In the *Dictionary* Johnson enters one of many biblical versions of the conviction under "spirit," an entry that may be especially significant because its attribution simply to "*Bible*" suggests that he quoted it from memory: "The *spirit*[3] shall return unto God that gave it." Forbes makes a similar reduction: "The lowest degree of faith, that can *quiet*[1] the soul of man, is a firm conviction that God is placable." The Common Prayer supplies this conviction in another form: "He pardoneth all them that truly repent, and *unfeignedly* believe his holy gospel" (here again, the lack of specificity in the attribution suggests that Johnson was quoting from memory). Compression of the dual fundamentals of religion puts an emphasis upon repentance that is characteristic of Johnson's religious writing. This emphasis shows up in the *Dictionary* in Johnson's energetic, pathetic definition of "penitence" and in many illustrative quotations. To give just one example, Hammond says, "The condition required of us is a constellation of all the gospel graces, every one of them rooted in the heart, though mixed with much weakness, and perhaps with many sins, so they be not wilfully, and *impenitently* lived and died in."

Faith and hope may be sufficient for the personal practice of religion, but religion also has a social aspect. The social meaning of religion is evident in a quotation from Camden under "anchor-hold": "The old English could express most aptly all the conceits of the mind in their own tongue, without borrowing from any; as for example: the holy service of God, which the Latins called *religion*, because it knitted the minds of men together, and most people of Europe have borrowed the same from them, they called most significantly *ean-fastness*, as the one and only assurance and fast *anchor-hold* of our souls health." This is a quintessential entry in Johnson's *Dictionary* because it so thoroughly combines the book's two main subjects, religion and philology; the combination is just as tight, though less surprising, in Johnson's treatment of some key religious words. Unlike Camden, Watts explains the social meaning of religion without invoking etymological support: "*Religion*[1] or virtue, in a large sense, includes duty to God and our neighbour. . . ." The social sense of religion also appears in Hooker's discussion of "church": "The *church*[1] being a supernatural society, doth differ from natural societies in this; that the persons unto whom we associate ourselves in the one, are men, simply considered as men; but they to whom we be joined in the other, are God, angels, and holy men." The specific human quality required for this religious fellowship is variously spoken of as charity, love, and mercy, and the terms are sometimes equated. Wake makes a point in the *Dictionary*'s book of fundamentals when he declares, "Charity *taken*[11] in its largest extent, is nothing else but the sincere love of God and our neighbour." The entries under the nominal, adjectival, and adverbial forms of "uncharitable" reiterate the point, which is summed up in Atterbury's simple and terrible remark, "Heaven and hell are the proper regions of mercy and *uncharitableness*."

The *Dictionary* treats human fellowship as a fundamental aspect of religious life and issues frequent reminders of its supernatural connections. Under "relation" Johnson allows Sprat some scope for a proper reminder of this kind: "Are we not to pity and supply the poor, though they have no *relation*[4] to us? no *relation*? that cannot be: the gospel styles them all our brethren; nay, they have a nearer *relation* to us, our fellow-members; and both these from their *relation* to our Saviour himself, who calls them his brethren." In Calamy's description, fellowship is equally sacred because it is part of God's plan: "There is no man but God puts excellent things into his possession, to be used for the common good; for men are made for society and mutual *fellowship*[1]." According to Bacon, even those living in the darkness before the advent of Christ achieved a sort of religious feeling by noticing "the supreme and indissoluable *consanguinity* and society between men in general; of which the heathen poet, whom the apostle calls to witness, saith, We are all his generation." The supreme practical lesson to be drawn from the existence of universal fellowship is the golden rule, and Locke provides one of its many articulations in

the *Dictionary*: "To love our neighbour as ourselves is such a fundamental truth for the regulating human society, that by that alone one
might determine all the cases in *social*[1] morality." South puts it a little
differently, but he maintains the crucial calculus of reciprocity: "Actions, that promote society and mutual fellowship, seem *reducible* to a
proneness to do good to others, and a ready sense of any good done by
others."

As an instance and an exponent of universal fellowship, friendship is
one of the chief blessings in the world of the *Dictionary*. Conversely,
solitude and bad fellowship are two of the vilest curses. In the words of
L'Estrange, "Good or bad company is the greatest blessing or greatest
plague[3] of life." South details the beneficial effects of friendship in
philosophical language: "Joy, like a ray of the sun, reflects with a
greater *ardour*[2] and *quickness*[1], when it rebounds upon a man from
the breast of his friend." Under "percase" Bacon uses the same
analogy to describe the effects of company on virtue, but elsewhere he
delivers the message in plainest speech: "A good sure friend is a better
help at a *pinch*[4], than all the stratagems of a man's own wit." Bacon is
also one of the *Dictionary*'s monitors on the danger of solitude: "It had
been hard to have put more truth and untruth together, in few words,
than in that speech; whosoever is delighted with *solitude*[1], is either a
wild beast or a god." Sidney lets us know where the untruth is in a
nearby quotation: "You subject yourself to *solitariness*, the sly enemy
that doth most separate a man from well doing." Johnson discusses the
matter in *Rambler* 138 and finds solitude one of the harshest sorrows to
which the learned are exposed. Indeed, the need of company is a proof
of the vanity of human learning: "No degree of knowledge attainable
by man is able to set him above the want of hourly assistance, or to
extinguish the desire of fond endearments, and tender officiousness"
(*Yale* 4: 364). Johnson thought friendship so essential that he once
wished he had learned to play cards for the sake of promoting it
(Boswell 5: 404). He himself clearly had a great personal need for
company, and he probably had the clubability that Boswell ascribes to
him, but his recorded statements on friendship and solitude should be
related to a public and long-standing tradition of religious remarks on
the subject before they are interpreted as expressions of his individual
personality. The *Dictionary* shows that friendship and solitude are
conventional subjects of great importance to the fundamentals of
religion that Johnson wished to promulgate in all his publications and,
no doubt, in many of his recorded conversations.

God is to the understanding*[1] of man, as the light of the sun is to our eyes, its first and most glorious object.* Tillotson.

The existence of God is not only the prime object of faith in the world of the *Dictionary*, it is also the foremost point of knowledge and, paradoxically, of ignorance. The knowledge of God is at the center of the controversy about innate ideas in the *Dictionary* and the exception to Locke's tabula rasa that is most frequently entertained. Tillotson further says, "God not only *rivetted*[2] the notion of himself into our natures, but likewise made the belief of his being necessary to the peace of our minds and happiness of society." Locke himself assigns a special place to knowledge of God, although he does not quite make it innate: "There is no truth which a man may more evidently *make*[49] out to himself, than the existence of a God."

Besides simply declaring that God's existence is obvious, the *Dictionary* also provides numerous proofs. Part of the evidence is the universal testimony of mankind. Citing a scholar famous for extending his researches as far as China, Stillingfleet reports, "Kircher *lays*[38] it *down* as a certain principle, that there never was any people so rude, which did not acknowledge and worship one supreme deity." Elsewhere Stillingfleet adds the testimony of the learned ancients: "Plato, and the *rest* of the philosophers, acknowledged the unity, power, wisdom, goodness, and providence of the supreme God." Under "poetical" and "link[1]" Hale brings in the oft-cited beginning of *Iliad* 8, and Hooker in another place adds, "The wise and learned amongst the very heathens themselves, have all acknowledged some first *cause*[1] whereupon originally the being of all things dependeth; neither have they otherwise spoken of that *cause*, than as an agent, which, knowing what and why it worketh, observeth, in working, a most exact order or law."

Hooker's remark adds to the testimonial evidence for God's existence, but he also alludes to the more rational demonstration of reasoning from the effects to the cause. The motto that Thomas Birch affixed to the collected works of Boyle sums up the proof of God that is most prominent in the *Dictionary*: *Ex rerum Causis Supremam noscere Causam.*[2] Tillotson lists this proof as an equally powerful alternative to direct instantiation of the knowledge that God exists: "We come to be assured that there is such a being, either by an internal impression of the notion of a God upon our minds, or else by such *external*[1] and visible effects as our reason tells us must be attributed to some cause, and which we cannot attribute to any other but such as we conceive God to be." The whole subject of natural history in the *Dictionary*, to which Boyle makes substantial contributions both in his own right and in the lectures he funded, is one continued proof of God's existence *ex rerum causis*. Wimsatt shows this conclusively in *Philosophic Words*, and an appreciation of the point tempts us to read Johnson's adduction of Cheyne under "to beget" as a statement in propria persona: "My whole intention was to *beget*[2], in the minds of men, magnificent sentiments of God and his works."

Boyle and the *Dictionary*'s other natural philosophers establish the wisdom, power, and glory of God as revealed in the creation, but his goodness is the attribute for which contributors to the *Dictionary* have most often to fight. The Manichean indictment of God as the author of evil is the adversary. Raleigh states the *Dictionary*'s orthodox view: "God is absolutely good, and so, *assuredly*, the cause of all that is good; but, of any thing that is evil, he is no cause at all." The arguments for this position tend not to be subtle in the *Dictionary* but to rely on assumptions about the nature of God. Hence, Hammond asks us merely to "consider the absurdities of that distinction betwixt the act and the obliquity, and the contrary being so *wide*[3] from the truth of scripture and the attributes of God, and so noxious to good life, we may certainly conclude, that to the perpetration of whatsoever sin, there is not at all any predestination of God." The Manichean conflation of foreknowledge and predetermination in the fall of man is the particular point of controversy here, as it is in South's similar defense of God's goodness: "To assert that God looked upon Adam's fall as a sin, and punished it as *such*[3], when, without any antecedent sin, he withdrew that actual grace, upon which it was impossible for him not to fall, highly reproaches the essential equity of the Divine Nature."

A fundamental point of religion correlative to belief in God is a belief in the existence and benevolence of providence. There are elaborate proofs of providence in Raleigh and Hakewill, and parts of their pious histories come into the *Dictionary*, but more widespread are simple assertions of providence as a necessary, logical result of God's own existence. South says, for example, "Creation must needs infer providence; and God's making the world, irrefragably proves that he governs it too; or that a being of a dependent nature remains *nevertheless* independent upon him in that respect." Hooker makes the declaration more metaphysical and sees providence as an aspect of God's omnipresence: "All things are therefore partakers of God; they are his offspring, his influence is in them, and the personal wisdom of God is for that very cause said to excel in *nimbleness* or agility, to pierce into all intellectual, pure and subtile spirits, to go through all, and to reach unto every thing which is." One of the reasons that the *Dictionary* is assiduous in its efforts to discourage pseudodoxical practices involving fortune and chance (above, pp. 71–72) is that belief in these notions is inconsistent with belief in providence. South makes this clear in a pair of consecutive quotations: first he says, "To say a thing is a chance, as it relates to second causes, signifies no more, than that there are some events *beside*[3] the knowledge, purpose, expectation, and power of second causes"; then he explains, "Providence often disposes of things by a method *beside*, and above the discoveries of man's reason."

As the divine efficiency, providence participates in the goodness of God. Woodward makes a declaration about providence with which all natural philosophers in the *Dictionary* agree: "If we look into its retired movements, and more secret *latent* springs, we may there trace out a steady hand producing good out of evil." One of Milton's many vindications of this theme appears under an important word in the *Dictionary*'s language of divinity:

> All is best, though we often doubt
> What th' *unsearchable* disposer
> Of highest wisdom brings about,
> And ever best found in the close.

Adversity tries this optimistic view of providence, and the *Dictionary* prepares its readers for such trials of faith with remarks like Wake's, "God proves us in this life, that he may the more *plenteously* reward us in the next." Characteristically, Addison finds a classical precedent for this point of Christian religion: "Plato *lays*[38] it *down* as a principle, that whatever is permitted to befal a just man, whether poverty or sickness, shall, either in life or death, conduce to his good."

Social inequity presents another threat to the notion that there is a just providence in the operation of the world, and the writers in the *Dictionary* find various ways of deflecting this threat. Addison simply denies it: "Providence, for the most part, set us upon a *level*[3], and observes a kind of proportion in its dispensations towards us." Grew confesses the apparent inequalities but says they have no significance from the divine point of view: "God values no man more or less, in

placing him high or low, but every one as he *maintains*[2] his post."
L'Estrange adds to this tranquilizing sermon, "Every man has his
post[5] assigned to him, and in that station he is well, if he can but think
himself so." These comforts bear a dangerous resemblance to denials,
like Soame Jenyns's, that there is any real evil in the world. The
difference between Jenyns's notion, which Johnson despised, and the
orthodox theodicy promulgated by the *Dictionary* is the difference
between arrogance and humility, as Locke demonstrates: "I think it a
good argument to say, the infinitely wise God hath made it so: and
therefore it is *best*[1]. But it is too much confidence of our wisdom, to
say, I think it *best*, and therefore God hath made it so."

The subject of providence rarely comes up in the *Dictionary* without
some reminder of human ignorance: we cannot see the total order and
are therefore unable to judge its benevolence. Dryden expresses
human ignorance of the divine will in terms of the great chain of being,
an image often associated with providence:

> *Purblind* man
> Sees but a part o' th' chain, the nearest links;
> His eyes not carrying to that equal beam,
> That poises all above.

Taylor draws the proper lesson from this reminder: "Submission is the
only reasoning between a creature and its Maker, and *contentment*[1] in
his will is the best remedy we can apply to misfortunes." Reminders of
ignorance are not quite as thoroughgoing on the subject of God's
person as they are on the subject of his governing will, but they are very
conspicuous. On Johnson's field of knowledge God has a paradoxical
position: he is the first and surest object of knowledge, and he is the
object that most conclusively proves our incurable ignorance. Hooker
beautifully sums up the paradox of God, "Whom although to know be
life, and joy to make mention of his name; yet our *soundest*[2] knowledge is to know that we know him not as he is, neither can know him:
and our safest eloquence concerning him is silence." Addison adds
testimonial evidence to the proposition that God is unknowable when
he reports, "Simonides, the more he contemplated the nature of the
Deity, found that he *waded*[2] but the more out of his depth, and that
he lost himself in thought." Probably reading the then misdated *Corpus
Hermeticum*, Taylor thinks he goes back even further to find, "The
Egyptians used to say, that unknown darkness is the first principle of

the world; by darkness they mean God, whose secrets are *pervious*[1] to no eye."

At the end of Bacon's *Works* appears his "Student's Prayer," a short monitory work that could well serve as the benediction for Johnson's whole feast of knowledge; Bacon prays that "human things may not prejudice such as are divine" and that "there may be given unto faith the things that are faith's" (*Works* 4: 488). Dryden provides the *Dictionary* with a versification of the theme (above, p. 56), and Prior seems to apply the warning to the lexicographer himself:

> Your God, forsooth, is found
> Incomprehensible and infinite;
> But is he therefore found? Vain searcher! no:
> Let your imperfect definition show,
> That nothing you, the weak *definer*, know.

Among the many failures of learning, is that no branch of it can perfect the knowledge of God. On the contrary, gaining knowledge of God is a process of perfecting ourselves in an unintellectual way. The important point to remember is what Atterbury argues under a key word in the language of learning: "Acquaintance with God is not a speculative knowledge, built on abstracted reasonings about his nature and essence, such as *philosophical*[2] minds often busy themselves in, without reaping from thence any advantage towards regulating their passions, but practical knowledge." Like other kinds of knowledge in the *Dictionary* but to an immeasurably higher degree, knowledge of God is attended with inevitable ignorance, and it is worthless unless it culminates in virtue.

9.3. Freedom

> Freely*[5] they stood who stood, and fell who fell:*
> *Not* free*[3], what proof could they have giv'n sincere*
> *Of true allegiance, constant faith, or love,*
> *Where only what they needs must do, appear'd;*
> *Not what they would?*
>   Milton's Paradise Lost, b. *iii.*

Another component of the *Dictionary*'s fundamental religious teaching is the doctrine of free will. Human freedom is essential to the vindication of God's goodness, and it is logically necessary to any concept of morality, as the *Dictionary* sees it. Milton's famous assertions of human freedom are quoted under "freely[5]," "free[3]," "freedom[4]," and "destiny[2]"; by choosing these illustrations Johnson emphasizes the religious and moral significance of freedom. Moreover, these famous quotations in obvious places are only the more visible traces of a deep and continuous vein of teaching on the subject. In less immortal lines, for example, Arbuthnot reiterates the pronouncements of Milton's God:

> Faultless thou dropt from his unerring skill,
> With the bare power to sin, since free of will;
> Yet charge not with thy guilt his bounteous love,
> For who has power to walk, has power to *rove*.

Johnson allocates valuable space to Hammond in order to explain one of the knottier problems of free will: "This *predetermination* of God's own will is so far from being the determining of ours, that it is distinctly the contrary; for supposing God to predetermine that I shall act freely; 'tis certain from thence, that my will is free in respect of God, and not predetermined."[3] Locke makes the point in the plainest possible way: "Our voluntary actions are the precedent causes of good and evil, which they *draw*[17] after them, and bring upon us."

Although many of Johnson's sources for quotations contain anti-Manichean arguments for freedom, the works of John Bramhall are exclusively concerned with the subject, and Johnson ensures an increase in his book's teaching on the subject by including many excerpts from *A Defence of True Liberty from Ante-Cedent and Extrinsecall Necessity* and *Castigations of Mr Hobbes His Last Animadversions, in the Case concerning Liberty, and Universal Necessity*. Bramhall attacks Hobbes in both these works on the grounds that his theory "makes second causes and outward objects to be the rackets, men to be but the balls of destiny. It makes the first cause, that is, God almighty, to be the introducer of all evil, and sin into the world . . ." (*Defence of True Liberty* 60). In the *Dictionary* Bramhall justifies his own literary efforts by saying, "To *clear*[3] the Deity *from* the imputation of tyranny, injustice, and dissimulation, which none do throw upon God with more presumption than those who are the patrons of absolute necessity, is both comely and christian." Most of Johnson's excerpts from Bramhall are

not as pithy and complete as this one, but they all make some
contribution to the establishment of freedom as a religious fundamental. Furthermore, Bramhall's very presence, along with Hobbes's absence, is significant: like many other eighteenth-century works, the
Dictionary is, in part, a reaction to Hobbes's deterministic theory and
the Manichean heresy it promotes. Some indication that Johnson
intended this part of his teaching in the *Dictionary* appears in Boswell's
account of a conversation in 1769 in which Boswell antagonistically
contended that "an universal prescience in the Deity" necessitates
predestination. Boswell reports that Johnson "mentioned Dr. Clarke,
and Bishop Bramhall on Liberty and Necessity, and bid me read
South's Sermons on Prayer; but avoided the question which has
excruciated philosophers and divines, beyond any other" (Boswell 2:
104). This is just what Johnson implicitly advises in the *Dictionary*, and
if he personally had doubts on this fundamental point, he allows his
readers to see no more of them than he allowed the religiously
confused Boswell to see in 1769.[4]

To the extent that it is separable from religion, freedom also has a
purely moral sense, the importance of which the *Dictionary* also
stresses. South is among those who talk about this separate but
essential value: "The *morality*[2] of an action is founded in the
freedom of that principle, by virtue of which it is in the agent's power,
having all things ready and requisite to the performance of an action,
either to perform or not perform it." Grew argues his way to the same
point: "To talk of compelling a man to be good, is a contradiction; for
where there is force, there can be no *choice*[2]. Whereas all moral
goodness consisteth in the elective act of the understanding will."
Johnson's inclusion of the last sentence here is an obvious indication of
the way his didactic purposes often led him to go above and beyond his
philological duty. The last sentence is philologically superfluous, but
because it drives home one of the most important lessons in Johnson's
book, it stands.

Johnson's most overt transmission of the message about freedom
and morality appears in his exuberant etymological note on "caitiff"
(above, p. 117). Johnson finds codified in several languages an inherent connection between meanness and slavery, and South corroborates
Johnson's finding: "The name of servants has of old been reckoned to
imply a certain meanness of mind, as well as *lowness*[3] of condition."
By an extension of the same reasoning, freedom is described as an
essential quality of the human spirit. Under "to link[6]" Locke says,

"the ideas of men and self-determination appear to be connected." When slavery takes away freedom, it destroys the rest of the spirit's powers along with virtue. Addison implies as much when he says, "There is a kind of sluggish *resignation*[2], as well as *poorness*[2] and degeneracy of spirit, in a state of slavery, that very few will recover themselves out of it." But sluggishness itself, as a failure to exercise freedom, is a decadent state of mind, whether or not it is imposed by social conditions. Another important word for this slavish frame of mind is said to grow out of the language of class, and Johnson affords Spelman unusual scope in his etymology of "lazy" in order to show also how the appellation survives its origins: ". . . Dividebantur antiqui Saxones, ut testatur Nithardus, in tres ordines; Edhilingos, Frilingos & Lazzos; hoc est nobiles, ingenuos & serviles: quam & nos distinctionem diu retinuimus. Sed Ricardo autem secundo pars servorum maxima se in libertatem vindicavit; sic ut hodie apud Anglos rarior inveniatur servus, qui mancipium dicitur. Restat nihilominus antiquæ appellationis commemoratio. Ignavos enim hodie *lazie* dicimus."[5]

Some of the material on freedom in the *Dictionary* bears political implications, but these are usually of a very broad and universally acceptable kind. Addison's political exhortation is representative in its acceptability to virtually all political positions: "Let freedom never perish in your hands! / But *piously* transmit it to your children." As Ben Jonson says, "Freedom we all *stand*[51] *for*." Milton and Locke get only a little closer to controversial ground when they describe political freedom as an inalienable, God-given right. Milton says,

> He gave us only over beast, fish, fowl,
> *Dominion*[1] absolute; that right we hold
> By his donation: but man over man
> He made not lord.

Locke adds, "He could not have private *dominion*[2] over that, which was under the private *dominion* of another." Locke here assumes the importance of individual political freedom, and from this same assumption he develops an argument against the divine right of kings that the *Dictionary* transmits. But in eighteenth-century England there was nothing especially controversial about this argument; Locke may have been used as a source of principles for the American revolution, but he was also a standard reference for completely conservative defenders of the Crown.[6] Moreover, Johnson is careful to qualify the panegyrics to freedom in his book, and often the same writers supply both praise and qualification. Locke and Milton are teamed up again

under the key word "license," which Johnson defines as "exorbitant
liberty; contempt of legal and necessary restraint":

> They baul for freedom in their senseless moods,
> And still revolt when truth would set them free;
> *Licence*[1] they mean, when they cry liberty.
>
> *Milton.*

Locke adds, "Though this be a state of liberty, yet it is not a state of
licence[1]. . . ."

The most important aspects of freedom in the *Dictionary* are religious and moral: throughout Johnson's book, the politics of the soul
are generally more important than the politics of states. True freedom
is the power to act morally. The tyranny that most endangers this
essential freedom is the internal psychological tyranny of the passions,
and against these usurpers the *Dictionary* is always eager to encourage
revolt. Dryden's Persius asks, "But if thy passions *lord* it in thy breast, /
Art thou not still a slave?" and Sidney pleads imperatively, "Let me
never know that any base affection should get any *lordship*[1] in your
thoughts." John Ray laments our failure to see the more important kind
of slavery when he says, "We are industrious to preserve our bodies
from slavery, but we make *nothing*[8] of suffering our souls to be slaves
to our lusts." Paradoxically, self-control in obedience to true religion
and morality is the only source of real freedom. As Tillotson says,
"True pleasure and perfect freedom are *nowhere* to be found but in the
practice of virtue."

9.4. Death and Judgment

> *If we* yield*[4] that there is a God, and that this God is almighty and
> just, it cannot be avoided but that, after this life [is] ended, he admin-
> isters justice unto men.* Hakewill.

> *The great incentive to virtue is the reflection that we must die.*
> (Rambler *78*, Yale *4: 50*)

In its attempts to understand the universal benevolence of providence mankind lacks a knowledge of how God will work things out in
the end. Our ignorance can only be redressed by a conviction that God

will rectify all the apparent injustices of this life by punishing the wicked and rewarding the good on the last day. Just such a conviction is unshakably strong in the *Dictionary* because it rests on the fundamental faith in God's goodness; moreover, the irregularities of fortune that threaten a faith in providence only serve to strengthen belief in the necessity of Judgment Day. Tillotson, for instance, declares, "No man, that considers the *promiscuous* dispensations of God's providence in this world, can think it unreasonable to conclude, that after this life good men shall be rewarded, and sinners punished." This line of reasoning is so strong to Watts's mind that he uses it as the model of one type of deduction: "God will one time or another make a difference between the good and the evil. *But*[3] there is little or no difference made in this world: therefore there must be another world, wherein this difference shall be made." Atterbury pursues the point: "It is equally necessary," he says, "that there should be a future state, to vindicate the justice of God, and solve the present irregularities of providence, whether the best men be *oftentimes* only, or always the most miserable."

Many more quotations in the *Dictionary* eschew argument and simply assert that the day of wrath must inevitably arrive. On one occasion Johnson reminds himself and his readers of this fact in his own voice: he explains the fourth sense of "to sleep" as "to be dead," and then he adds with some reverence, "death being a state from which man will some time awake." But, as usual, the theme is carried primarily in the illustrative quotations. The standard vision of Judgment Day is predictably juridical (see the first epigraph to this section). Dryden modifies the standard just slightly and imagines "the last assizes" (s.v. "to wake[1]"), and the same branch of law occurs to Donne when he describes the human condition:

> We are but farmers of ourselves; yet may,
> If we can stock ourselves and thrive, *uplay*
> Much, much good treasure for the great rent-day.

More terribly, South depicts criminal proceedings: "O the inexpressible horrour that will seize upon a sinner, when he stands arraigned at the bar of divine justice! when he shall see his accuser, his judge, the witnesses, all his *remorseless* adversaries."

The *Dictionary*'s natural philosophers make almost as many contributions to the pious belief in the world's end as they do to the orthodox view of its creation. Cheyne is one of many who turn scientific

language to religious uses; he thus departs entirely from the legal
vision of the *dies irae*, and writes about it in electromagnetic terms: "If
the principle of reunion has not its energy in this life, whenever the
attractions of sense cease, the acquired principles of *dissimilarity* must
repel these beings from their centre; so that the principle of reunion,
being set free by death, must drive these beings towards God their
centre, and the principle of *dissimilarity* forcing him to repel them with
infinite violence from him, must make them infinitely miserable."
In squaring God's actions with the laws of nature Cheyne follows
Thomas Burnet's example in *The Sacred Theory of the Earth*, an attempt
to show that the primordial earth collapsed into an underlying ocean,
thus causing the flood, when God's anger at man's sinfulness and the
erosive action of sea and sun climaxed simultaneously. Johnson took
quotations from all parts of Burnet's work, including those that
describe the fiery destruction of the earth on the last day. Burnet's
words under *deluge*[1] are somewhat predictable, but another of his
reminders surprisingly appears under "cold": "To see a world in
flames, and an host of angels in the clouds, one must be much of a
stoick to be a *cold*[4] and unconcerned spectator." Tillotson agrees with
Burnet's conclusion about the manner of the earth's destruction: "By a
general conflagration mankind shall be destroyed, with the form and
all the *furniture*[2] of the earth." Rogers concentrates on slightly
different phenomena, but the message is the same: "Reflect on that
day, when earth shall be again in travail with her sons, and at one
fruitful *throe*[1] bring forth all the generations of learned and unlearned, noble and ignoble dust." But the important and continually
restated point is Hakewill's: "Whatever be the manner of the world's
end, most certain it is an end it shall have, and as certain that then we
shall appear before the judgment *seat*[2] of Christ, that every man may
receive according to that which he hath done in his body, whether it be
good or evil." Johnson himself owned a pocket watch inscribed with an
eschatological reminder from the Septuagint version of Isaiah, νὺξ
ἔρχεται (night cometh), and he makes sure that owners of the
Dictionary also encounter such reminders. Raleigh perhaps comes
closest to a periphrasis of the passage in Isaiah: "The devil is now more
laborious than ever, the long day of mankind drawing fast towards an
evening, and the world's tragedy and time near at an end."

The moral value of remembering the *dies irae* is obvious, but the
Dictionary does not hesitate to repeat it often. Locke is probably the
most assiduous in this respect, and Johnson allows him a pair of

consecutive quotations on the subject under "prospect": "To him, who hath a *prospect*[5] of the different state of perfect happiness or misery, that attends all men after this life, the measures of good and evil are mightily changed"; but, "If there be no *prospect* beyond the grave, the inference is right; let us eat and drink, for to-morrow we shall die."[7] Allestree calls "contemplation of the last judgment" a "*catholicon* against all*" sin, and Rogers implies as much when he urges us to "live in a constant and serious *expectation*[2] of that day, when we must appear before the Judge of heaven and earth." The *Dictionary* heightens this expectation in its readers, and anyone who spends much time with Johnson's book knows exactly the meaning of Tillotson's rhetorical question: "Is not he imprudent, who, seeing the tide making haste towards him *apace*[1], will sleep till the sea overwhelm him?"

The stream of reminders about the day of judgment is confluent in the *Dictionary* with a steadier flow of memento mori. Like all of Johnson's works, the *Dictionary* is dotted with death's heads that recall us to the serious, religious business of life. In *The Rambler* Johnson excels in compositions on this theme, and he seldom fails to explain its moral and religious usefulness. In number 17 he writes, "A frequent and attentive prospect of that moment, which must put a period to all our schemes, and deprive us of all our acquisitions, is, indeed, of the utmost efficacy to the just and rational regulation of our lives; nor would ever any thing wicked, or often any thing absurd, be undertaken or prosecuted by him who should begin every day with a serious reflection, that he is born to die" (*Yale* 3: 92). The *Dictionary* embodies the doctrine of *Rambler* 78 that "the remembrance of death ought to predominate in our minds . . ." (*Yale* 4: 47). On a few interesting occasions Johnson acts on this doctrine without regard to the usual lexicographical aims of his book by printing gratuitous reminders of death; under the second sense of "to rest" and the twelfth sense of "measure," for example, he enters some verses on death out of the Greek Anthology (above, p. 117). On other occasions he seems spontaneously to deviate into the subject of death. After defining "preparedness" rather unsatisfactorily as "state or act of being prepared," he adds, "as, *he's in a* preparedness *for his final exit*." The same preoccupation appears in Johnson's treatment of "periphrasis": "Circumlocution; use of many words to express the sense of one: as, for *death*, we may say, *the loss of life*." The occasion of the last *Idler* stimulated Johnson to "make a secret comparison between a part and the whole," and to reflect that "the termination of any period of life reminds us that life itself has likewise its termination . . ." (*Yale* 2: 315).

In the *Dictionary* the occasion of writing the entry for the word "last" also arouses Johnson's "secret horrour of the last": he defines the third sense, with elegiac overtones, as "beyond which there is no more," and Cowley, Addison, and Prior echo Johnson's elegiac tone with couplets ending in "bell" and "knell"; "try'd" and "dy'd"; and "adieu" and "tear."

Although the topic of death is extremely common in all the literature in the period covered by the *Dictionary*'s illustrative quotations, Johnson ensured a heavier than usual concentration by his choice of certain sources specifically devoted to the subject. Jeremy Taylor's *Holy Dying* dependably fills Johnson's pages with advice like the following: "If you have served God in a holy life, send away the women and the *weepers*[1]: tell them it is as much intemperance to weep too much as to laugh too much: if thou art alone, or with fitting company, die as thou should'st; but do not die impatiently, and like a fox catched in a trap." For Taylor, dying is such a fundamental subject that it brings in all the topics of moral living, but William Wake's *Preparation for Death* consistently speaks specifically to the topic of dying. Wake's little work describes itself on the title page as "a Letter sent to a Young Gentlewoman in France, in a dangerous distemper, of which she died." Wake attempts to reconcile his correspondent to death by convincing her that the things of this world are nothing but vanity: "'tis the tying of our affections so much to this World, that above any thing indisposes us to think of another" (19). In volume 1 of the *Dictionary* Johnson quotes Wake's short duodecimo at least forty-three times, and almost every quotation is another memento mori. The entries under "to encounter" and "indeed" are representative: "They who have most dread of death, must in a little time be content to *encounter*[2] with it, whether they will or no"; "There is nothing in the world more generally dreaded, and yet less to be feared, than death: *indeed*[3], for those unhappy men whose hopes terminate in this life, no wonder if the prospect of another seems terrible and amazing." A third book that contributes mainly to the topic of death is John Graunt's *Natural and Political Observations . . . made upon the Bills of Mortality*. Though this is a sort of social study, complete with statistics, Graunt did not neglect its obvious opportunities for morally beneficial reminders of death. He intended that the Bills themselves "shall not be onley as Death's-heads to put men in minde of their *Mortality* but also as *Mercurial Statues* to point out the most dangerous ways, that lead us into it" (36–37). Graunt adds morbidity to the *Dictionary*'s treatment of death by describing the final stages of some illnesses and by giving advice on the handling of corpses; he appears appropriately, for instance, under "rickets," "sickliness," and "sexton."

In his unpublished and invaluable dissertation on the books marked up for making the *Dictionary* E. J. Thomas suggests that Johnson's melancholy led him in 1749 to read and take excerpts from the poetry of Garth (101). This is no doubt true, and I think the *Dictionary* contains ample evidence of Johnson's personality and even of some of his personal emotional weather. But more: Johnson's whole bibliography and the body of illustrative quotations that he excerpted from it represent enduring human and educational concerns. Death figures prominently in these concerns, as almost every page of the *Dictionary* shows. Ecclesiastes 7.2 is the text for a sizable portion of Johnson's book, and the verse itself appears in illustration of "to lay": "It is better to go to the house of mourning than to go to the house of feasting; for that is the end of all men, and the living will *lay*[19] it to his heart." L'Estrange writes an important commentary on this passage: "'Tis the great business of life to fit ourselves for our *end*[8], and no man can live well that has not death in his eye."

Simple and blunt reminders of the inevitability of death are the most common contributions to the topic. Raleigh points out, "Nature assureth us by *never*[5]-failing experience, and reason by infallible demonstration, that our times upon the earth have neither certainty nor durability." Elsewhere he makes the sentiment more memorable in couplets:

> The sun may set and rise:
> But we, *contrariwise*[2],
> Sleep, after our short light,
> One everlasting night.

Davies makes the arresting perception, "Our bodies, ev'ry footstep that they make, / *March*[2] towards death, until at last they die." Necessity and abruptness are important qualities of death's approach; Prior expresses their unsettling combination:

> To *morrow*[2] comes; 'tis noon; 'tis night;
> This day like all the former flies;
> Yet on he runs to seek delight
> To *morrow*, till tonight he dies.

Prior's lines are reminiscent of Macbeth's "Tomorrow and tomorrow . . . ," and Rogers's similar focus on "tomorrow" suggests that it may be one of the key words in the genre of the memento mori: "How know we that our souls shall not this night be required, laden with those *unpardoned*[1] sins, for which we proposed to repent tomorrow." But repetition of any unit of time is also characteristic in expressions of this theme. Whether or not Johnson had the phonology necessary for an appreciation of Jacques' pun, his illustration of "to rot" must have seemed to him pure truth-telling melancholy: "From hour to hour we ripe and ripe, / And then from hour to hour we *rot* and *rot*."

Sir Thomas Browne uses a more philosophical image of sidereal time to describe the demise of man: "Upon the tropick, and first descension from our solstice, we are scarce sensible of declination; but declining farther, our *decrement* accelerates: we set apace, and in our last days precipitate into our graves." Johnson may have been influenced by Browne when in 1749, while he was at work excerpting quotations for the *Dictionary*, he emended line 20 of "The Vanity" from "And restless enterprise impells to death" to "And restless fire precipitates on death." As there is in Browne's language, there is also a Johnsonian ring to some of the many ironic little stories in the *Dictionary* that turn on someone's failure to remember the inevitability of death. Johnson gives Bacon room enough for a fairly elaborate tale of this sort under "grandfather": "One was saying that his great grandfather, and *grandfather*, and father died at sea: said another, that heard him, an' I were as you, I would never come at sea. Why, saith he, where did your great grandfather, and *grandfather*, and father die? He answered, where but in their beds? He answered, an' I were as you, I would never come in bed." Death may have been the definitive joke for Johnson, as this quotation from Pope suggests:

> Link towns to towns with avenues of oak,
> Inclose whole downs in walls, 'tis all a *joke!*
> Inexorable death shall level all.

Johnson's profound appreciation of this cosmic joke is probably what moved him to such stupendous laughter on the night when he and Boswell walked home after celebrating a friend's triumph in completing his will. Reflecting on this "achievement," according to Boswell, "Johnson could not stop his merriment, but continued it all the way till we got without the Temple-gate. He then burst into such a fit of laughter, that he appeared to be almost in a convulsion; and, in order to support himself, laid hold of one of the posts at the side of the foot pavement, and sent forth peals so loud, that in the silence of the night his voice seemed to resound from Temple-bar to Fleet-ditch" (Boswell 2: 262).

Riches, power, beauty, youth, and knowledge all show their ephemeral colors in the face of death and serve as foils to heighten its effect. The reader encounters Dryden's "Riches cannot *rescue* from the grave, / Which claims alike the monarch and the slave"; Shakespeare's "The scepter, learning, physic must / All follow this, and come to *dust*[2]"; and his sharper remark, "He was skilful enough to have lived still, if knowledge could be *set*[61] *up* against mortality." Johnson's entries under "bridal" show how images of youthfulness and beauty are especially useful foils. The illustration of the adjective begins with Shakespeare's lines:

> Our wedding chear to a sad fun'ral feast,
> Our solemn hymns to sullen dirges change,
> Our *bridal* flowers serve for a buried corse.

The entry following for the noun begins with an ironic illustration from *Othello* and juxtaposes Herbert's beautiful lines,

> Sweet day, so cool, so calm, so bright,
> The *bridal* of the earth and sky,
> Sweet dews shall weep thy fall to-night;
> For thou must die.

Johnson's treatment of the two forms of "bridal" ends as grimly as it begins. The last verses come from Dryden:

> In death's dark bow'rs our *bridals* we will keep,
> And his cold hand
> Shall draw the curtain when we go to sleep.

The illustration of "bridal" is altogether so morbid and ironic that it reads like an expression of Johnson's grief for his wife, who was ill and dying while he composed volume 1 of the *Dictionary*. However, a conflation of the themes of youthful beauty, love, and death is a conventional characteristic of amorous and elegiac poetry, and Johnson did not have to look hard to find such melancholy associations. He used them in profusion because they suited his overall educational purposes, perhaps because he was temperamentally drawn to them, and perhaps because they suited his melancholy mood; it is impossible completely to disentangle these possible personal motives from the deeper, cultural forces at work in shaping the *Dictionary*.

Much of education and, indeed, a good part of living, in the world of the *Dictionary*, seems to be a preparation for death. Herbert supplies a formula for avoiding this gloomy sense of life: "This hour is mine; if for the next I care, I grow too wide, / And do *encroach*[2] upon death's side." But this kind of concentration cannot last, and the only way to overcome death is with the faith that it is not final. Rogers represents the view of the *Dictionary* as a whole when he says, "Human nature could not sustain the reflection of having all its schemes and expectations to determine with this frail and *perishable* composition of flesh and blood." Nor does the *Dictionary* fail to assist its readers in achieving the necessary conviction. Donne supplies a strengthening couplet, in a surprising place: "Think then, my soul! that death is but a *groom*[1] / Which brings a taper to the outward room." Davies likewise tries to naturalize the thought of death; speaking of the soul he says,

> And when thou think'st of her eternity
> Think not that death *against*[7] her nature is;
> Think it a birth: and when thou go'st to die,
> Sing like a swan, as if thou went'st to bliss.

The most comforting remarks on the subject of death avoid mentioning the dissolution of the body and soul altogether, in order to focus on the scene of eternal joy. Tillotson provides a preface to this group of remarks when he says, with some apparent complacence, "It is *for*[31] wicked men to dread God; but a virtuous man may have undisturbed thoughts, even of the justice of God." Boyle goes one step beyond the ugliness of physical death: "Those departed friends, whom at our last separation we saw disfigured by all the *ghastly*[1] horrours of death, we shall then see assisting about the majestick throne of Christ, with their once vile bodies transfigured into the likeness of his glorious body, mingling their glad acclamations with the hallelujahs of thrones, principalities and powers." When Hooker explains the metaphysics of heavenly translation, he too gives the mind something other than horror with which to fill its conception of death: "The soul being, as it is active, perfected by love of that infinite good, shall, as it is *receptive*, be also perfected with those supernatural passions of joy, peace and delight." The heaven imagined in the *Dictionary* is sometimes very appropriately suited to the life of learning that it encourages. John Ray suggests a continuity between his celestial activity and the work of his most famous book when he says, "It may be a part of our employment in eternity, to contemplate the works of God, and give him the glory of his wisdom *manifested* in the creation." But the most appropriate heavenly vision of all appears in illustration of "class." The *Dictionary* addresses an audience of learners, and Watts aptly describes their heaven as a kind of celestial sixth form: "We shall be seized away from this lower *class*[2] in the school of knowledge, and our conversation shall be with angels and illuminated spirits."

10. Happiness

Our main*[1] interest is to be as happy as we can, and as long as possible.* Tillotson's Sermons.

> *Happiness, object of that waking dream,*
> *Which we call life, mistaking:* fugitive*[1] theme*
> *Of my pursuing verse, ideal shade,*
> Notional*[1] good, by fancy only made.* Prior.

As the *Dictionary* represents it, human life is and should be a search for happiness. Locke takes this view completely when he nearly identifies the self with the quest for happiness (s.v. "to resolve[3]"): ". . . this every intelligent man must grant, that there is something that is himself, that he would have happy." Tillotson is almost as extreme, naming happiness as the test of useful existence: "The contemplation of things, that do not serve to promote our happiness, is but a more specious and ingenious sort of idleness, a more pardonable and *creditable*[2] kind of ignorance." Yet, despite the general consent that happiness is the proper goal of human life, an equally insistent current of opinion in the *Dictionary* declares that happiness cannot be attained. As Prior says, "We happiness *pursue*[4]; we fly from pain; / Yet the pursuit, and yet the flight is vain." For Rogers too, happiness is an ignis fatuus: "Restless and impatient to try every scheme and overture of present happiness, he hunts a *phantom*[2] he can never overtake." This is the condition of human life; in Atterbury's words, "We find our souls disordered and *restless*[2], tossed and disquieted by passions, ever seeking happiness in the enjoyments of this world, and ever missing what they seek."

It should come as no surprise that the solution to this paradox of life is religion. Locke sums up the point: "If there remains an eternity to us after the short revolution of time, we so swiftly *run*[12] over here, 'tis clear, that all the happiness, that can be imagined in this fleeting state, is not valuable in respect of the future." A calculus designed to maximize happiness and therefore best perform the business of life must conclude in a recommendation of religion. Locke again: "This life is a scene of vanity, that soon passes away, and affords no solid satisfaction but in the consciousness of doing well, and in the hopes of another life: this is what I can say upon experience, and what you will find to be true when you come to *make*[59] *up* the account." In less arithmetical terms, South comes to the same conclusion: "Nothing can make a man happy, but that which shall last as long as he lasts; for an immortal soul shall *persist* in being not only when profit, pleasure and honour, but when time itself shall cease." In the *Dictionary* the subject of happiness, which might belong to psychology or ethical philosophy in a modern encyclopedia, serves religion. In serving religion it is no different from natural philosophy or most other topics in Johnson's book, but its service is particularly great because the search for happiness is so generally agreed to be the purpose of life. Tillotson describes the special contribution of happiness to the *Dictionary*'s work on religion when he says, "He, that would do *right*[1] to religion, cannot take a more effectual course, than by reconciling it with the happiness of mankind."

10.1. Human Life

Many subjects fall under the consideration of an author, which being limited by nature can admit only of slight and accidental diversities. . . . Different poets describing the spring or the sea would mention the zephyrs and the flowers, the billows and the rocks; reflecting on human life, they would, without any communication of opinions, lament the deceitfulness of hope, the fugacity of pleasure, the fragility of beauty, and the frequency of calamity. (Rambler *143*, Yale *4: 395)*

To live is perpetually to be exposed to the chances of unhappiness. The body of quotation in the *Dictionary* on the topic of life substantiates Johnson's view in *Rambler* 143, and it may have evoked the grand amplification in his expression. Under the second sense of "life" Johnson includes twelve lines from Dryden and a quatrain more from Prior to assert the uncertainty of life (above, p. 30). The expenditure of valuable space is itself significant, and the frequency with which similar contributions are made suggests that Johnson may

have intended the uncertainty of life to be a prominent theme in his
book, or even that he was constitutionally drawn to expressions of it as he read through his sources. In any case, "the frequency of calamity" is one of the most visible themes in the literature recorded in the *Dictionary*. The message is ancient, appearing, for instance, in the tales of happy men told by Solon to Croesus. Dryden alludes to these discouraging stories:

> I hasten to our own; nor will relate
> Great Mithridates, and rich Crœsus' fate;
> Whom Solon wisely counsell'd to *attend*[12]
> The name of happy, till he knew his end.

Solon gave "the name of happy" only to men who, typically, performed a glorious deed and died upon receiving their laurels, or who enjoyed untypical good fortune.

Most remarks on life in the *Dictionary* focus directly on the unhappiness of life and its propensity to fall out from under us when we least expect it. South provides a question and answer that sound like parts of Johnson's "Vanity": "Is a man confident of his present strength? An unwholesome blast may shake in pieces his *hardy*[2] fabrick." The most general pessimistic statements on the topic of life receive the most exemplification and converge with the *Dictionary*'s continuous stream of memento mori. Here is a small sample of the choicest contributions:

> This is the state of man; to-day he puts forth
> The tender leaves of hopes, to-morrow blossoms,
> And bears his blushing honours thick upon him;
> The third day comes a frost, a killing frost;
> And when he thinks, good easy man, full surely
> His greatness is a *ripening*, nips his root;
> And then he falls as I do.
>> *Shakesp. Henry VIII.*

> So many accidents may deprive us of our lives, that we can never say, that he who neglects to secure his salvation today, may without danger *put*[36] it *off* to to-morrow. *Wake.*

> We are but of *yesterday*, and know nothing, because our days upon earth are a shadow. *Job* viii.9.

Life's but a walking *shadow*[1], a poor player,
That struts and frets his hour upon the stage,
And then is heard no more.

Shakesp.

Courts are theatres, where some men *play*[14]
Princes, some slaves, and all end in one day.

Donne.

Man's life's a tragedy; his mother's womb,
From which he enters, is the *tiringroom*;
This spacious earth the theatre; and the stage
That country which he lives in; passions, rage,
Folly, and vice, are actors.

Wotton.

We bring into the world with us a poor *needy* uncertain life,
short *at*[4] the longest, and unquiet *at* the best. *Temple.*

This days ensample hath this *lesson*[2] dear
Deep written in my heart with iron pen,
That bliss may not abide in state of mortal men.

Fa[erie] *Qu*[eene].

According to the *Dictionary*, instability is the only constant quality of
life; in Raleigh's words, "The life of man is always either increasing
towards ripeness and perfection, or declining and decreasing towards
rottenness and *dissolution*[6]." Although Johnson's book recognizes
both of these movements in its depiction of human life, its emphasis is
on decline and dissolution. Johnson seems at times purposely to
intensify this emphasis. For example, whereas he pays no special
attention to any of its antonyms, he seems to indulge his gloomy view
of things with a lavish definition of "fall" in the sixth sense: "Downfall;
loss of greatness; declension from eminence; degradation; state of
being deposed from a high station; plunge from happiness or greatness
into misery or meanness." Similarly, a "winner" for Johnson is simply
"one who wins," but a "loser" is "one that is deprived of any thing, one
that forfeits any thing; one that is impaired in his possession or hope,
the contrary to winner or gainer." In another instance too, I think
Johnson may reveal his impulse to dwell on the sad changes of life: he
defines "to alter" at first with philosophic neutrality as "to become

otherwise than it was," but spontaneously he adds, "as, *the weather*
alters *from bright to cloudy.*"

These few instances are representative of the generally pessimistic view of human life that the *Dictionary* expresses, and the proof, as usual, must be sought in the whole body of illustrative quotation. Ongoing decay and degradation is a commonplace derived from Hesiod that many writers in the *Dictionary* employ when they characterize life. Roscommon's words are typical:

> Time sensibly all things impairs;
> Our fathers have been worse than theirs,
> And we than ours; next age will see
> A race more *profligate* than we,
> With all the pains we take, have skill enough to be.

Swift seems to hearken back to Cicero's Hesiodic thought—"*O tempora, o mores!*"—when he exclaims,

> Less should I dawb it o'er with transitory praise,
> And *watercolours* of these days:
> These days! where e'en th' extravagance of poetry
> Is at a loss for figures to express
> Men's folly, whimsies, and inconstancy.

Even when it is not actually getting worse, life is generally unhappy as the *Dictionary* describes it. Wake says, "Ours is [a] melancholy and *uncomfortable*[1] portion here below! A place, where not a day passes, but we eat our bread with sorrow and cares: the present troubles us, the future amazes; and even the past fills us with grief and anguish." Rogers sums up the human situation thus: "We are weak, dependant creatures, *insufficient* to our own happiness, full of wants which of ourselves we cannot relieve, exposed to a numerous train of evils which we know not how to divert."

Morally and ethically, man lives in a middle state. Perhaps Shakespeare expresses this most memorably: "The web of our life is of a mingled *yarn*, good and ill together. . . ." South likewise recognizes that "in most things good and evil lie *shuffled*[1], and thrust up together in a confused heap. . . ."[1] But whether this state is examined in the case of the individual or in the case of the whole race together, the portion of evil is almost always seen to outweigh the good. Johnson might have been surveying his illustrative quotations in the *Dictionary* when he remarked in *Rambler* 175, "None of the axioms of wisdom which recommended the ancient sages to veneration, seems to have required less extent of knowledge or perspicacity of penetration than the remark of Bias, that οἱ πλέονες κακοί, 'the majority are wicked' " (*Yale* 5: 159–60). For this reason, as Otway says, "To *rise*[5] i' th' world, / No wise man that's honest should expect." But the Biatic proportion is said to hold just as firmly in the individual soul. Allestree seems to vindicate the vast extent of moralizing in the *Dictionary* when he says, "Man's nature is so *unattentive* to good, that there can scarce be too many monitors." Recognizing human depravity serves religion and exalts the passion of Christ, but in the *Dictionary* the emphasis is very often on the depravity. Addison's quotation under "expiation" is fuller than most but representative: "Let a man's innocence be what it will, let his virtues rise to the highest pitch of perfection, there will be still in him so many secret sins, so many human frailties, so many offences of ignorance, passion and prejudice, so many unguarded words and thoughts, that without the advantage of such an *expiation*[2] and atonement, as Christianity has revealed to us, it is impossible he should be saved." Rogers's celebration of the same divine event makes a more direct expression of the Biatic proportion of human evil that stands throughout the *Dictionary*'s descriptions of human life: "He assists us with a measure of grace, sufficient to overbalance the corrupt *propensity*[1] of the will."

When an exact concordance to Johnson's *Dictionary* is finally prepared, it will show that the majority of sentences in which the word "man" appears discourage pride and vanity by attesting to human weakness and corruption. Part of the entry under "man" in this speculative concordance will read as follows:

> That *crawling*[1] insect, who from the mud began;
> Warm'd by my beams, and kindled into man!
> *Dryd*[en].

> The vile worm, that yesterday began
> To *crawl*[1]; thy fellow-creature, abject man!
> *Prior.*

> Man is a very worm by birth,
> Vile reptile, weak and vain!

A while he *crawls*[2] upon the earth,
Then shrinks to earth again.

Swift.

Alas, said I, man was made in vain! How is he *given*[23] *away* to misery and mortality! *Addison's Spectator*, No. 159.

Man! Proud man!
Drest in a little brief authority,
Most ignorant of what he's most assur'd:
His *glassy*[2] essence, like an angry ape,
Plays such fantastick tricks before high heav'n,
As makes the angels weep.

Shakes. Meas. for Measure.

Poor *orphan* in the wide world scattered,
As budding branch rent from native tree,
And thrown forth until it be withered:
Such is the state of man.

Fairy Queen, b. ii.

Man is but a *topsyturvy* creature: his head where his heels should be, grovelling on the earth. *Swift.*

10.2. Human Wishes

No mortal was ever so much at ease, but his shoe wrung *him somewhere.* L'Estrange.

Of night impatient, we demand the day*[1]*;
The day arrives, then for the night we pray:
The night and day successive come and go,
Our lasting pains no interruption know.

Blackmore's Creation.

A due recognition of the uncertainty and degeneracy of human life might make it possible to avoid some pain, but happiness in this life is logically impossible because of an essential incompatibility between the concepts of life and happiness as the *Dictionary* describes them. An important definition of happiness occurs in consecutive quotations from Locke: "Who is *content*[1], is happy," and "A man is perfectly *content*[1] with the state he is in, when he is perfectly without any uneasiness." But uneasiness is an essential ingredient in Locke's description of human life: "We are seldom at ease, and free enough from the solicitation of our natural or *adopted*[2] desires; but a constant succession of uneasiness, out of that stock, which natural wants, or *acquired* habits, have heaped up, take the will in their turns." Moreover, throughout the *Dictionary* Johnson prints volumes of testimony in agreement with Locke's perception that "we be in this world *beset*[2] with sundry uneasinesses, distracted with different desires." For instance, Atterbury says, "The happiest of mankind overlooking those solid blessings which they already have, set their hearts upon somewhat which they want; some *untry'd*[2] pleasure, which, if they could but taste, they should then be compleatly blest." Swift puts it more bluntly: "So endless and *exorbitant*[3] are the desires of men, that they will *grasp*[1] at all, and can form no scheme of perfect happiness with less."

Because desire is an inseparable accompaniment of human life, it is inextinguishable, and the *Dictionary* more often attempts to regulate than to quell it. The closest Johnson's book comes to recommending a stoical repudiation of desire is in a vein of remarks on the theme of *contemptus mundi*. Taylor is the most radical contributor, with such remarks as "He that despises the world, and all its *appendant*[2] vanities, is the most secure." The morals that L'Estrange wrote for his Aesop sometimes further this theme: "A due consideration of the vanities of the world, will naturally *bring*[9] us to the contempt of it; and the contempt of the world will as certainly *bring* us home to ourselves." Burnet writes about the inevitable result of failing to reject the things of this world when he says, "We *dote* upon this present world, and the enjoyments of it; and 'tis not without pain and fear, and reluctancy, that we are torn from them, as if our hopes lay all within the compass of this life." As Burnet suggests, hopes and fears and all the forms of desire are most profitably turned from this world to the next. South sums up the *Dictionary*'s survey of mundane joy: "Should a man *run*[15] over the whole circle of earthly pleasures, he would be forced to complain that pleasure was not satisfaction."

On the other hand, "The pleasure of the religious man," says South, "is an easy and *portable* pleasure. . . ." Religious pleasure, as the *Dictionary* usually represents it, is a positive satisfaction and not just the evacuation of earthly desires. This is abundantly evident in Tillot-

son's statement that "religion tends to the ease and pleasure, the peace
and tranquillity of our minds, which all the wisdom of the world did always *aim at*, as the utmost felicity of this life." Rogers goes a little further and sees a happy cooperation between the properly regulated desire for earthly things and religious desire: "Those proportions of the good things of this life, which are most consistent with the interests of the soul, are also most *conducive* to our present felicity." But Atterbury has the ne plus ultra in his reconciliation of earthly and spiritual pleasures: "Take delight in the good things of this world, so as to remember that we are to part with them, and to *exchange*[1] them for more excellent and durable enjoyments." This turns the theme of *contemptus mundi* upside down, and the remarks similar to it through-out the *Dictionary* counteract Johnson's more extreme interdictions of desire.

Total satisfaction is impossible in this vale of tears no matter what the object of desire, but the particular wishes of men carry with them their own particular torments. Addison traces to Socrates the John-sonian wisdom (in "The Vanity of Human Wishes") that "Fate wings with ev'ry wish th'afflictive dart," when he says: "Socrates meeting Alcibiades going to his devotions, and observing his eyes fixed with great seriousness, tells him that he had reason to be thoughtful, since a man might bring down evils by his prayers, and the things which the gods send him at his request might *turn*[9] to his destruction." One of the ways in which earthly wishes can be destructive is by sheer excess. Some of the best entries on this theme are taken from South; he says, for example, "The most voluptuous person, were he tied to follow his hawks and his hounds, his dice and his courtships every day, would find it the greatest torment that could befal him: he would fly to the mines and the *gallies*[2] for his recreation, and to the spade and the mattock for a diversion from the misery of a continual uninterrupted pleasure."[2] The irony is even sharper in Milton's "Rest, that gives all men life, gave him his death, / And too much breathing put him out of *breath*[4]." Pope applies this principle to the wish of authors: "Praise to a wit is like rain to a tender flower; if it be moderately bestowed, it chears and revives; but if too *lavishly*, overcharges and depresses him." Bacon may not have intended it, but he seems to present the pattern of this kind of destructive pleasure when he says, "It is a common experience, that if you do not pull off some blossoms the first time a tree *bloometh*[1], it will blossom itself to death."

Although every human wish is subject to dangerous excess, the particular desire that most requires regulation is the desire for money. Wealth is the typical worldly desire, and its treatment makes a subtopic in the *Dictionary*. In *Rambler* 131 Johnson observes the archetypal place occupied by the wish for wealth: "There is scarcely any sentiment in which, amidst the innumerable varieties of inclination that nature or accident have scattered in the world, we find greater numbers concurring than in the wish for riches; a wish indeed so prevalent that it may be considered as universal and transcendental, as the desire in which all other desires are included, and of which the various purposes which actuate mankind are only subordinate species and different modifications" (*Yale* 4: 331). The great object of moral writers, "who," as Johnson says, "have undertaken the unpromising task of moderating desire" (*Yale* 5: 110), is to show the fallacy of the wish for wealth. One flank of Johnson's assault on this master-wish isolates the physical dangers of wealth. Temple says, "Persons in those posts are usually born of families noble and rich, and so derive a weakness of constitution from the ease and luxury of their ancestors, and the *delicacy*[7] of their own education."[3] L'Estrange contributes a transparent allegory for Johnson's readers to repeat whenever the wish for money causes uneasiness: "The heifer, that valued itself upon a smooth coat and a *plump* habit of body, was taken up for a sacrifice; but the ox, that was despised for his raw bones, went on with his work still." Bacon very credibly extends the *Dictionary*'s warning about the dangers of wealth to psychological well-being when he observes, "Men in great fortunes are strangers to themselves, and while they are in the *puzzle* of business, they have no time to tend their health either of body or mind."

The perilous spiritual condition to which the rich are exposed is the most common dissuasive to the general envy that their position attracts. As Temple justly remarks, "The love of money is the *root*[4] of all evil, is a truth universally agreed in." The foundation of the agreement can be traced first to St. Paul: "The love of money is the root of all evil; which while some coveted after, they have *pierced*[1] themselves through with many sorrows." Paul's authority for citing the danger of riches is Jesus himself, as South reports: "Does not our Saviour himself speak of the intolerable difficulty which they cause in men's passage to heaven? Do not they make the narrow way much narrower, and contract the gate which leads to life to the streightness of a needle's *eye*[11]?" In his inimitable fashion Swift makes the sentiment modern and blunt: "Few bankers will to heav'n be *mounters*."

Under key words in the language of wealth Hooker declares, "*Prosperity* . . . doth prove a thing dangerous to the souls of men," and Addison reflects, "Riches expose a man to pride and *luxury*[1], and a foolish elation of heart."

For all his warnings about riches, however, Johnson does not transmit an entirely naive recommendation of poverty, either in the *Dictionary* or elsewhere. Hooker makes a simple point to which Johnson often returns in his remarks on social issues: "In as much as righteous life *presupposeth* life, in as much as to live virtuously it is impossible except we live; therefore the first impediment, which naturally we endeavour to remove, is penury and want of things, without which we cannot live." In his tenth definition of "poor" Johnson himself provides the grounds for a criticism of those who sing the praises of virtuous poverty: "*The* Poor. [collectively.] Those who are in the lowest rank of the community; those who cannot subsist but by the charity of others; but it is sometimes used with laxity for any not rich." As Thomson has it, what is required is "An elegant *sufficiency*[3], content, / *Retirement*[2]. . . ." Rogers comes close to summing up the *Dictionary*'s balanced view of the desirability of riches: "When he considers the manifold temptations of poverty and riches, and how fatally it will affect his happiness to be overcome by them, he will join with Agur in petitioning God for the safer *portion*[2] of a moderate convenience."

Concerning the wish for fame, the moralist's task is more complicated because immortal yearnings are involved. In *Rambler* 49 Johnson delivers his opinion: "Upon an attentive and impartial review of the argument, it will appear that the love of fame is to be regulated, rather than extinguished; and that men should be taught not to be wholly careless about their memory, but to endeavour that they may be remembered chiefly for their virtues, since no other reputation will be able to transmit any pleasure beyond the grave" (*Yale* 3: 266). Like so many of Johnson's opinions, this one too may be gathered from the illustrative quotations in the *Dictionary*, in some of which fame, glory, and renown are spoken of as extremely valuable acquisitions. Herbert's lines, for instance, contrast the value of fame to that of mere money:

> What *skills*[2] it, if a bag of stones or gold
> About thy neck do drown thee? raise thy head,
> Take stars for money; stars not to be told,

By any art: yet to be purchas'd.
None is so wasteful as the scraping dame,
She loseth three for one; her soul, rest, fame.

Some form of the wish for fame is universal, as Swift suggests: "There is in most people a reluctance and *unwillingness* to be forgotten. We observe, even among the vulgar, how fond they are to have an inscription over their grave." But Bacon carefully discriminates varieties of the universal wish, and these are expressed in terms of the objects to which the wish attaches itself: "The best temper of minds desireth good name and true honour; the lighter, *popularity*[1] and applause; the more depraved, subjection and tyranny." Along with its praise of the highest kind of fame, the *Dictionary* issues warnings about the meanness and deceitfulness of the lesser kinds. Locke talks about the lowest level of fame in Bacon's scheme when he says justly, "Honour and renown are bestowed on conquerours, who, for the most part, are but the great *butchers*[2] of mankind." Testimony to the transience of political and military glory comes in from many sources, but perhaps the most poignant is delivered in the royal plural by King Charles I: "Experience we have of the vanity of human glory, in our scatterings and *eclipses*[2]." Corbet brings in the trusty example of Wolsey:

> Wolsey, who from his own great store might have
> A palace or a college for his grave,
> Lies here interr'd:
> Nothing but earth to earth, no pond'rous *weight*[3]
> Upon him, but a pebble or a quoit:
> If thus thou lie'st neglected, what must we
> Hope after death, who are but shreds of thee?

The votaries of the lesser kind of literary fame, popularity, suffer the same fate as those who seek glory through power. Just as in "The Vanity of Human Wishes" poets receive a "tardy bust" (162), so in the *Dictionary* Garth says, "Dryden wants a poor square foot of stone, to shew where the ashes of one of the greatest poets on earth are *deposited*[1]." Pope issues a more general warning about the wish for literary fame:

> How vain that second life in others breath,
> Th' estate which wits inherit after death!

Ease, health, and life for this they must resign,
Unsure the tenure, but how vast the *fine*[3]!

Happiness

Under a key word in this subtopic a quotation from Shakespeare contributes a piece of ironic wisdom that seems to me characteristic of the *Dictionary*'s treatment of life and death in general:

> *Glory*[3] is like a circle in the water,
> Which never ceaseth to enlarge itself,
> 'Till by broad spreading it disperse to nought.

Even though "all is vanity," however, the main way to content in the *Dictionary* is not through the extinction of wishes: what cannot be extinguished except with life itself must be regulated. Moreover, a certain degree of wealth is not only desirable but necessary to happiness, and certain kinds of fame are fit objects of hope. Hooker's key to happiness is found in the *Dictionary* in the most obvious place: "*Happiness*[1] is that estate whereby we attain, so far as possibly may be attained, the full possession of that which simply for itself is to be desired, and containeth in it after an eminent sort the contentation of our desires, the highest degree of all our perfection." In the great chain of wishes, fame is higher than wealth; virtue is inherently more valuable than fame because virtue is what one should be famous for; but the anchoring point of this chain, as of the chain of being, is God himself. "*Virtue*[1] only makes our bliss below," says Pope, but Cheyne adds, "Nothing but the uncreated Infinite can adequately *fill*[3] and *superabundantly* satisfy the desire." Comparing the top to the bottom of this chain Allestree argues, "He that has inured his eyes to that divine splendour, which results from the beauty of holiness, is not dazzled with the glittering *shine*[2] of gold, and considers it as a vein of the same earth he treads on."

10.3. Work

> *My labour will* sustain*[3] me.*
> Milton.

The great antidote to the forces of degeneration and decay inherent in human life is useful activity. This is the message in a significant number of places in the *Dictionary*, and, more importantly, it is transmitted implicitly in the fact of the work itself. Working is, first of all, a way of escaping the demonic proliferation of human wishes; South draws the crucial antithesis between wishing and working: "A *wish*[1] is properly the desire of a man sitting or lying still; but an act of the will, is a man of business vigorously going about his work." Wishing is a form of desire and therefore a part of perpetual discontent and unhappiness. In another place South shows us the perenially unhappy entertainer of wishes: "The sot cried, *Utinam hoc esset laborare,* while he lay *lazing* and lolling upon his couch" (above, p. 116). The wish of wishes is a wish not to be wishing, but the only way to achieve the better life is by acting.

As Johnson suggests in a rare quotation from his own *Irene*, idleness is hell on earth: "Immur'd and busied in perpetual sloth, / That gloomy slumber of the *stagnant* soul." In *Rambler* 85 he says, "to be idle is to be vicious" (*Yale* 4: 87), and the same thought stimulates him to write hortatory definitions of many words relating to sloth. "To mope," for example, is "to be stupid; to drowse; to be in a constant daydream; to be spiritless, unactive and inattentive; to be stupid and delirious." It is clear that we are equally to avoid being called a "loiterer": "A lingerer; an idler; a lazy wretch; one who lives without business; one who is sluggish and dilatory." The nine synonyms of "sluggish" are like a series of pokes and prods: "Dull; drowsy; lazy; slothful; idle; insipid; slow; inactive; inert." Even "to yawn" is a grotesquerie to be avoided; it is "to gape; to oscitate; to have the mouth opened involuntarily by fumes, as in sleepiness." Elsewhere Johnson adduces Quincy to show in medical terms that idleness is a species of vice: "*Lassitude* generally expresses that weariness which proceeds from a distempered state, and not from exercise, which wants no remedy but rest: it proceeds from an increase of bulk, from a diminution of proper evacuation, or from too great a consumption of the fluid necessary to maintain the spring of the solids, as in fevers; or from a vitiated secretion of that juice, whereby the fibres are not supplied." Perhaps the hope that when dried and ingested they would cure this terrible condition by treating a principal cause is what made Johnson so assiduous in his collection of laxative orange peels.

The really serious consequences of laziness are not in this world but the next. Dryden says, "Let Epicurus give *indolency*[2] as an attribute to his gods, and place in it the happiness of the blest: the divinity which we worship has given us not only a precept against it, but his own example to the contrary." Turning to the metaphorical language of the

Old Testament, Seed reminds us that "the author of nature and the
scriptures[2] has expressly enjoined, that he who will not work, shall not
eat." This recalls the language of Proverbs: "I went by the field of the
slothful, and by the vineyard of the man void of understanding; and lo,
it was all grown[2] over with thorns, and nettles had covered the face
thereof." The positive side of the story also appears in Proverbs: "Seest
thou a man diligent[1] in his business? he shall stand before kings."
Rogers explains properly, without eliminating the literal sense of work:
"God will judge every man according to his works; to them, who by
patient continuance in well[13]-doing, endure through the heat and
burden of the day, he will give the reward of their labour." Work is the
way to eternal life, and so the concepts of work and life are closely
associated in the intellectual world that Johnson put together in the
Dictionary. A close and frightening analogy between work and the life
of man appears in the line from Isaiah that Johnson used to illustrate
two terrifying meanings in his book: "Behold, ye are of nothing[6], and
your work of nought[1]." Like the Dictionary Johnson himself came
close to identifying life and work, as has been conclusively shown by
Paul Fussell, W. J. Bate, and others. The identification appears most
dramatically in Johnson's frequent references to the parable of the
talents. Clearly, he saw the sum of his work as the basis for his claim to
eternal life. He makes it plain that he saw the Dictionary as an
important part of his life's work in the prayer he composed on the
occasion of beginning the second volume, 3 April 1753: "O God who
hast hitherto supported me enable me to proceed in this labour & in
the Whole task of my present state that when I shall render up at the
last day an account of the talent committed to me I may receive pardon
for the sake of Jesus Christ. Amen" (Yale 1: 50).

The Dictionary is Johnson's work, and so it is very nearly his life in
spiritual terms, but it was also his life in a somewhat more mundane
way. With its very numerous and relatively discrete parts the Dictionary
was for Johnson a way of marking time in terms of work, and therefore
it was a mode of realizing his existence. His great book served for
Johnson some of the purposes of a diary or commonplace book: it
provided him with a way of knowing where the time went and of seeing
that it was not wasted. When he had finally completed the near
innumerable corrections that he made to the Dictionary between 1755
and 1773,[4] he sought more lexicographical work. To Boswell's statement that "in 1773 his only publication was an edition of his folio
Dictionary," G. B. Hill appends the following note:

It should seem that this dictionary work was not unpleasant to Johnson; for Stockdale records (*Memoirs*, ii. 179) that about 1774, having told him that he had declined to edit a new edition of Chambers's *Dictionary of the Arts and Sciences*, Johnson replied, "that if I would not undertake it, he would. . . . I took the liberty to express my astonishment, that he, in his easy, and happy circumstances, should think of preparing a new edition of a voluminous, tedious, and scientifick dictionary. 'Sir,' said he, 'I like that *muddling* work.' He allowed some time to go by, during which another editor was found. Immediately after this intelligence, he called on me; and his first words were:—'It is gone, Sir.' " (Boswell 2: 203–4n)

Johnson spoke to Stockdale in words appropriate to shocked bereavement because a new alphabet of which to beat the track meant a renovation of life to him. In writing and revising the *Dictionary* he exhibited the same desire for perpetuating existence in perpetual expression that shows up more evidently in open-ended or circular encyclopedic works like *Jubilate Agno* and *Finnegans Wake*. That Johnson found a useful, morally beneficial, and financially sustaining form in which to embody this powerful desire testifies to his profoundly healthy sense of public and personal responsibility.

Notes

Introduction

1. See Wimsatt, *Philosophic Words* 24, for some other readers of Johnson's *Dictionary*. See Murray 235 for an account of Browning's intention to read every word of the *OED*.

2. See Boswell 1: 218–19; Wimsatt, *Philosophic Words* 53; and Sledd and Kolb, *Dr. Johnson's Dictionary* 19–25.

3. An examination of the John Johnson Collection of Proposals, which is full of prospectuses of dictionaries and encyclopedias, suggests this observation. I wish to thank Eric Buckley, the Printer to Oxford University, for allowing me to examine this collection.

4. J. A. Comenius, for example, focused his plans for "human omni-science" on the production of a vast dictionary, and his prospectus sounds much like Chambers's. In *A Patterne of Universall Knowledge* Comenius resolves:

> therefore, that a Booke should be compiled, for the containing all things which are necessary to be knowne and done, believed and hoped for by man, in respect of this and the life to come, *viz.* an entire narration of those things which we know already, with an exact Index of such things as we are ignorant of, whether they be those whose knowledge is altogether unattainable, or those that are left for further search. And all these things to that end, and in that order, that the mindes of men by *medium's* may be (as it were by a kind of artificiall Ladder) advanced from the first to the last, the lowest to the highest, even to him from whom, by whom, and for whom are all things. (4)

Comenius's consummate lexicographical effort has only recently been printed, but he did numerous works preparatory to the *Lexicon Reale Pansophicum*, and his idea of the dictionary as a great book of all things, even when considered fanciful, is present to the tradition of European lexicography in which Johnson labored.

5. Thomas Edwards to D. Wray, 23 May 1755, MS Bodley 1012, p. 211. See Sledd and Kolb, *Dr. Johnson's Dictionary* 135. Although I have examined these documents myself, I am nonetheless indebted to these earlier investigators.

6. This letter is in the Johnson Birthplace Museum. I am grateful to Dr. Nicholls, the curator, for showing it to me.

7. For accounts of the early printing history of the *Dictionary* see Sledd and Kolb, *Dr. Johnson's Dictionary* 105–10; and Cochrane 21–29. I have also received help in this matter from Dr. J. D. Fleeman who has, unlike myself, examined all the pertinent documents, including Strahan's printing ledger.

8. There is a suggestion of the connection in *Letters* 1: 10, and Chapman emphasizes it by indexing Johnson's remark under "Literature" (Index V) with the subheading "*scholarship*" and the description, " 'learning' *not* distinguished from literature" (*Letters* 3: 454).

9. Isaac Watts, for example, laments the loss of esteem for systematic learning

indicated by the relatively small bulk of the volumes published in his day (*Logick* 219).

10. See Fleeman, "Revenue of a Writer" 212; and Chapple.

11. A recently published book by John A. Vance, *Samuel Johnson and the Sense of History*, precedes me in exploding the myth. Vance shows Johnson's extensive interest in history and maintains that "his was one of the best historical minds of the eighteenth century" (3).

12. Like the initiative for so much seventeenth-century intellectual activity, the initiative for intellectual history of the sort Johnson wrote in the *Dictionary* and elsewhere comes straight out of Bacon's *Advancement of Learning*. Bacon says: "History is natural, civil, ecclesiastical, and literary, whereof the three first I allow as extant, the fourth I note as deficient. For no man hath propounded to himself the general state of learning to be described and represented from age to age, as many have done the works of nature, and the state civil and ecclesiastical, without which the history of the world seemeth to me to be as the *statua* of *Polyphemus* with his eye out, that part being wanting which doth most shew the spirit and life of the person . . ." (*Works* 2: 455).

13. This is the phraseology in Bailey's *Universal Etymological Dictionary* (London, 1721), but nearly the same thing appears in his *Dictionarium Britannicum* in both the 1730 and 1736 editions. Johnson used the latter in preparing the *Dictionary*; see Wimsatt, *Philosophic Words* 21.

14. For the transcription and other information pertaining to the manuscript I am indebted to Sledd and Kolb, *Dr. Johnson's Dictionary* 46–58. A facsimile of the manuscript, including the versos, appears in volume 2 of *The R. B. Adam Library*.

15. This is also the finding of Paul Korshin and of Sledd and Kolb (*Dr. Johnson's Dictionary* 54).

16. In the address to the reader in the 1696 edition, augmented by Augustus Buchner, Cellarius complains, "Historias ceteri, philosophorum maxime, vel sententias &t παροιμίας Græcorum adiecerunt, non inutiles quidem iuventuti, ad lexicon autem Latinum non pertinentes." That is, some of the earlier compilers "threw in histories, chiefly of philosophers, or wise sayings and aphorisms of the Greeks, which are not useless for students but do not belong in a Latin dictionary."

17. No. 230 in *The Sale Catalogue* is "Basilii fabri thesaurus eruditionis scholasticæ, Lips. 1696." Lot 15167 in the *Harleian Catalogue* (2: 989) is "Fabri Thesaurus Eruditionis Scholasticæ, 2 Vols.—Lipsiæ 1717" and has subjoined the note "Lexicon Fabri laudatissimum est, derivata primitivis subjiciuntur." The *Harleian Catalogue* also lists two copies of a 1604 *Forum Romanum*: no. 599 (5: 38) and no. 15144 (2: 988); after the latter appears the note, "Auctor huijus Libri fere omnia Rob. Stephano debere fertur." This is probably neither Curione's work nor Johnson's note. No. 1186 (3: 98) strikes me as more likely to be the work of a prospective lexicographer, and it seems to provide more evidence of the connection between Johnson and a Renaissance tradition of significant lexicography:

> 1186 Doleti Commentaria Linguæ Latinæ, 2 vol. *Lugd. apud Seb. Gryph.* 1536
>
> Though *Stephanus Doletus* was no good Poet, yet he was an excellent Printer. He applied himself with the utmost Assiduity and Attention to the Study of the *Greek*, *Latin*, and *French* Languages. Before he arrived at the Age of thirty-nine, he was burnt at *Paris* for Atheism, *Aug.* 3, 1546. Some have upbraided him with having stolen all the Materials of this Work from

Robert Stephanus. Be that as it will, it is certain he ought to be highly commended for having disposed in a clear and proper Order many Words and Things, which are found dispersed in *Stephanus* without any Method or Regularity. . . .

18. Wimsatt (*Philosophic Words* 152) cites Boswell 5: 323 and the preface to *The Preceptor.*

19. Johnson also cites at least once a similar work by the precocious fifteen-year-old Jacques Ozenham, *Récréations Mathématiques et Physiques.*

20. Introducing Gilbey's translation of Robert Grosseteste's *Testaments*, another book quoted in the *Dictionary*, Richard Day makes a similar admonition: "Looke upon Iacob, O you Parents, peruse the 12 godly Fathers in time and order: learne of him & his, to pray to God in Christ his name for your Children, have regard to their instruction: the want of the former, your children shall mis: the neglecte of the latter, you your selves shall bewaile. For the harty prayer of a father to the Almighty for his Children is a right singular benifit: but he that for foolish pity giveth them the bridle, is before God accounted a guilty partner of their sinfull race" (Grosseteste A2v).

21. Quoted in the *Dictionary* under "childless" from Bacon's essay "Of Parents and Children."

22. See also "pure[4]," "induction[2]," "sweet[1]," and "incident[1]."

23. These are almost matched in generality and directness by Howell's example of a "chronogram"—"Gloria lausque *Deo*, sæ*CL*or*VM* in sæ*CV*la sunt" (Glory and praise to God forever and ever)—and Addison's "motto"—"*Inservi Deo & lætare*" (Serve God and be cheerful).

24. See Wimsatt, "Johnson's Treatment of Bolingbroke in the *Dictionary.*"

25. There is an interesting contrast between Johnson's ironic presentation of himself as Ulysses and Boswell's attempt to present him unironically as the same character (1: 12). One of the main things missing from Boswell's *Life* is an adequate presentation of Johnson's capacity for satire and parody of himself as well as others.

26. The vanity of human learning is the subject of "The Vision of Theodore" and of the section on the student in "The Vanity of Human Wishes." It is also prominent in "Γνῶθι Σεαυτόν," but the closest approximation to Erasmus's notion that "the love of true holiness makes all human learning contemptible" is in Johnson's story of Pertinax in *Rambler* 95. Pertinax is a typical Menippean hero, a *philosophus gloriosus* who loses himself in the mazes of vain learning. Science leads Pertinax away from the most important truth, and he recovers it only by unscientifically subordinating reason to religion. The epigraph from Horace that Johnson prefixed to *Rambler* 95 is a suitable motto for a good part of the *Dictionary* as well as for many other "creative treatments of exhaustive erudition" in the Menippean tradition; in Francis's translation of the lines, they have a Christian cast that makes them even better suited to the *Dictionary* than in their original Latin:

> A fugitive from heav'n and prayer,
> I mock'd at all religious fear,
> Deep scienc'd in the mazy lore
> Of mad philosophy; but now
> Hoist sail, and back my voyage plow
> To that blest harbour, which I left before.
>
> (*Yale* 4: 143).

27. See chapter 2 below.

28. Locke confirms this tripartite division of the intellectual world in the conclusion to his *Essay concerning Human Understanding*: there the three great branches of knowledge are φυσική, or "the Knowledge of Things, as they are in their own proper Beings"; πρακτική, or "the Skill of Right applying our own Powers and Actions, for the Attainment of Things good and useful"; and σημειωτική, or "*the Doctrine of Signs*; the most usual whereof being Words" (720).

29. The thesaurus was appended to volume 7 of the fourth edition (1751) of *Clarissa*, a copy of which Richardson gave to Johnson (Keast 436n).

30. When I had finished all but the last draft of this book I finally saw the unpublished dissertation of Robert Carroll Miller, "Johnson's *Dictionary* Categorized." Miller's categories, like mine, display the *Dictionary* as an encyclopedic work that focuses on basic subjects in the curriculum, such as language, literature, religion, law, and science. My book is, happily, a complement to Miller's, and does not duplicate much of his effort. Miller lists the words appropriate to the topics he treats and is mainly interested in how Johnson defines the words belonging to the vocabulary of each topic. I, on the other hand, am mostly interested in the content of Johnson's illustrative quotations and have sought material relevant to my topics under every related and unrelated word in the *Dictionary*.

Chapter 1

1. Also see Locke under "abyss[3]" (see *Essay* 533).

2. Also see the quotation from Hooker under "deduction[1]," which asserts, "all truth, out of any truth, may be concluded."

3. "The work that God performs forever from the beginning to the end."

4. It also has a middle ground in generality, but at that level general knowledge is superficial and misleading. Hooker, in fact, sees it as evidence of our incurable human ignorance: see "generality[1]," "unlimited[2]," and "infirmity[3]."

5. Also see Bacon under "to collate[1]" and Watts under "quarto" and "systematical."

6. If the frontispiece is indicative of Chambers's sense of the episteme, his refusal to call his book an encyclopedia, despite his publisher's entreaties, may have had something to do with a reluctance to portray the field of knowledge as whole and harmonious; John Nichols (*Literary Anecdotes* 5: 659–60n) tells this story in a footnote quoting Bowyer, and I hasten to add that Chambers apparently objected to adding the "en-" primarily because he thought it made no difference in the meaning of the word. He rejected Bowyer's philological argument that the added "en-" makes the word more accurate than "cyclopædia," which could be construed as meaning education of a circle rather than in a circle. Chambers added his reasons for rejecting "en-" to his article on "cyclopædia" and took the occasion to reiterate his faith in the Lockean theory that words get their meanings entirely by convention.

7. As Locke's use of "dark" suggests, the surest sort of experience in the *Dictionary* is visual. Johnson seems to assent to this preference when he defines "intuition" as "sight of any thing." A pair of couplets from Watts, though they hope to be memorable in sound, also exalt sight:

> Sounds which address the ear, are lost and die
> In one short hour; but that which strikes the eye,

Lives long upon the mind: the faithful sight
Engraves[3] the knowledge with a beam of light.

8. Also see Locke under "extrinsical" and "proper": "Outward objects, that are *extrinsical* to the mind, and its own operations, proceeding from powers intrinsical and *proper*[1] to itself, which become also objects of its contemplation, are the original of all knowledge."

9. An example of what was excluded is a passage alluding to the Platonic notion of knowledge as anamnesis in which Johnson underlined three words: "it was not *without* some kind of probability that some of the ancients thought that Science was little else than memory or reminiscence, a discovery of which was in the soul before. But whatever may be said of other matters, certainly the first *draughts* and *strictures* of natural religion and morality are naturally in the mind" (Bodley Dep. c. 25, 63).

10. Hale is allowed to say, for example, "Those implanted anticipations are, that there is a god, that he is *placable*, to be feared, honoured, loved, worshipped and obeyed."

11. See Tillotson under "to rivet[2]" and South under "cultivation[2]."

12. Also see Locke under the key word "to implant."

13. See also the reiteration by Watts under the same word.

14. See also Bacon under "amplitude[2]" and Milton under "to fetch[9]."

15. See also Fairfax under "greedy[2]" and Dryden under "broad[1]."

16. Tillotson explains the principle in negative terms: "The Scripture represents wicked men as without understanding; not that they are destitute of the natural faculty: they are not blind, but they *wink*[1]."

17. See also Rogers under "wisely": "Admitting their principles to be true, they act *wisely*: they keep their end, evil as it is, steadily in view."

18. See also South under "policy[2]."

19. In addition to those cited below see his entry under "to avoid[1]."

20. Prior follows Hooker when he describes wisdom as "this great *empress*[2] of the human soul."

Chapter 2

1. See Kolb and Kolb 71. Having checked a great many quotations myself, I agree with the Kolbs' findings, although there are exceptions to the rule.

2. Also see Glanvill under "crepusculous" and South under "diminutive."

3. See also Allestree: "Men are so possessed with their own fancies, that they take them for oracles; and are arrived to some extraordinary revelations of truth, when indeed they do but dream dreams, and amuse themselves with the *fantastick*[2] ideas of a busy imagination."

4. Under the same word see also Watts's identification of complication with error: "By admitting a *complication*[3] of ideas, and taking too many things at once into one question, the mind is dazzled and bewildered."

5. The errors of Aristotle are noted with some regularity in the *Dictionary*; see, for instance, Johnson's citation of Cowley under "female rhyme."

6. Another excerpt of the same passage appears under "new[1]."

7. Also see Holder under "diphthong."

8. Also see Locke under "angel[1]" and "to coexist[1]."

9. Addison's entry under "biggest[1]" is clearly influenced by Locke's notion. See also Prior's lines under "to illude."

10. Quotations by Browne and Blackmore under "problem" suggest other imponderables. Blackmore says, "This *problem* let philosophers resolve, / What makes the globe from West to East revolve," and Browne, "Although in general one understood colours, yet were it not an easy *problem* to resolve, why grass is green?"

11. See also Boyle under "dogmatical."

12. See Boyle under "judiciary."

13. See also Browne under "illimitable."

Chapter 3

1. Johnson's scrupulousness about lying is one result of this attitude. In a famous passage of the *Life* Boswell records a piece of Johnsonian educational advice that demonstrates the point: " 'Accustom your children (said he) constantly to this; if a thing happened at one window, and they, when relating it, say that it happened at another, do not let it pass, but instantly check them; you do not know where deviation from truth will end' " (3: 228). The admonitions against lying in the *Dictionary* are equally strict, and they rest on an equally strong sense of truth as whole and absolute.

2. Further excerpts from this passage appear under "onset[1]" and "battery[2]."

3. This Lucretian image is also present in *Rambler* 52 and in "The Vanity of Human Wishes."

4. For two of the many quotations in the *Dictionary* that make this point, see Browne under "to emancipate" and Raleigh under "to cast[1]."

5. See Hooker's support for Tillotson under "fact[1]."

6. Also see Swift under "upon[13]."

7. Hale makes much the same distinction under "inductive[2]," and under "quillet" Digby describes the mental balancing in "the scale of reason." Watts, however, is closer to both Locke's and Johnson's language when he says, "By putting every argument on one side and the other into the balance, we must form a judgment which side *preponderates*[2]."

8. Addison speaks a little less scientifically about the *inclination*[2] of the soil to produce certain plants in certain places.

9. The methodological priority extended to analysis in the *Dictionary* is also evident in Locke's remark that "to observe every the least difference that is in things, keeps the understanding steady and right in its *way*[4] to knowledge."

Chapter 4

1. For example, see Glanvill under "intelligibility[2]," Addison under "litigation" and "to disencumber[1]," and Watts under "consciousness[1]."

2. Also see *Rambler* 42, where restlessness of attention is a sign of the "celestial nature of the soul" (*Yale* 3: 222).

3. Also see Davies under "fine[7]" and Collier under "to scour[6]."

4. Glanvill adds, "'Tis no *disparagement*[3] to philosophy, that it cannot deify us."

5. See Watts again under "signature[1]."

6. Under "species" Dryden favorably describes imagination in terms reminiscent of Hobbes: "Wit in the poet, or wit-writing, is no other than the faculty of the imagination in the writer, which searches over all the memory for the *species*[4] or ideas of those things which it designs to represent."

7. Also see Burnet under "clear[6]."

Chapter 5

1. To give one example among many, under "intermission" we find Ben Jonson's translation of part of the epigraph to the *Dictionary* (see below, p. 170).

2. Yet, his editorial comments frequently enough register his sense that such Romanization is illegitimate. Johnson often applies to Thomson, Philips, Milton, and others the sort of criticism that Dryden makes: "He did too much *romanize* our tongue, leaving the words, he translated, almost as much Latin as he found them." (See below, p. 171). Harold B. Allen counts thirteen instances in which Johnson censures Latinism (172).

3. "I have endured hardships at the hands of the rude or untutored."

4. "There are words and formulas with which you may ease this grief."   ·

5. "Nature would suffer if it were denied such things."

6. "On all counts complete." See also "glade," "garnish[4]," and "maxim[5]."

7. Johnson marked out only 55 passages in Burton (see Thomas 126–27).

8. "The dead are the best counselors."

9. "If only this were work."

10. "However, passing through their midst, Jesus departed" (see Luke 4.30 in the Vulgate). Under "glossary" Johnson provides more Latin when he lets stand Stillingfleet's citation of Varro; the citation both recommends the ancients and gives point to Johnson's campaign against idolatry: "when *delubrum* was applied to a place, it signified such a one, *in quo dei simulachrum dedicatum est*" (in which there was an image dedicated to a god).

11. "Silver cut up into little images and inscriptions" (Satire 14.291; Ramsay 285).

12. "The day of slavery destroys fully half of virtue."

13. "He sleeps a holy sleep: say not the noble suffer death" (Callimachus, Ep. 2.2).

14. "Three decades and twice three years did the heavenly augurs fix as the measure of my life. I am content therewith" (*Greek Anthology* 7: 157; Paton 2: 88–89).

15. "The amice, with which the neck is caught fast and the breast concealed, bespeaks the purity of the inner man; for it covers the heart, lest it contemplate vanities, and further, it binds in the neck, lest falsehood make its way up to the tongue."

16. "My ruddy wing gives me a name, but my tongue is a delicacy to gluttons. What if my tongue were to speak?" (13.71; Ker 417). I think Johnson would have liked Housman's interpretation of "garrula" as "telltale," an alternate translation in Ker.

17. "Magpie poetesses" (Prologue 13; Ramsay 311).

18. "They bring the towels with the teaseled nap" (*Georgics* 4.377).

19. "Paler or greener than grass [am I]" (Lobel and Page's 31.14).

20. "His body is starred with bright-coloured spots" (Miller 271).

21. "A woman of easy repute."

22. "Golden Aphrodite."

23. "To the stars extols . . . his courage and his golden virtue" (*Odes* 4.11.23; Bennett 289).

24. "This festal day, each time the year revolves, shall draw a well-pitched cork forth from a jar set to drink the smoke in Tullus' consulship" (Bennett 209).

25. "A man in whose garden sage grows, why should he die?"

26. For example, see Hooker under "proper[1]" and Atterbury under "to set[33]."

27. Also see Shakespeare under "noun." The extent to which an attack on grammar is an attack on learning is evident in Johnson's definition of "grammar school" as "a school in which the learned languages are grammatically taught."

28. Also see "to beat[13]."

29. The exception is Bacon under "schoolmen[2]," but Donne, Baker, and Pope follow hard on his heels with satire under the same word and sense.

30. See also Addison under "to disinter" and Felton under "to crust[1]."

31. See Carlson.

32. Burton section 1.2.15 (Bodleian Dep. c. 25, 68 and following); I think the great amount of Latin, most of which would have had to have been excised for the English *Dictionary*, deterred Johnson from marking his Burton more heavily (see above, p. 116 and n. 7).

33. See also "excrementitious."

34. "Straitened domestic circumstances."

35. Also see L'Estrange under "ado[3]" and South under "to maintain[6]."

36. See also "subtilely[2]" and successive quotations under "to trouble[2]."

37. See the *Literary Magazine* 2.13 (1757): 171–75; 2.14: 251–53; 2.15: 299–304.

38. Atterbury agrees with Addison under "to set[59]."

39. Swift seems to underwrite this judgment in illustration of the same word, but his faithful readers will recognize that the sentence comes from Gulliver's description of the Houyhnhnms' educational practices and is therefore subject to irony.

40. Also see Locke under "discouragement[3]."

41. Locke makes a similar remark under "broad[2]."

42. An example of Swift's irony appears under "mama": "Little masters and misses are great impediments to servants; the remedy is to bribe them, that they may not tell tales to papa and *mama*." Johnson further indulged a temptation to print ironic advice on breeding in his citations from Jane Collier's *Essay on the Art of Ingeniously Tormenting . . . With some instructions for Plaguing all your Acquaintance*.

43. Under "to elapse" Richardson imagines education as architecture on a larger scale.

44. The condition of these students is part of the universal condition of fallen man, as Hooker suggests: "By reason of that original weakness in the instruments, without which the understanding part is not able in this world by *discourse*[1] to work, the very conceit of painfulness is a bridle to stay us."

45. The warning about conversation is related, of course, to a more general warning about company. For quotations on the dangers of company see, for example, Ascham under "to breed[2]," Bacon under "to sort[2]," Taylor under "misgovernment[2]," and Locke under "to misbecome."

46. A similar excision occurs under "breeder[2]" (c.f. Ascham 74).

47. "This book" is *Il Cortegiano*.

48. Also see "doctrinal" and "primer" for moral and religious exemplification of the language of education.

Chapter 6

1. See, for instance, his *New and Easy Institution of Grammer*.

2. Swift says about the same thing under "to jumble," but he does not mention Hobbes.

3. Also see "misguidance," "afloat," "demagogue," and "to league" for more of South's warnings about the moral dangers of language.

4. Another version of this appears under "to take[48]."

5. Browne provides another example of this kind of equivocation under "wolf[2]"; also see Baker under "drug[1]" and Hervey under "misconception."

6. The first example means either "don't fear to kill the king; that is a good thing" or "don't kill the king; it is good to fear him," depending upon how the line is broken. The second example means "to get (i.e., understand) jokes" or "to get (i.e., catch) rabbits": his example of equivocation is doubly equivocal.

7. See Locke again under "inveterateness" and "obstinacy."

8. Johnson's assent to this notion is the subject of Wimsatt's book *Philosophic Words*, and the impression the passage made upon him may be reflected in the famous remark in his preface to Shakespeare, "the mind can only repose on the stability of truth" (*Yale* 7: 62).

9. *Ars Poetica* 72–73. Brink and other modern editors have *ius* where Johnson prints *vis*. In the translation by Francis the lines read: "If custom will, whose arbitrary sway, / Words, and the forms of language, must obey" (Horace, *Works* 347).

10. See also Swift under "antiquary."

11. See also "far[7]," and for Dryden's different praise of Greek see "russet" and "rusticity[1]."

12. "If it come from a Greek original."

13. Harold B. Allen counts 17 authorial complaints against Gallicism in the *Dictionary* (172).

14. Hughes also says, "If any will rashly blame such his choice of old and unwonted words, him may I more justly blame and condemn, either of witless *headiness* in judging, or of *headless* hardiness in condemning."

15. Also see "to fall[44]" and "to fill[7]."

16. For a full treatment of the "brands" Johnson used, see Allen.

Chapter 7

1. Johnson thinks of syntax mainly as inflection, so he finds it almost irrelevant to English: "Wallis therefore has totally omitted it; and [Ben] Johnson, whose desire of following the writers upon the learned languages made him think a syntax indispensably necessary, has published such petty observations as were better omitted" (see subheading "Syntax" in the "Grammar").

2. As a man of science, Murray was inclined to include more indecent words than his publishers allowed him. At the Pembroke College Conference com-

memorating the two-hundrèth anniversary of Johnson's death, D. T. Siebert gave a paper on Johnson's inclusions of low and bad words, "Propriety in the *Dictionary*." Siebert identified many funny and playful inclusions in his paper, but not so many as to alter substantially the point I am making here. The most indecent word I know of in the *Dictionary* is "fart," which Johnson defines as "wind from behind." In "Samuel Johnson and the Authoritarian Principle" Allen catalogues eight words that Johnson brands as "vulgar," and in Appendix 3 he compares Johnson's treatment of "four-letter" words to the treatment they receive in other dictionaries.

3. Pope's correspondents include Berkeley, Bolingbroke, Swift, and Gay.

4. A possible exception is Ainsworth's English-Latin *Thesaurus*, but the use of Ainsworth is not visibly tendentious, whereas Calmet is clearly present to make reading the Bible easier.

5. "The dead are the best counsellors." In his own "Apophthegms" Bacon alludes to an older source of the sentiment: in No. 137 he reports that Alonzo of Aragon said "of himself, that he was a great necromancer, for that he used to ask counsel of the dead; meaning of books" (*Works* 3: 276). Johnson, imperfectly remembering his reading in Bacon, continues the tradition of this remark in *Rambler* 87: "It was the maxim, I think, of Alphonsus of Arragon, that 'dead counsellors are safest.'" He goes on to make the maxim his own with a characteristic commentary: "The grave puts an end to flattery and artifice, and the information that we receive from books is pure from interest, fear, or ambition. Dead counsellors are likewise most instructive; because they are heard with patience and with reverence" (*Yale* 4: 96–97).

6. Also see "believer[2]."

7. Watts's Vario resembles Johnson's Quisquillius (*Yale* 4: 64–70).

8. Johnson makes a similar distinction under "to scruze."

9. Curiously, Swift makes just this appropriation in the very next quotation. The irony of the juxtaposition is to his cost as well as "the sex's."

10. See More under "subderisorious" for a little greater liberality.

Chapter 8

1. Johnson's interest in censuring Milton's errors does not prevent him from vindicating Milton's use of "to obey[2]," and criticizing Addison's erroneous censure of it.

2. Perhaps the most interesting and personal exception to this rule in the *Dictionary* is the case of Bolingbroke, whom Johnson censures as often as he mentions him. The reasons for this are ideological, but the censure usually takes a philological form. Unlike other authors from whom Johnson did not directly take illustrative quotations, Bolingbroke is not allowed the safety of obscurity. Under the fifth sense of "to owe," for instance, Johnson writes, "A practice has long prevailed among writers, to use *owing*, the active participle of *owe*, in a passive sense, for *owed* or *due*. Of this impropriety *Bolinbroke* was aware, and, having no quick sense of the force of English words, has used *due*, in the sense of consequence or imputation, which by other writers is only used of *debt*. We say, the money is *due* to me; *Bolinbroke* says, the effect is *due* to the cause." See Wimsatt, "Johnson's Treatment of Bolingbroke in the *Dictionary*."

3. But a dissenting view is expressed by Bentley under "defoedation."

4. For the similar birth of Cibber see Pope under "reading[1]."

5. Johnson's third sense of "science" shows how relevant to science South's definition is: science is regulated art or "Art attained by precepts, or built on principles."

6. Ben Jonson also locates critical reality in the audience when he says, "Plays in themselves have neither hopes nor fears; / Their fate is only in their *hearers* ears."

7. It is worth noting that Johnson makes the formula less extreme than it sounds by listing it under the tenth sense of "nature": "Sentiments or images adapted to nature, or conformable to truth and reality."

8. Also see Dryden under "undeniably": "I grant that nature all poets ought to study: but then this *undeniably* also follows, that those things which delight all ages, must have been an imitation of nature."

9. Also see Dryden under "painter."

10. "Verses void of thought, and sonorous trifles" (Horace, *Ars Poetica* 332; Fairclough 477).

11. Horace, *Epistles* 1.2.3–4; in the Loeb edition the first four lines run: "While you, Lollius Maximus, declaim at Rome, I have been reading afresh at Praeneste the writer of the Trojan War [Homer]; who tells us what is fair, what is foul, what is helpful, what not, more plainly and better than Chrysippus or Crantor [the moralists]" (Fairclough 263).

12. Prior further describes the effect of dependence upon poetic honesty and casts Boileau in a different light:

> When once the poet's honour ceases,
> From reason far his transports rove;
> And Boileau, for eight hundred *pieces*[8],
> Makes Louis take the wall of Jove.

13. "Asterisk" gets a "*," and the third definition of "crotchet" is "hooks in which words are included [thus]"; there are examples of brevier, pica, and bourgeois type, but no cuts anywhere in the book.

14. For other quotations that seem to mention the amanuenses, see Matthew 23 under "to shut[7]," Grew under "scribe[1]," and 1 Maccabees 4 under "offence." Also see above, p. 119.

15. "The man elect for Chancellor of all England's realm, see you, will be the first object of petition by the fretting mind, for he it is who revokes the kingdom's unjust laws and devises the equity in a pious prince's biddings."

Chapter 9

1. For a good example of how Hammond combines the political and the Lactantian, see his message "To the Reader" prefatory to *A Practical Catechism* (*Works* 1).

2. "From the causes of things to come to know the Supreme Cause."

3. See Pope under "to charge[3]" and Broome under "decree[1]" for other versions of the thought.

4. The *Dictionary* does sometimes lament the tragic domination of fate. See, for example, Milton under "inevitable," Spenser under "destiny[2]," and Shakespeare

under "to play[15]." But these lamentations seem to me less numerous by far than the assertions of freedom and the denigrations of such hypostatic, possibly sacrilegious notions as fortune and chance.

5. "According to Nithard, the ancient Saxons were divided into three classes: Edhilingas, Frilingas, and Lazzas—that is, nobles, freemen, and slaves, in a distinction long retained. But during the reign of Richard the Second the greater part of the slaves achieved liberty. So today among the English a slave is rarely found who is said to be owned. Nevertheless there is a memory of the ancient name, for even today we call an ignoble person *lazy*."

6. See Dunn, "Politics of Locke." I have reserved a full-scale account of the politics of Johnson's *Dictionary* for separate treatment in an article.

7. Also see Locke under "punishment" and his third contribution under "to look[3]."

Chapter 10

1. Also see Temple under "comparatively," Pope under "isthmus," and Addison under "to checker."

2. See South again under "recreation[2]."

3. Under "to endure" Temple repeats the folk wisdom that the rich and lazy are more susceptible to gout.

4. Alan Reddick sheds further light on how much correction Johnson did apart from the huge revision for the fourth edition. James Basker of Harvard University has shown, contrary to earlier findings, that Johnson made some changes in the third edition of 1765 (personal conversation, 1984). My sense is that he was almost continually correcting and emending in a habitual and perhaps even a compulsive way.

Bibliography

Abbot, George. *A Brief Description of the Whole Worlde. Wherein are Particularly described al the Monarchies, Empires, and Kingdomes of the same: with their severall titles and situations thereunto adioyning.* London, 1600.

The R. B. Adam Library Relating to Dr. Samuel Johnson and His Era. 3 vols. London: privately printed, 1929.

Agrippa, Henri Cornelius. *Of the Vanitie and Uncertaintie of Arts and Sciences.* Trans. James Sanford. London, 1569.

Ainsworth, Robert. *Thesaurus Linguae Latinae Compendius.* London, 1736.

Allen, Harold B. "Samuel Johnson and the Authoritarian Principle in Linguistic Criticism." Ph.D. diss. Univ. of Michigan, 1940.

Allestree, Richard. *The Causes of the Decay of Christian Piety.* London, 1677.

———. *The Government of the Tongue.* 3rd ed. London, 1675.

Ascham, Roger. *The Schoolmaster.* Ed. James Upton. London, 1743. See *Sale Catalogue*, nos. 558 and 276.

Atterbury, Francis. *Fourteen Sermons Preach'd on Several Occasions.* London, 1708.

Ayliffe, John. *Pareregon Canonici Anglicani or, A Commentary by Way of Supplement to the Canons and Constitutions of the Church of England.* London, 1726. See *Sale Catalogue*, no. 119.

Bacon, Francis. *Works.* 4 vols. London, 1740. See Wimsatt, *Philosophic Words* 148–49.

Bailey, Nathan. *Dictionarium Britannicum.* London, 1730, 1736.

———. *An Universal Etymological English Dictionary.* London, 1721.

Baker, Thomas. *Reflections upon Learning; Wherein is Shewn the Insufficiency Thereof, in its several Particulars: in order to Evince the Usefulness and Necessity of Revelation.* 7th ed. London, 1738.

Barker, Jane. *The Entertaining Novels of Mrs. Jane Barker.* 2nd ed. 2 vols. London, 1719.

Bate, Walter Jackson. *Samuel Johnson.* New York: Harcourt Brace Jovanovich, 1977.

Bentley, Richard. *The Folly and Unreasonableness of Atheism Demonstrated from the Advantage and Pleasure of a Religious Life.* London, 1693.

Boethius. *The Consolation of Philosophy.* Trans. S. J. Tester. Loeb Classical Library. London: Heinemann, 1973.

Boswell, James. *The Life of Samuel Johnson.* Ed. G. B. Hill; rev. L. F. Powell. 6 vols. Oxford: Clarendon, 1934–50.

Bourde, Andrew. *The Fyrst boke of the Introduction of Knowledge. The whych doth teache a man to Speake part of all manner of languages, and to know the usage and fashion of all manner of countreys.* London, n.d.

Boyle, Robert. *Works.* 5 vols. London, 1744.

Bramhall, Joseph. *Castigations of Mr Hobbes His Last Animadversions, in the Case concerning Liberty, and Universal Necessity.* London, 1658.

———. *A Defence of True Liberty from Ante-Cedent and Extrinsecall Necessity, Being an answer to a late Book of Mr Thomas Hobbs of Malmesbury, intituled, A Treatise of Liberty and Necessity.* London, 1655.

Brerewood, Edward. *Enquiries Touching the Diversity of Languages and Religions, through the Chiefe Parts of the World*. London, 1622.

Browne, Sir Thomas. *Pseudodoxia Epidemica*. London, 1646. See *Sale Catalogue*, no. 579.

Burgess, Daniel. Commonplace Book. Bodleian MS Eng. misc. f. 20.

Burke, Kenneth. *The Philosophy of Literary Form*. Berkeley: Univ. of California Press, 1973.

Burnet, Thomas. *The Sacred Theory of the Earth*. London, 1690. See Wimsatt, *Philosophic Words* 151; *Sale Catalogue*, no. 453.

Burton, Robert. *Anatomy of Melancholy*. 8th ed. London, 1676. (Bodleian Library Dep. c. 25 is the copy Johnson used.)

Camden, William. *Camden's Britannia*. Trans. Edmund Gibson. London, 1695.

Carew, Richard. *The Survey of Cornwall and An Epistle concerning the Excellencies of the English Tongue*. London, 1723.

Carlson, W. R. "Dialectic and Rhetoric in Pierre Bayle." Ph.D. diss. Yale Univ., 1973.

Chambers, Ephraim. *Considerations Preparatory to a Second Edition*. N.p., n.d.

———. *Cyclopædia or, A Universal Dictionary of Arts and Sciences*. 4th ed. 2 vols. London, 1741. See Wimsatt, *Philosophic Words* 151; *Sale Catalogue*, no. 487.

Chapple, J. A. V. "Samuel Johnson's *Proposals for Printing the History of the Council of Trent*." *Bulletin of the John Rylands Library* 45 (1963): 340–69.

Chaucer, Geoffrey. *The Works of Geoffrey Chaucer . . . Together with a Glossary by a student of the same College*. Ed. John Urrey. London, 1721.

Cheyne, George. *Philosophical Principles of Religion: Natural and Reveal'd*. 2nd ed. London, 1715.

Clifford, James. *Dictionary Johnson*. New York: McGraw Hill, 1979.

Cochrane, J. A. *Dr. Johnson's Printer: The Life of William Strahan*. London: Routledge and Kegan Paul, 1974.

Coleridge, Samuel T. *Biographia Literaria*. Ed. James Engel and W. Jackson Bate. 2 vols. Vol. 7 of *The Collected Works of Samuel Taylor Coleridge*. Princeton: Princeton Univ. Press, 1983.

———. *The Notebooks of Samuel Taylor Coleridge*. Ed. Kathleen Coburn. 3 vols. Princeton: Princeton Univ. Press, 1973–.

Collier, Jane. *An Essay on the Art of Ingeniously Tormenting . . . With some instructions for Plaguing all your Acquaintance*. London, 1753.

Collier, Jeremy. *Essays*. 6th ed. London, 1722.

Comenius, J. A. *A Patterne of Universall Knowledge, In a plaine and true Draught*. Trans. Jeremy Collier. London, 1651.

Corbet, Dr. Richard. *Poems*. 3rd ed. London, 1672.

Curione, Caelius Secundus. *Thesaurus Linguae Latine Sive Forum Romanum*. Basel, 1561.

Davies, John. *A Discovery of the True Causes Why Ireland was never Entirely Subdued nor brought under the Obedience of the Crowne of England, untill the Beginning of his Majesties happie Raigne*. London, 1612.

Derham, William. *Physico-Theology: or, a Demonstration of the Being and Attributes of God from His Works of Creation*. 2nd ed. London, 1714. See Wimsatt, *Philosophic Words* 152.

Digby, Sir Kenelm. *Of Bodies* and *Of the Immortality of Man's Soul*. London, 1669.

Dodds, E. R. *Missing Persons*. Oxford: Clarendon, 1977.

————, ed. *Gorgias*. Oxford: Clarendon, 1959.

Dodsley, Robert. *The Preceptor*. 2 vols. London, 1748.

Douglas, David C. *English Scholars 1660–1730*. 2nd ed. London: Eyre and Spottiswood, 1951.

Dunn, John. "The Politics of Locke in England and America in the Eighteenth Century." *John Locke: Problems and Perspectives*. Ed. John W. Yolton. Cambridge: Cambridge Univ. Press, 1969. 45–80.

Eco, Umberto. *Semiotics and the Philosophy of Language*. Bloomington: Indiana Univ. Press, 1984.

Edwards, Thomas. Letters. MS Bodleian 1012.

Elledge, Scott. "The Naked Science of Language 1747–86." *Studies in Criticism and Aesthetics, 1600–1800*. Ed. Howard Anderson and John S. Shea. Minneapolis: Univ. of Minnesota Press, 1967. 266–295.

Ellis, Henry. *A Voyage to Hudson's Bay*. London, 1748.

Erasmus, Desiderius. *The Praise of Folly*. Trans. Clarence H. Miller. New Haven: Yale Univ. Press, 1979.

[Estienne, Robert] Stephanus. *Thesaurus Linguae Latinae*. London, 1734–35.

Faber, Basilius. *Thesaurus Eruditis Scholasticae*. Leipzig, 1587.

————. *Thesaurus Eruditis Scholasticae*. Ed. Augustus Buchner and Christophorus Cellarius. Leipzig, 1696.

Felton, Henry. *A Dissertation on Reading the Classics and Forming a Just Style*. London, 1713.

Ficino, Marsilino. *Marsilino Ficino: The Philebus Commentary*. Ed. Michael J. B. Allen. Los Angeles: Univ. of California Press, 1975.

Fiddes, Richard. *Practical Discourses on Several Subjects*. London, 1712. See *Sale Catalogue*, nos. 212, 355, and 599.

Fleeman, J. D., ed. *Early Biographical Writings of Dr. Johnson*. Farnborough, Hants: Gregg, 1973. Facsimile reprints of early editions.

————. *A Preliminary Handlist of Copies of Books associated with Dr. Samuel Johnson*. Oxford Bibliographical Society Occasional Publications, No. 17. Oxford: Oxford Bibliographical Society, 1984.

————. *A Preliminary Handlist of Documents & Manuscripts of Samuel Johnson*. Oxford Bibliographical Society Occasional Publications, No. 2. Oxford: Oxford Bibliographical Society, 1967.

————. "The Revenue of a Writer: Johnson's Literary Earnings." *Studies in the Book Trade*. Oxford: Oxford Bibliographical Society, 1975. 211–30.

————. "Some of Dr. Johnson's Preparatory Notes for His *Dictionary*, 1755." *Bodleian Library Record* 7.4 (1964): 205–10.

Fraser, Russell. *The Language of Adam: On the Limits and Systems of Discourse*. New York: Columbia Univ. Press, 1977.

Freed, Lewis. "The Sources of Johnson's *Dictionary*." Ph.D. diss. Cornell Univ., 1939.

Frye, Northrop. *Anatomy of Criticism*. Princeton: Princeton Univ. Press, 1957.

Fussell, Paul. *Samuel Johnson and the Life of Writing*. New York: Harcourt Brace Jovanovich, 1971.

Garretson, J. *English Exercises for school-boys to translate into Latin, Comprizing All the Rules of Grammar*. 11th ed. London, 1706.

Glanvill, Joseph. *Scepsis Scientifica: or, Confest Ignorance the way to Science*. London, 1665. See Wimsatt, *Philosophic Words* 152.

Γραφαυτάρχεια, *or the Scriptures' Sufficiency Practically Demonstrated, wherein whatever is contain'd in Scripture Respecting Doctrine, Worship or Manners, is reduced to its proper Head.* N.p., n.d.

Graunt, John. *Natural and Political Observations Mentioned in a Following Index, and Made upon the Bills of Mortality.* London, 1662; rpt. Baltimore: Johns Hopkins Univ. Press, 1939. See Wimsatt, *Philosophic Words* 153.

Greek Anthology. Trans. W. R. Paton. 5 vols. Loeb Classical Library. London: Heinemann, 1916; rpt. 1980.

Greene, Donald, ed. *Samuel Johnson's Library: An Annotated Guide.* English Literary Studies Monograph Series, No. 1. Vancouver: Univ. of British Columbia, 1975.

Grew, Nehemiah. *Cosmologia Sacra.* London, 1701.

Grosseteste, Robert [Grosthead]. *The Testaments of the twelve Patriarches, the Sonnes of Iacob.* Trans. A. Gilby. London, 1606. Prefatory address "To the Christian Reader" by Richard Day.

Hakewill, George. *An Apologie or Declaration of the Power and Providence of God in the Government of the World.* London, 1635.

Hale, Matthew. *The Primitive Origination of Mankind Considered and Examined According to the Light of Nature.* London, 1677. (Bodleian Dep. c. 25 is Johnson's copy; see Fleeman, *Handlist* [1967] 107.)

Hammond, Henry. *Works.* 4 vols. London, 1684. Volume 1 contains *A Practical Catechism* and *Of Fundamentals.*

[*Harleian Catalogue*] *Catalogus Bibliothecæ Harleianæ.* 5 vols. London, 1743–45.

Harris, John. *Lexicon Technicum: or, an Universal English Dictionary of Arts and Sciences: Explaining not only the Terms of Art, but the Arts themselves.* 2 vols. London, 1704. See Wimsatt, *Philosophic Words* 153.

Holder, William. *Elements of Speech: An Essay of Inquiry into the Natural Production of Letters with an Appendix concerning persons Deaf and Dumb.* London, 1669. See Wimsatt, *Philosophic Words* 154.

Hooker, Richard. *Works.* London, 1676.

Horace. *The 'Ars Poetica.'* Ed. C. O. Brink. Vol. 2 of *Horace on Poetry.* Cambridge: Cambridge Univ. Press, 1971.

————. *Satires, Epistles and Ars Poetica.* Trans. H. R. Fairclough. Loeb Classical Library. London: Heinemann, 1926; rpt. 1978.

————. *The Works of Horace.* Trans. Philip Francis. London, 1807.

Howell, James. *Dodona's Grove, or the Vocal Forest.* Cambridge, 1645.

[Johnson, Samuel]. *A Compleat Vindication of the Licensers of the Stage, from the Malicious and Scandalous Aspersions of Mr. Brooke, Author of Gustavus Vasa.* London, 1739.

Johnson, Samuel. *A Dictionary of the English Language.* 2 vols. London, 1755.

————. *A Dictionary of the English Language* [corrected and annotated sheets from the first edition comprising A-Pumper with a few sections missing]. London, 1755. See *Sale Catalogue* 106; this is the Sneyd-Gimbel copy now in the Beinecke Library, Yale University.

————. *A Dictionary of the English Language* [corrected and annotated sheets from the first and third editions, comprising A-I with some selections missing]. London, 1755 and 1765. British Museum C.45. k.3; see *Sale Catalogue* 106.

————. *A Dictionary of the English Language.* 2 vols. London, 1773.

————. *Johnsonian Miscellanies.* Ed. G. B. Hill. 2 vols. 1897; rpt. New York:

Barnes and Noble, 1970.

———. *The Letters of Samuel Johnson.* Ed. R. W. Chapman. 3 vols. Oxford: Clarendon, 1952.

———. *Works.* 11 vols. Oxford, 1825.

———. *The Yale Edition of the Works of Samuel Johnson.* Ed. Allen T. Hazen, John Middendorf, et. al. New Haven: Yale Univ. Press, 1958–.

Jonson, Benjamin. *Works.* London, 1692.

Junius, Franciscus. *Etymologicon Anglicanum.* Ed. Edward Lye. Oxford, 1743.

Juvenal. *Juvenal and Persius.* Trans. G. G. Ramsay. Loeb Classical Library. London: Heinemann, 1940; rpt. 1979.

Keast, W. R. "The Two Clarissas in Johnson's *Dictionary.*" *Studies in Philology* 54 (1957): 429–39.

King, William. *The Art of Cookery: A Poem in Imitation of Horace's Art of Poetry by the Author of a Tale of a Tub.* London, 1708.

Knowlson, James. *Universal Language Schemes in England and France: 1600–1800.* Toronto: Univ. of Toronto Press, 1975.

Kolb, Gwin J., and Ruth A. Kolb. "The Selection and Use of the Illustrative Quotations in Dr. Johnson's *Dictionary.*" *New Aspects of Lexicography.* Ed. Howard Weinbrot. Carbondale: Univ. of Illinois Press, 1972. 61–72.

Korshin, Paul J. "Johnson and the Renaissance Dictionary." *Journal of the History of Ideas* 35 (1974): 300–312.

Lactantius. *The Divine Institutes.* Trans. Rev. William Fletcher. The Ante-Nicene Fathers, 7. Rpt. Grand Rapids: Erdmans, 1979.

L'Estrange, Roger. *The Fables of Aesop and Other Eminent Mythologists: with Morals and Reflections.* London, 1692.

Levine, Joseph. "Ancients, Moderns, and History: The Continuity of English Historical Writing in the Later Seventeenth Century." *Studies in Change and Revolution: Aspects of English Intellectual History 1640–1800.* Ed. Paul Korshin. Menston, Yorkshire: Scolar, 1972. 43–75.

———. *Dr. Woodward's Shield.* Berkeley: Univ. of California Press, 1977.

Locke, John. *The Educational Writings of John Locke.* Ed. James Axtell. Cambridge: Cambridge Univ. Press, 1968.

———. *An Essay concerning Human Understanding.* Ed. Peter Nidditch. Oxford: Clarendon, 1975.

———. Notebooks. Bodleian MS Locke c. 25.

———. *Works.* 3 vols. London, 1727.

McAdam, E. L. "Inkhorn Words before Dr. Johnson." *Eighteenth-Century Studies.* Ed. W. H. Bond. New York: Grolier Club, 1970. 187–206.

Macrobius. *Opera.* Cologne, 1523. See *Sale Catalogue,* no. 191.

———. *Saturnalia.* Trans. Percival Vaughn Davies. New York: Columbia Univ. Press, 1969.

Malcolm X. *The Autobiography of Malcolm X.* New York: Grove Press, 1964.

Martial. *Epigrams.* Trans. Walter C. A. Ker. 2 vols. Loeb Classical Library. Rpt. London: Heinemann, 1968.

Matthaeus Westmonasteriensis. *Elegans, Illustris, et Facilis Rerum Praesertim Britannicarum, et Aliarum Obiter, Notatu Dignarum, a Mundi Exordio ad Annum Domini. 1307.* N.p., 1567.

Middendorf, John H. "Johnson, Locke, and the Edition of Shakespeare." *English Writers of the Eighteenth Century.* Ed. J. H. Middendorf. New York: Columbia Univ. Press, 1971. 249–272.

Miller, Robert Carroll. "Johnson's *Dictionary* Categorized: A Selection for Eighteenth-Century Studies." Ph.D. diss. Texas A & M, 1975.

Milton, John. *Paradise Lost*. Ed. Thomas Newton. 2 vols. London, 1749.

More, Henry. *An Antidote against Atheisme, or An Appeal to the Natural Faculties of the Minde of Man, whether there be not a God*. London, 1653. See Wimsatt, *Philosophic Words* 155.

———. *Divine Dialogues*. London, 1668. See Wimsatt, *Philosophic Words* 156.

Morery, Lewis. *The Great Historical, Geographical and Poetical Dictionary*. Trans. Anon. Ed. Johann LeClerc. 6th ed. 2 vols. London, 1694.

Murray, Elizabeth K. M. *Caught in the Web of Words*. New Haven: Yale Univ. Press, 1977.

Nicholas Cusanus. *De Docta Ignorantia, Of Learned Ignorance*. Trans. Fr. Germain Heron. London: Routledge and Kegan Paul, 1954.

———. *Opera*. 2 vols. Venice, 1490.

Nichols, John. *Literary Anecdotes of the Eighteenth Century*. 9 vols. London, 1812–16.

Norris, John. *A Collection of Miscellanies*. 3rd ed. London, 1699. See *Sale Catalogue*, no. 111.

Ozenham, Jacques. *Récréations Mathématiques et Physiques*. Trans. Anon. London, 1708.

Pattison, Mark. *Essays*. Ed. Henry Nettleship. 2 vols. Oxford, 1889.

Peacham, Henry. *The Compleat Gentleman*. London, 1622.

———. *Graphice: or the Most Auncient and Excellent Art of Drawing and Limning*. London, 1612.

Persius. *Juvenal and Persius*. Trans. G. G. Ramsay. Loeb Classical Library. London: Heinemann, 1940; rpt. 1979.

Phillips, Edward. *A New Worlde of English Words or, a General Dictionary Containing the Interpretations of such hard words as are derived from other Languages*. London, 1658.

Quincy, John. *Lexicon Physico-Medicum*. London, 1719.

Raleigh, Sir Walter. *The History of the World*. London, 1614.

Reddick, Alan. "The Making of Johnson's *Dictionary*, 1746–55 and 1771–73." Ph.D. diss. Columbia Univ., 1985.

Richardson, Charles. *A New Dictionary of the English Language*. 2nd ed. 2 vols. London, 1839.

Rogers, John. *Nineteen Sermons on Several Occasions*. London, 1735.

Rogers, Pat. *Grub Street: Studies in a Subculture*. London: Methuen, 1972.

The Sale Catalogue of Samuel Johnson's Library: A Facsimile Edition. Ed. J. D. Fleeman. English Literary Studies Monograph Series, No. 2. Vancouver: Univ. of British Columbia, 1975.

Scaliger, Joseph. *De Emendatione Temporum*. Paris, 1583.

Schwartz, Richard. "Johnson's 'Vision of Theodore.'" *New Rambler* C, 14 (1973): 31–39.

Skinner, Stephen. *Etymologicon Linguae Anglicanae*. London, 1671.

Sledd, James, and Gwin J. Kolb. *Dr. Johnson's Dictionary: Essays in the Biography of a Book*. Chicago: Univ. of Chicago Press, 1955.

———. "Johnson's Definitions of *Whig* and *Tory*." *PMLA* 67 (September 1952): 882–85.

South, Robert. *Twelve Sermons Preached on Several Occasions*. London, 1692.

———. *Twelve Sermons Preached on Several Occasions*. London, 1694. The volume that Johnson marked is in the Lichfield Cathedral Library; see Fleeman, *Handlist* (1984) 59.

Starnes, Dewitt, and Gertrude Noyes. *The English Dictionary from Cawdrey to Johnson*. Chapel Hill: Univ. of North Carolina Press, 1946.

Sternhold, Thomas, and Isaac Hopkins. *The Whole Booke of Psalms*. Geneva, 1569.

Stillingfleet, Edward. *A Defence of the Discourse concerning the Idolatry Practiced in the Church of Rome in Answer to a Book entituled, Catholicks no Idolaters*. London, 1676.

Taylor, Jeremy. *The Rule and Exercise of Holy Dying*. 2nd ed. London, 1652.

_____. *The Rule and Exercise of Holy Living together with Prayers Containing the Whole Duty of a Christian*. 10th ed. London, 1674. See *Sale Catalogue*, nos. 213, 351, and 477.

Thomas, E. J. "A Bibliographical and Critical Analysis of Johnson's *Dictionary* with Special Reference to Twentieth-Century Scholarship." D.Phil. diss. Univ. of Aberystwyth, 1974.

Tillotson, John. *Sermons Preach'd upon Several Occasions*. London, 1671.

_____. *Six Sermons*. London, 1694.

Vance, John A. *Samuel Johnson and the Sense of History*. Athens, Ga.: Univ. of Georgia Press, 1984.

Wake, William. *Preparation for Death. Being A Letter Sent to a Young Gentlewoman in France, in a dangerous Distemper; of which She died*. London, 1687.

Walker, William. *English Examples of the Latine Syntaxis*. London, 1683.

Wallis, John. "Grammatica Linguae Anglicanae." *Opera Quaedam Miscellanea*. 1653; rpt. Oxford, 1699.

Ward, Seth. *Concerning the Sinfulness of Infidelity*. London, 1670.

Watts, Isaac. *The Improvement of the Mind*. London, 1741.

_____. *Logick*. 8th ed. London, 1745.

Wells, Ronald A. *Dictionaries and the Authoritarian Tradition*. The Hague: Mouton, 1973.

Wesley, John. *The Complete English Dictionary*. 2nd ed. Bristol, 1764.

Wilkins, John. *An Essay towards a Real Character and a Philosophical Language*. London, 1668.

_____. *Mathematical Magick; or the Wonders that May be Performed by Mechanical Geometry*. London, 1648. See Wimsatt, *Philosophic Words* 159.

Wimsatt, William K. "Johnson's *Dictionary*: April 15, 1955." *New Light on Dr. Johnson: Essays on the Occasion of His 250th Birthday*. Ed. Frederick W. Hilles. New Haven: Yale Univ. Press, 1959. 65–90.

_____. "Johnson's Treatment of Bolingbroke in the *Dictionary*." *Modern Language Review* 43 (January 1948): 78–80.

_____. *Philosophic Words*. New Haven: Yale Univ. Press, 1948.

Wiseman, Richard. *Eight Chirurgical Treatises*. London, 1676.

Index of Words Cited
in the *Dictionary*

Index of Authors Cited
in the *Dictionary*

General Index

Abbot, George, 16, 150
Adam Library. See *R. B. Adam Library*.
Addison, Joseph, 17, 108, 149
Agrippa, Henri Cornelius, 23
Ainsworth, Robert, 12, 114, 276 (n. 4)
Allestree, Richard, 16, 192, 195
Amanuenses: in Johnson's employ, 4, 116, 119, 225
America, 150
Amphibology, 160
Anaximander, 74
Antediluvian language, 164
Archaism, 171
Aristotle, 14, 63–64, 74, 90, 110, 204, 207, 271 (n. 5)
Ascham, Roger, 16, 138, 148
Athenaeus, 31
Atterbury, Francis, 224
Audience, 11, 19, 75, 104, 118, 132, 144, 203
Augustine, Saint, Bishop of Hippo, 65
Ausonius, 214
Axtell, James, 106–7

Bacon, Francis, 5, 11, 17–18, 35, 101, 132, 186, 188, 199, 203, 207; *Essays*, 19, 24, 35, 58, 71, 80, 148; *Advancement of Learning*, 35, 40, 186, 228, 268 (n. 12); "Apophthegms," 35, 75, 276 (n. 5); *Sylva Sylvarum*, 35, 128, 188–89; *Valerius Terminus*, 104; "Student's Prayer," 152, 237; *New Atlantis*, 188
Bailey, Nathan, 12, 15, 111, 268 (n. 13)
Baker, Thomas, 23, 61, 200
Bate, Walter Jackson, 11, 265
Bayle, Pierre, 129
Berkeley, George, 52, 276 (n. 3)
Bias, 256
Bible, 6, 17, 23–24, 36, 61, 108, 183, 229
Birch, Thomas, 4, 233

Boethius, 27–28, 31
Boileau-Despréaux, Nicolas, 212, 277 (n. 12)
Bolingbroke, Henry St. John, 1st Viscount, 276 (n. 2)
Boswell, James, 10, 19, 139, 186, 247; *Life of Johnson*, 4, 9, 52, 62, 216, 232, 239, 248, 265, 267 (n. 2), 269 (n.25)
Bourde, Andrew, 16
Boyle, Robert, 11, 23, 233
Bramhall, John, 16, 238
Breeding: as part of education, 106
Broome, William, 108, 150, 183
Browne, Sir Thomas, 23, 61, 70, 247
Browning, Robert, 3
Bruno, Jacobus Pancratius, 117
Bunyan, John, 55
Burgess, Daniel, 34
Burke, Kenneth, 32, 215
Burnet, Thomas, 28, 243
Burton, Robert, 31, 116, 129

Callimachus, 117
Calmet, Augustin, 9, 109, 183
Camden, William, 9, 109
Carlyle, Thomas, 19, 87
Cawdrey, Robert, 11
Cellarius, Christopher, 15
Chambers, Ephraim, 4–6, 153, 270 (n. 6); *Considerations Preparatory to a Second Edition*, 4, 6, 187; *Cyclopaedia*, 4–8, 36, 43, 47, 61, 111, 154–55, 266
Chapman, John, 108
Chapone, Hester, 19
Chaucer, Geoffrey, 8, 109, 172, 202, 208, 214
Cheyne, George, 17, 242
China, 150
Cibber, Colley, 210
Cicero, Marcus Tullius, 180, 217
Clarke, John, 113, 239

Thomas, E. J., 49, 246
Tillotson, John, 18
Tooke, Horne, 8, 163

Understanding, 96
Unities, the, 202
Usage, 167, 173

Varro, 31
Vergil, 108, 110, 118, 203, 214
Verstegan, Richard, 111

Wake, William, 9, 245
Walker, William, 13, 17
Wallis, John, 113, 167
Warburton, William, 17
Watts, Isaac, 16, 153, 187, 196; *The Improvement of the Mind*, 36, 99, 147; *Logick*, 267–68 (n. 9)
Webster's Third New International Dic-

tionary, 162–63
Welsted, Leonard, 209
Wesley, Charles, 185
Wesley, John, 185
West, Gilbert, 108
Whitehead, Alfred North, 11
Whorf, Benjamin, 158
Wilkins, John, 16, 167–68, 188
Will, 97
Wimsatt, William K., xi, 19, 167, 182–83, 234, 267 (n. 2), 268 (n. 13), 269 (n. 24), 276 (n. 2)
Wiseman, Richard, 221
Wit, 97, 99
Women, 11, 72, 186, 190, 192
Wotton, Sir Henry, 220
Wotton, William, 10
Wray, Daniel, 7

Xenophanes, 61